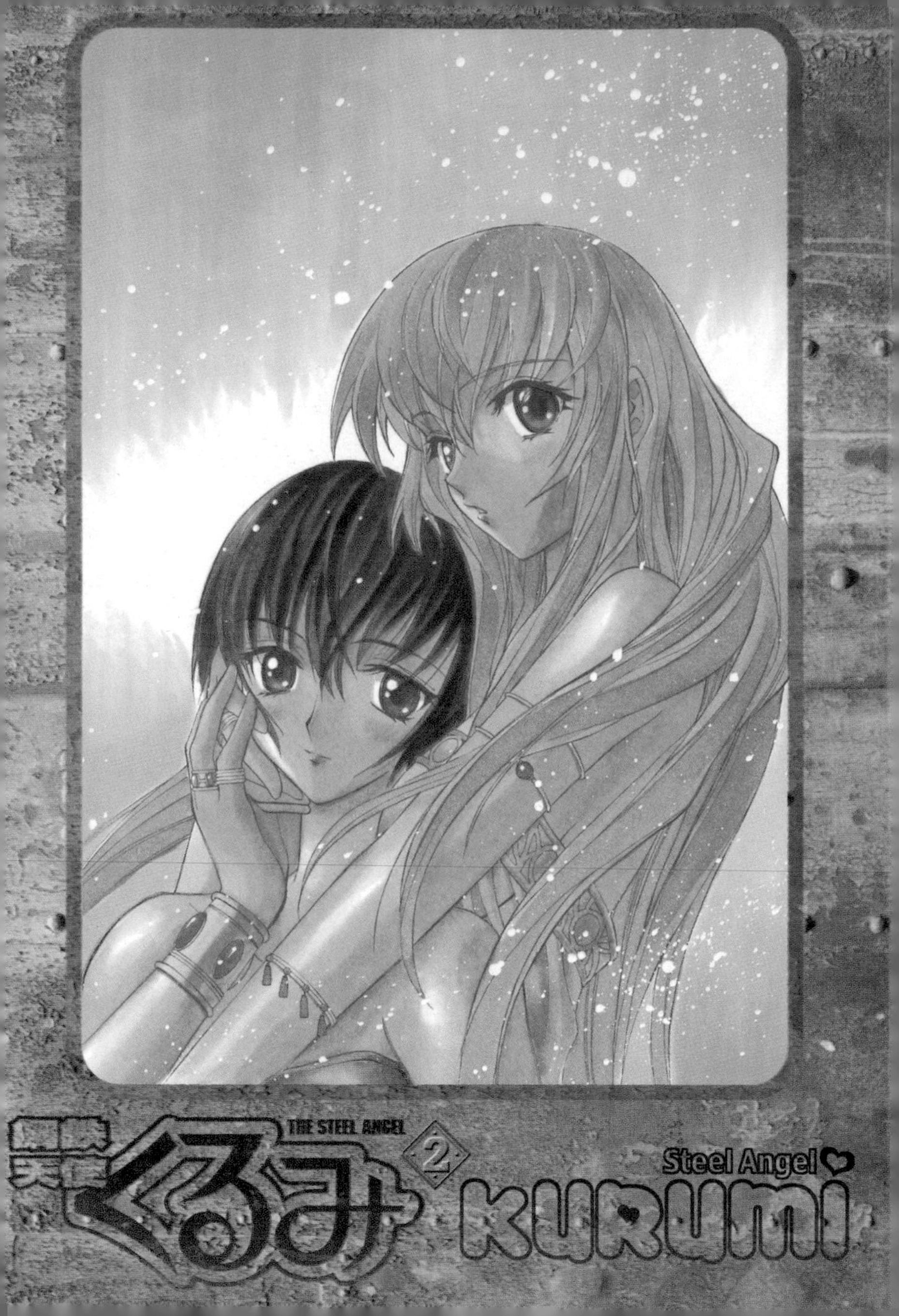

鋼鉄天使くるみ 2

THE STEEL ANGEL

Steel Angel KURUMI

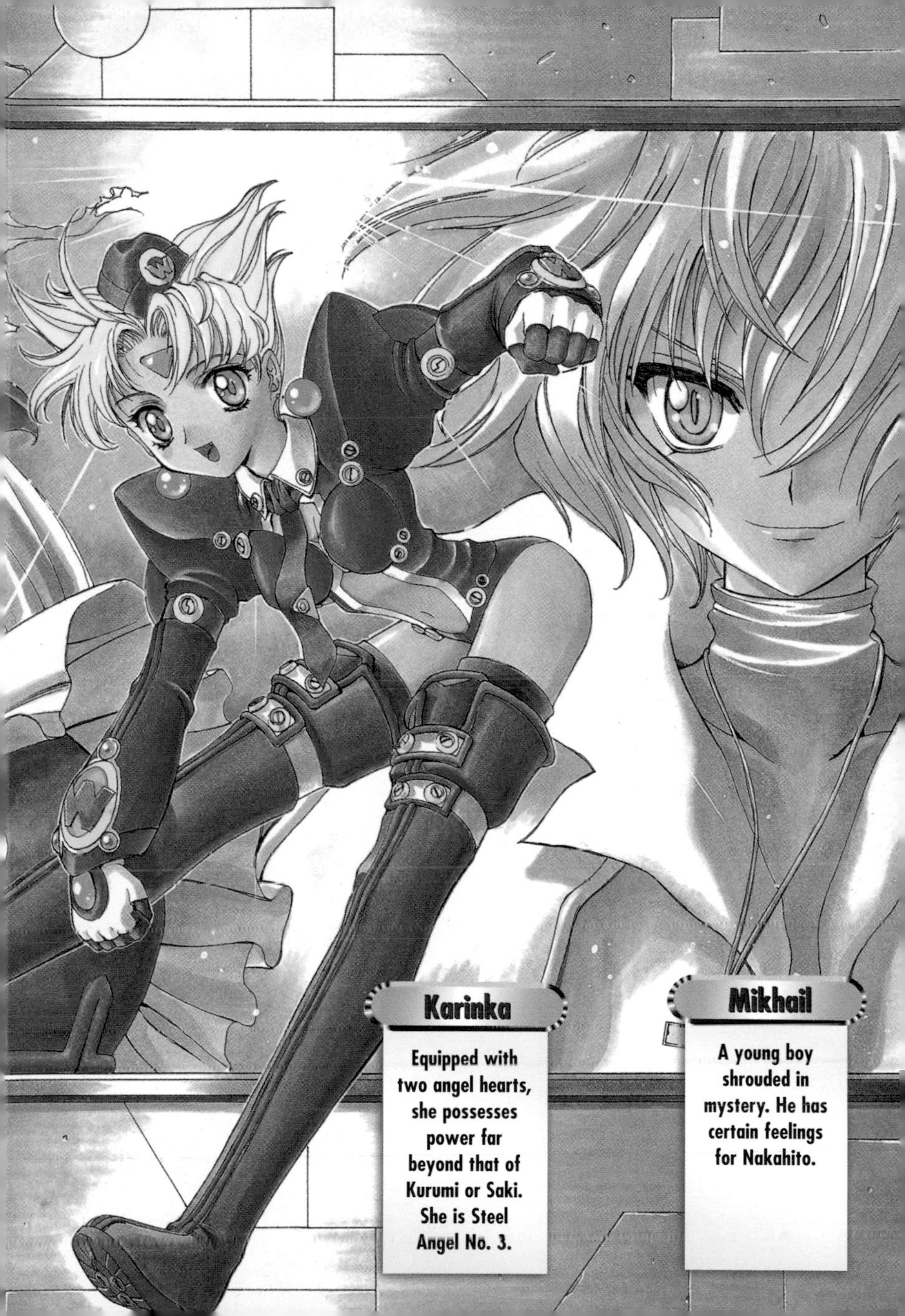
Mikhail
A young boy shrouded in mystery. He has certain feelings for Nakahito.
Karinka
Equipped with two angel hearts, she possesses power far beyond that of Kurumi or Saki. She is Steel Angel No. 3.

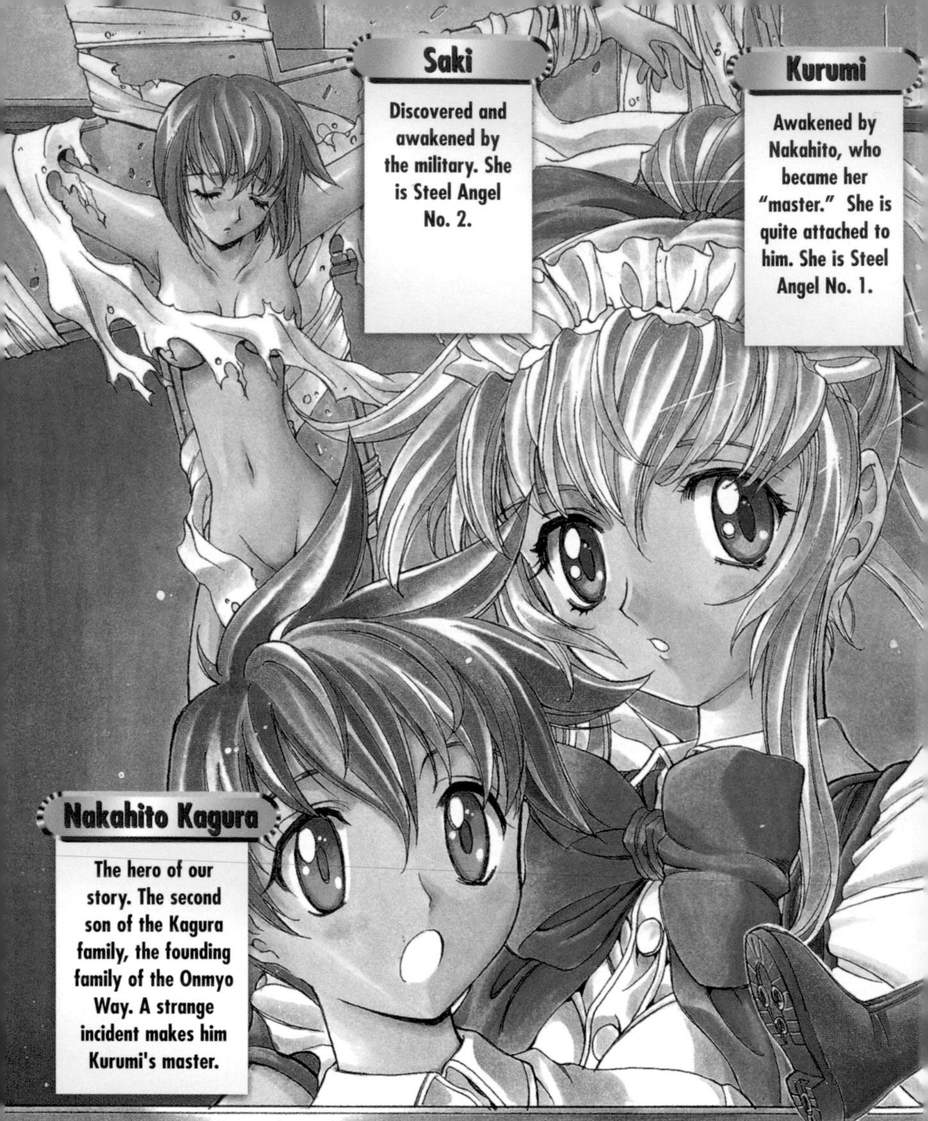
Saki
Discovered and awakened by the military. She is Steel Angel No. 2.
Kurumi
Awakened by Nakahito, who became her "master." She is quite attached to him. She is Steel Angel No. 1.
Nakahito Kagura
The hero of our story. The second son of the Kagura family, the founding family of the Onmyo Way. A strange incident makes him Kurumi's master.

The Story So Far

The Steel Angel Kurumi, a synthesis of science and magic, was awakened by Nakahito's kiss. However, Dr. Ayanokoji (who developed Kurumi) was abducted by his nemesis, Dr. Walski. The "Angel Heart," the powe source of the Steel Angels, was also taken.

With the cooperation of Dr. Amagi of the Japanese Imperial Army, Nakahito plans to rescue Dr. Ayanokoji. Around that time a mysterious boy named Mikhail approaches Nakahito and Kurumi. Kurumi and Saki (Steel Angel No. 2) are forced to figh Karinka, the super-strong Steel Angel built by Dr. Walski.

GUARD☆ANGEL

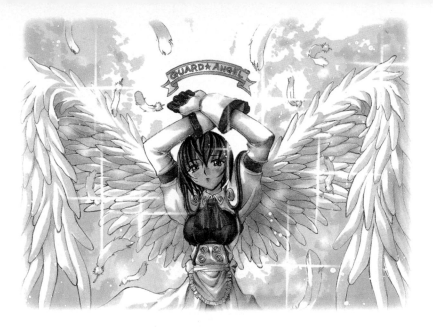

Contents

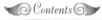

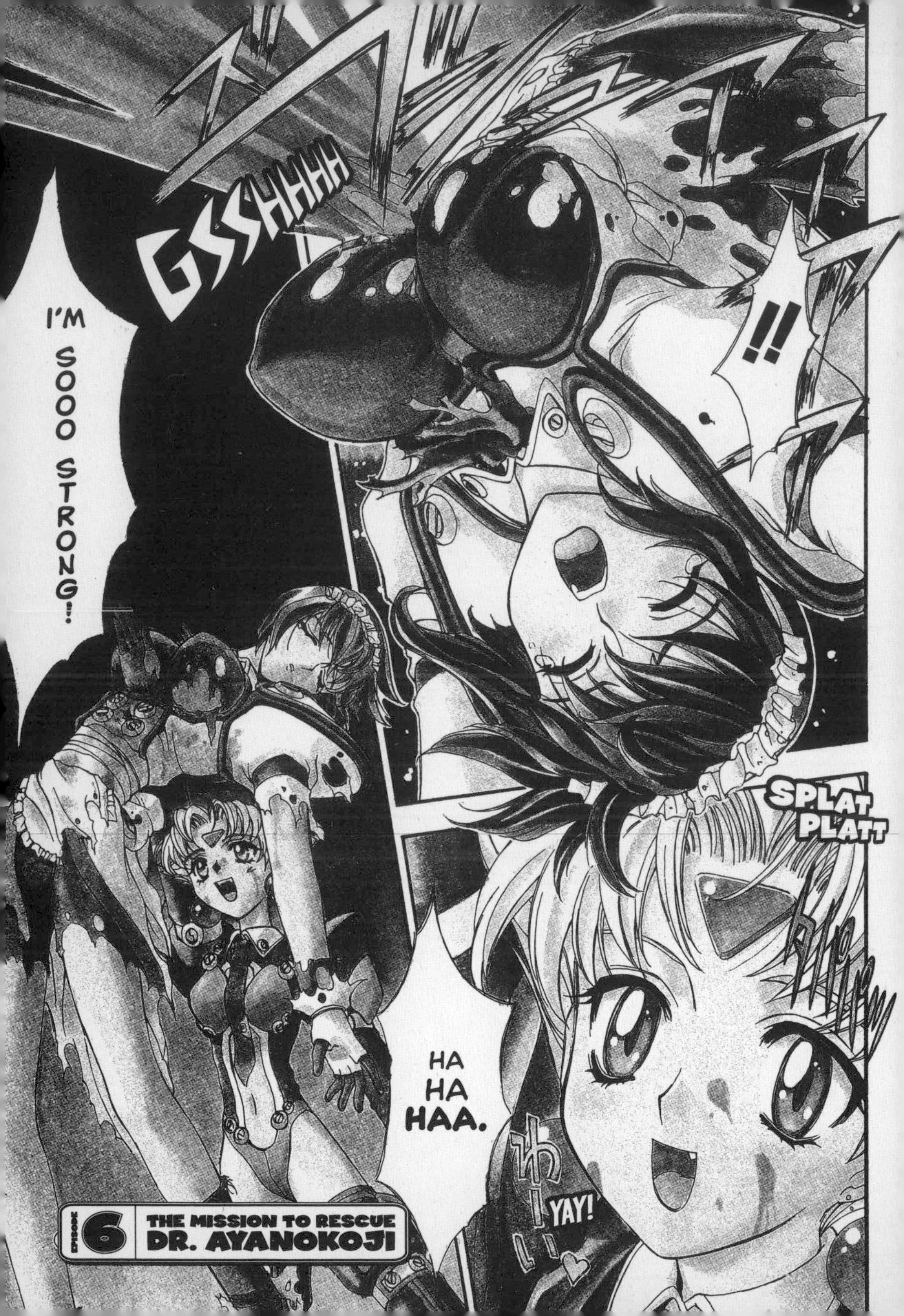
GSSHHHH
!!
I'M SOOO STRONG!
SPLAT PLATT
HA HA HAA.
YAY!
EPISODE 6 THE MISSION TO RESCUE DR. AYANOKOJI

EPISODE 6 THE MISSION TO RESCUE DR. AYANOKOJI

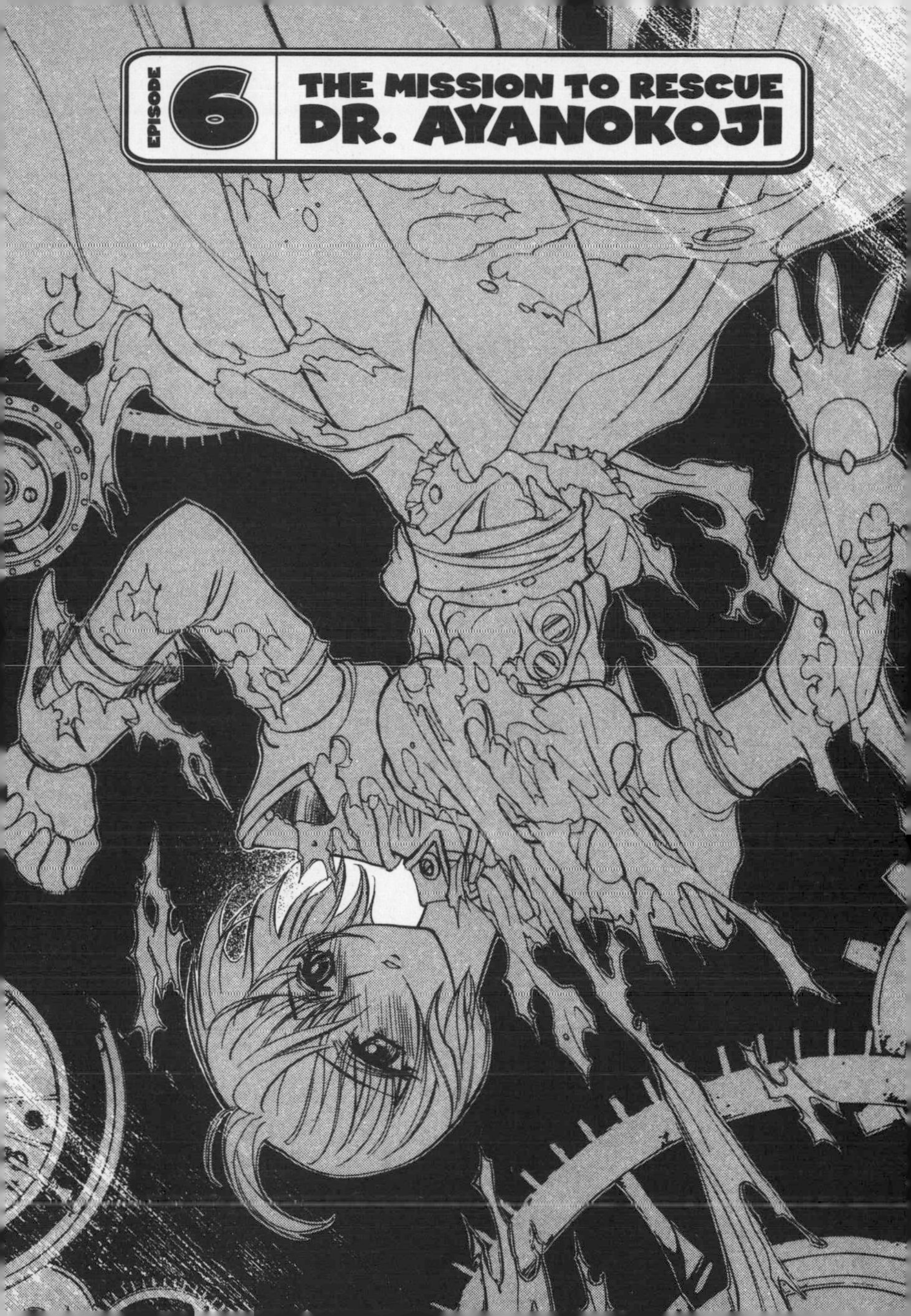

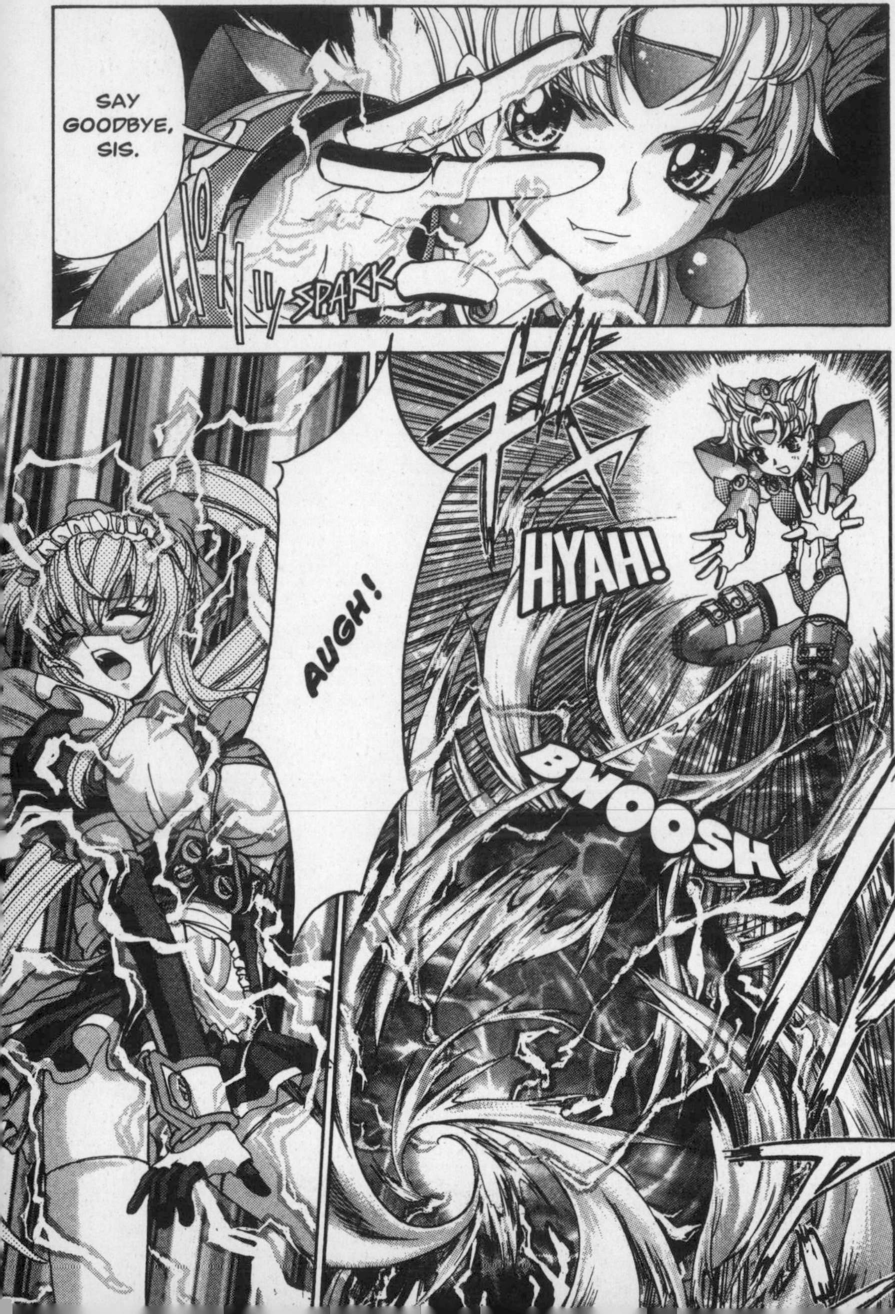
SAY GOODBYE, SIS.
SPAKK
HYAH!
AUGH!
BWOOSH

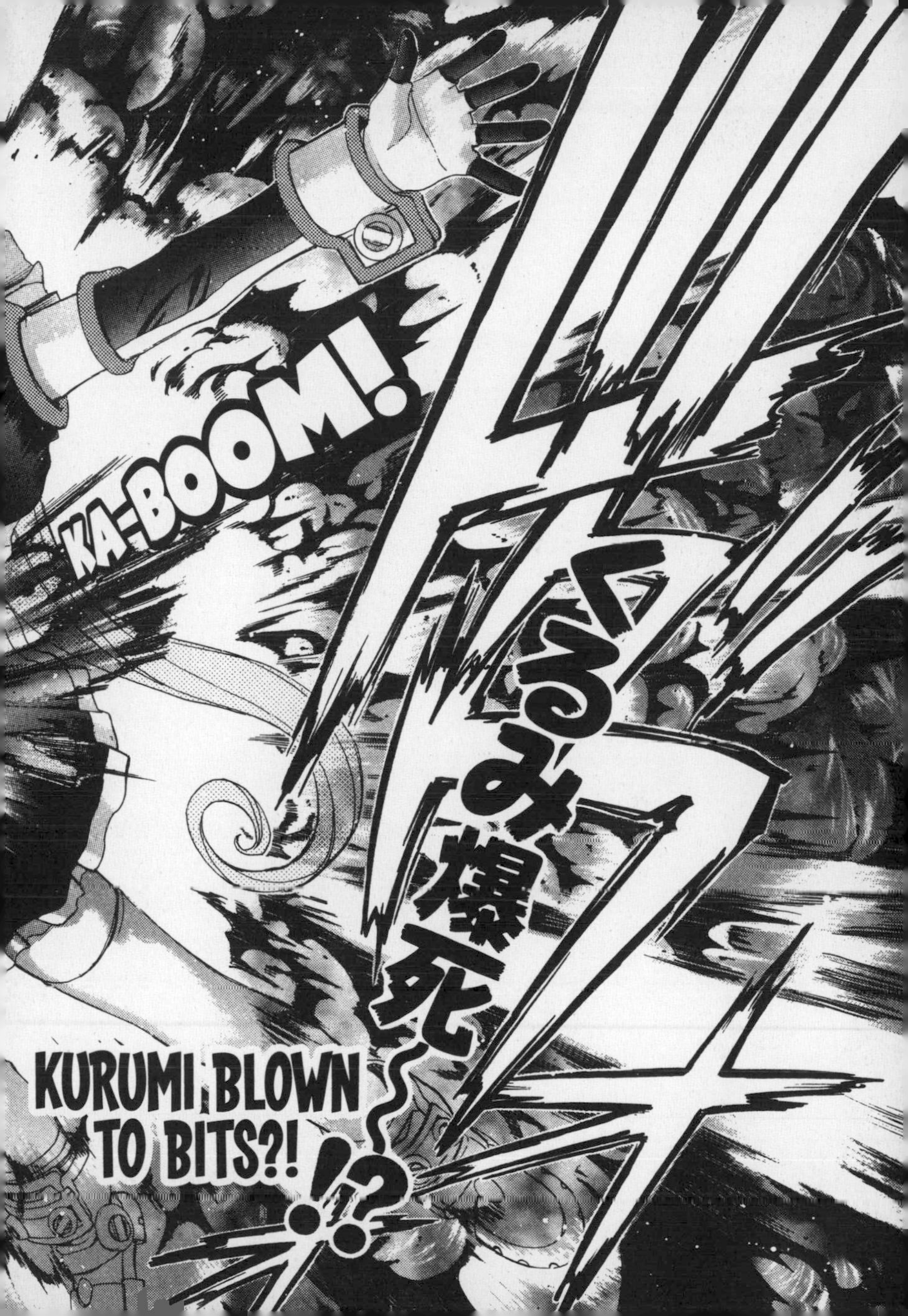
KA-BOOM!
くるみ爆死～!?
KURUMI BLOWN TO BITS?!

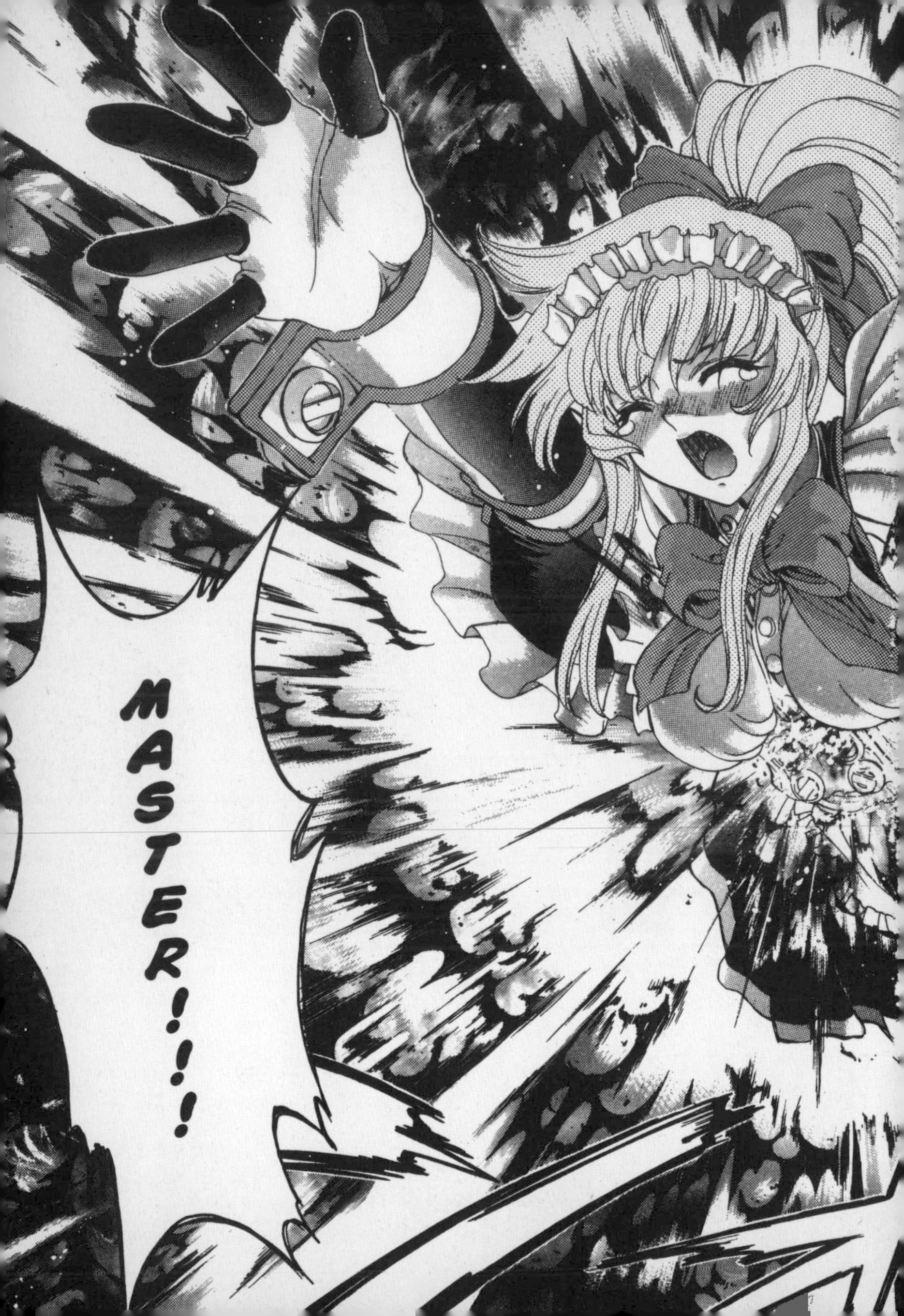
MASTER!!!

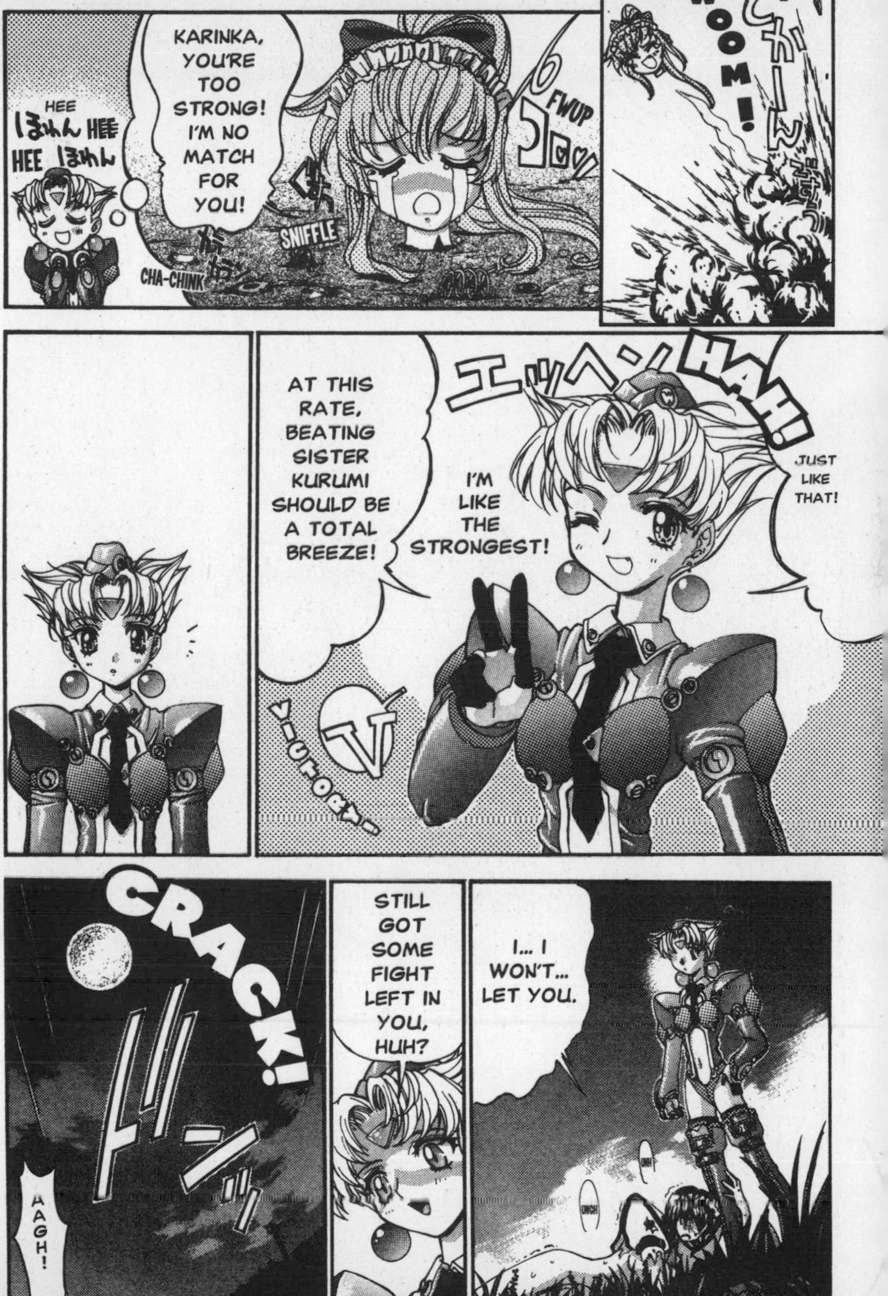
WOOM!
FWUP
KARINKA, YOU'RE TOO STRONG! I'M NO MATCH FOR YOU!
SNIFFLE
CHA-CHINK
HEE ほわん HEE
HEE ほわん
HAH!
JUST LIKE THAT!
I'M LIKE THE STRONGEST!
AT THIS RATE, BEATING SISTER KURUMI SHOULD BE A TOTAL BREEZE!
VICTORY!
I... I WON'T... LET YOU.
UNGH
UNGH
STILL GOT SOME FIGHT LEFT IN YOU, HUH?
CRACK!
AAGH!

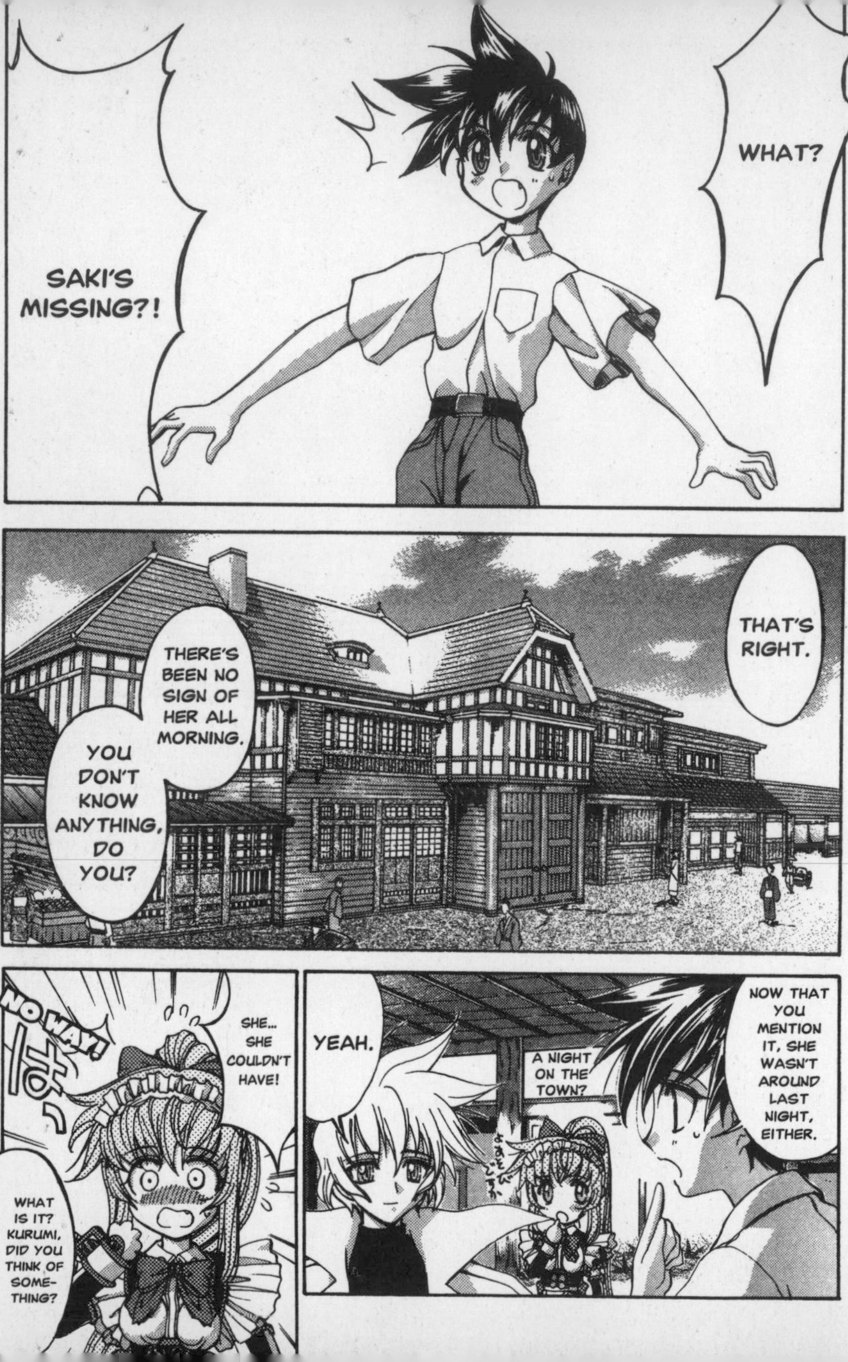
WHAT?
SAKI'S MISSING?!
THAT'S RIGHT.
THERE'S BEEN NO SIGN OF HER ALL MORNING.
YOU DON'T KNOW ANYTHING, DO YOU?
NOW THAT YOU MENTION IT, SHE WASN'T AROUND LAST NIGHT, EITHER.
A NIGHT ON THE TOWN?
YEAH.
SHE... SHE COULDN'T HAVE!
NO WAY!
WHAT IS IT? KURUMI, DID YOU THINK OF SOME-THING?

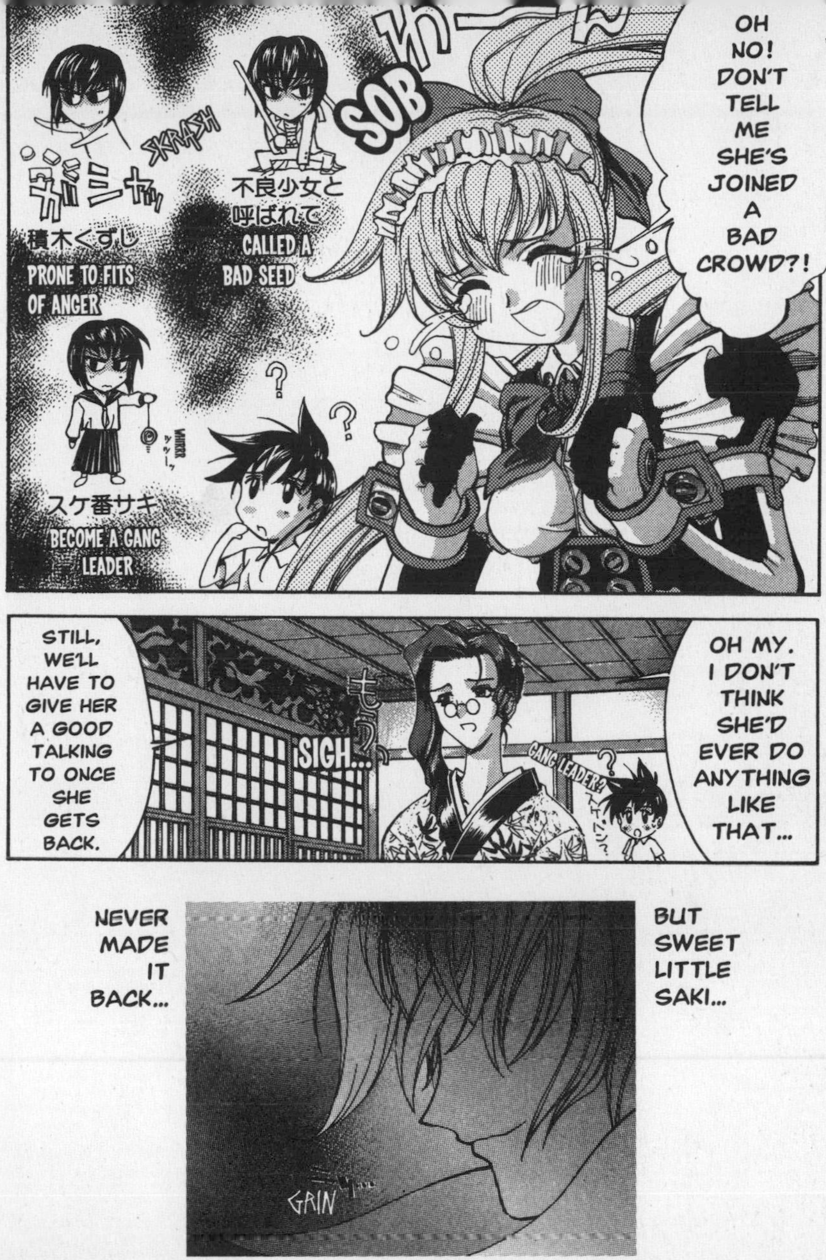
OH NO! DON'T TELL ME SHE'S JOINED A BAD CROWD?!
SOB
不良少女と呼ばれて
CALLED A BAD SEED
SKRASH
ガシャッ
積木くずし
PRONE TO FITS OF ANGER
スケ番サキ
BECOME A GANG LEADER
WHIRR
OH MY. I DON'T THINK SHE'D EVER DO ANYTHING LIKE THAT...
GANG LEADER?
SIGH...
STILL, WE'LL HAVE TO GIVE HER A GOOD TALKING TO ONCE SHE GETS BACK.
BUT SWEET LITTLE SAKI...
GRIN
NEVER MADE IT BACK...

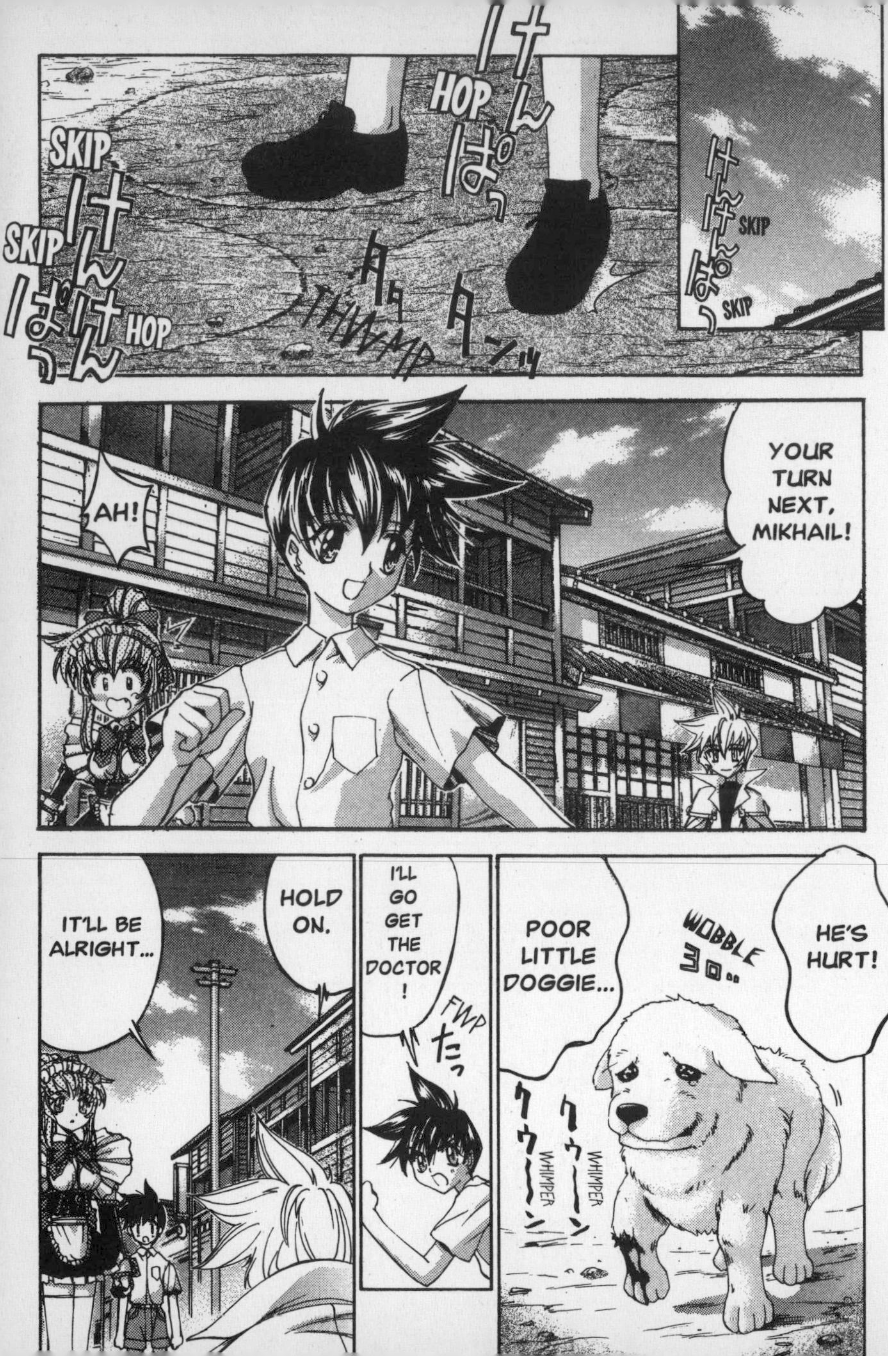
けんけんぱっ
SKIP
SKIP
けんぱっ
HOP
タンッ
タタ
THWAMP
けんけんぱっ
SKIP
SKIP
HOP
YOUR TURN NEXT, MIKHAIL!
AH!
HE'S HURT!
WOBBLE
ヨロ..
POOR LITTLE DOGGIE...
クゥーン
WHIMPER
クゥーン
WHIMPER
I'LL GO GET THE DOCTOR!
FWP
たっ
HOLD ON.
IT'LL BE ALRIGHT...

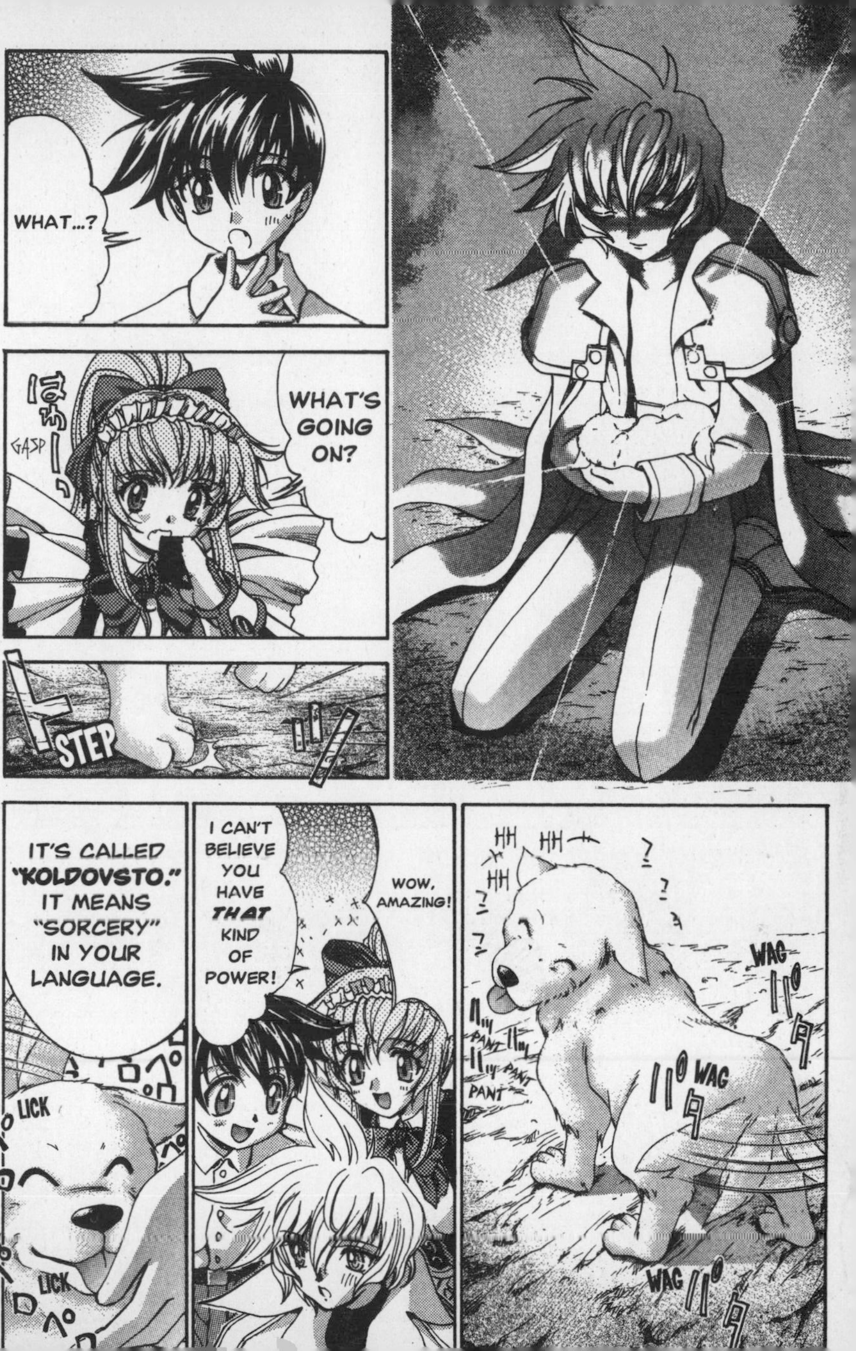
WHAT...?
はわー
GASP
WHAT'S GOING ON?
STEP
HH HH
WAG
PANT PANT PANT
WAG
WAG
WOW, AMAZING!
I CAN'T BELIEVE YOU HAVE ***THAT*** KIND OF POWER!
IT'S CALLED "**KOLDOVSTO.**" IT MEANS "SORCERY" IN YOUR LANGUAGE.
LICK
LICK
LICK

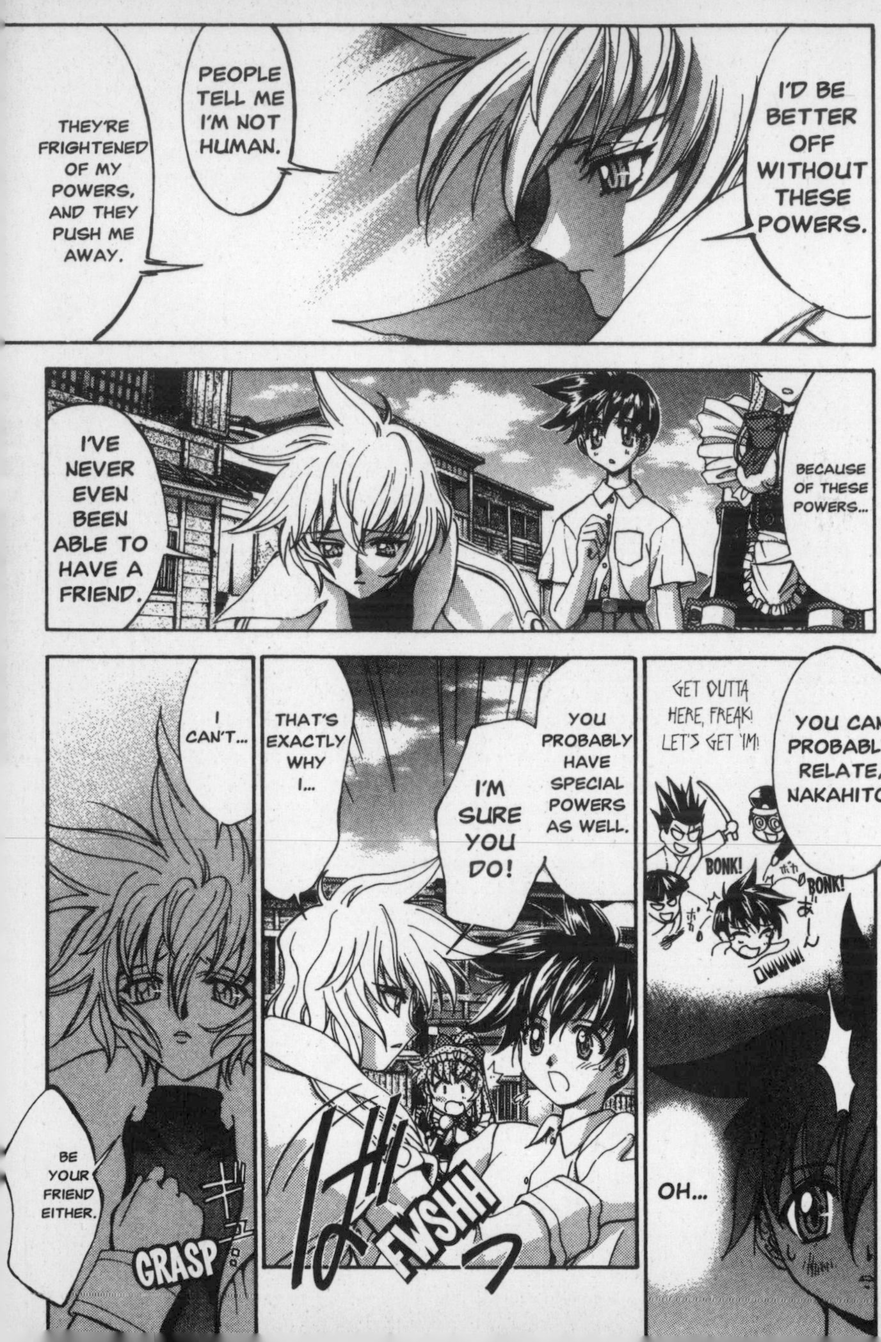
I'D BE BETTER OFF WITHOUT THESE POWERS.
PEOPLE TELL ME I'M NOT HUMAN.
THEY'RE FRIGHTENED OF MY POWERS, AND THEY PUSH ME AWAY.
BECAUSE OF THESE POWERS...
I'VE NEVER EVEN BEEN ABLE TO HAVE A FRIEND.
YOU CAN PROBABLY RELATE, NAKAHITO.
GET OUTTA HERE, FREAK! LET'S GET 'IM!
BONK!
BONK!
OWWW!
OH...
YOU PROBABLY HAVE SPECIAL POWERS AS WELL.
I'M SURE YOU DO!
THAT'S EXACTLY WHY I...
FWSHH
I CAN'T...
BE YOUR FRIEND EITHER.
GRASP

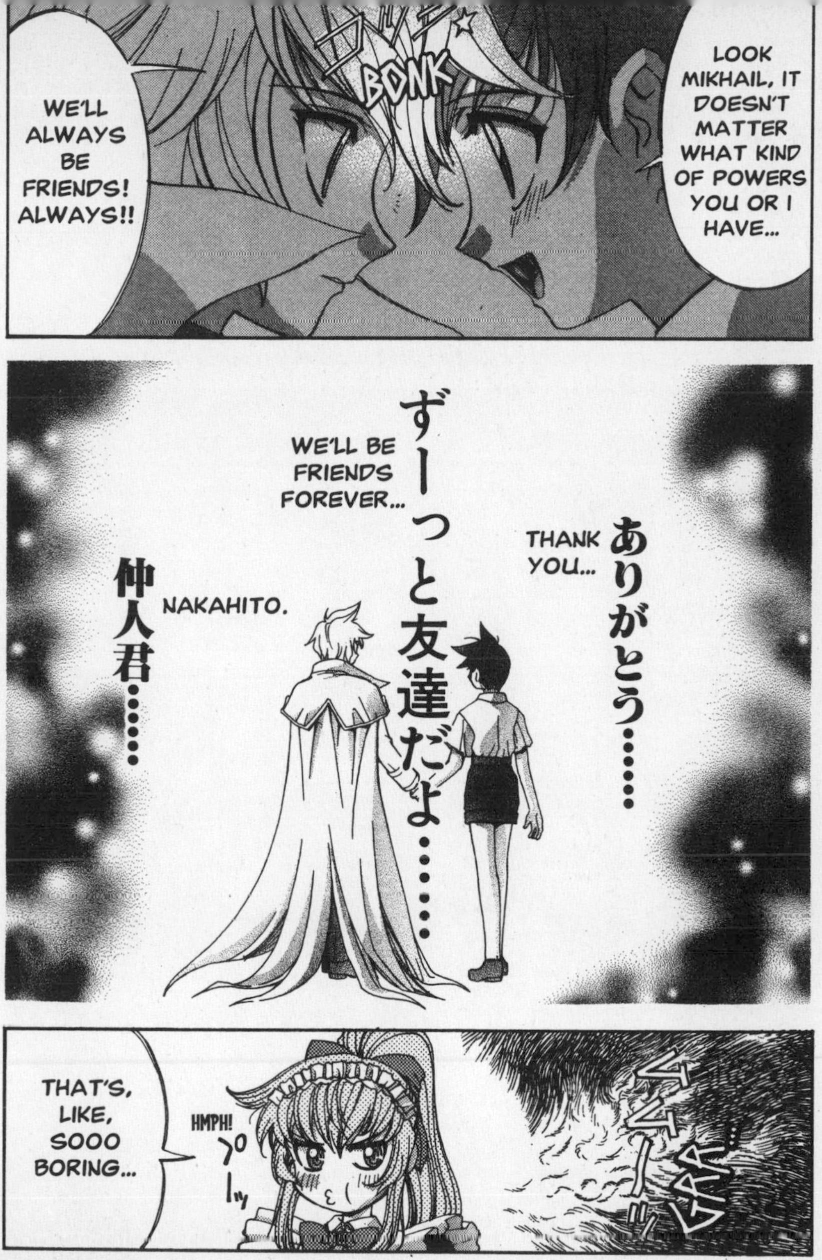
BONK
LOOK MIKHAIL, IT DOESN'T MATTER WHAT KIND OF POWERS YOU OR I HAVE...
WE'LL ALWAYS BE FRIENDS! ALWAYS!!
ありがとう……
THANK YOU...
ずーっと友達だよ……
WE'LL BE FRIENDS FOREVER...
仲人君……
NAKAHITO.
GRR...
HMPH!
THAT'S, LIKE, SOOO BORING...

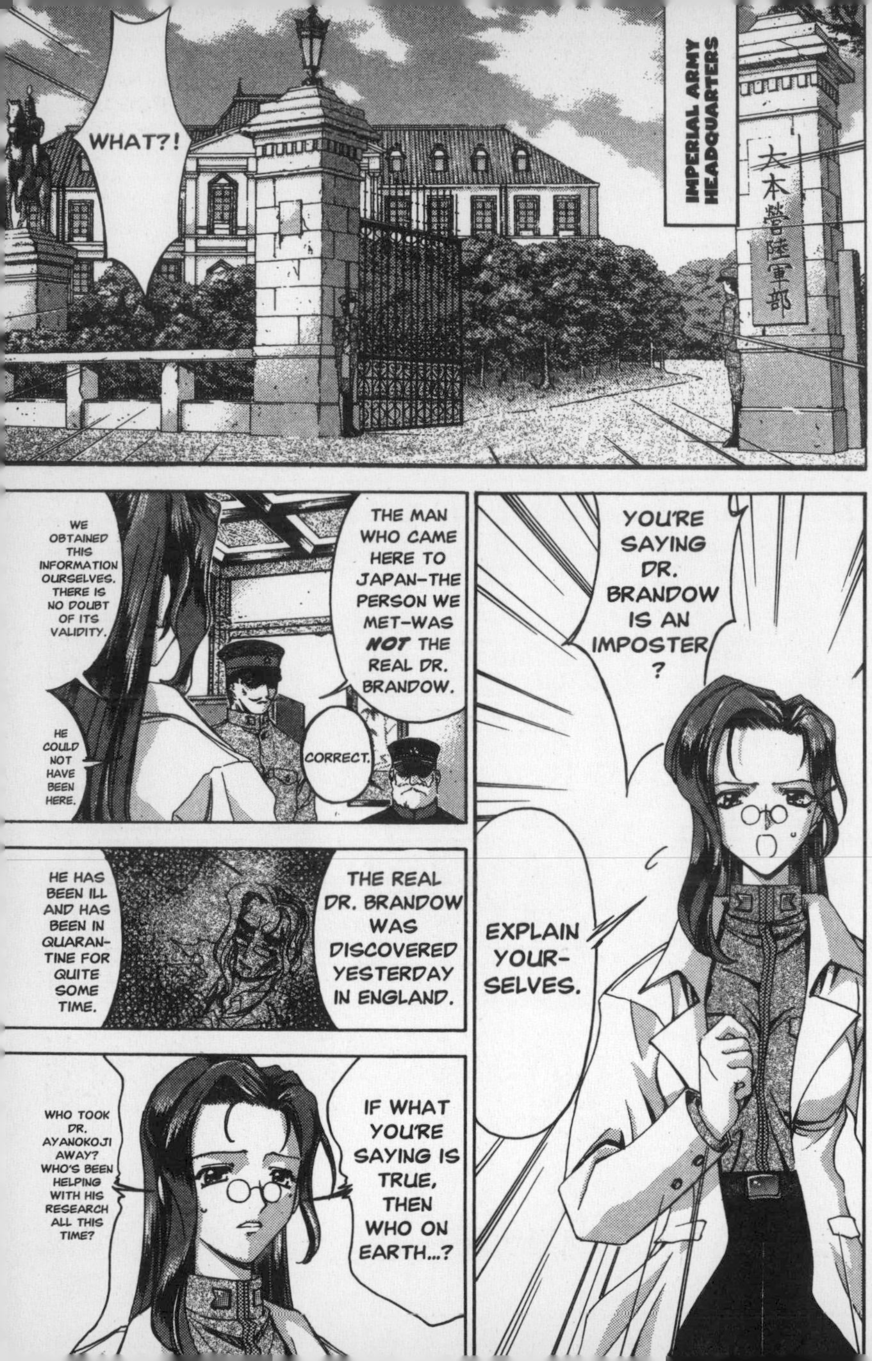
IMPERIAL ARMY HEADQUARTERS
大本營陸軍部
WHAT?!
YOU'RE SAYING DR. BRANDOW IS AN IMPOSTER?
EXPLAIN YOUR-SELVES.
THE MAN WHO CAME HERE TO JAPAN—THE PERSON WE MET—WAS NOT THE REAL DR. BRANDOW.
WE OBTAINED THIS INFORMATION OURSELVES. THERE IS NO DOUBT OF ITS VALIDITY.
CORRECT.
HE COULD NOT HAVE BEEN HERE.
THE REAL DR. BRANDOW WAS DISCOVERED YESTERDAY IN ENGLAND.
HE HAS BEEN ILL AND HAS BEEN IN QUARAN-TINE FOR QUITE SOME TIME.
IF WHAT YOU'RE SAYING IS TRUE, THEN WHO ON EARTH...?
WHO TOOK DR. AYANOKOJI AWAY? WHO'S BEEN HELPING WITH HIS RESEARCH ALL THIS TIME?

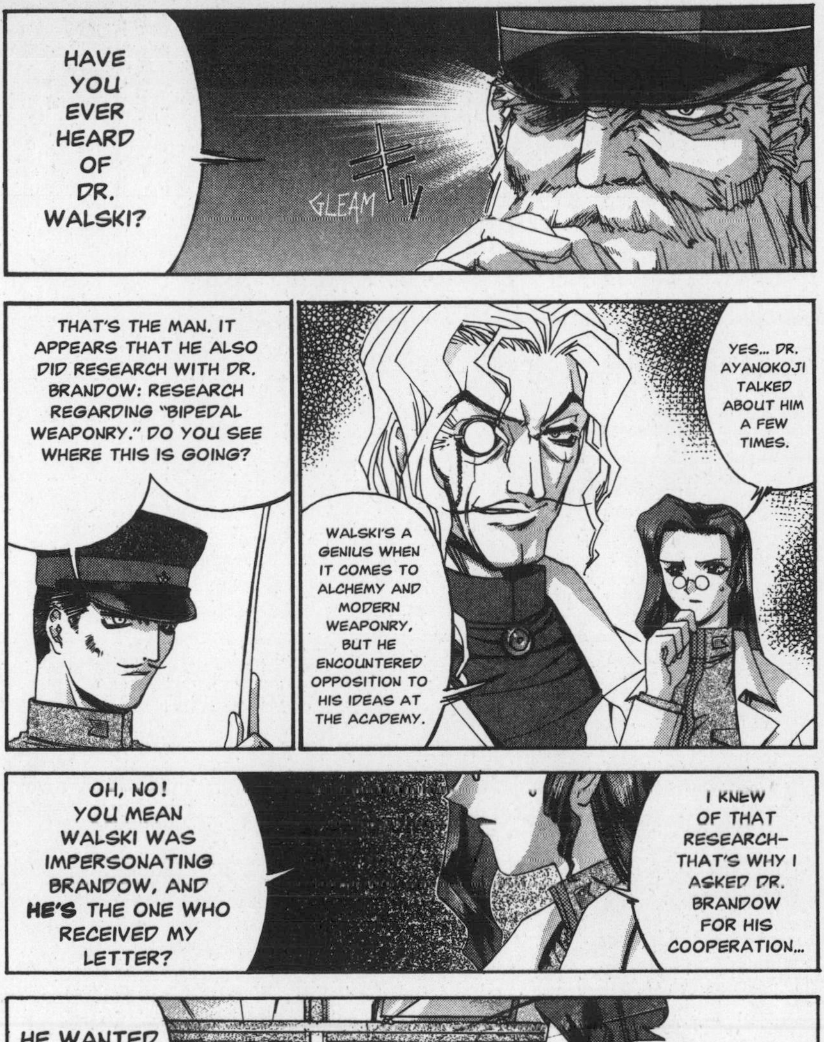
HAVE YOU EVER HEARD OF DR. WALSKI?
GLEAM
YES... DR. AYANOKOJI TALKED ABOUT HIM A FEW TIMES.
WALSKI'S A GENIUS WHEN IT COMES TO ALCHEMY AND MODERN WEAPONRY, BUT HE ENCOUNTERED OPPOSITION TO HIS IDEAS AT THE ACADEMY.
THAT'S THE MAN. IT APPEARS THAT HE ALSO DID RESEARCH WITH DR. BRANDOW: RESEARCH REGARDING "BIPEDAL WEAPONRY." DO YOU SEE WHERE THIS IS GOING?
OH, NO! YOU MEAN WALSKI WAS IMPERSONATING BRANDOW, AND **HE'S** THE ONE WHO RECEIVED MY LETTER?
I KNEW OF THAT RESEARCH— THAT'S WHY I ASKED DR. BRANDOW FOR HIS COOPERATION...
HE WANTED TO GET HIS HANDS ON OUR RESEARCH ALL ALONG.
SNAP!
CORRECT. WE'VE BEEN HAD!

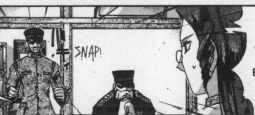

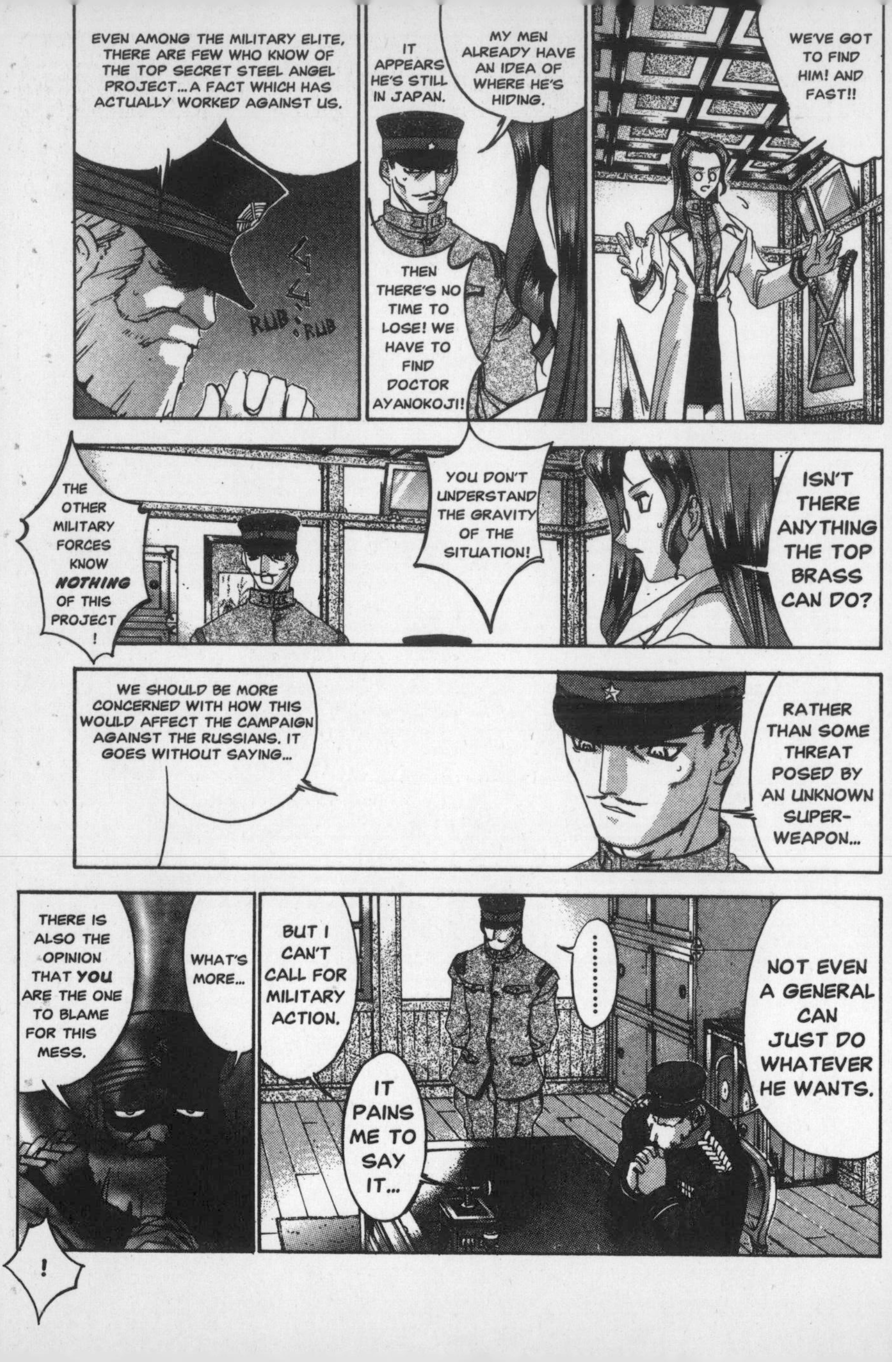
WE'VE GOT TO FIND HIM! AND FAST!!
MY MEN ALREADY HAVE AN IDEA OF WHERE HE'S HIDING.
IT APPEARS HE'S STILL IN JAPAN.
THEN THERE'S NO TIME TO LOSE! WE HAVE TO FIND DOCTOR AYANOKOJI!
EVEN AMONG THE MILITARY ELITE, THERE ARE FEW WHO KNOW OF THE TOP SECRET STEEL ANGEL PROJECT... A FACT WHICH HAS ACTUALLY WORKED AGAINST US.
RUB RUB
ISN'T THERE ANYTHING THE TOP BRASS CAN DO?
YOU DON'T UNDERSTAND THE GRAVITY OF THE SITUATION!
THE OTHER MILITARY FORCES KNOW **NOTHING** OF THIS PROJECT!
RATHER THAN SOME THREAT POSED BY AN UNKNOWN SUPER-WEAPON...
WE SHOULD BE MORE CONCERNED WITH HOW THIS WOULD AFFECT THE CAMPAIGN AGAINST THE RUSSIANS. IT GOES WITHOUT SAYING...
NOT EVEN A GENERAL CAN JUST DO WHATEVER HE WANTS.
....
BUT I CAN'T CALL FOR MILITARY ACTION.
IT PAINS ME TO SAY IT...
WHAT'S MORE...
THERE IS ALSO THE OPINION THAT **YOU** ARE THE ONE TO BLAME FOR THIS MESS.
!

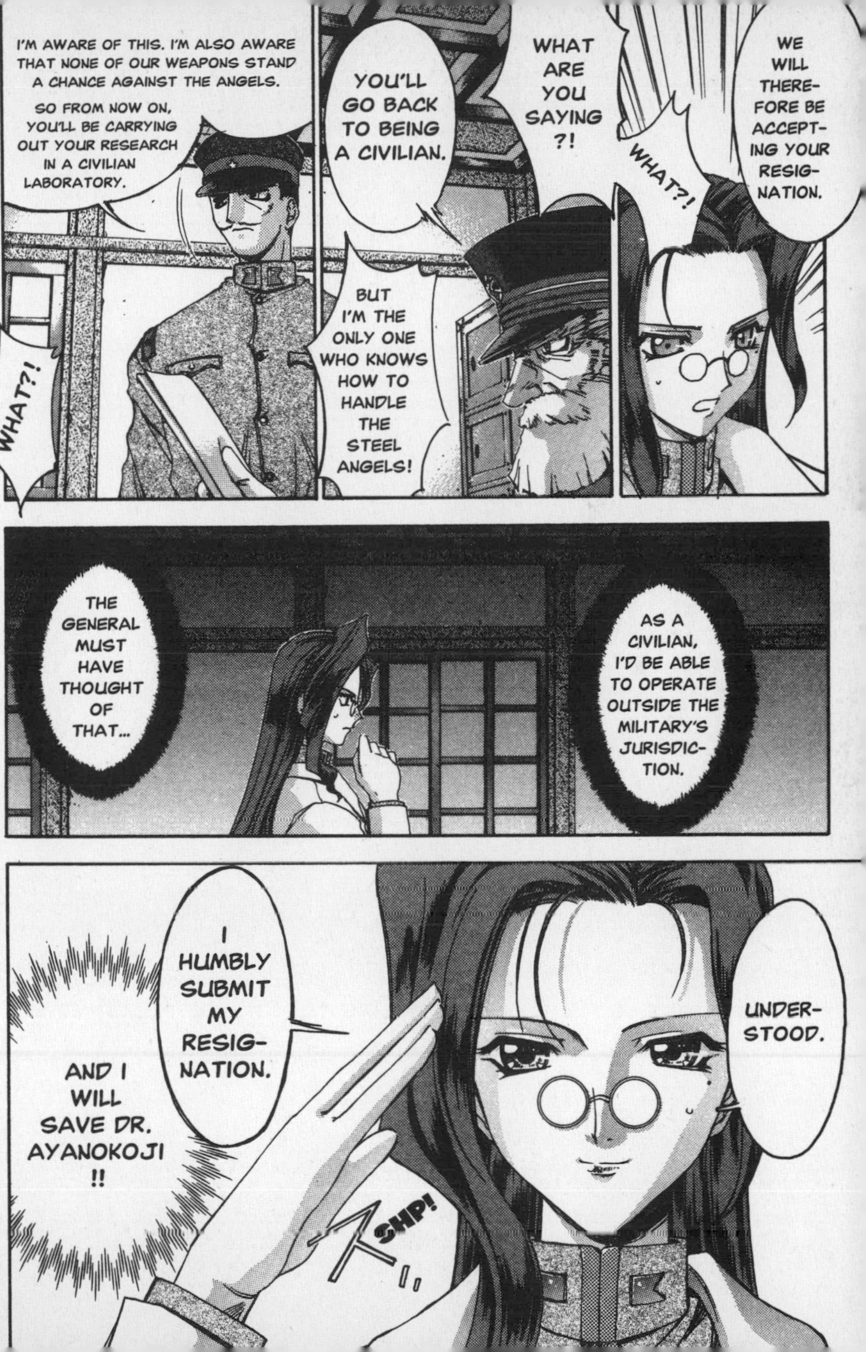
WE WILL THEREFORE BE ACCEPTING YOUR RESIGNATION.
WHAT?!
WHAT ARE YOU SAYING ?!
YOU'LL GO BACK TO BEING A CIVILIAN.
BUT I'M THE ONLY ONE WHO KNOWS HOW TO HANDLE THE STEEL ANGELS!
I'M AWARE OF THIS. I'M ALSO AWARE THAT NONE OF OUR WEAPONS STAND A CHANCE AGAINST THE ANGELS.
SO FROM NOW ON, YOU'LL BE CARRYING OUT YOUR RESEARCH IN A CIVILIAN LABORATORY.
WHAT?!
AS A CIVILIAN, I'D BE ABLE TO OPERATE OUTSIDE THE MILITARY'S JURISDICTION.
THE GENERAL MUST HAVE THOUGHT OF THAT...
UNDERSTOOD.
I HUMBLY SUBMIT MY RESIGNATION.
AND I WILL SAVE DR. AYANOKOJI !!
SHP!

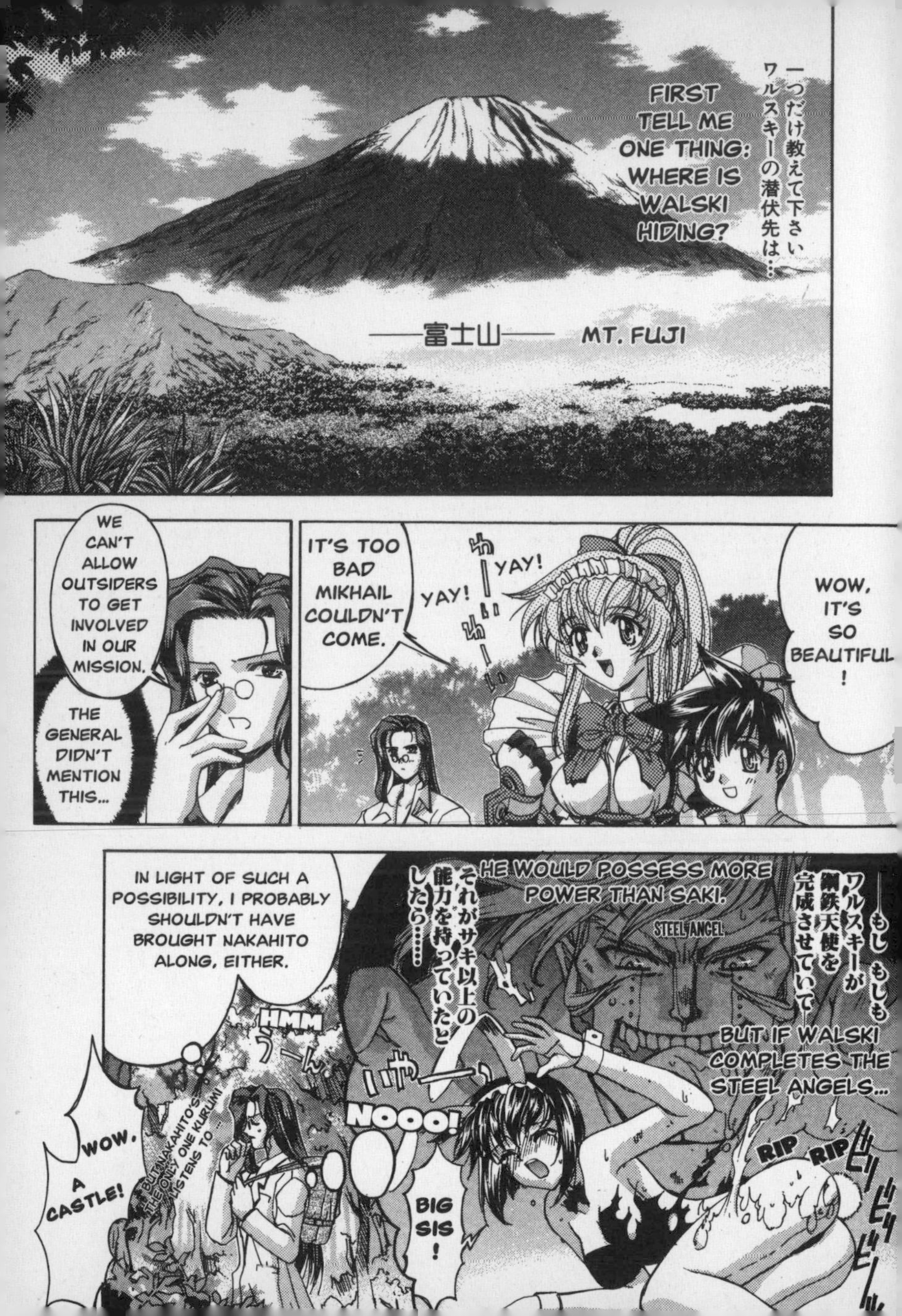
一つだけ教えて下さい
ワルスキーの潜伏先は…
FIRST TELL ME ONE THING: WHERE IS WALSKI HIDING?
——富士山——
MT. FUJI
WOW, IT'S SO BEAUTIFUL!
YAY!
YAY!
IT'S TOO BAD MIKHAIL COULDN'T COME.
WE CAN'T ALLOW OUTSIDERS TO GET INVOLVED IN OUR MISSION.
THE GENERAL DIDN'T MENTION THIS...
—もしもしも
ワルスキーが
鋼鉄天使を
完成させていて
BUT IF WALSKI COMPLETES THE STEEL ANGELS...
それがサキ以上の
能力を持っていたと
したら……
HE WOULD POSSESS MORE POWER THAN SAKI.
STEEL ANGEL
RIP
RIP
いやー
NOOO!
BIG SIS!
IN LIGHT OF SUCH A POSSIBILITY, I PROBABLY SHOULDN'T HAVE BROUGHT NAKAHITO ALONG, EITHER.
HMM
うーん
BUT NAKAHITO'S THE ONLY ONE KURUMI LISTENS TO
WOW, A CASTLE!

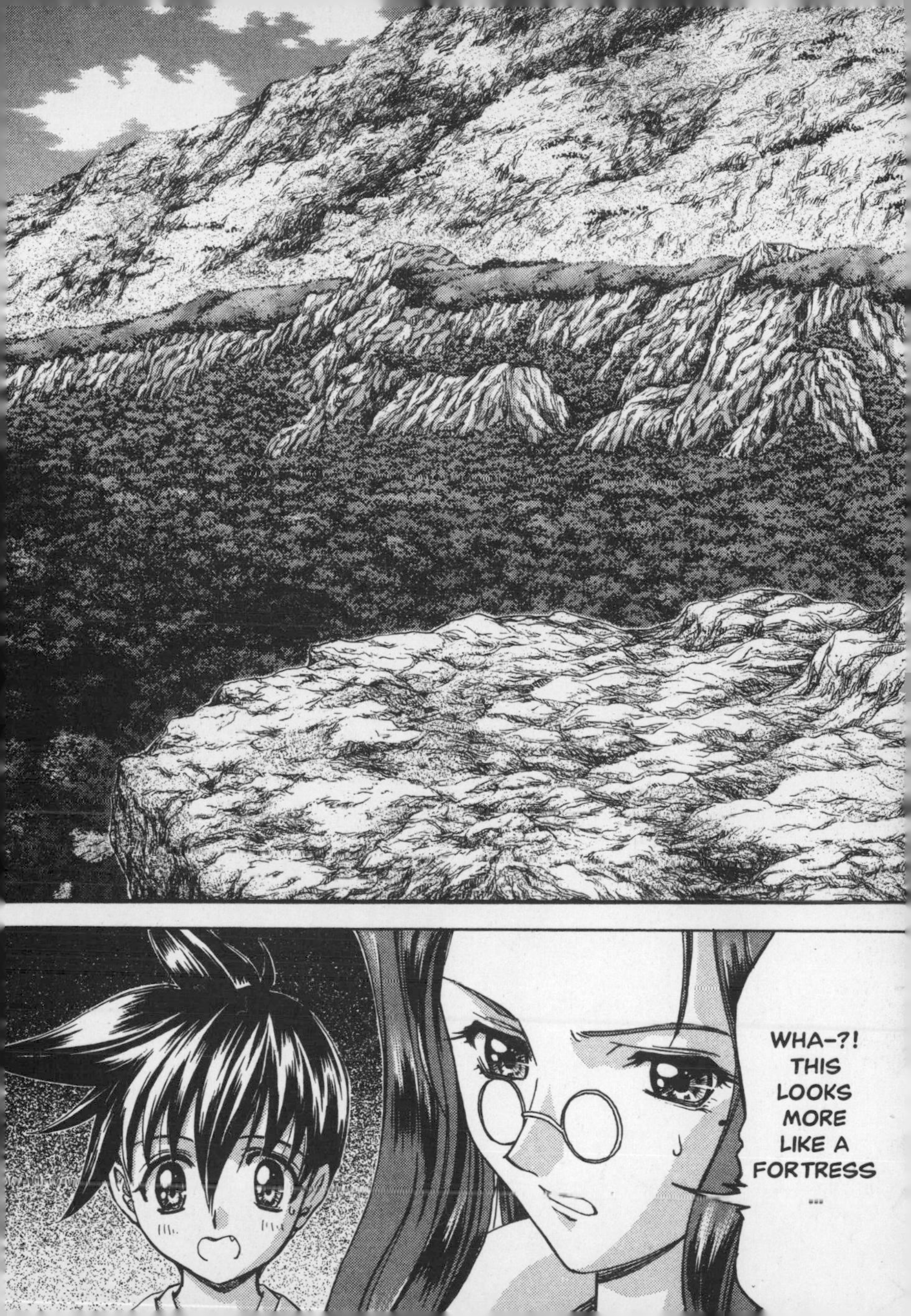
WHA-?! THIS LOOKS MORE LIKE A FORTRESS ...

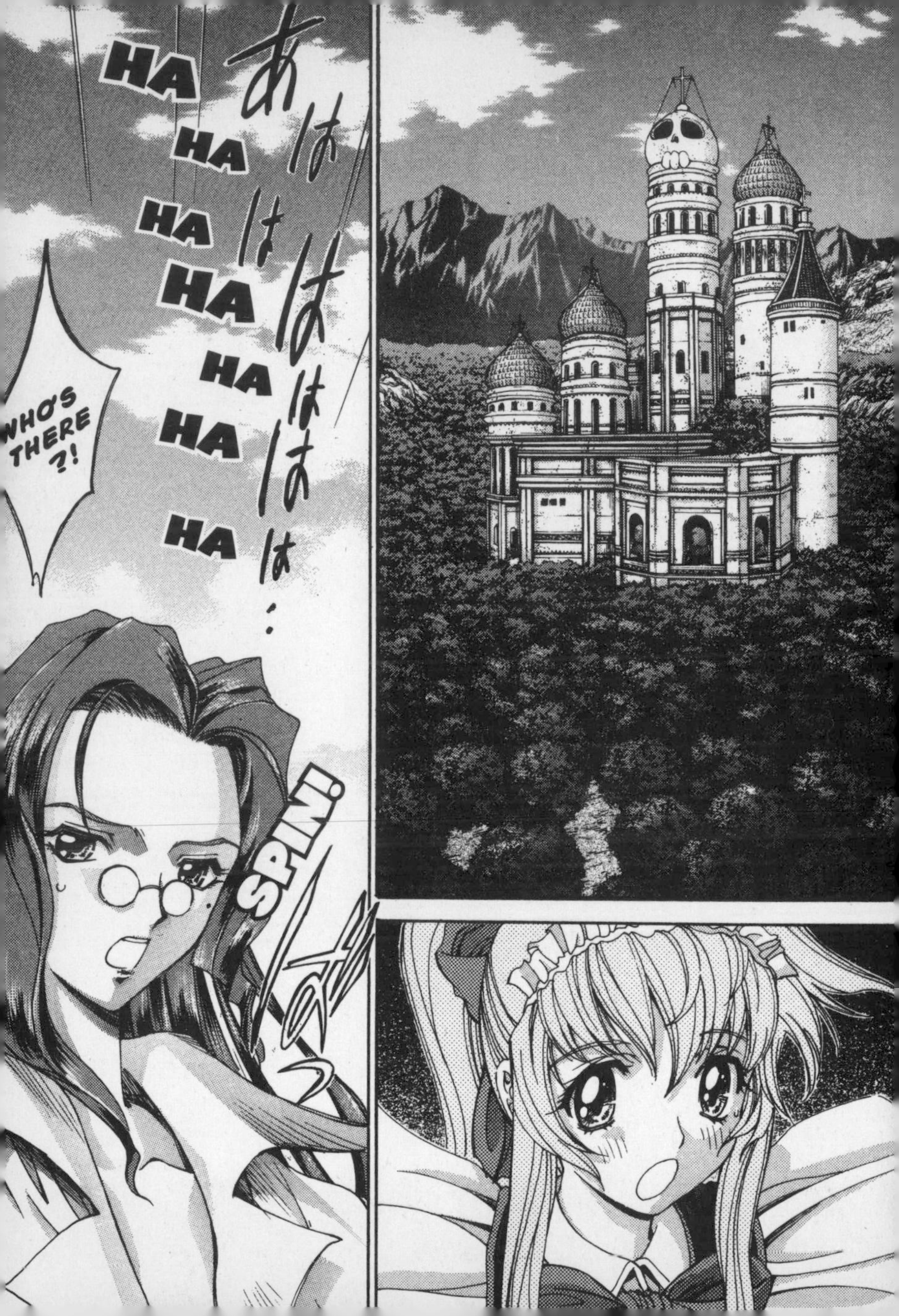

あはははははは…
HA HA HA HA HA HA HA
WHO'S THERE ?!
SPIN!

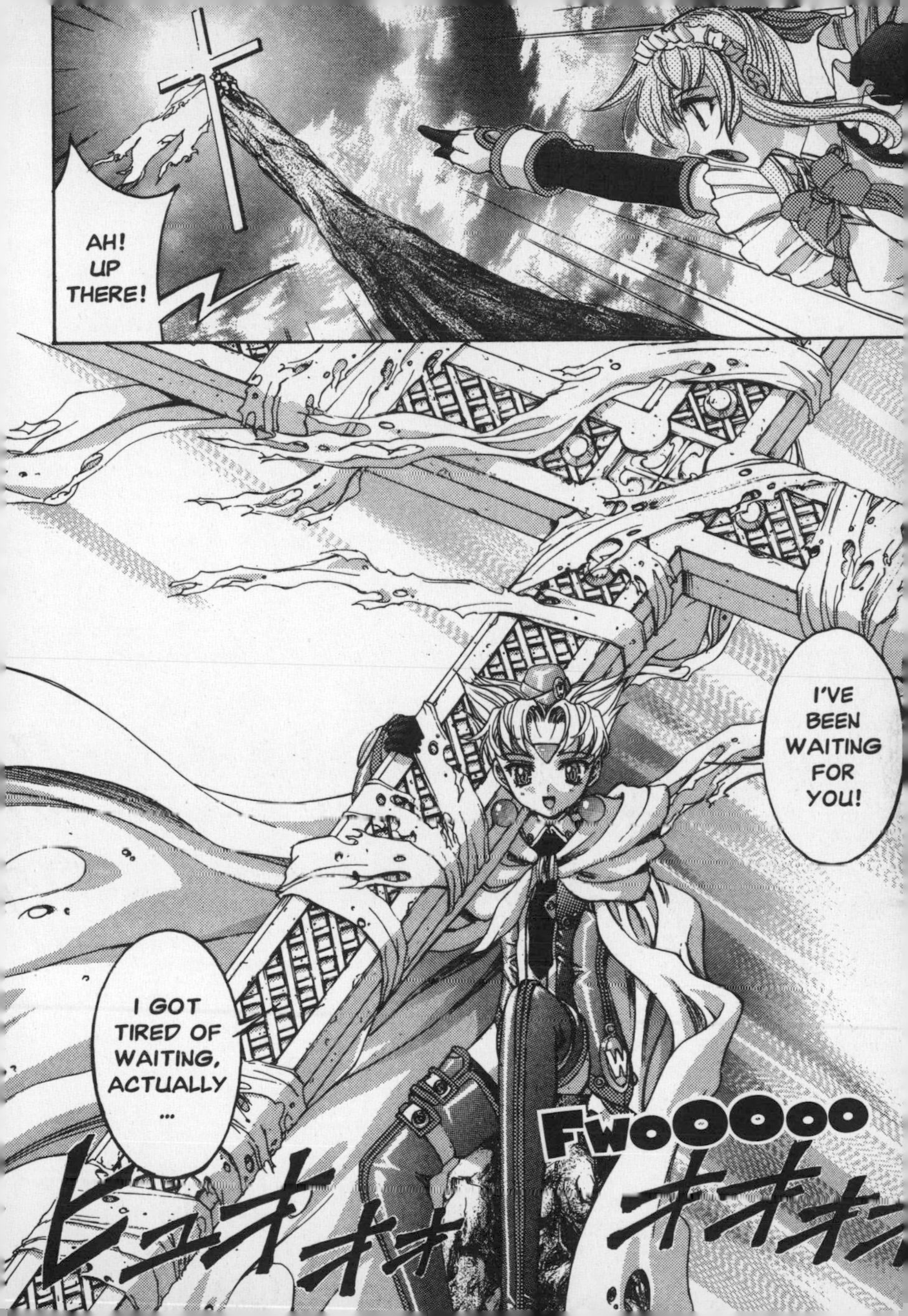
AH! UP THERE!
I'VE BEEN WAITING FOR YOU!
I GOT TIRED OF WAITING, ACTUALLY ...
FWOOOOO
ヒュオオオ
オオオン

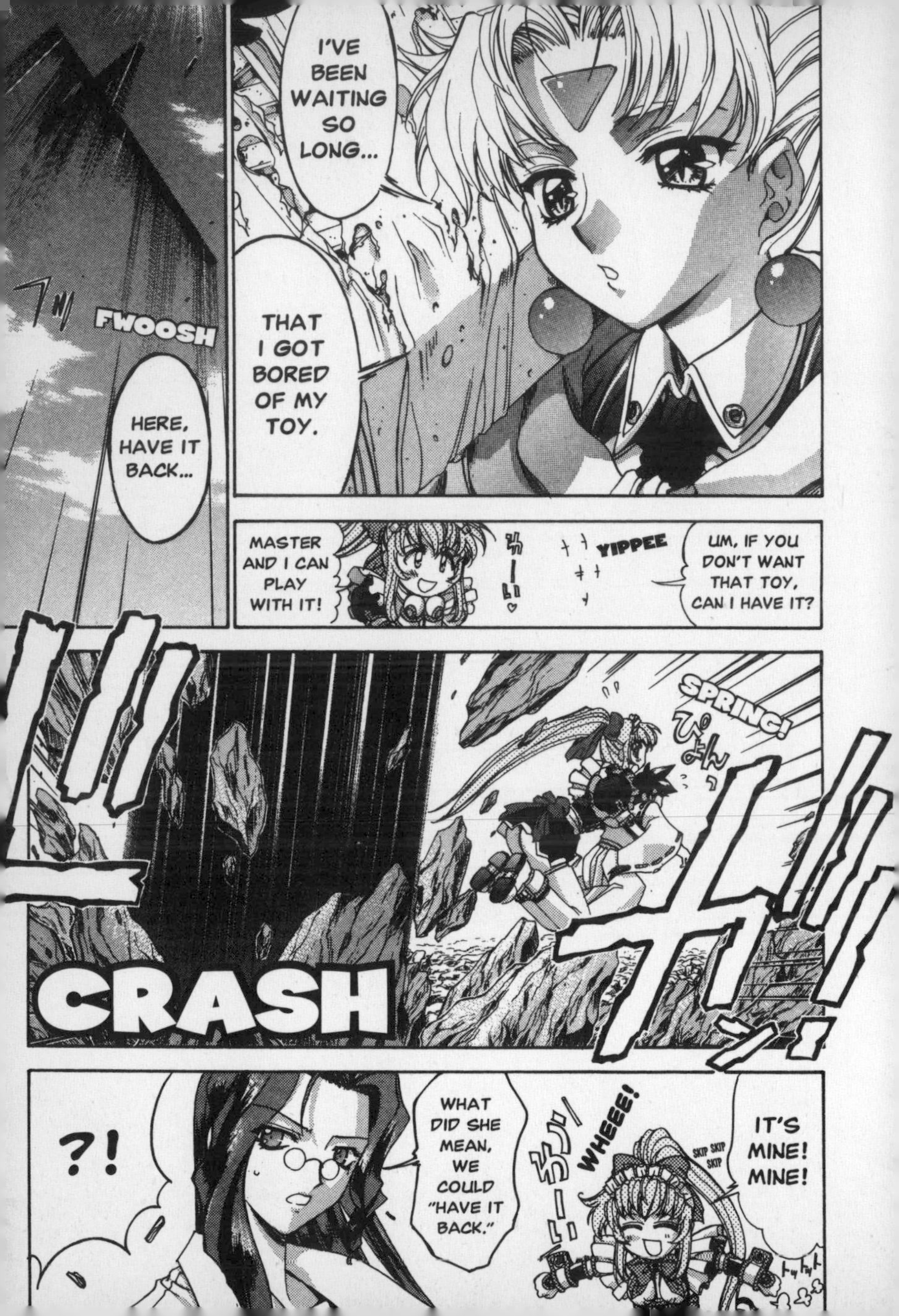
I'VE BEEN WAITING SO LONG...
THAT I GOT BORED OF MY TOY.
UM, IF YOU DON'T WANT THAT TOY, CAN I HAVE IT?
YIPPEE
MASTER AND I CAN PLAY WITH IT!
FWOOSH
HERE, HAVE IT BACK...
SPRING!
CRASH
IT'S MINE! MINE!
SKIP SKIP SKIP
WHEEE!
WHAT DID SHE MEAN, WE COULD "HAVE IT BACK."
?!

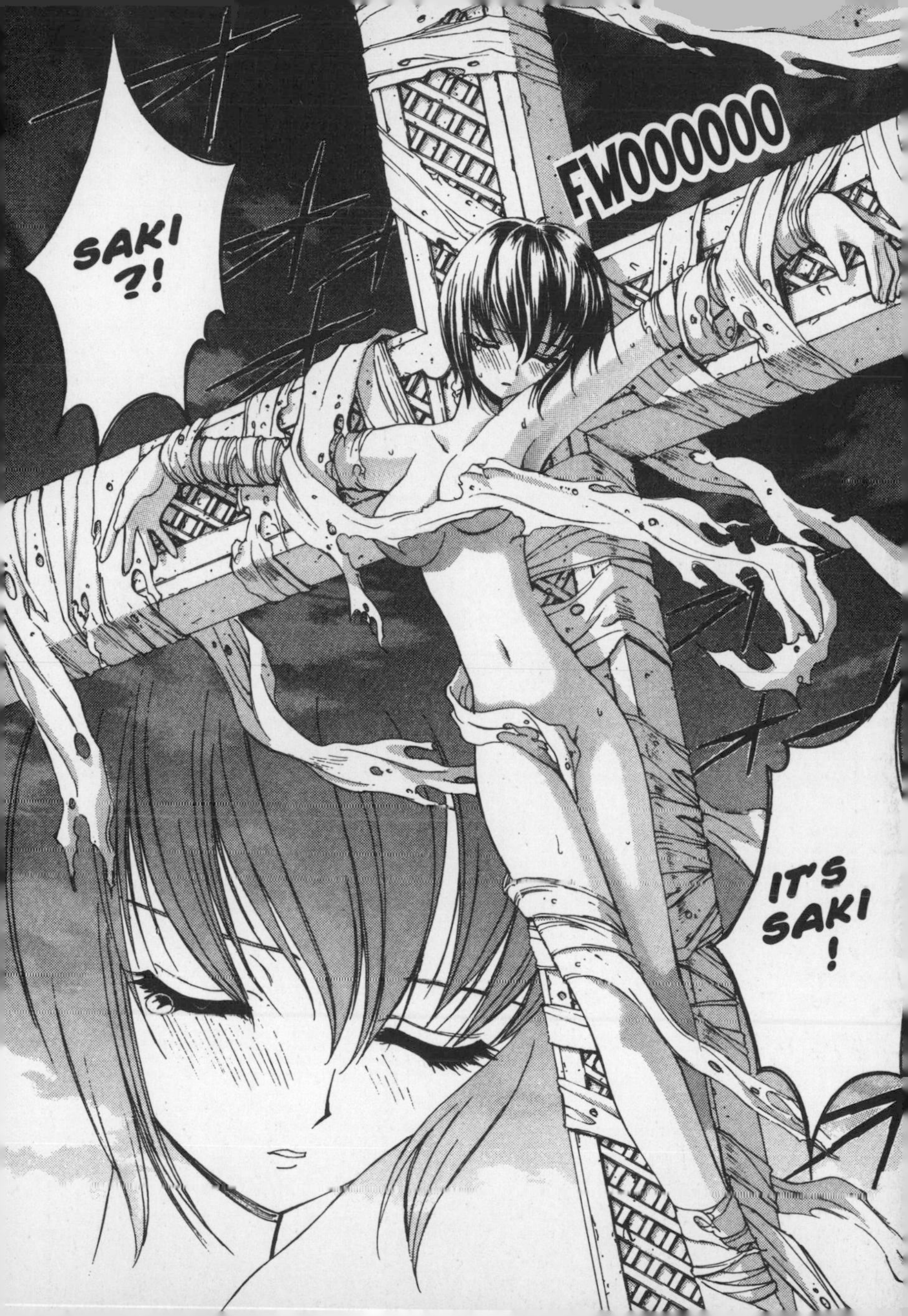
FWOOOOOO
SAKI?!
IT'S SAKI!

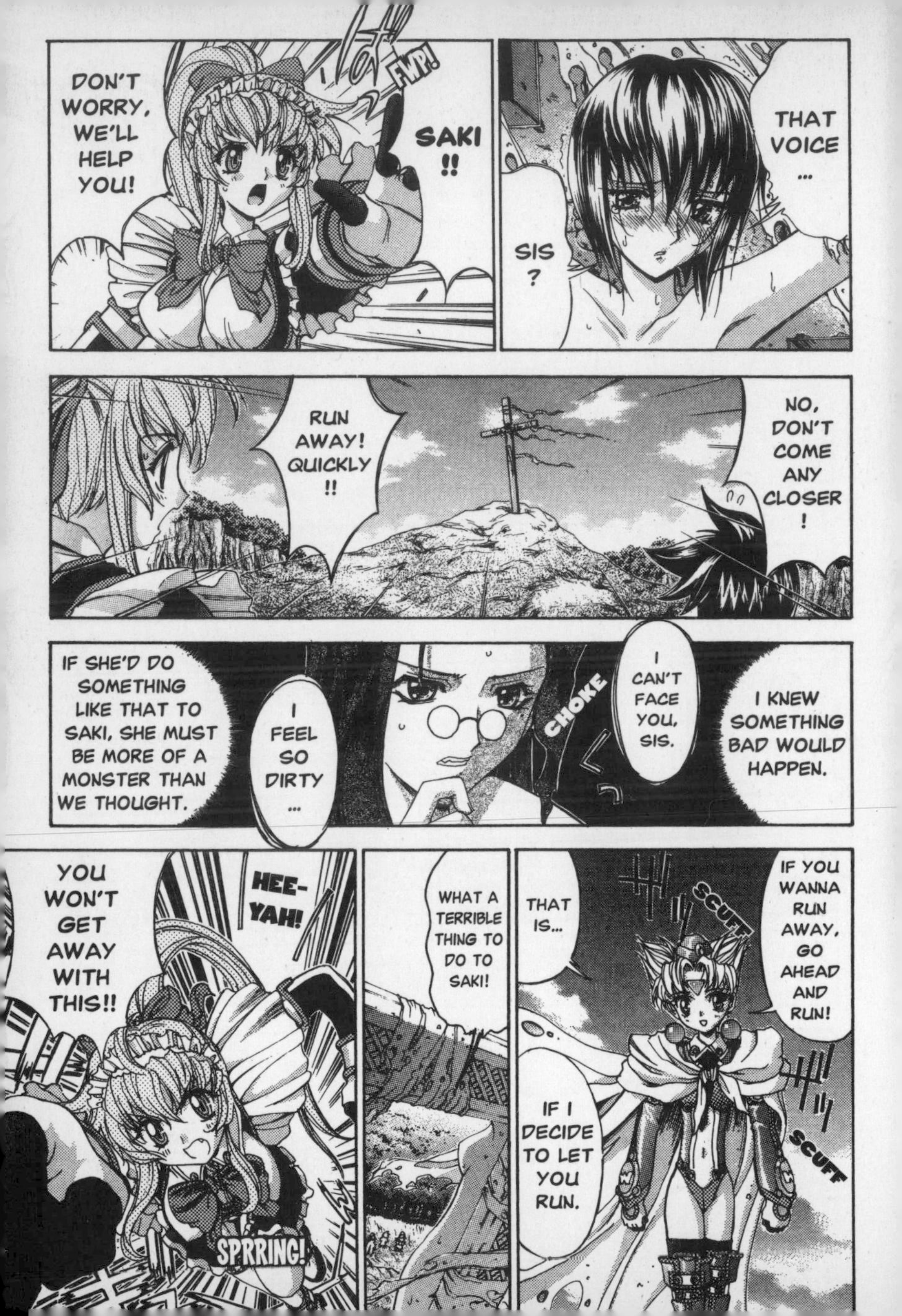
THAT VOICE ...
SIS ?
FWP!
SAKI !!
DON'T WORRY, WE'LL HELP YOU!
NO, DON'T COME ANY CLOSER !
RUN AWAY! QUICKLY !!
I KNEW SOMETHING BAD WOULD HAPPEN.
I CAN'T FACE YOU, SIS.
CHOKE
I FEEL SO DIRTY ...
IF SHE'D DO SOMETHING LIKE THAT TO SAKI, SHE MUST BE MORE OF A MONSTER THAN WE THOUGHT.
IF YOU WANNA RUN AWAY, GO AHEAD AND RUN!
SCUFF
THAT IS...
IF I DECIDE TO LET YOU RUN.
SCUFF
WHAT A TERRIBLE THING TO DO TO SAKI!
HEE-YAH!
YOU WON'T GET AWAY WITH THIS!!
SPRRING!

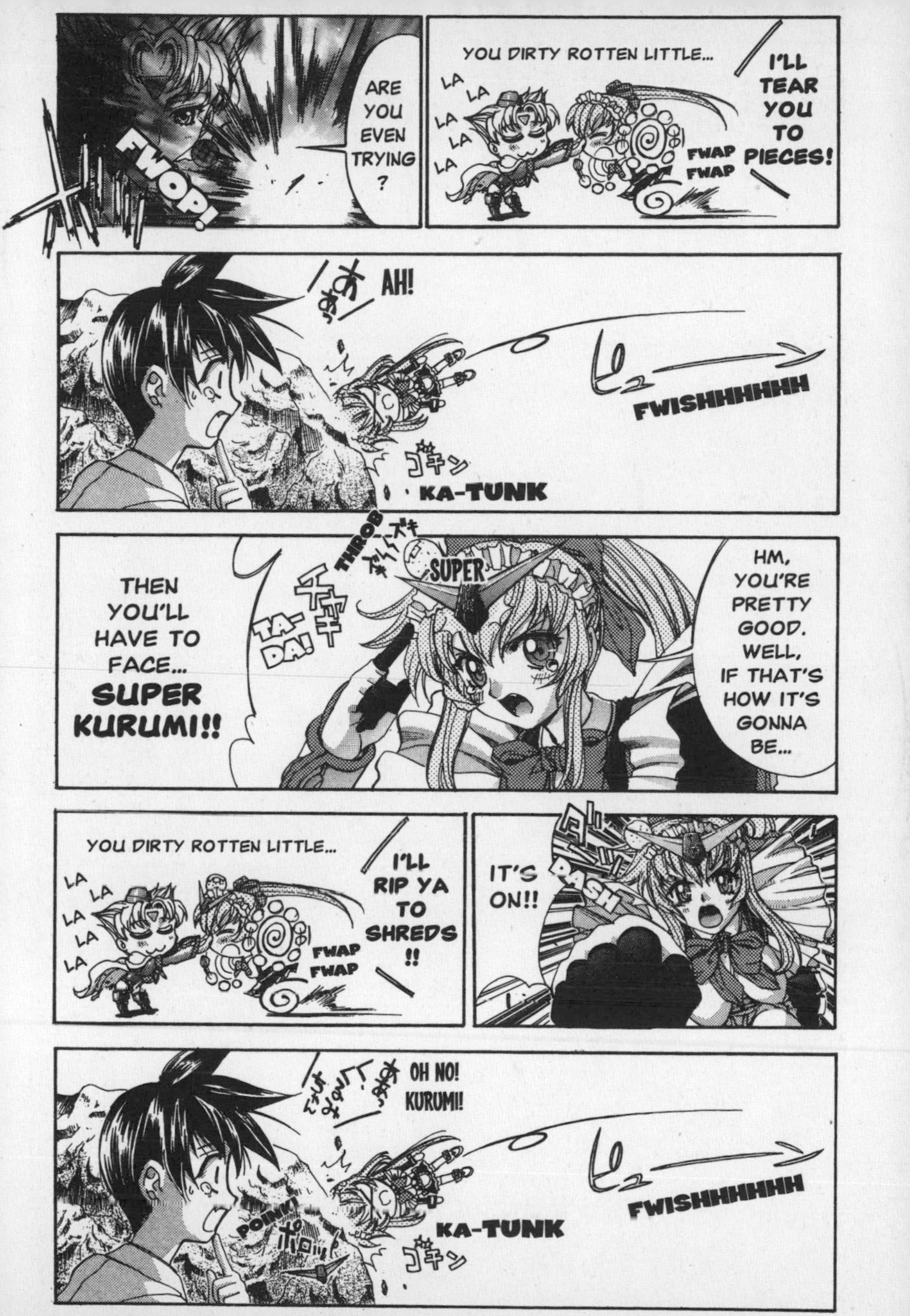
YOU DIRTY ROTTEN LITTLE...
I'LL TEAR YOU TO PIECES!
LA LA LA LA LA
FWAP FWAP
ARE YOU EVEN TRYING?
FWOP!
AH!
FWISHHHHHH
KA-TUNK
HM, YOU'RE PRETTY GOOD. WELL, IF THAT'S HOW IT'S GONNA BE...
SUPER
THROB
THEN YOU'LL HAVE TO FACE... SUPER KURUMI!!
TA-DA!
IT'S ON!!
DASH
YOU DIRTY ROTTEN LITTLE...
I'LL RIP YA TO SHREDS!!
LA LA LA LA LA
FWAP FWAP
OH NO! KURUMI!
FWISHHHHHH
KA-TUNK
POINK!

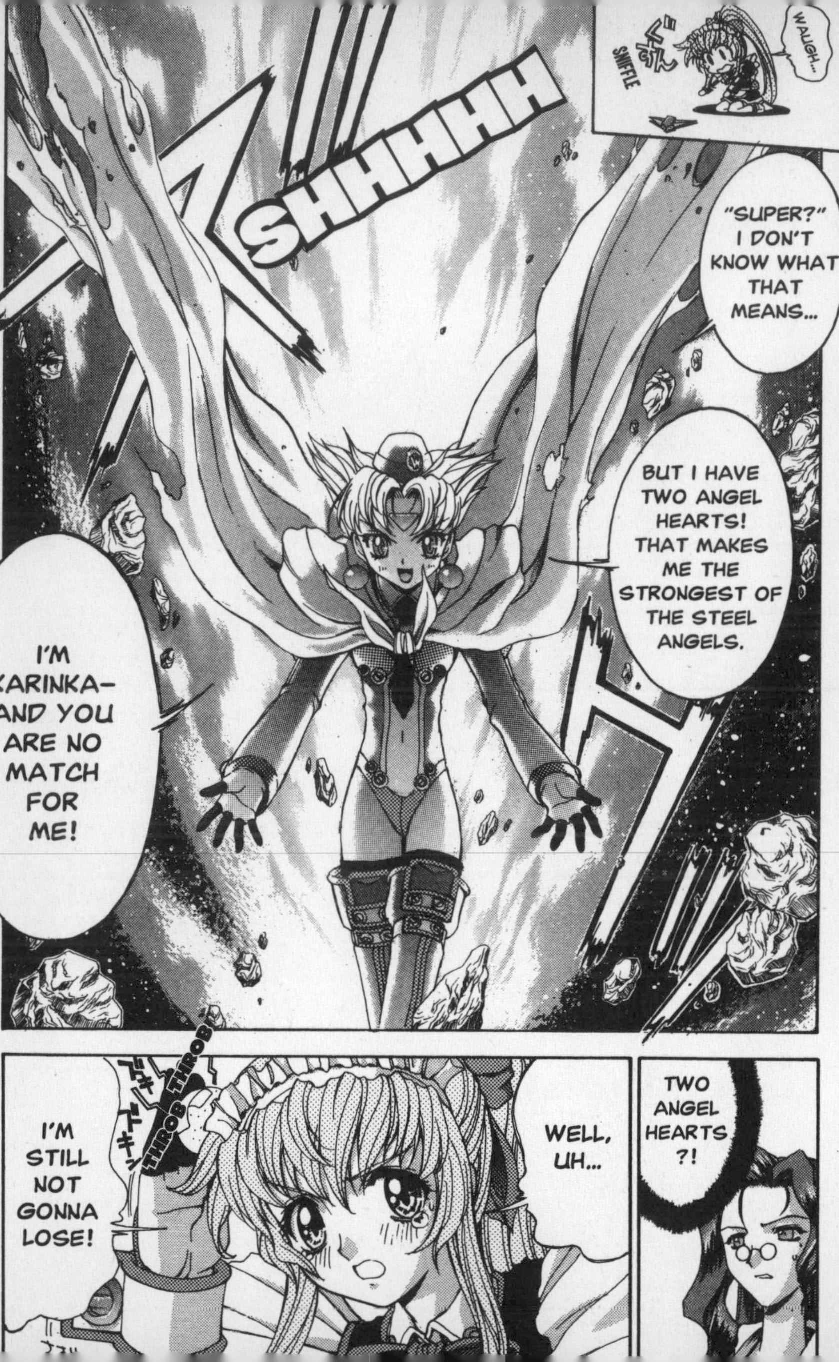
WAUGH...
SNIFFLE
SHHHHHH
"SUPER?" I DON'T KNOW WHAT THAT MEANS...
BUT I HAVE TWO ANGEL HEARTS! THAT MAKES ME THE STRONGEST OF THE STEEL ANGELS.
I'M KARINKA- AND YOU ARE NO MATCH FOR ME!
TWO ANGEL HEARTS ?!
WELL, UH...
THROB THROB
I'M STILL NOT GONNA LOSE!

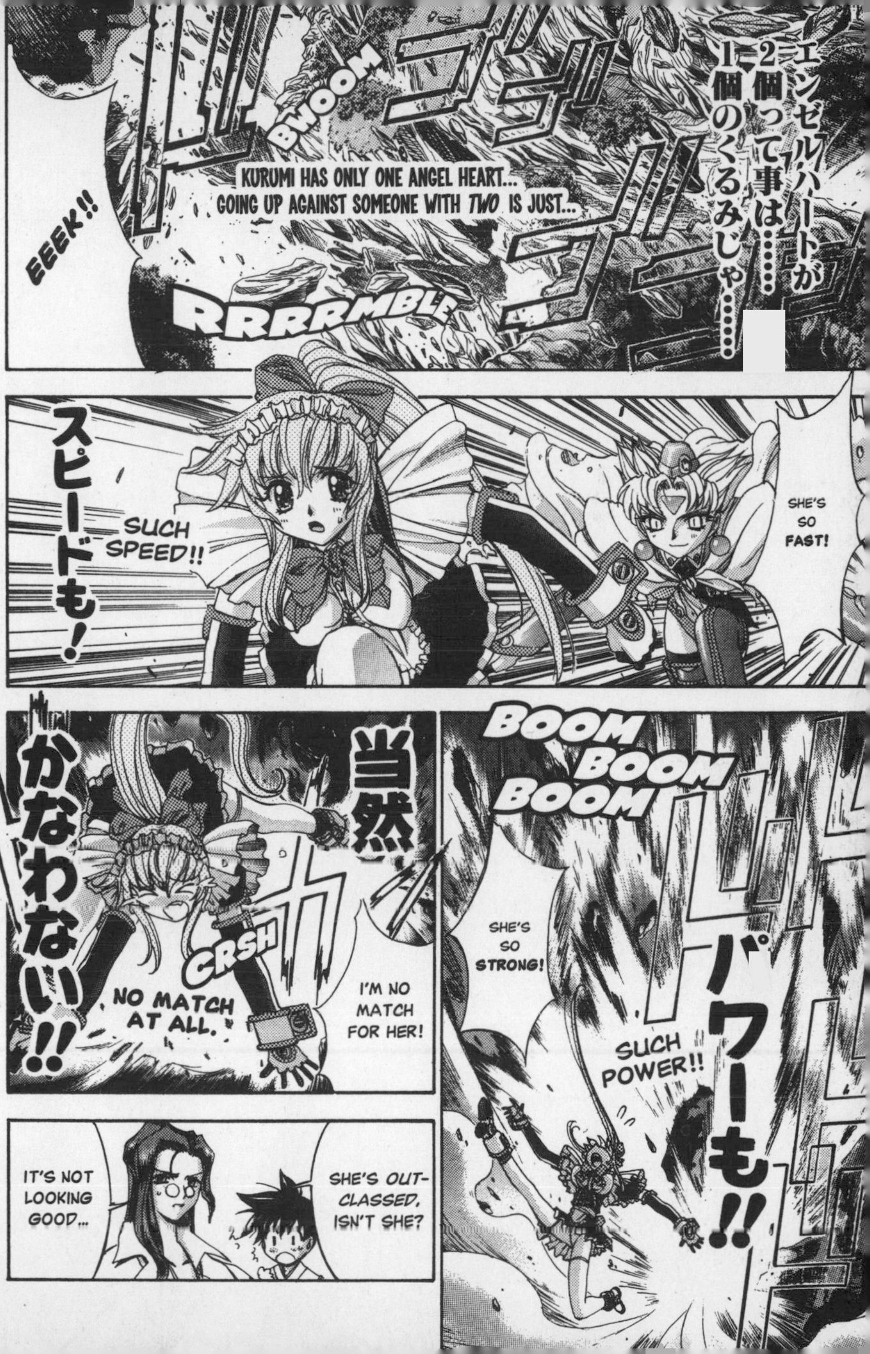
エンゼルハートが2個って事は……1個のくるみじゃ……
KURUMI HAS ONLY ONE ANGEL HEART... GOING UP AGAINST SOMEONE WITH *TWO* IS JUST...
BWOOM
RRRRMBLE
EEEK!!
SHE'S SO FAST!
スピードも!
SUCH SPEED!!
BOOM BOOM BOOM
パワーも!!
SHE'S SO STRONG!
SUCH POWER!!
当然
I'M NO MATCH FOR HER!
CRSH
かなわない!!
NO MATCH AT ALL.
SHE'S OUT-CLASSED, ISN'T SHE?
IT'S NOT LOOKING GOOD...

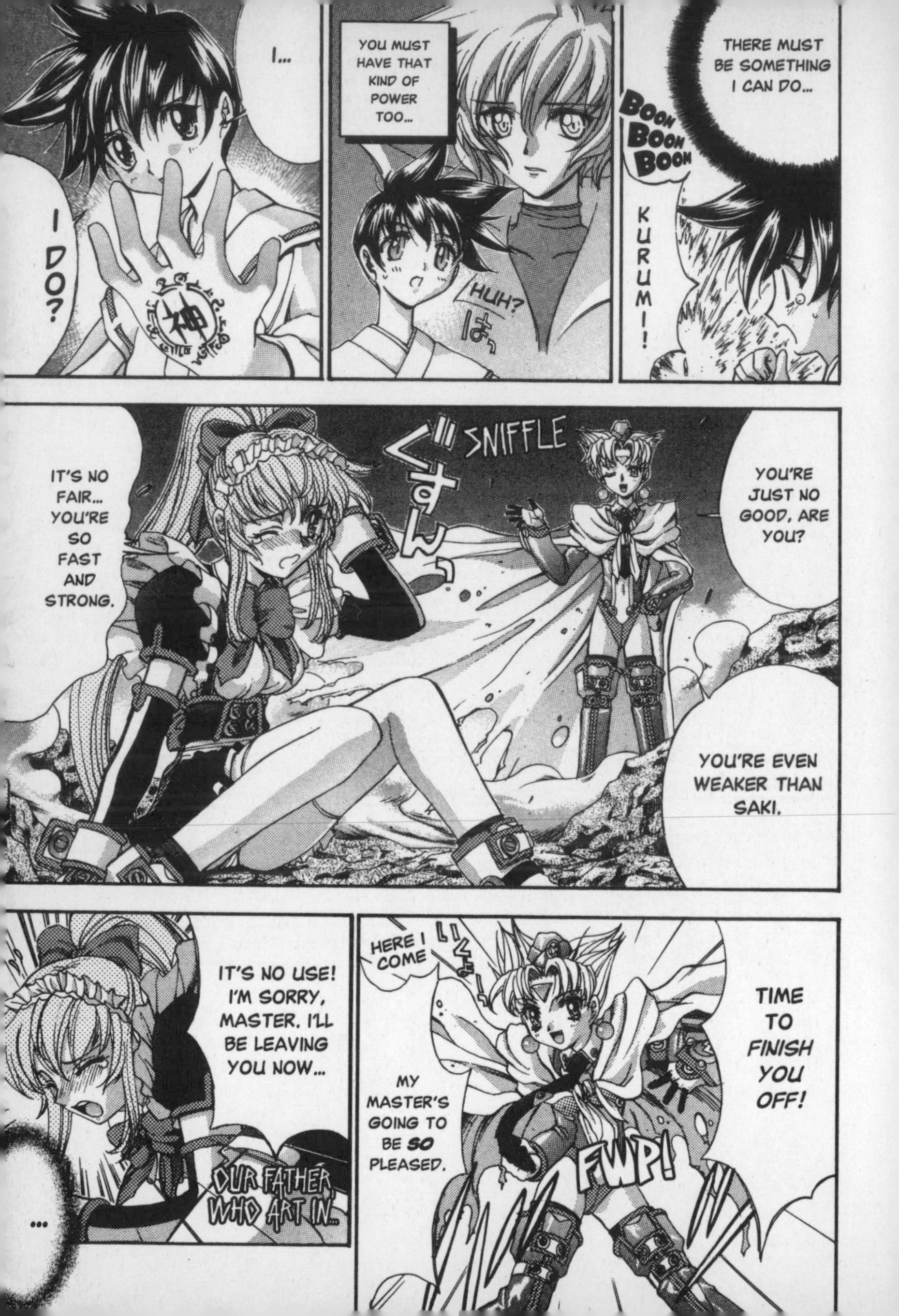
THERE MUST BE SOMETHING I CAN DO...
BOOM BOOM BOOM
KURUMI!
YOU MUST HAVE THAT KIND OF POWER TOO...
HUH?
はっ
I...
I DO?
YOU'RE JUST NO GOOD, ARE YOU?
SNIFFLE
ぐすん
IT'S NO FAIR... YOU'RE SO FAST AND STRONG.
YOU'RE EVEN WEAKER THAN SAKI.
TIME TO FINISH YOU OFF!
HERE I COME
MY MASTER'S GOING TO BE SO PLEASED.
FWP!
IT'S NO USE! I'M SORRY, MASTER. I'LL BE LEAVING YOU NOW...
OUR FATHER WHO ART IN...
...

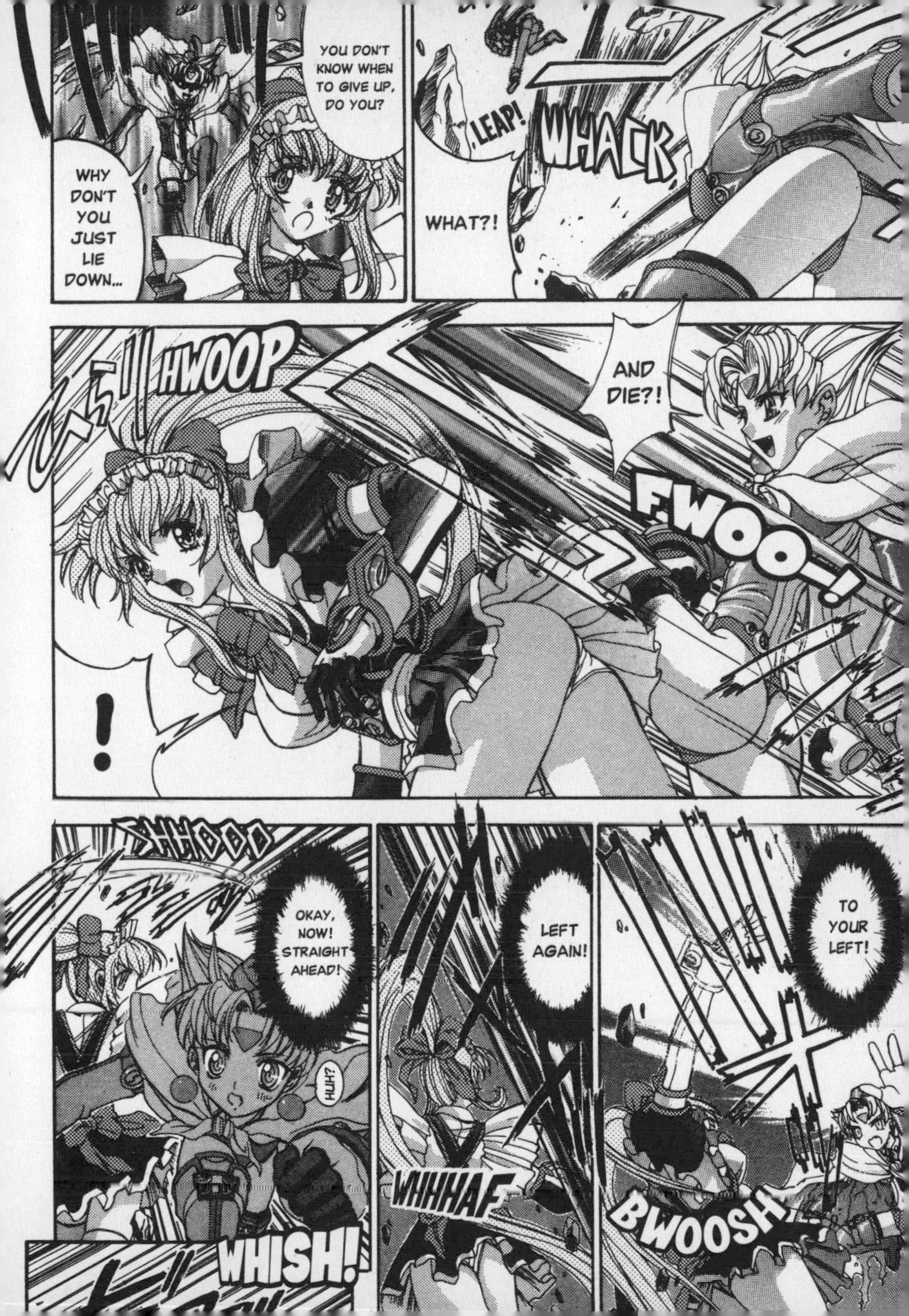
WHACK
LEAP!
WHAT?!
YOU DON'T KNOW WHEN TO GIVE UP, DO YOU?
WHY DON'T YOU JUST LIE DOWN...
AND DIE?!
HWOOP
FWOO-!
!
TO YOUR LEFT!
BWOOSH
LEFT AGAIN!
WHHHAF
OKAY, NOW! STRAIGHT AHEAD!
HUH?!
WHISH!

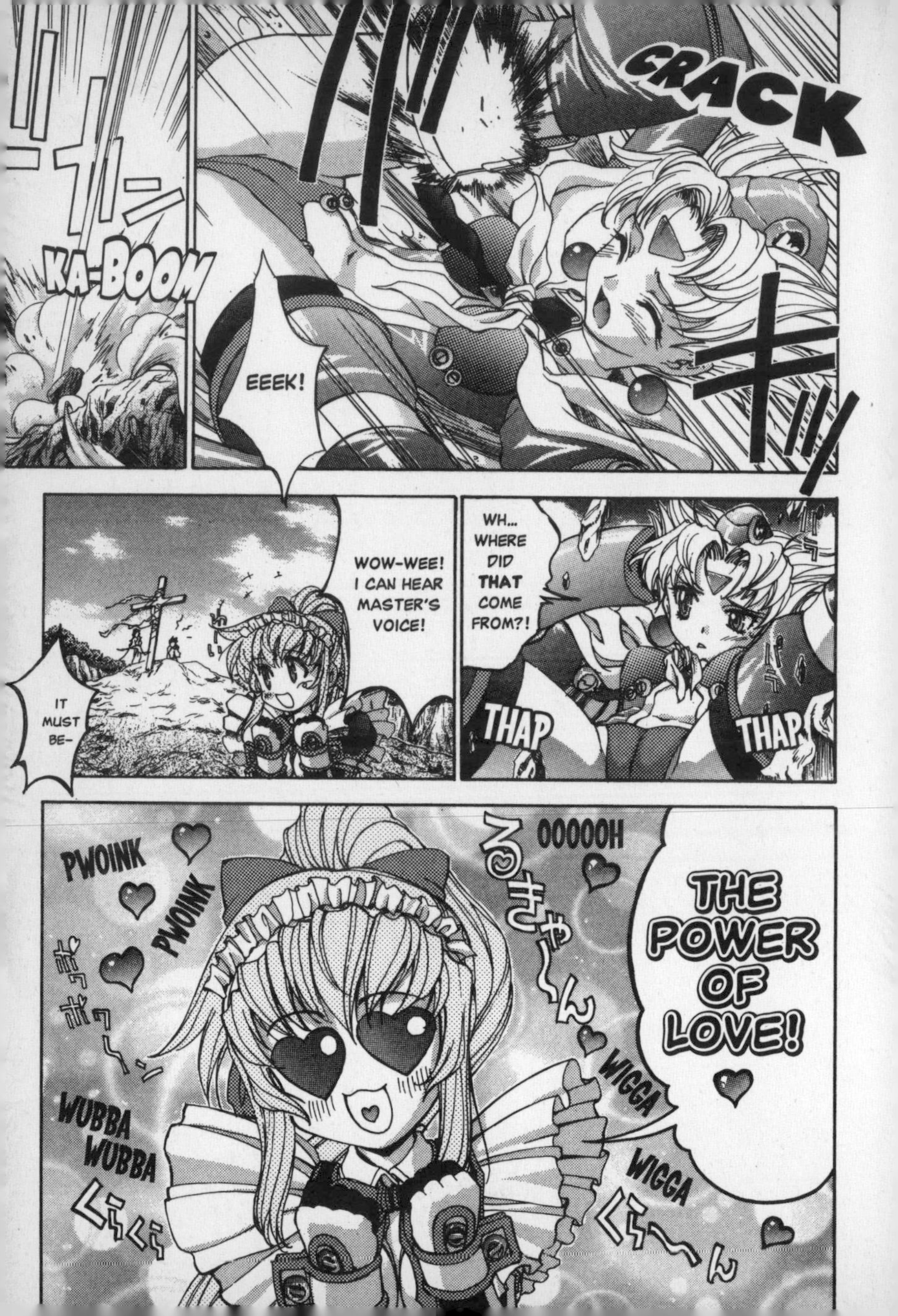
CRACK
EEEK!
KA-BOOM
WH... WHERE DID THAT COME FROM?!
THAP
THAP
WOW-WEE! I CAN HEAR MASTER'S VOICE!
IT MUST BE-
THE POWER OF LOVE!
OOOOOH
WIGGA
WIGGA
PWOINK
PWOINK
WUBBA WUBBA

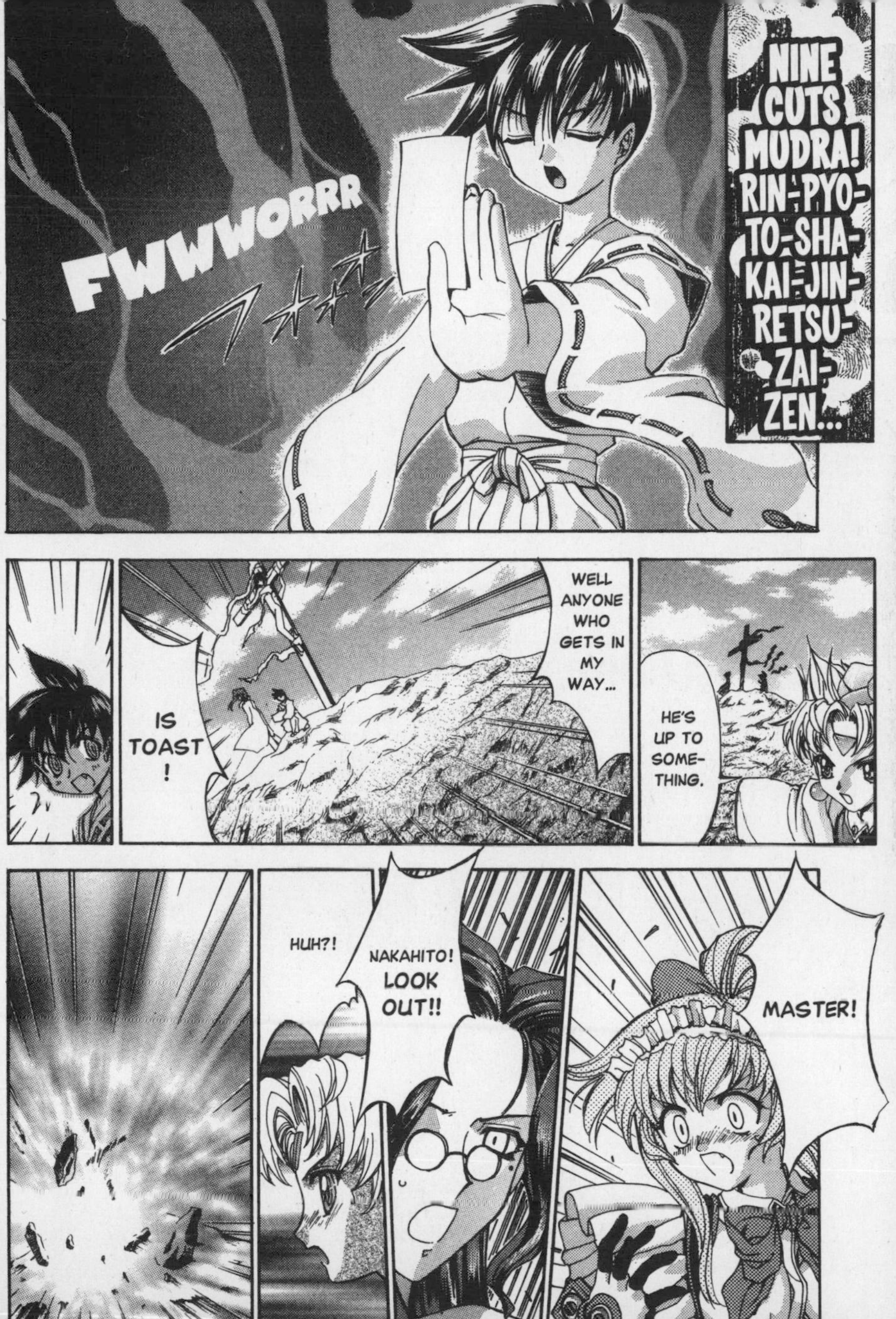
NINE CUTS MUDRA! RIN-PYO-TO-SHA-KAI-JIN-RETSU-ZAI-ZEN...
FWWWORRR
HE'S UP TO SOMETHING.
WELL ANYONE WHO GETS IN MY WAY...
IS TOAST!
MASTER!
NAKAHITO! LOOK OUT!!
HUH?!

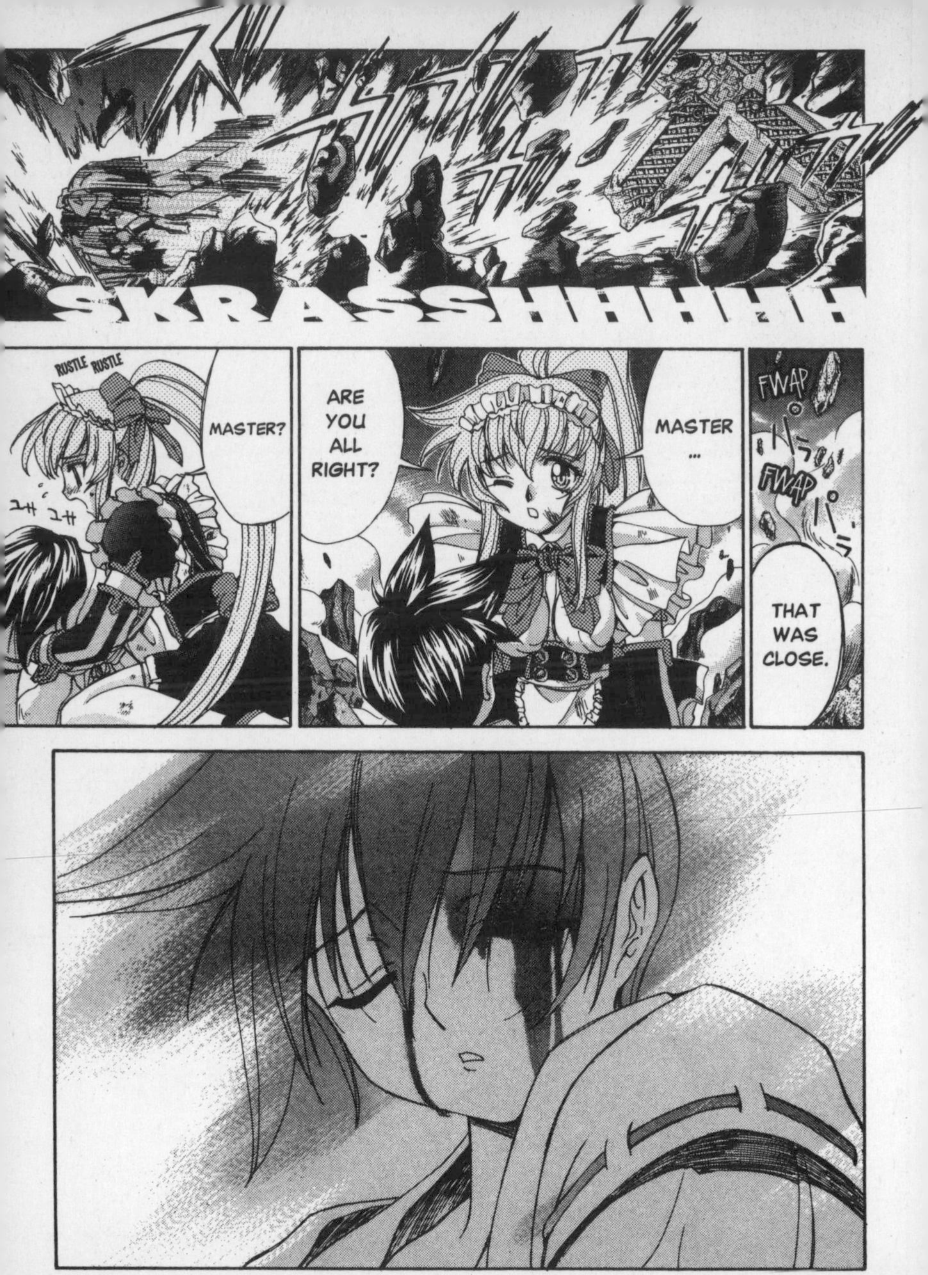
SKRASSH!!!!!!
FWAP
FWAP
THAT WAS CLOSE.
MASTER ...
ARE YOU ALL RIGHT?
RUSTLE RUSTLE
MASTER?

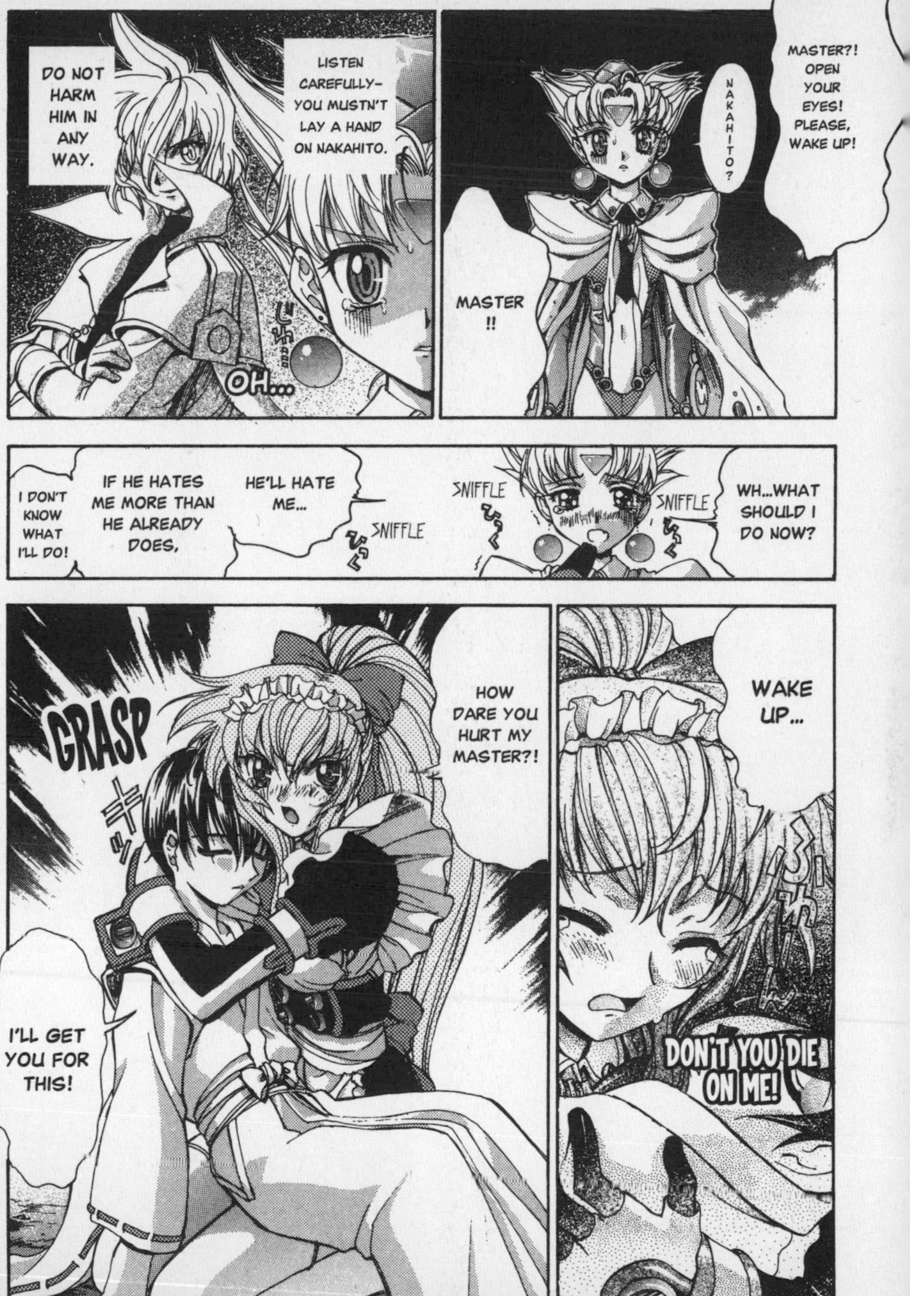
MASTER?! OPEN YOUR EYES! PLEASE, WAKE UP!
NAKAHITO?
MASTER !!
LISTEN CAREFULLY- YOU MUSTN'T LAY A HAND ON NAKAHITO.
DO NOT HARM HIM IN ANY WAY.
OH...
WH...WHAT SHOULD I DO NOW?
SNIFFLE
SNIFFLE
SNIFFLE
HE'LL HATE ME...
IF HE HATES ME MORE THAN HE ALREADY DOES,
I DON'T KNOW WHAT I'LL DO!
WAKE UP...
DON'T YOU DIE ON ME!
HOW DARE YOU HURT MY MASTER?!
GRASP
I'LL GET YOU FOR THIS!

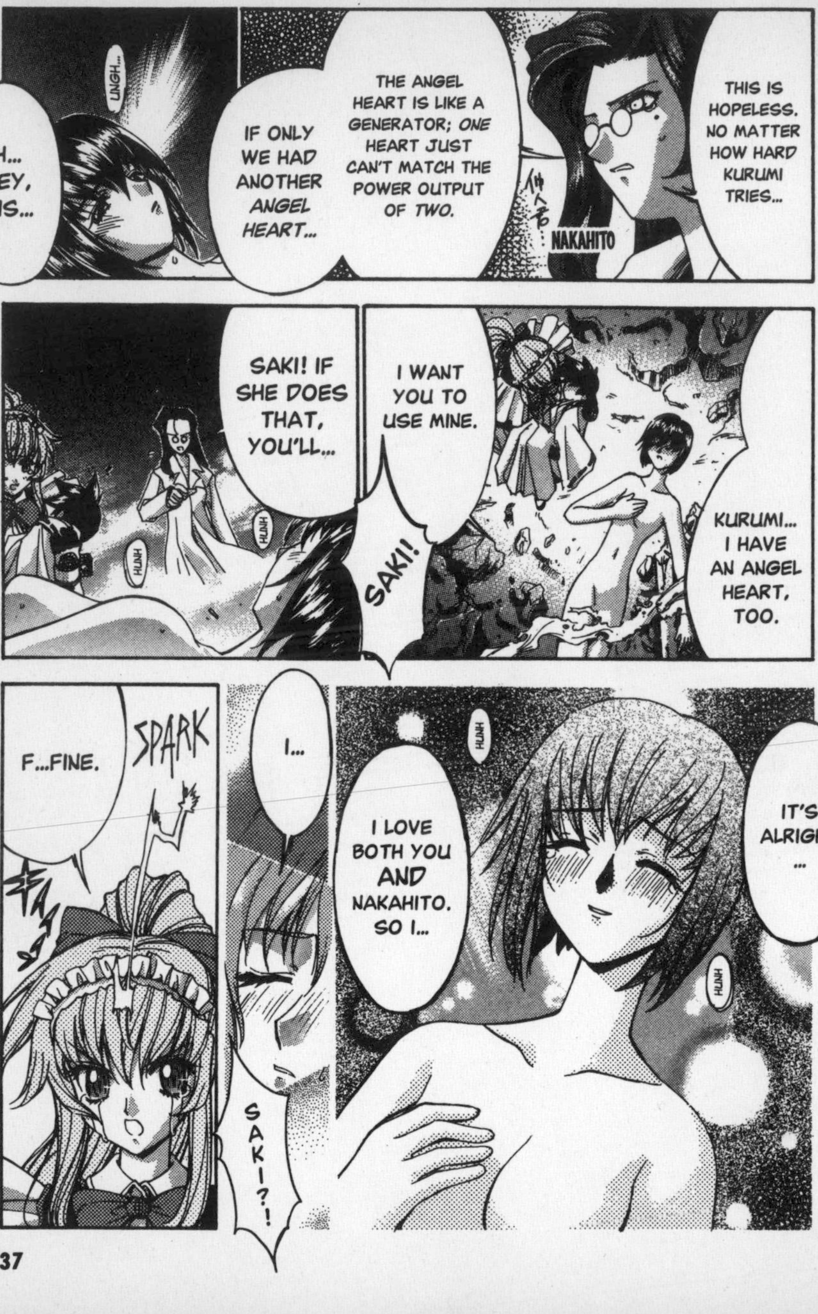
THIS IS HOPELESS. NO MATTER HOW HARD KURUMI TRIES...
NAKAHITO
THE ANGEL HEART IS LIKE A GENERATOR; *ONE* HEART JUST CAN'T MATCH THE POWER OUTPUT OF *TWO*.
IF ONLY WE HAD ANOTHER *ANGEL HEART*...
UNGH...
H... HEY, SIS...
KURUMI... I HAVE AN ANGEL HEART, TOO.
I WANT YOU TO USE MINE.
SAKI!
HUNH
HUNH
SAKI! IF SHE DOES THAT, YOU'LL...
IT'S ALRIGHT ...
HUNH
I LOVE BOTH YOU AND NAKAHITO. SO I...
HUNH
I...
SAKI?!
SPARK
F...FINE.

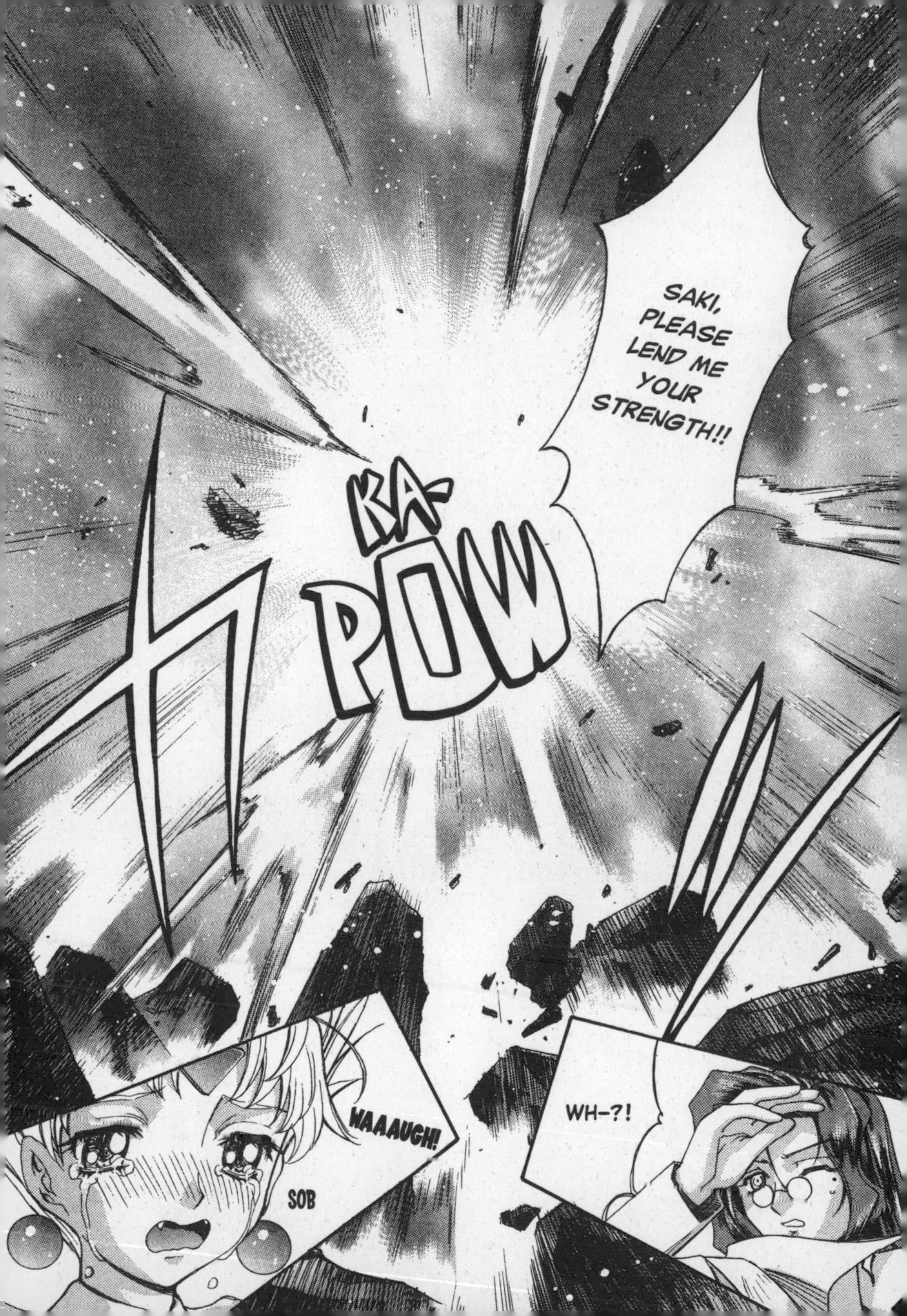
SAKI, PLEASE LEND ME YOUR STRENGTH!!
KA-POW
WH-?!
WAAAUGH!
SOB

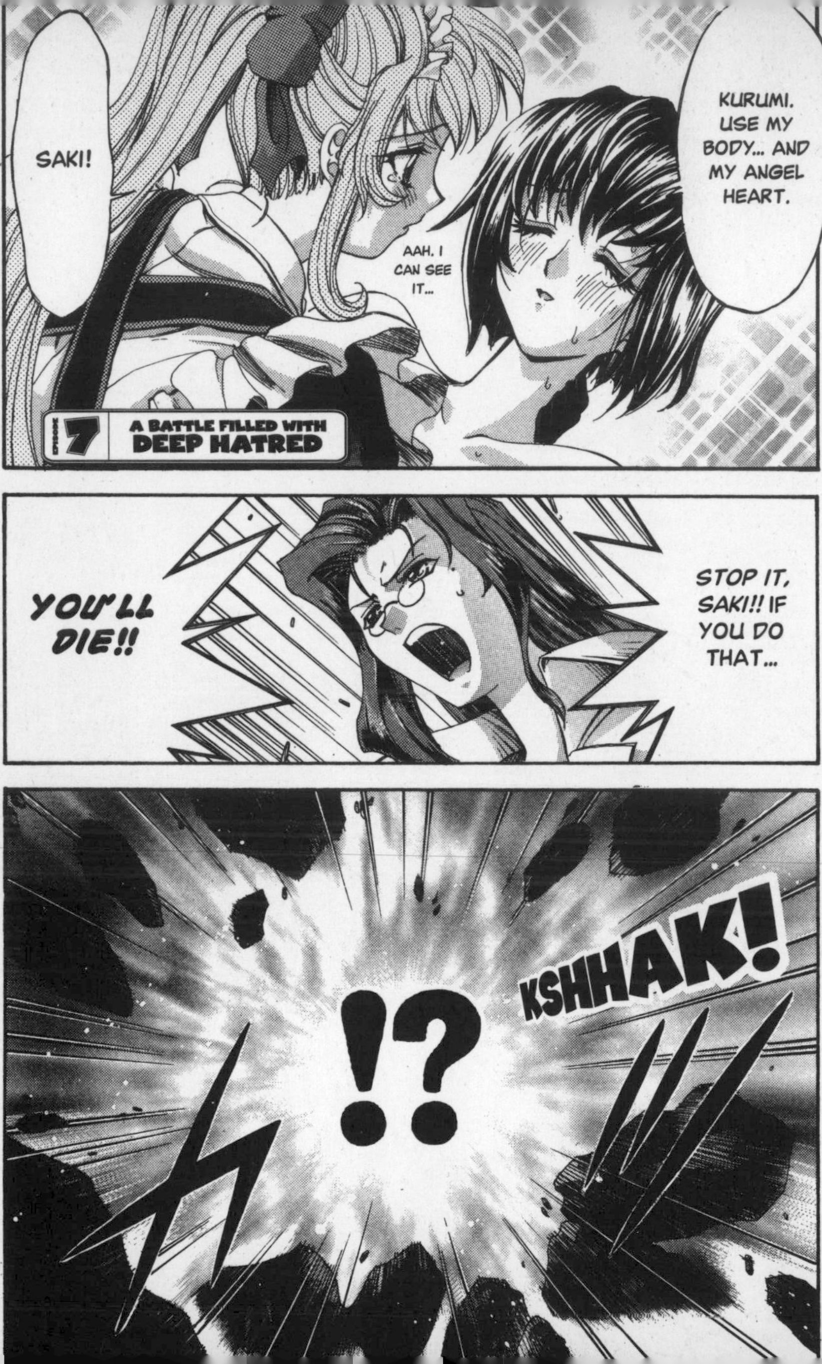
KURUMI. USE MY BODY... AND MY ANGEL HEART.
AAH, I CAN SEE IT...
SAKI!
EPISODE 7 A BATTLE FILLED WITH DEEP HATRED
STOP IT, SAKI!! IF YOU DO THAT...
YOU'LL DIE!!
KSHHAK!
!?

EPISODE 7 A BATTLE FILLED WITH DEEP HATRED

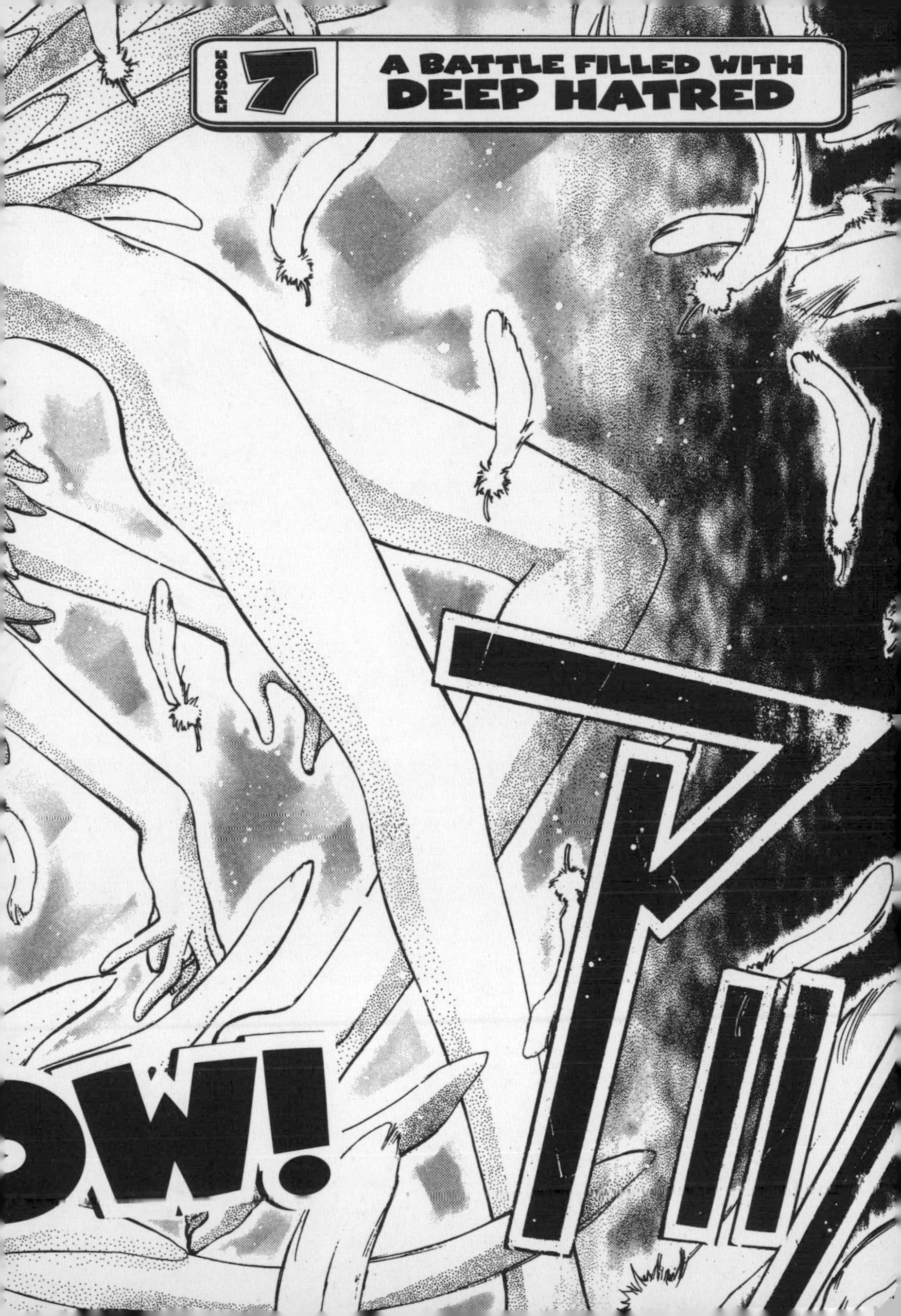
OW!

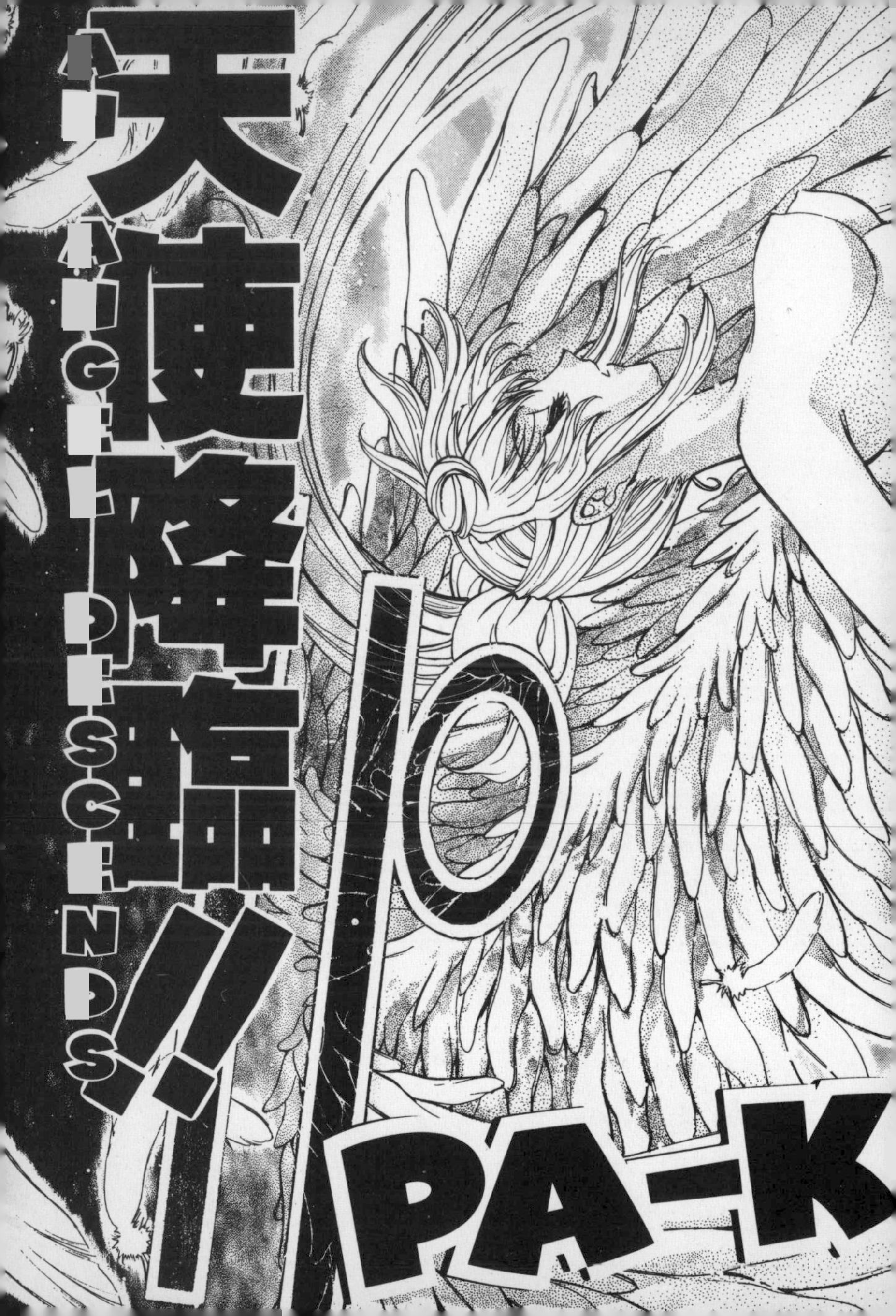
天使降臨!!
ANGEL DESCENDS
PA-K

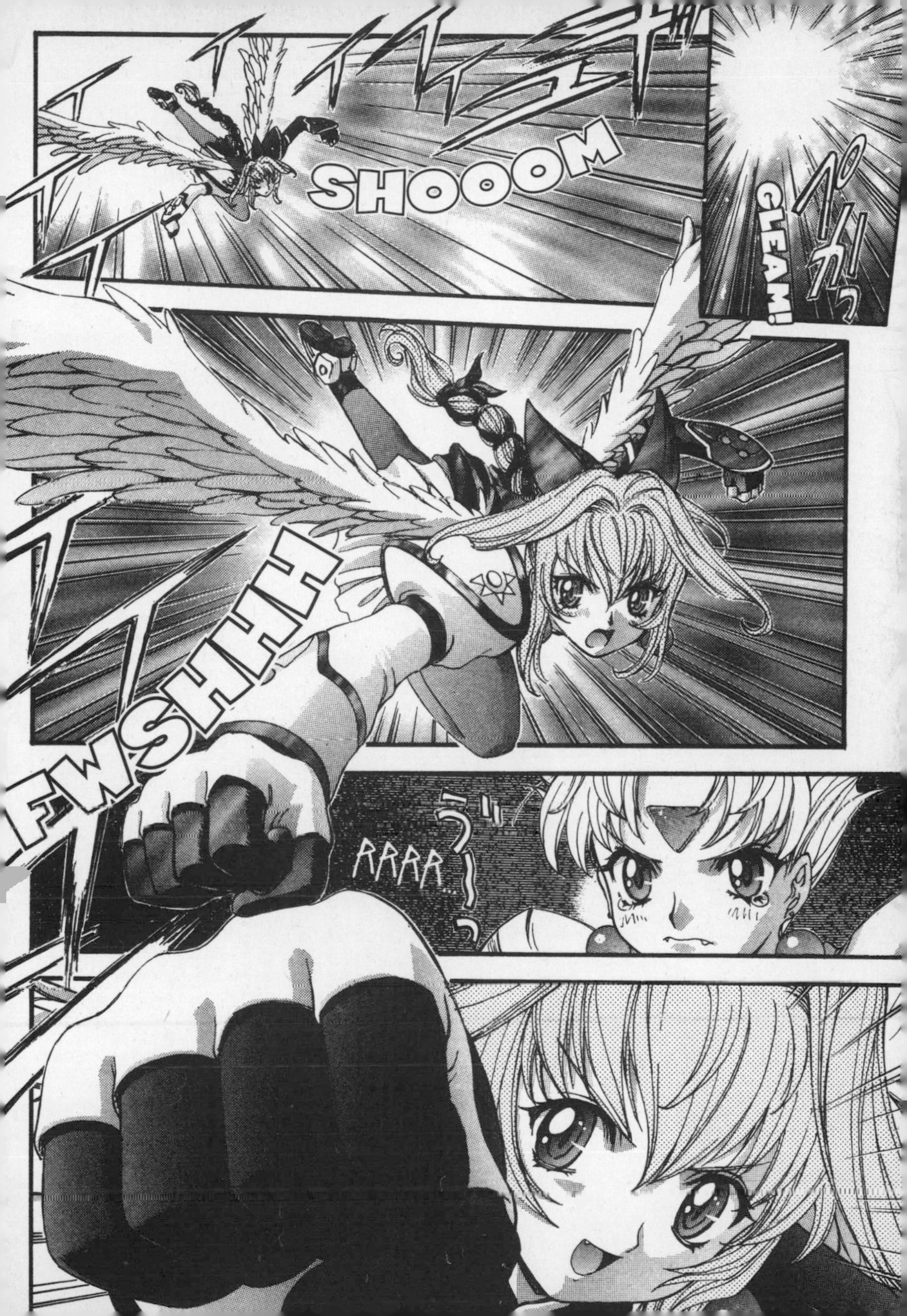
GLEAM!
SHOOOM
FWSHHH
RRRR...

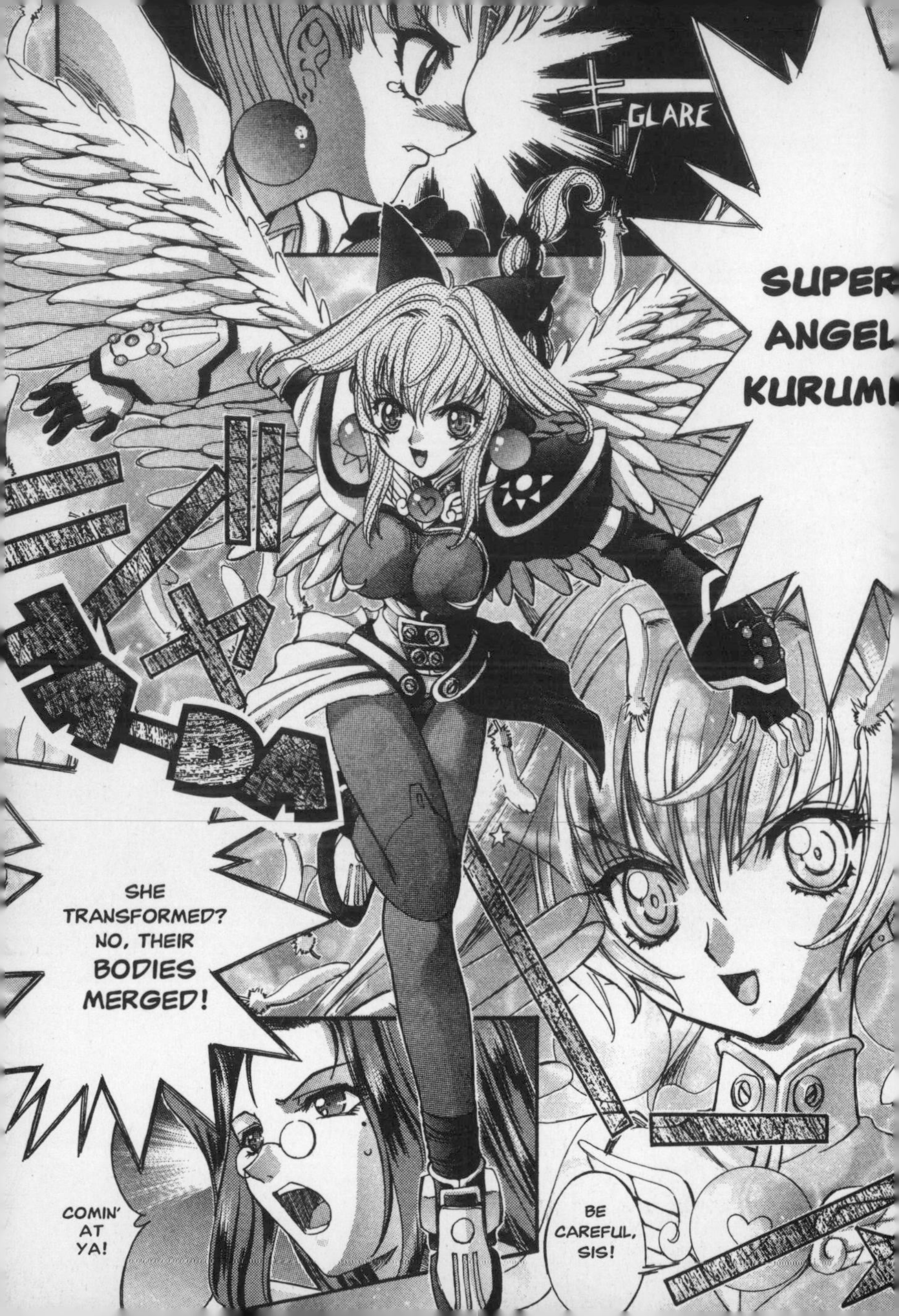
GLARE
SUPER ANGEL KURUM
DA
SHE TRANSFORMED? NO, THEIR BODIES MERGED!
BE CAREFUL, SIS!
COMIN' AT YA!

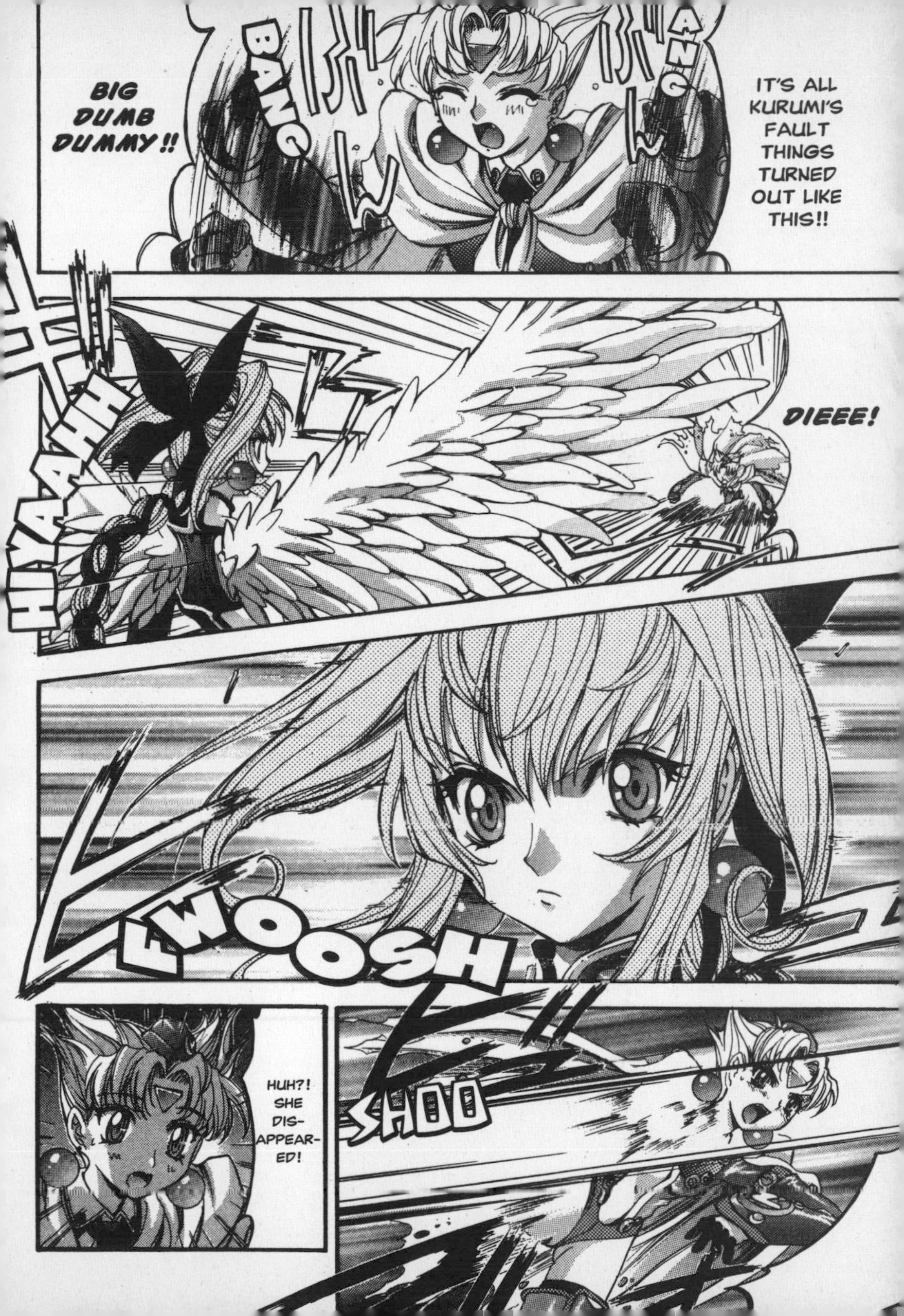
ANG
IT'S ALL KURUMI'S FAULT THINGS TURNED OUT LIKE THIS!!
BANG
BIG DUMB DUMMY!!
DIEEE!
HIYAAHH
FWOOSH
SHOO
HUH?! SHE DIS-APPEARED!

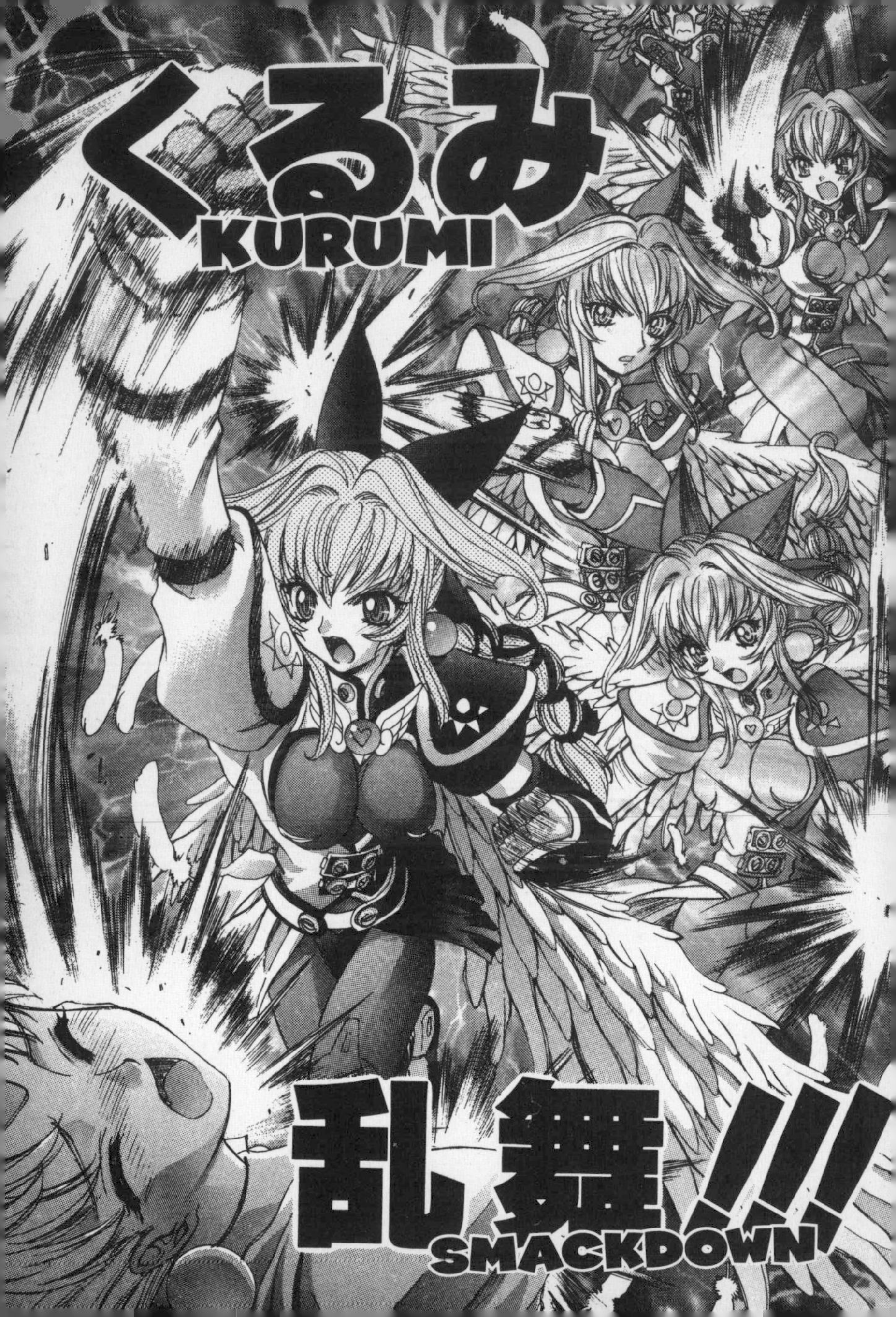
くるみ
KURUMI
乱舞!!!
SMACKDOWN

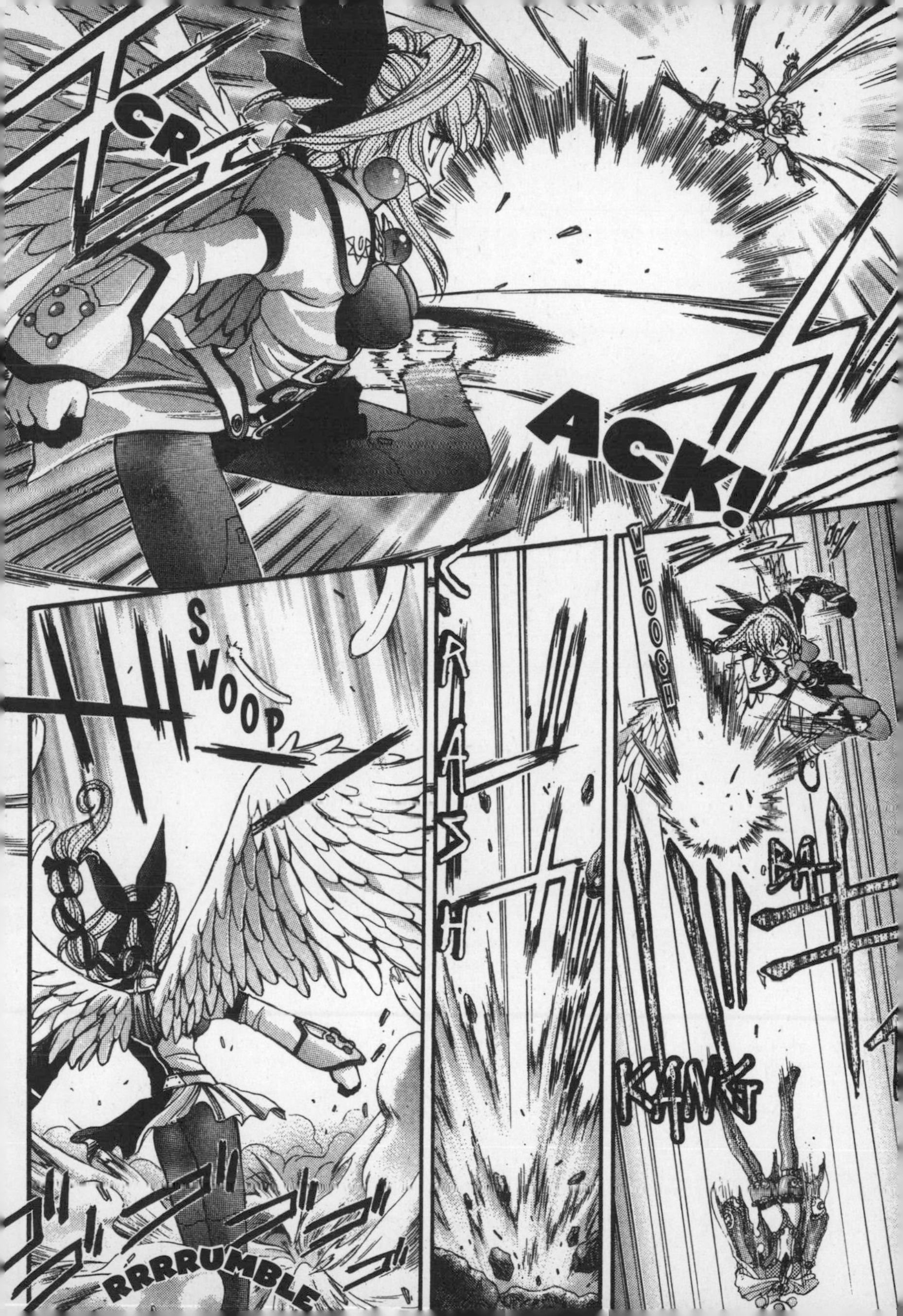
CR
ACK!
WHOOSH
CRASH
SWOOP
RRRRUMBLE

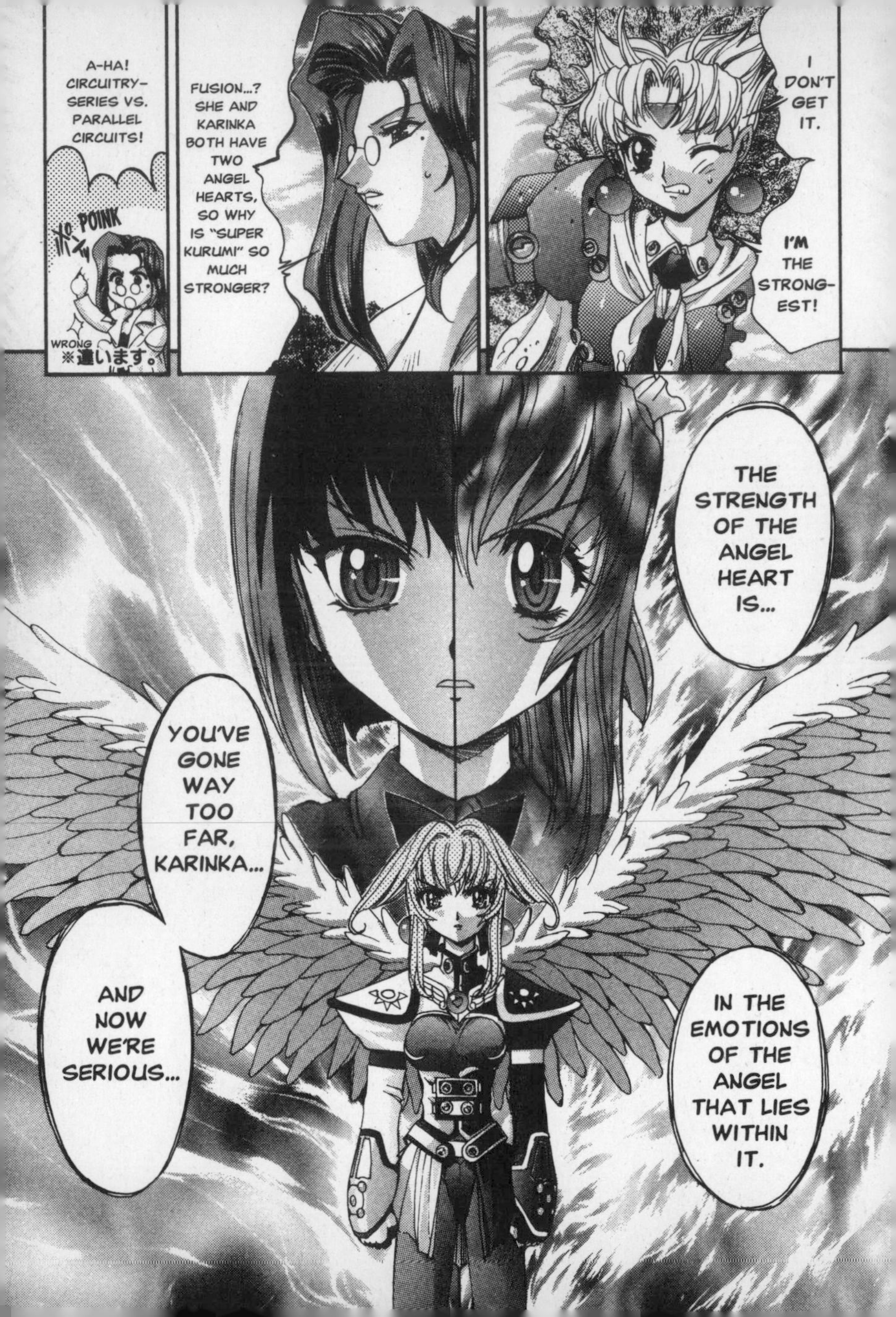
I DON'T GET IT.
I'M THE STRONGEST!
FUSION...? SHE AND KARINKA BOTH HAVE TWO ANGEL HEARTS, SO WHY IS "SUPER KURUMI" SO MUCH STRONGER?
A-HA! CIRCUITRY-SERIES VS. PARALLEL CIRCUITS!
POINK
WRONG
※違います。
THE STRENGTH OF THE ANGEL HEART IS...
YOU'VE GONE WAY TOO FAR, KARINKA...
IN THE EMOTIONS OF THE ANGEL THAT LIES WITHIN IT.
AND NOW WE'RE SERIOUS...

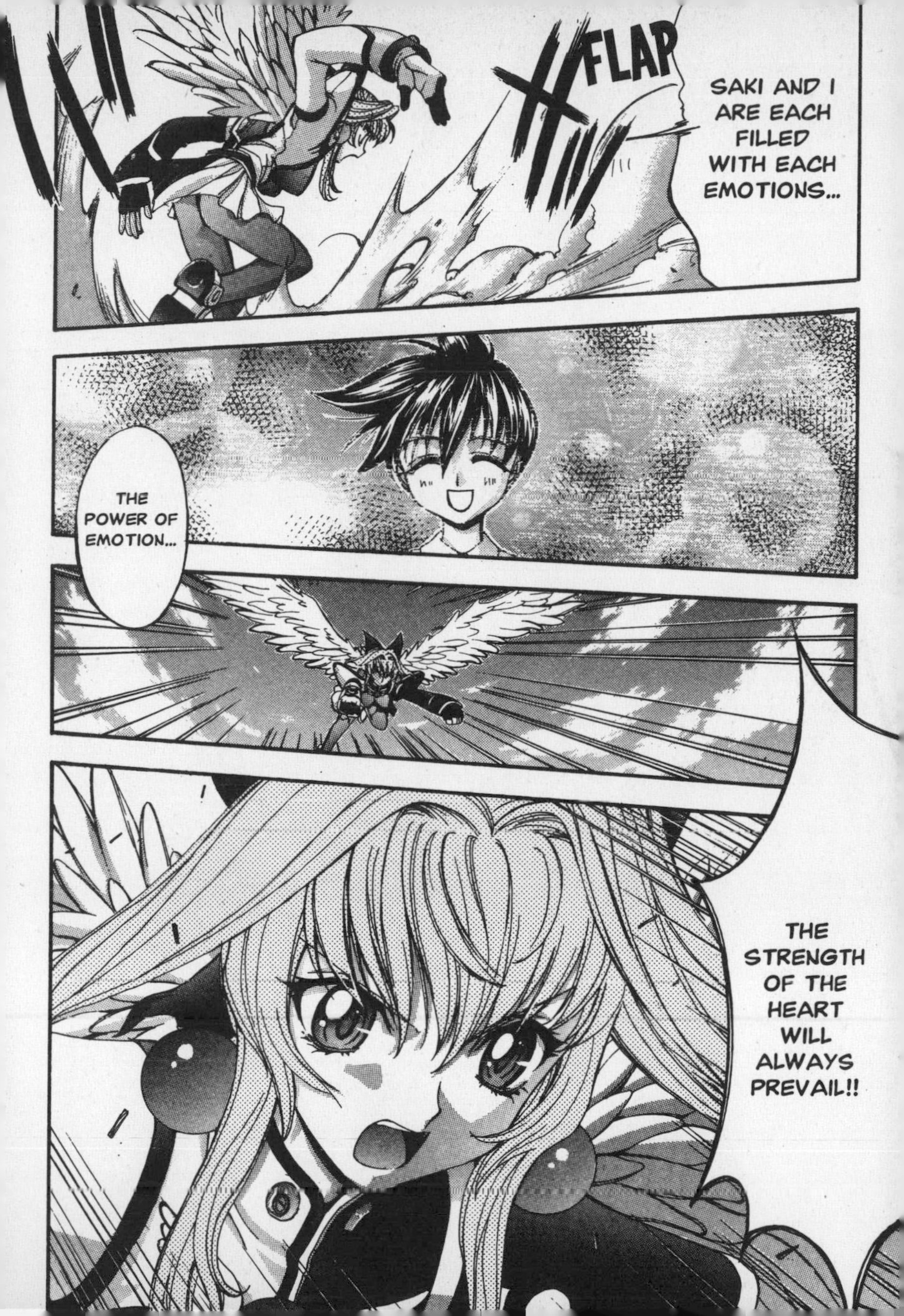
FLAP
SAKI AND I ARE EACH FILLED WITH EACH EMOTIONS...
THE POWER OF EMOTION...
THE STRENGTH OF THE HEART WILL ALWAYS PREVAIL!!

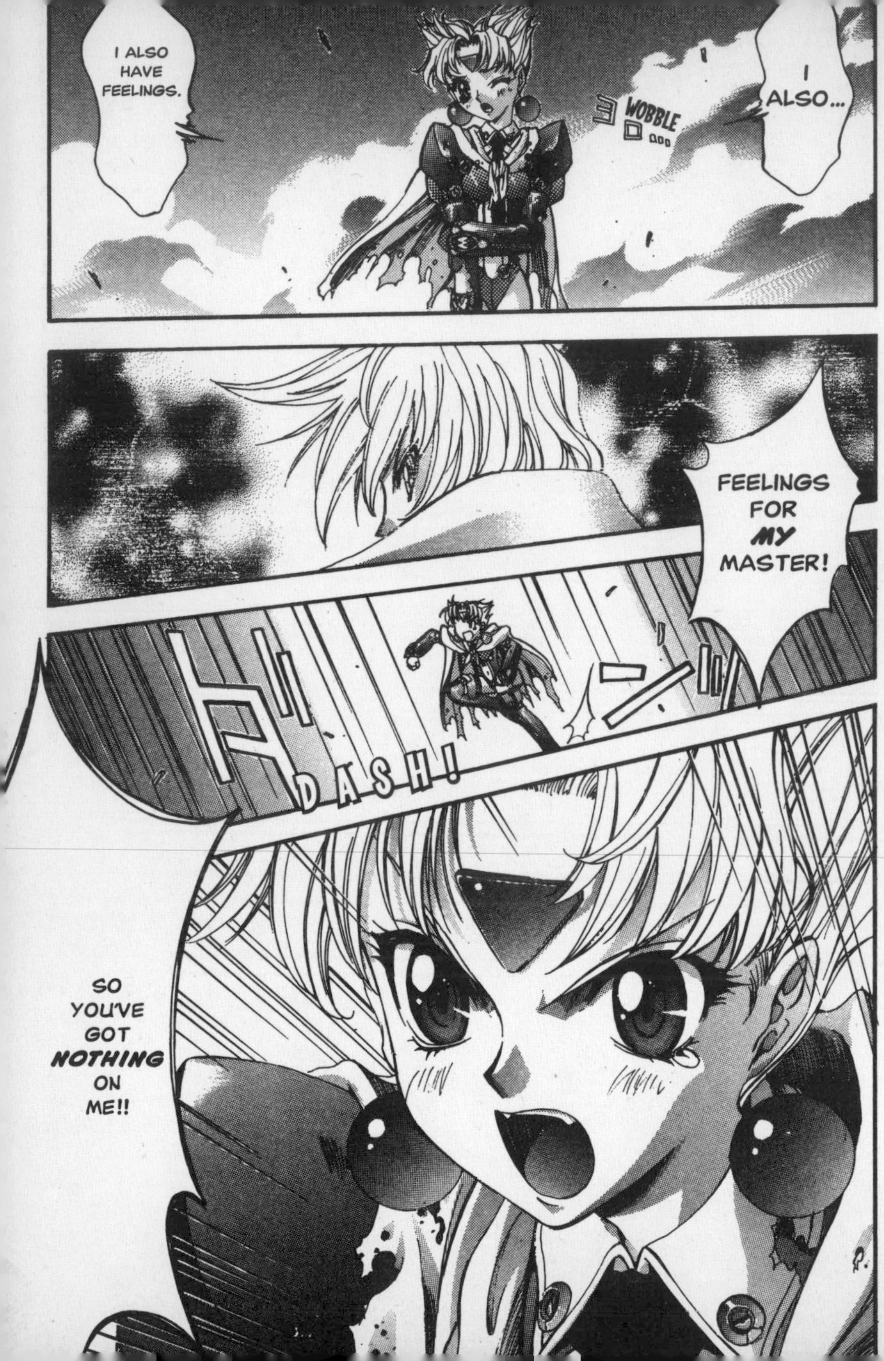
I ALSO...
I ALSO HAVE FEELINGS.
WOBBLE
FEELINGS FOR *MY* MASTER!
DASH!
SO YOU'VE GOT *NOTHING* ON ME!!

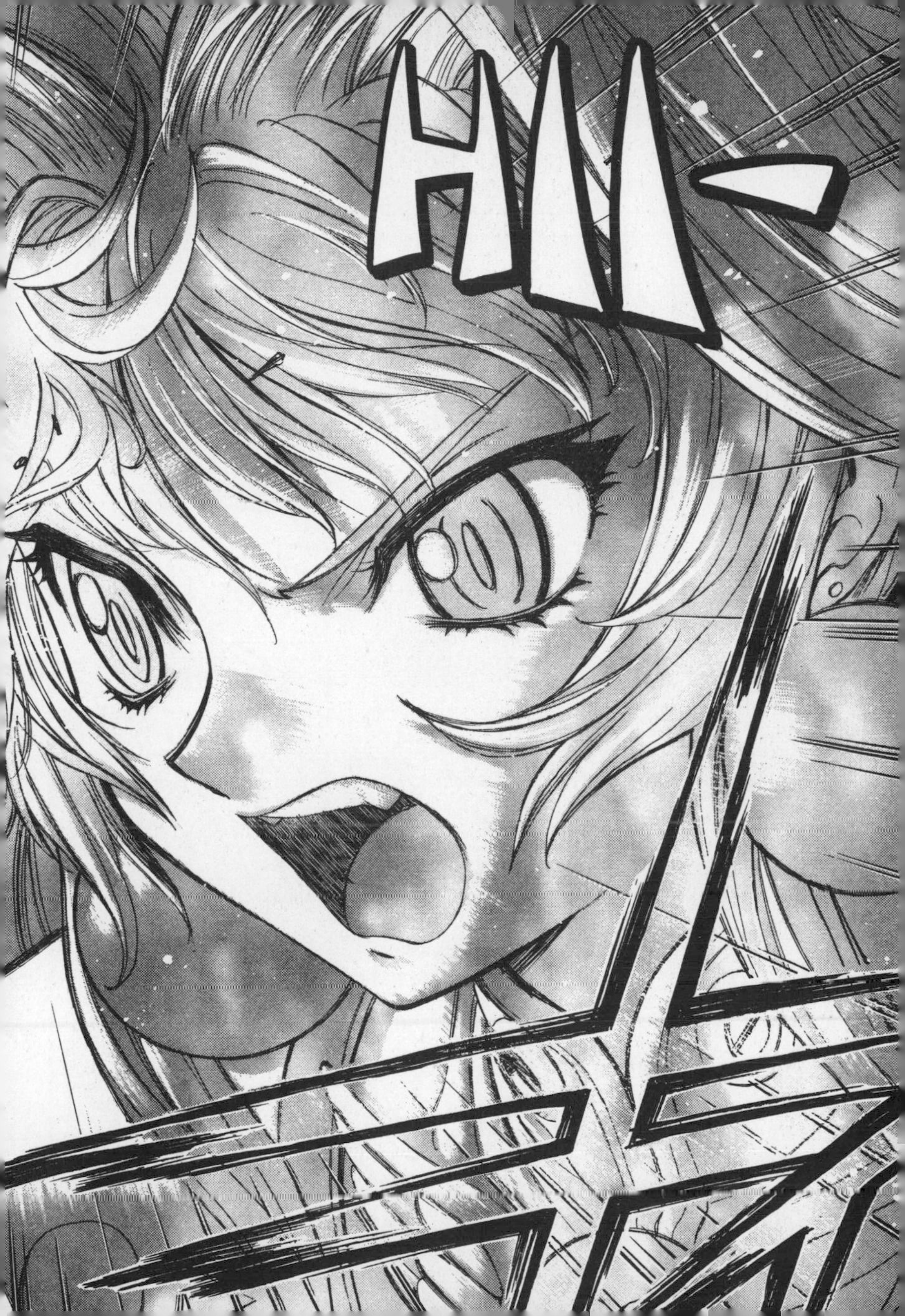
HII-

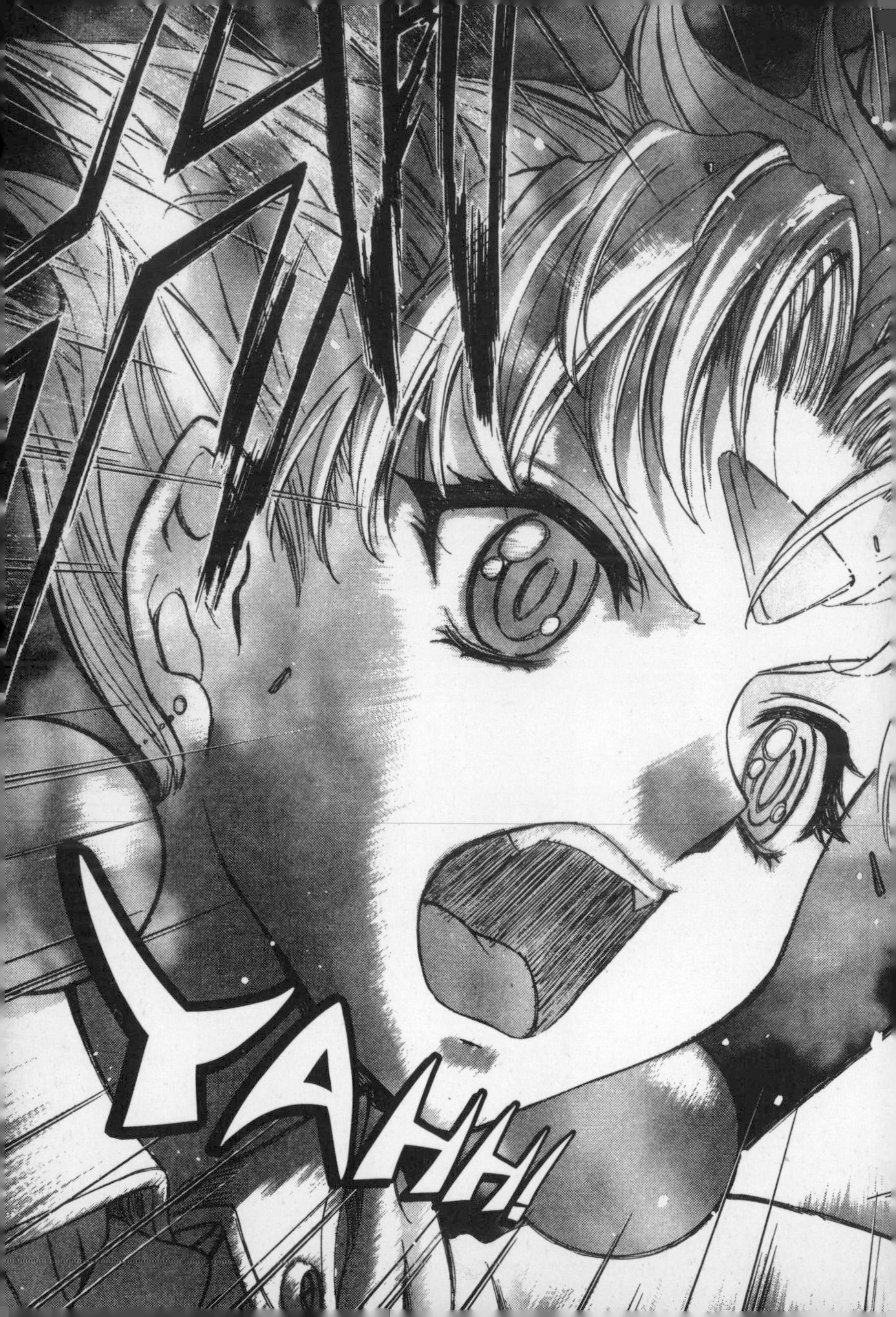
YAHH!

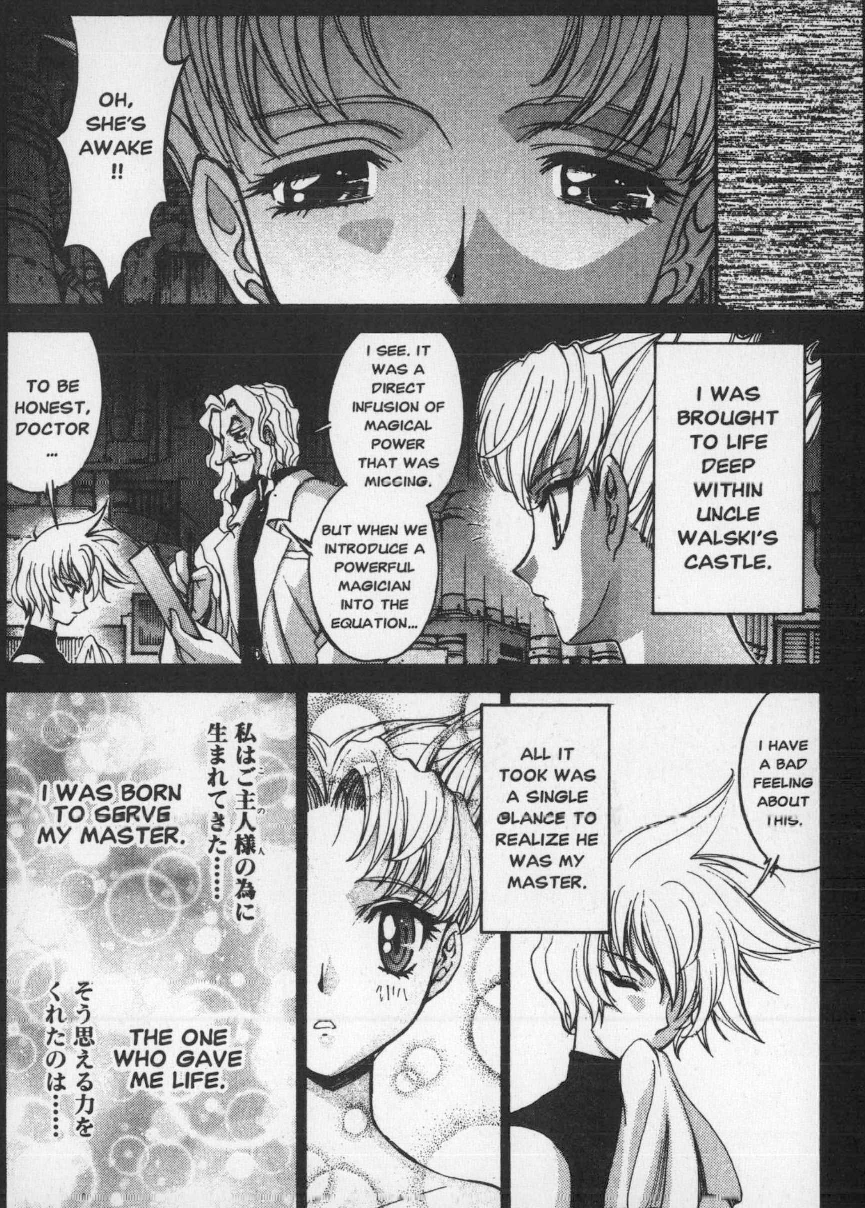
OH, SHE'S AWAKE !!
I WAS BROUGHT TO LIFE DEEP WITHIN UNCLE WALSKI'S CASTLE.
I SEE. IT WAS A DIRECT INFUSION OF MAGICAL POWER THAT WAS MISSING.
BUT WHEN WE INTRODUCE A POWERFUL MAGICIAN INTO THE EQUATION...
TO BE HONEST, DOCTOR ...
I HAVE A BAD FEELING ABOUT THIS.
ALL IT TOOK WAS A SINGLE GLANCE TO REALIZE HE WAS MY MASTER.
私はご主人様の為に生まれてきた……
I WAS BORN TO SERVE MY MASTER.
そう思える力をくれたのは……
THE ONE WHO GAVE ME LIFE.

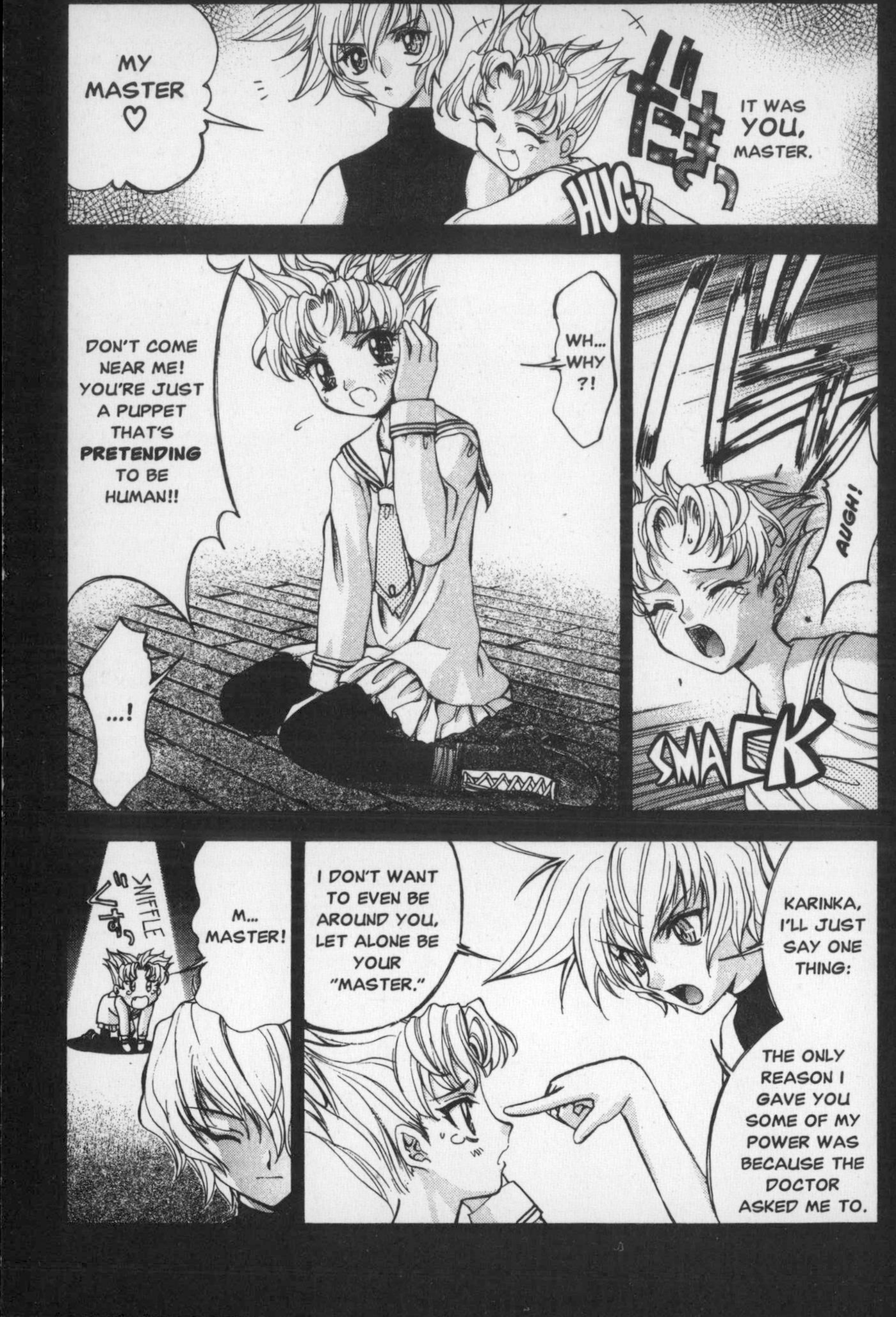
IT WAS YOU, MASTER.
HUG
MY MASTER ♡
AUGH!
SMACK
WH... WHY ?!
DON'T COME NEAR ME! YOU'RE JUST A PUPPET THAT'S **PRETENDING** TO BE HUMAN!!
...!
KARINKA, I'LL JUST SAY ONE THING:
THE ONLY REASON I GAVE YOU SOME OF MY POWER WAS BECAUSE THE DOCTOR ASKED ME TO.
I DON'T WANT TO EVEN BE AROUND YOU, LET ALONE BE YOUR "MASTER."
SNIFFLE
M... MASTER!

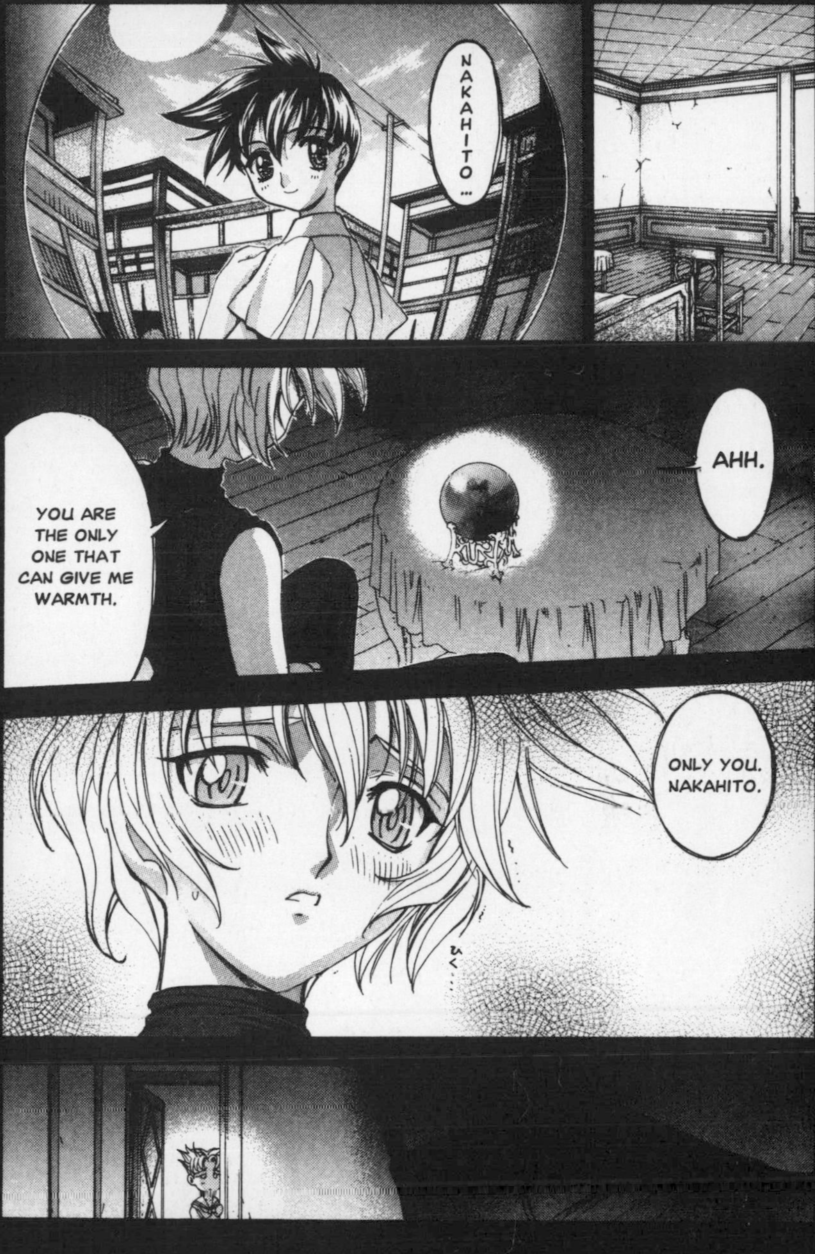
NAKAHITO...
AHH.
YOU ARE THE ONLY ONE THAT CAN GIVE ME WARMTH.
ONLY YOU. NAKAHITO.

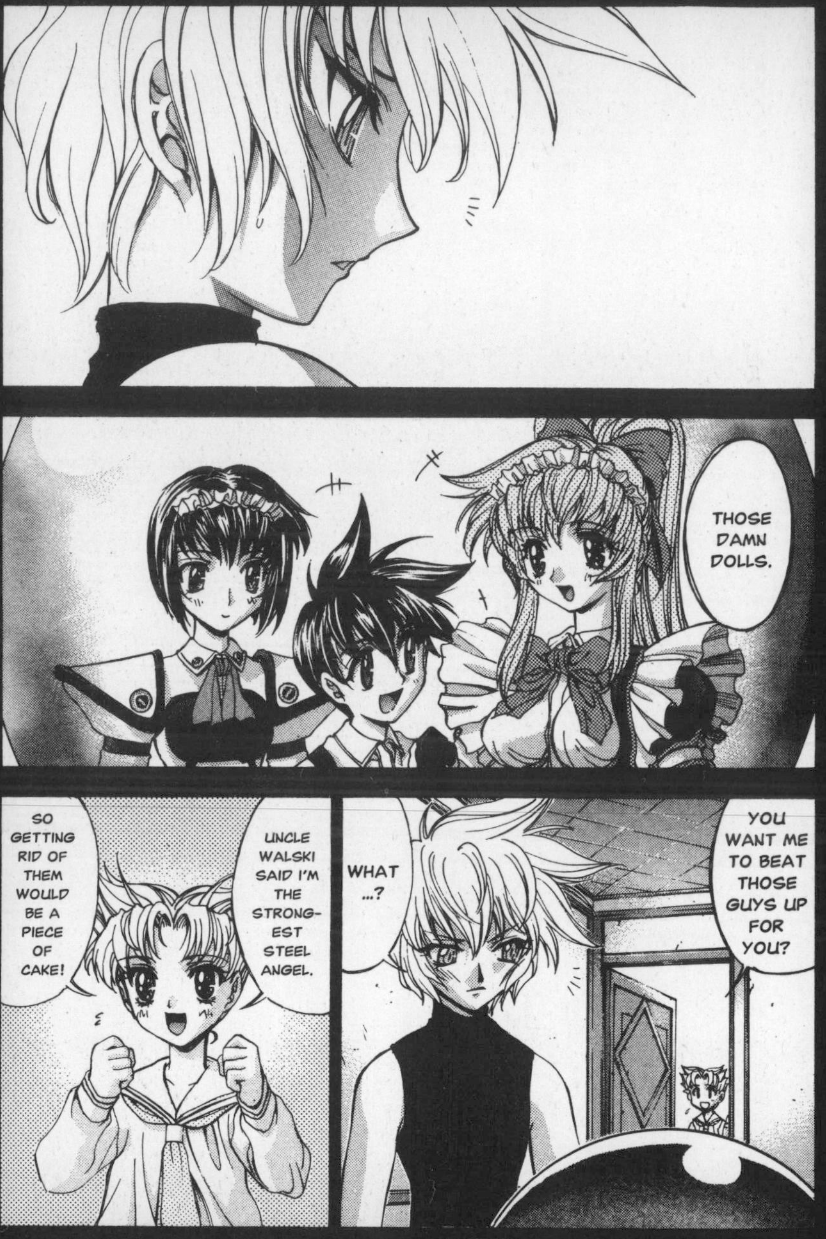
THOSE DAMN DOLLS.
YOU WANT ME TO BEAT THOSE GUYS UP FOR YOU?
WHAT ...?
UNCLE WALSKI SAID I'M THE STRONG-EST STEEL ANGEL.
SO GETTING RID OF THEM WOULD BE A PIECE OF CAKE!

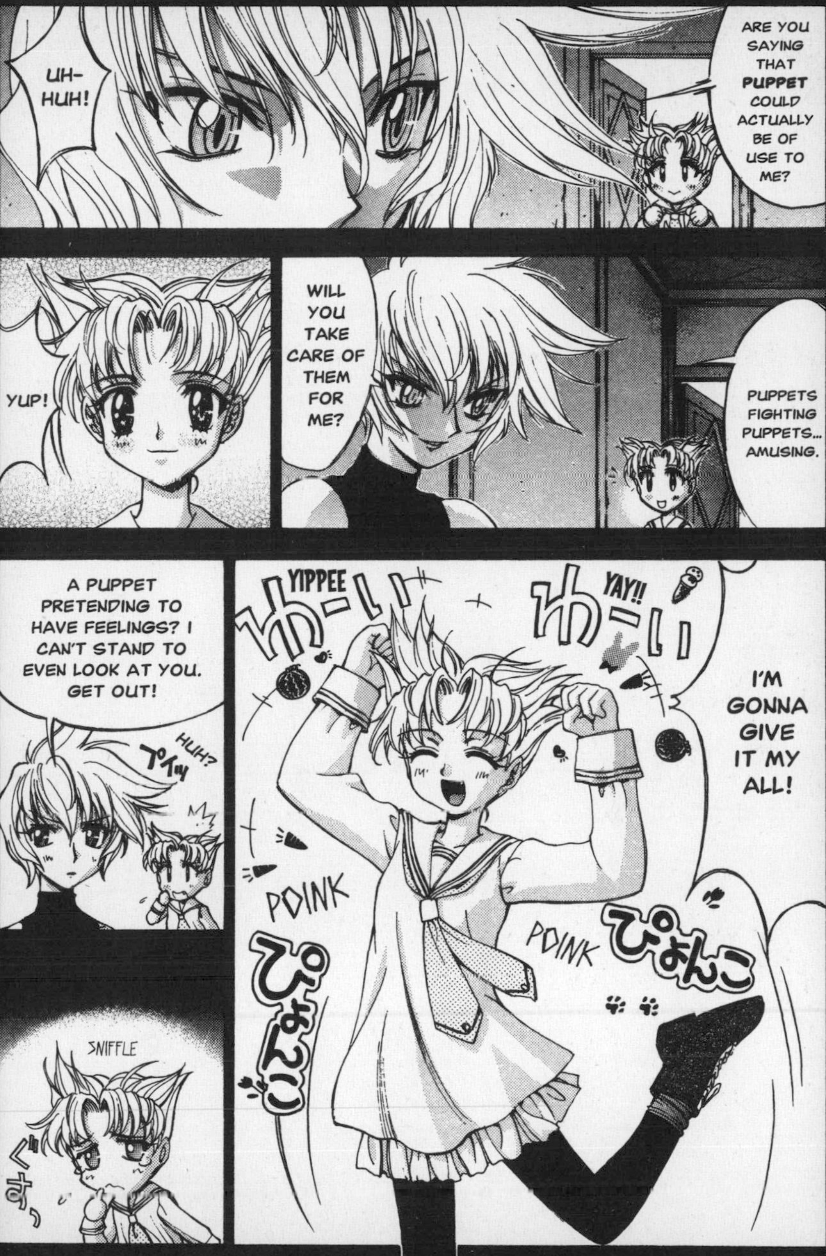
ARE YOU SAYING THAT PUPPET COULD ACTUALLY BE OF USE TO ME?
UH-HUH!
PUPPETS FIGHTING PUPPETS... AMUSING.
WILL YOU TAKE CARE OF THEM FOR ME?
YUP!
YAY!!
わーい
I'M GONNA GIVE IT MY ALL!
YIPPEE
わーい
ぴょんこ
POINK
POINK
ぴょんこ
A PUPPET PRETENDING TO HAVE FEELINGS? I CAN'T STAND TO EVEN LOOK AT YOU. GET OUT!
HUH?
プイッ
SNIFFLE
ぐすっ

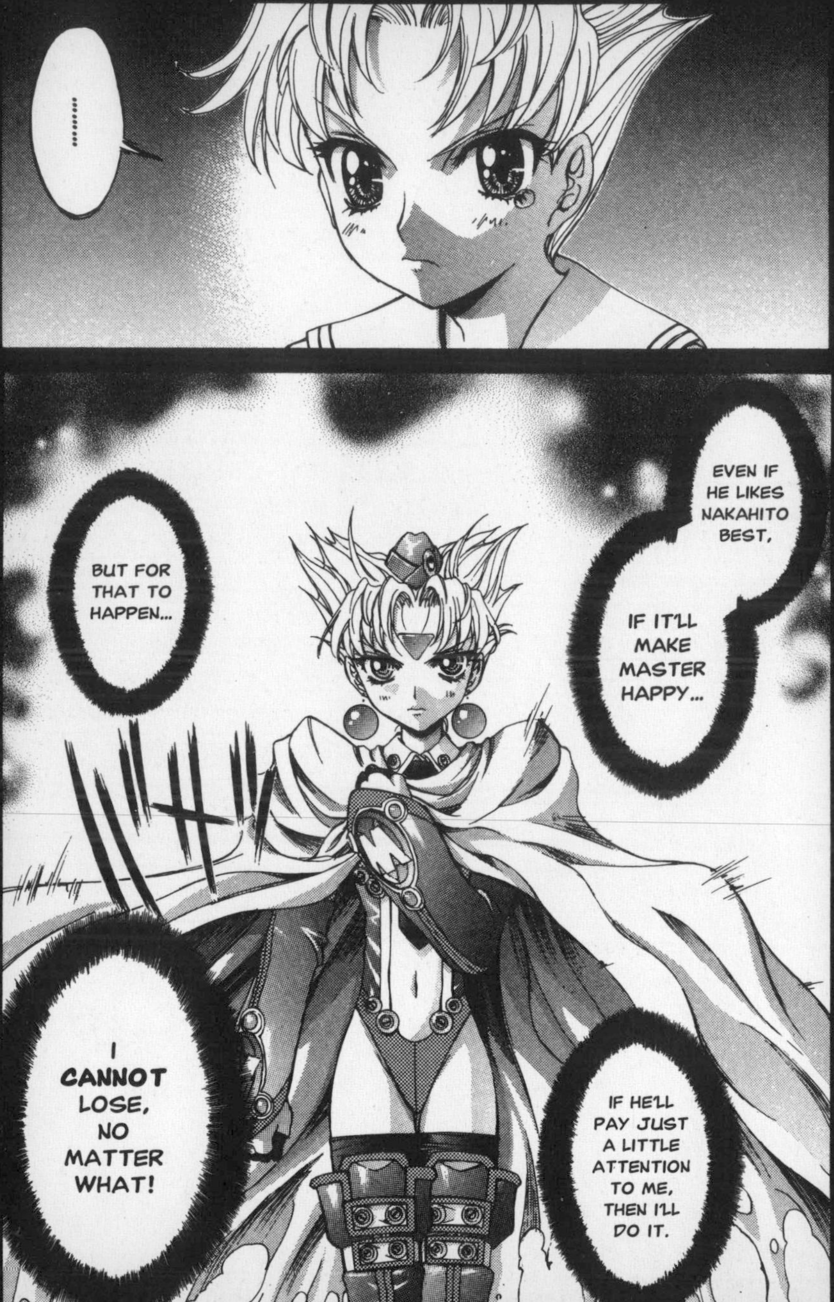
....
EVEN IF HE LIKES NAKAHITO BEST,
IF IT'LL MAKE MASTER HAPPY...
IF HE'LL PAY JUST A LITTLE ATTENTION TO ME, THEN I'LL DO IT.
BUT FOR THAT TO HAPPEN...
I CANNOT LOSE, NO MATTER WHAT!

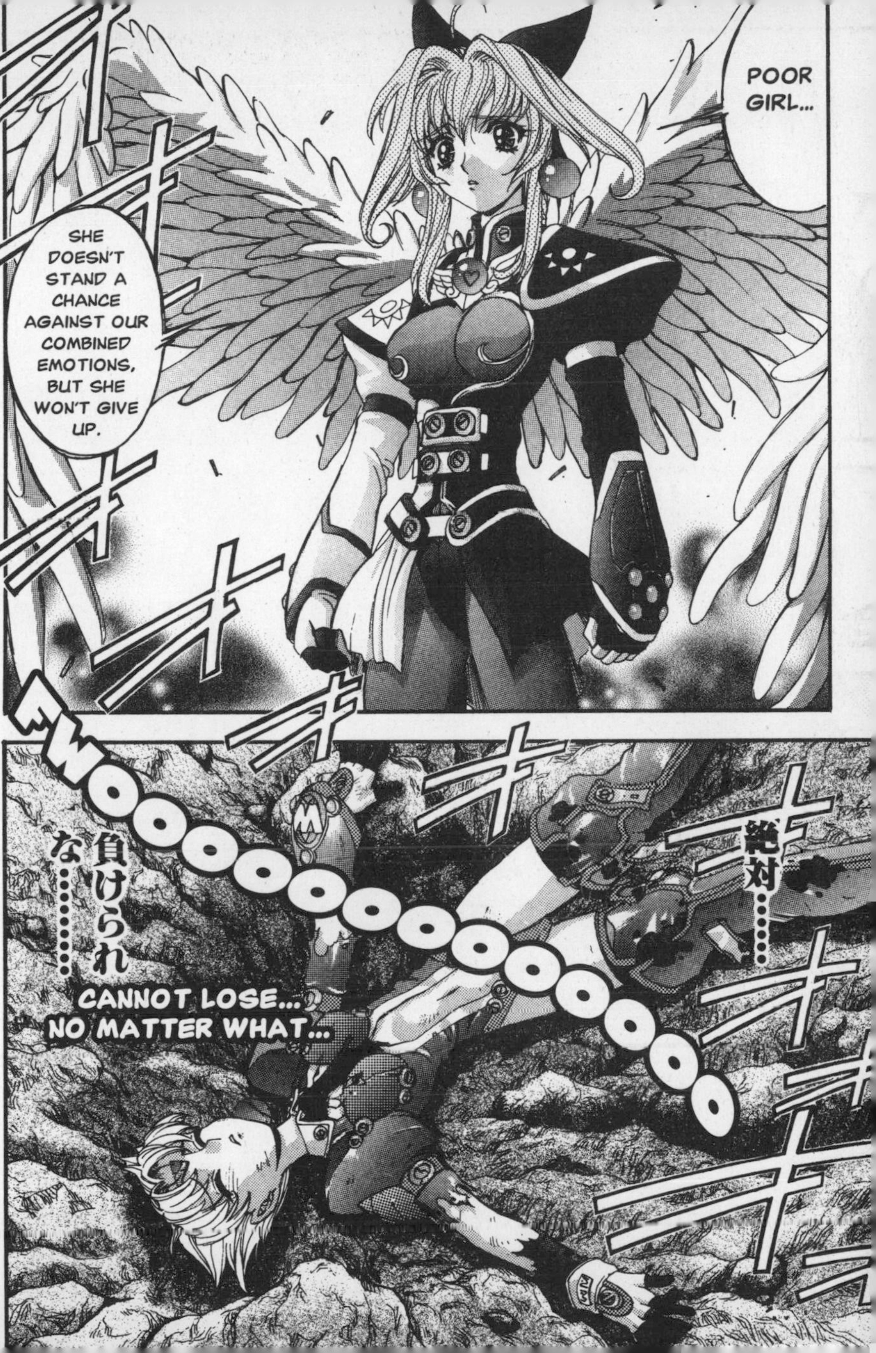
POOR GIRL...
SHE DOESN'T STAND A CHANCE AGAINST OUR COMBINED EMOTIONS, BUT SHE WON'T GIVE UP.
FWOOOOOOOOOOOOOO
絶対……
負けられな……
CANNOT LOSE... NO MATTER WHAT...

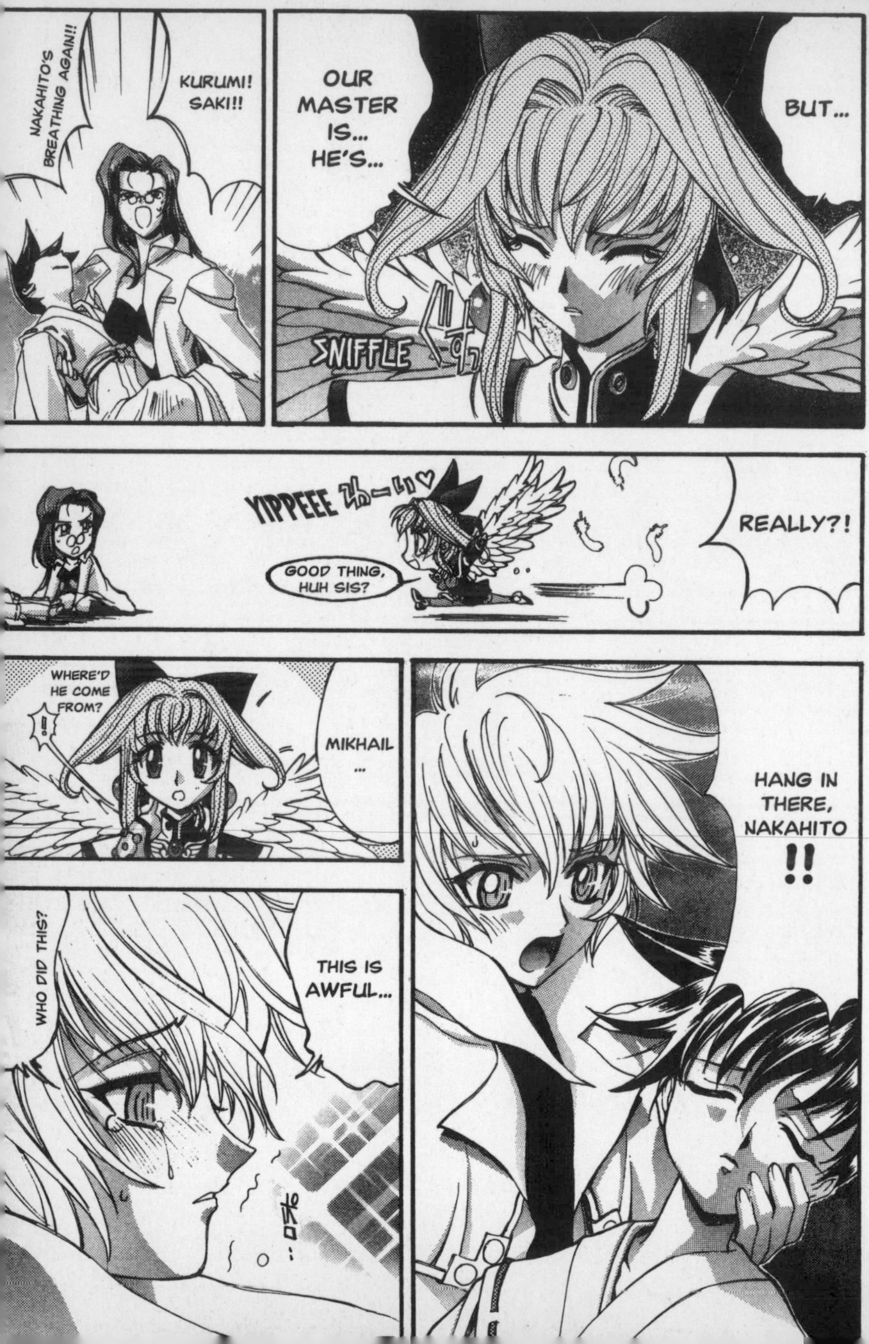
OUR MASTER IS... HE'S...
BUT...
SNIFFLE
KURUMI! SAKI!!
NAKAHITO'S BREATHING AGAIN!!
REALLY?!
YIPPEEE
GOOD THING, HUH SIS?
HANG IN THERE, NAKAHITO !!
MIKHAIL ...
WHERE'D HE COME FROM?
!!
THIS IS AWFUL...
WHO DID THIS?

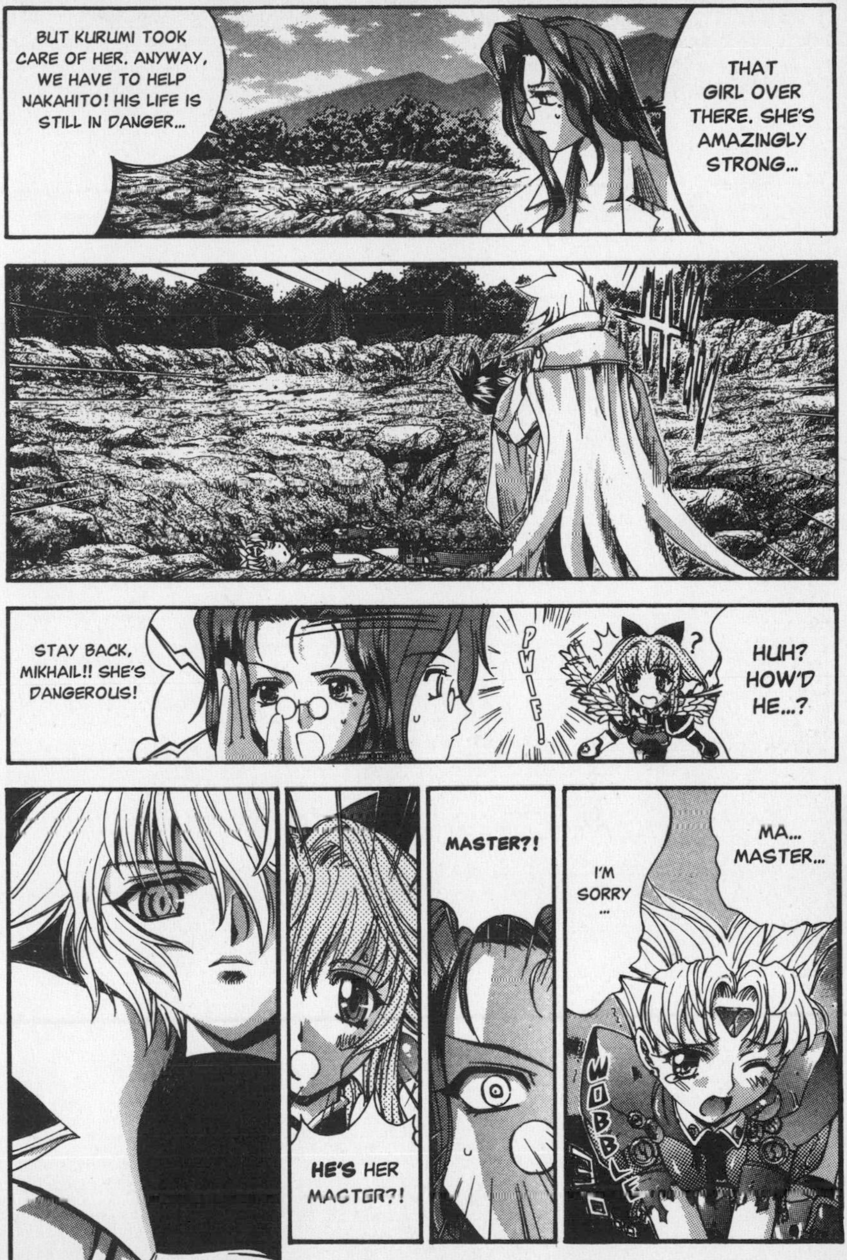
THAT GIRL OVER THERE. SHE'S AMAZINGLY STRONG...
BUT KURUMI TOOK CARE OF HER. ANYWAY, WE HAVE TO HELP NAKAHITO! HIS LIFE IS STILL IN DANGER...
HUH? HOW'D HE...?
?
PWIF!
STAY BACK, MIKHAIL!! SHE'S DANGEROUS!
MA... MASTER...
I'M SORRY ...
WOBBLE...
MASTER?!
HE'S HER MASTER?!

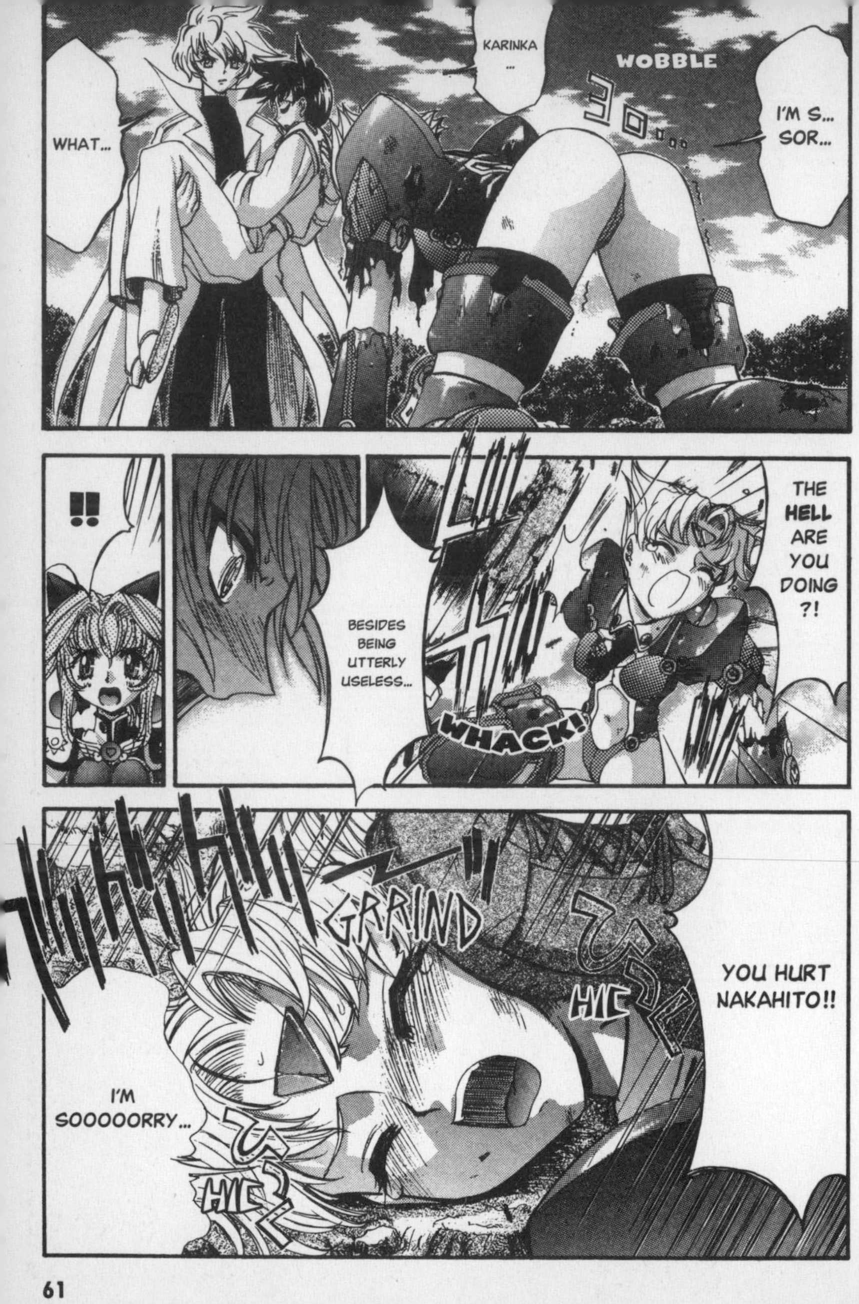
I'M S... SOR...
WOBBLE
KARINKA ...
WHAT...
THE **HELL** ARE YOU DOING ?!
WHACK!
BESIDES BEING UTTERLY USELESS...
!!
YOU HURT NAKAHITO!!
GRRIND
HIC
I'M SOOOOORRY...
HIC

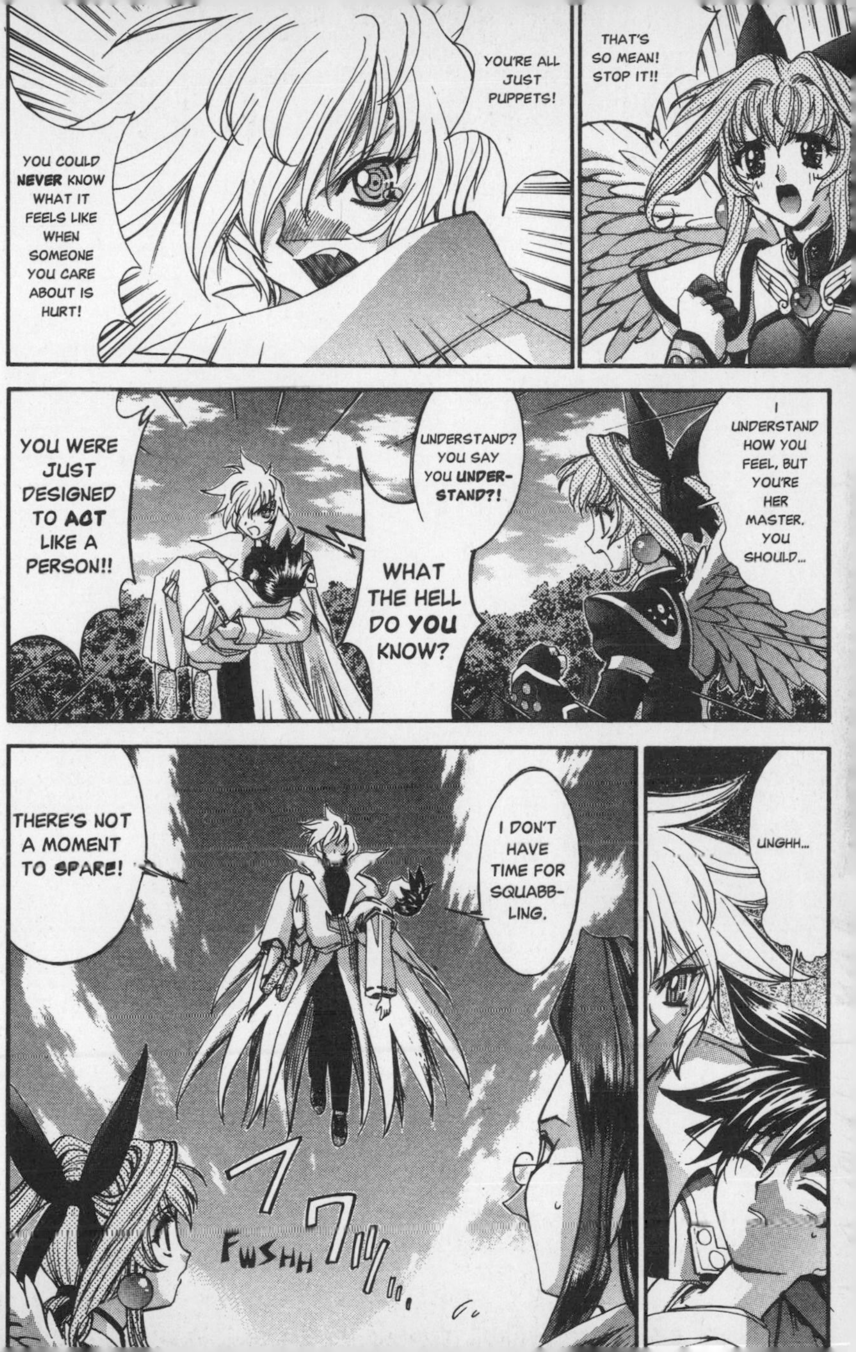
THAT'S SO MEAN! STOP IT!!
YOU'RE ALL JUST PUPPETS!
YOU COULD NEVER KNOW WHAT IT FEELS LIKE WHEN SOMEONE YOU CARE ABOUT IS HURT!
I UNDERSTAND HOW YOU FEEL, BUT YOU'RE HER MASTER. YOU SHOULD...
UNDERSTAND? YOU SAY YOU UNDER-STAND?!
WHAT THE HELL DO YOU KNOW?
YOU WERE JUST DESIGNED TO ACT LIKE A PERSON!!
UNGHH...
I DON'T HAVE TIME FOR SQUABB-LING.
THERE'S NOT A MOMENT TO SPARE!
FWSHH

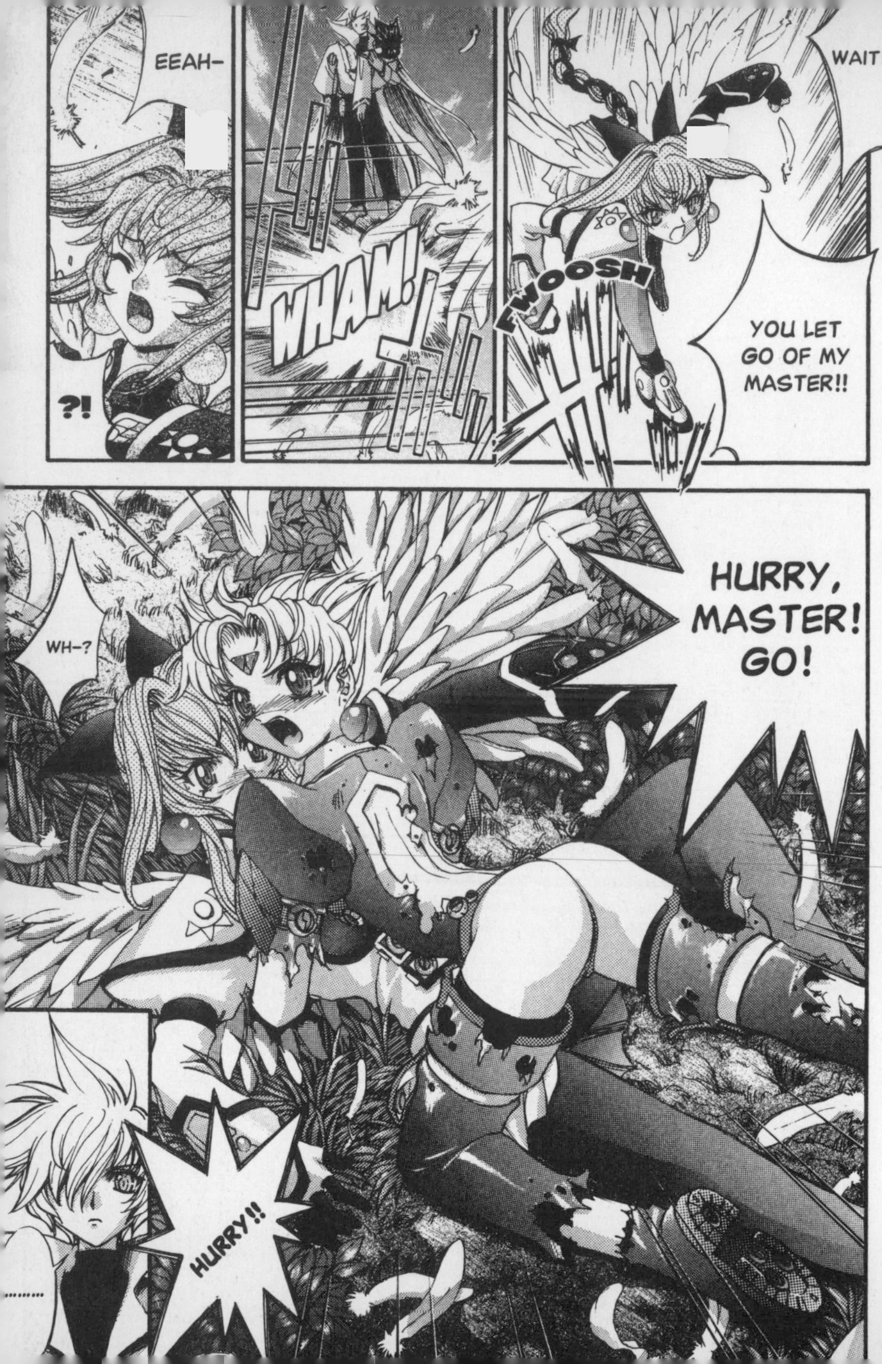
WAIT!
FWOOSH
YOU LET GO OF MY MASTER!!
WHAM!
EEAH-
?!
HURRY, MASTER! GO!
WH-?
HURRY!!
....

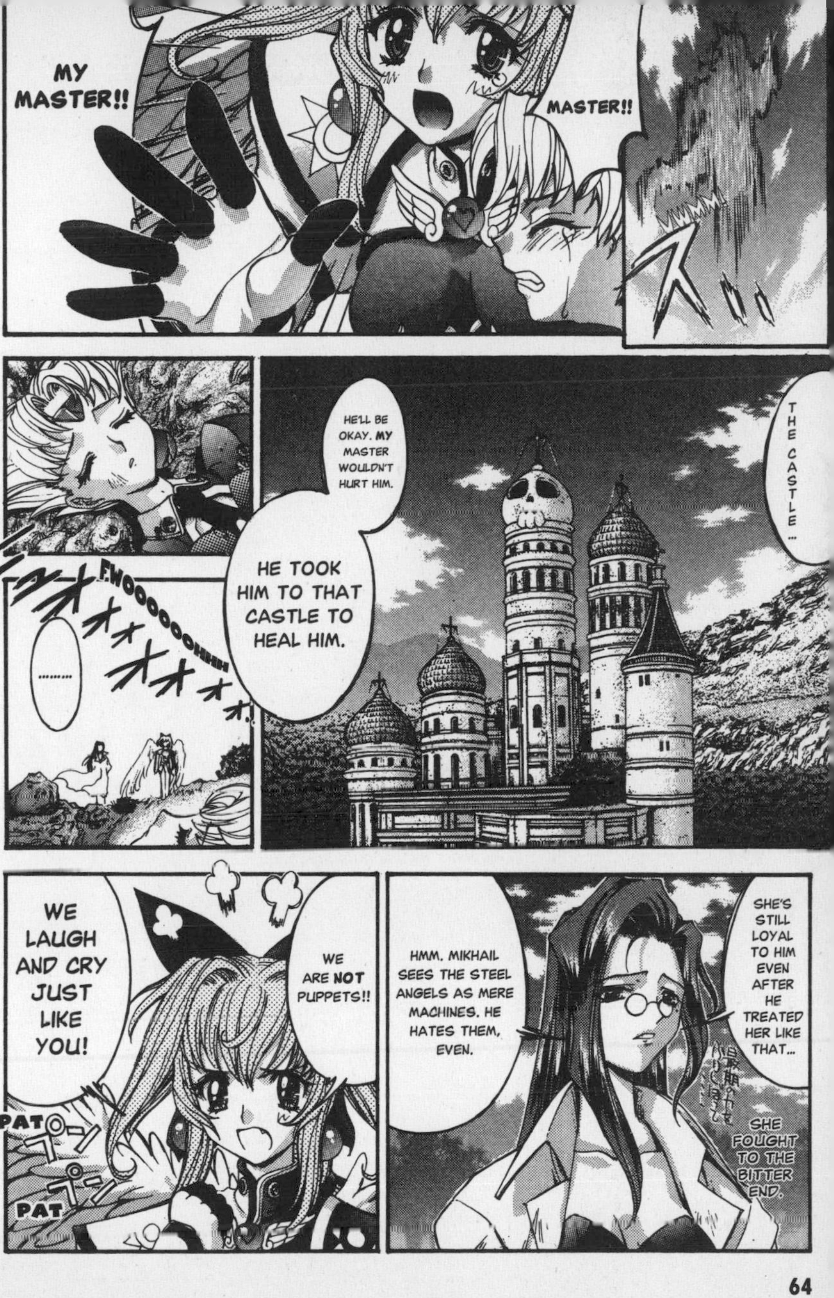
MASTER!!
MY MASTER!!
THE CASTLE ...
HE'LL BE OKAY. MY MASTER WOULDN'T HURT HIM.
HE TOOK HIM TO THAT CASTLE TO HEAL HIM.
FWOOOOOOOHHH
....
SHE'S STILL LOYAL TO HIM EVEN AFTER HE TREATED HER LIKE THAT...
HMM. MIKHAIL SEES THE STEEL ANGELS AS MERE MACHINES. HE HATES THEM, EVEN.
SHE FOUGHT TO THE BITTER END.
WE ARE NOT PUPPETS!!
WE LAUGH AND CRY JUST LIKE YOU!
PAT
PAT

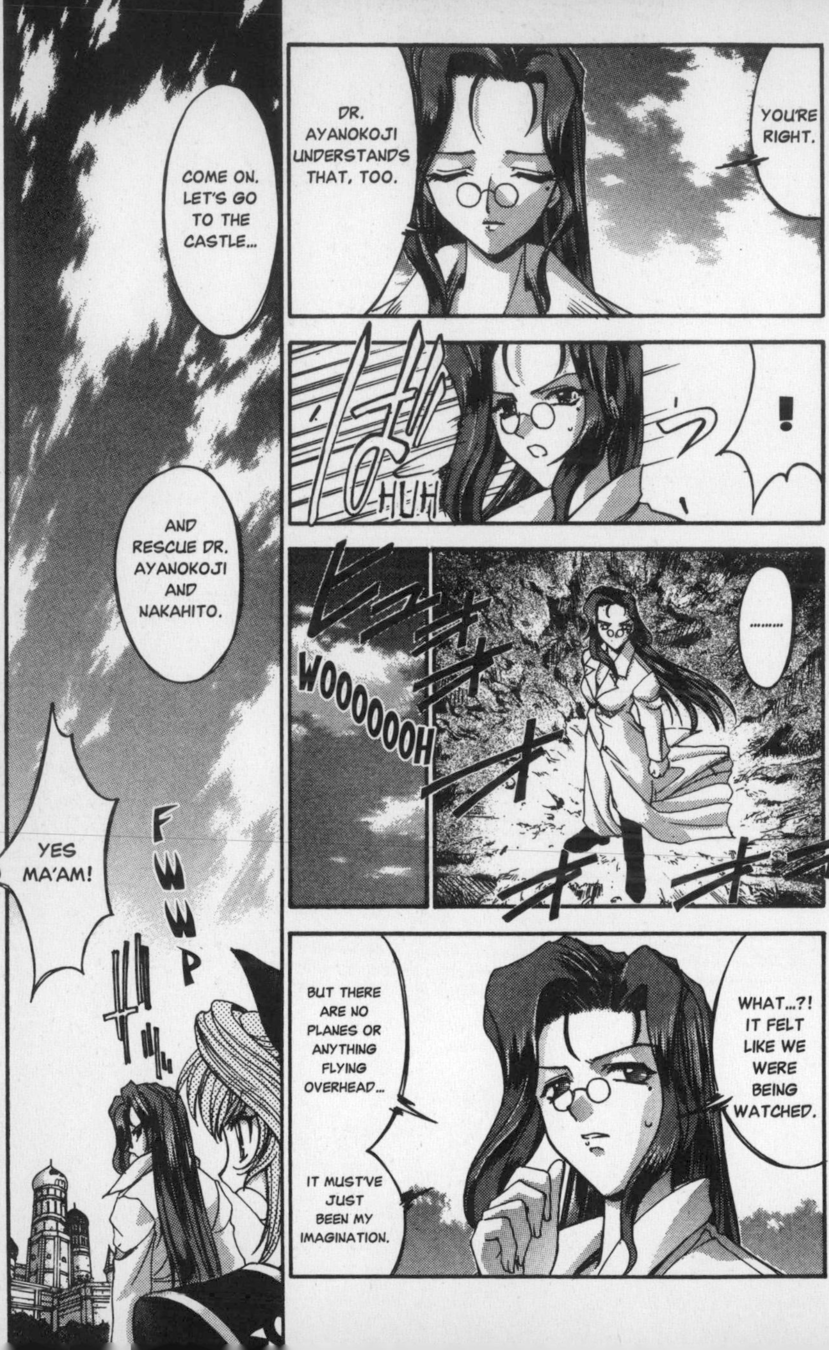
YOU'RE RIGHT.
DR. AYANOKOJI UNDERSTANDS THAT, TOO.
!
HUH
....
WOOOOOOOH
WHAT...?! IT FELT LIKE WE WERE BEING WATCHED.
BUT THERE ARE NO PLANES OR ANYTHING FLYING OVERHEAD...
IT MUST'VE JUST BEEN MY IMAGINATION.
COME ON. LET'S GO TO THE CASTLE...
AND RESCUE DR. AYANOKOJI AND NAKAHITO.
YES MA'AM!
FWWP

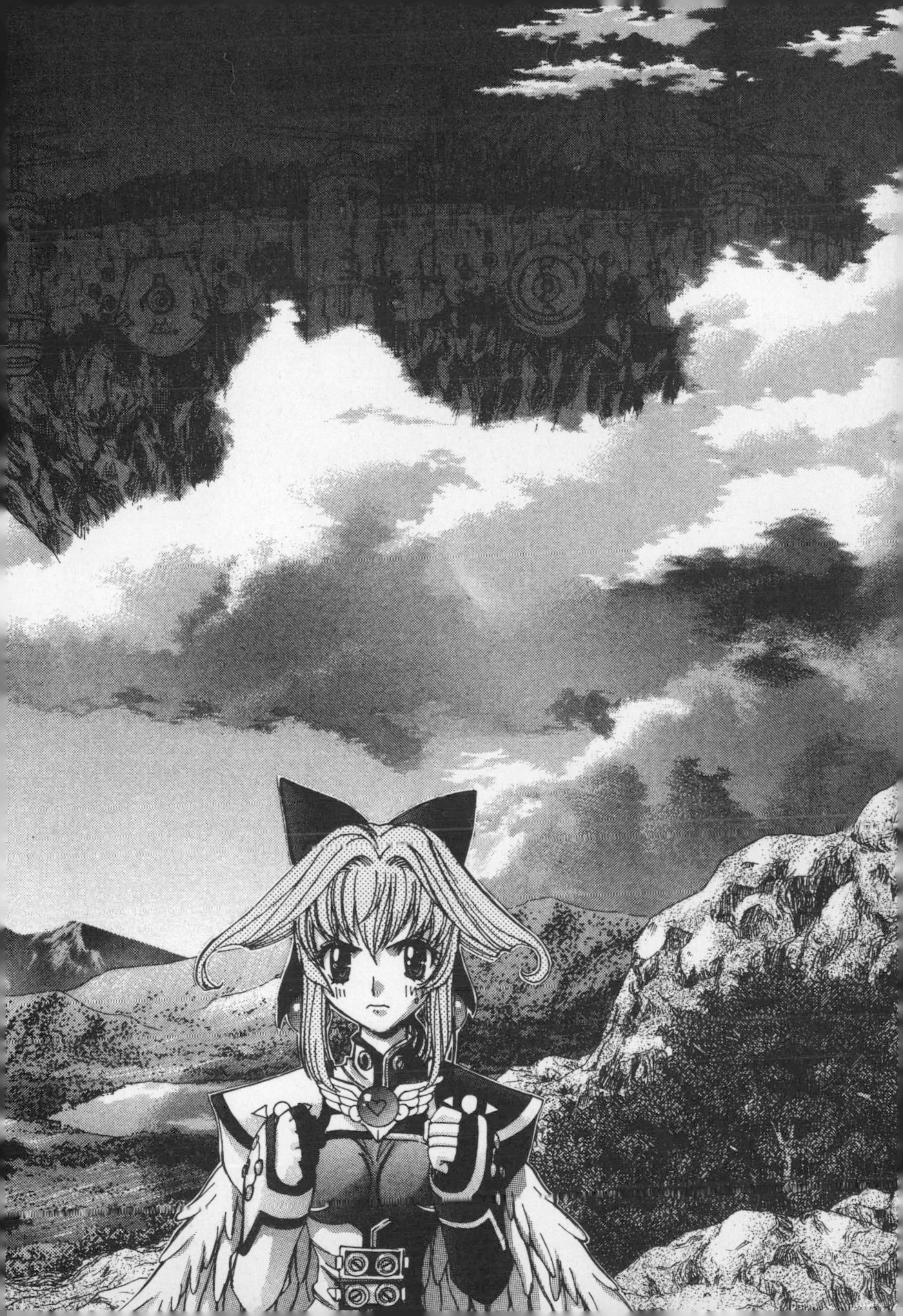

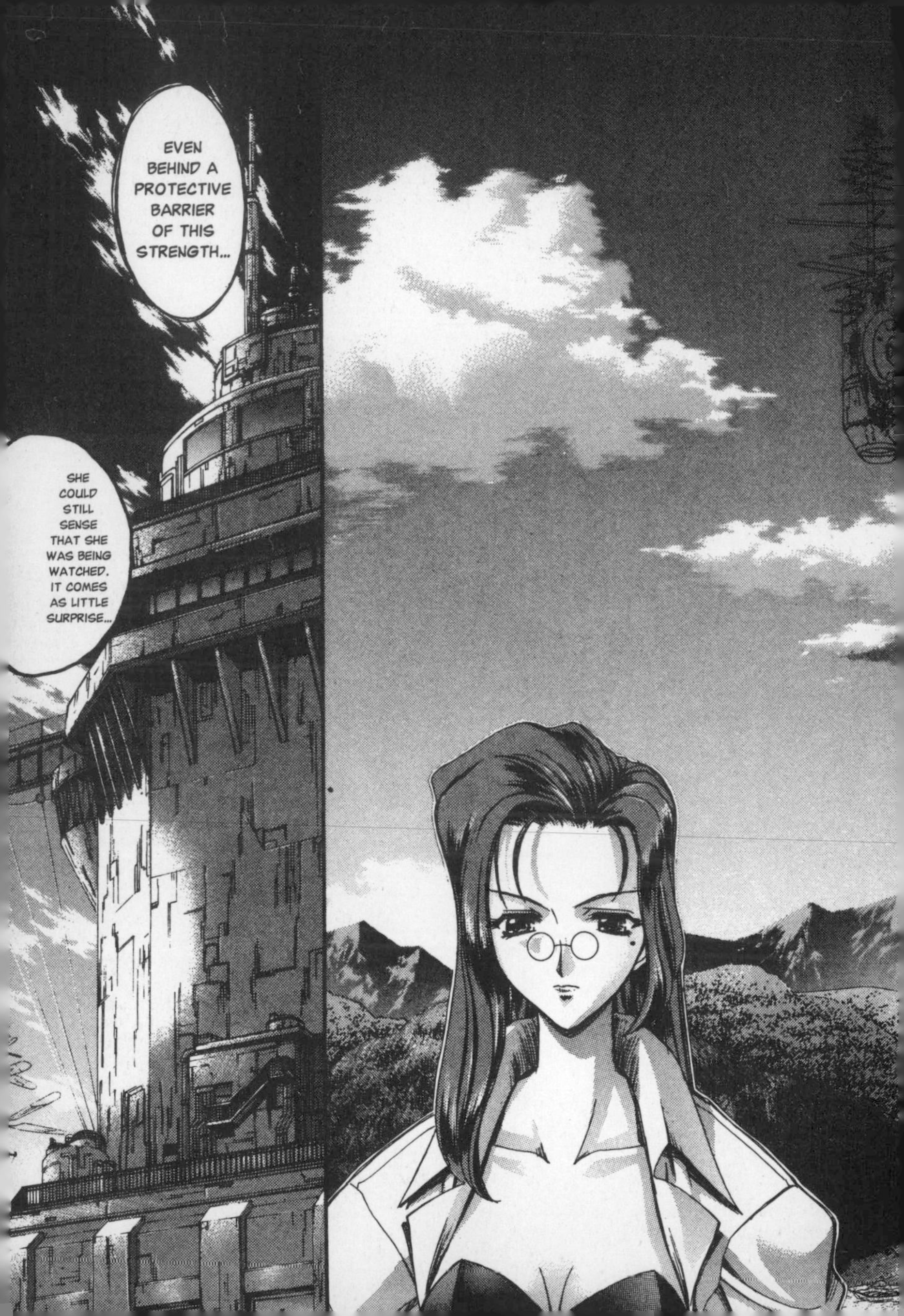
EVEN BEHIND A PROTECTIVE BARRIER OF THIS STRENGTH...
SHE COULD STILL SENSE THAT SHE WAS BEING WATCHED. IT COMES AS LITTLE SURPRISE...

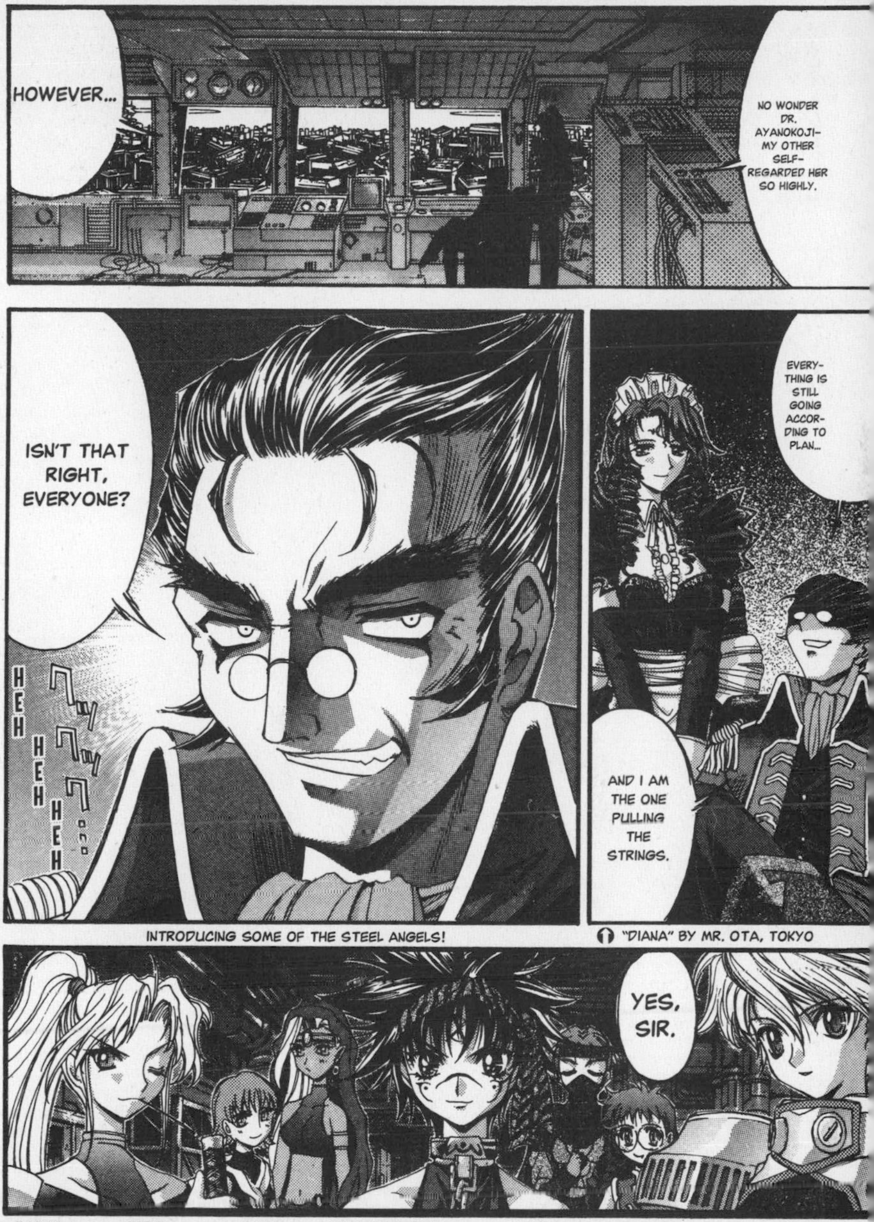
NO WONDER DR. AYANOKOJI—MY OTHER SELF—REGARDED HER SO HIGHLY.
HOWEVER...
EVERYTHING IS STILL GOING ACCORDING TO PLAN...
AND I AM THE ONE PULLING THE STRINGS.
ISN'T THAT RIGHT, EVERYONE?
HEH HEH HEH HEH
"DIANA" BY MR. OTA, TOKYO
INTRODUCING SOME OF THE STEEL ANGELS!
YES, SIR.

ZANKAN (BY HISANAO DOI, FROM TOKYO) TOMO (BY AKIRA HANAOKA, FROM OKAYAMA PREF.) SUMIRE (BY "PERSONA," FROM TOKYO) THE LEADER—KAGA, ANGEL OF DESTRUCTION (BY MR. SHICHINOHE, FROM TOKYO) KASUMI (BY TAKESHI SAKAYA, FROM CHIBA PREF.) KURON BY NA-NI-NU-NE-NO THE ALIEN, FROM AOMORI PREF.) LEOPOLD (BY YASUHIDE OKABE, FROM SAITAMA PREF.)

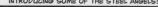

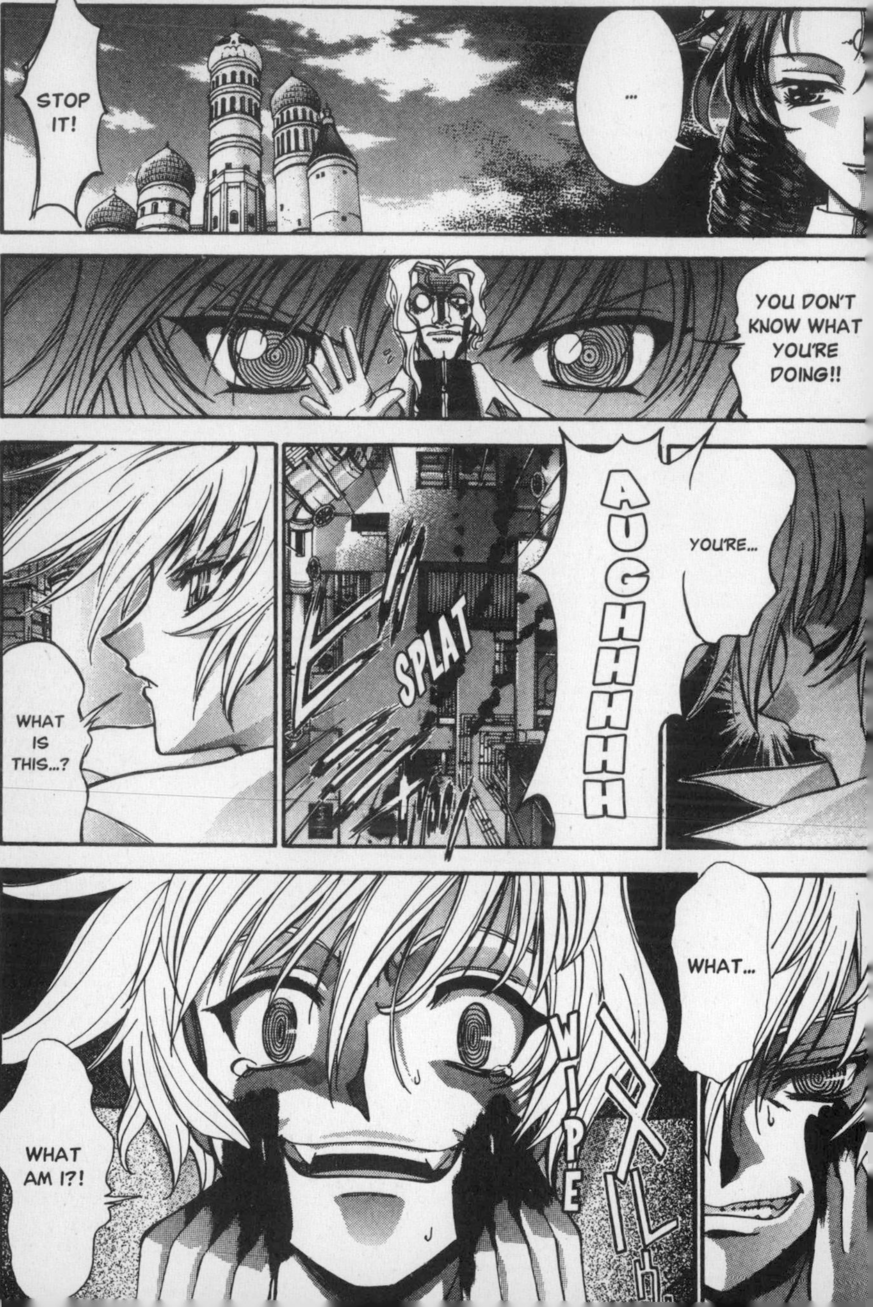
...
STOP IT!
YOU DON'T KNOW WHAT YOU'RE DOING!!
YOU'RE...
AUGHHHHHH
SPLAT
WHAT IS THIS...?
WHAT...
WIPE
WHAT AM I?!

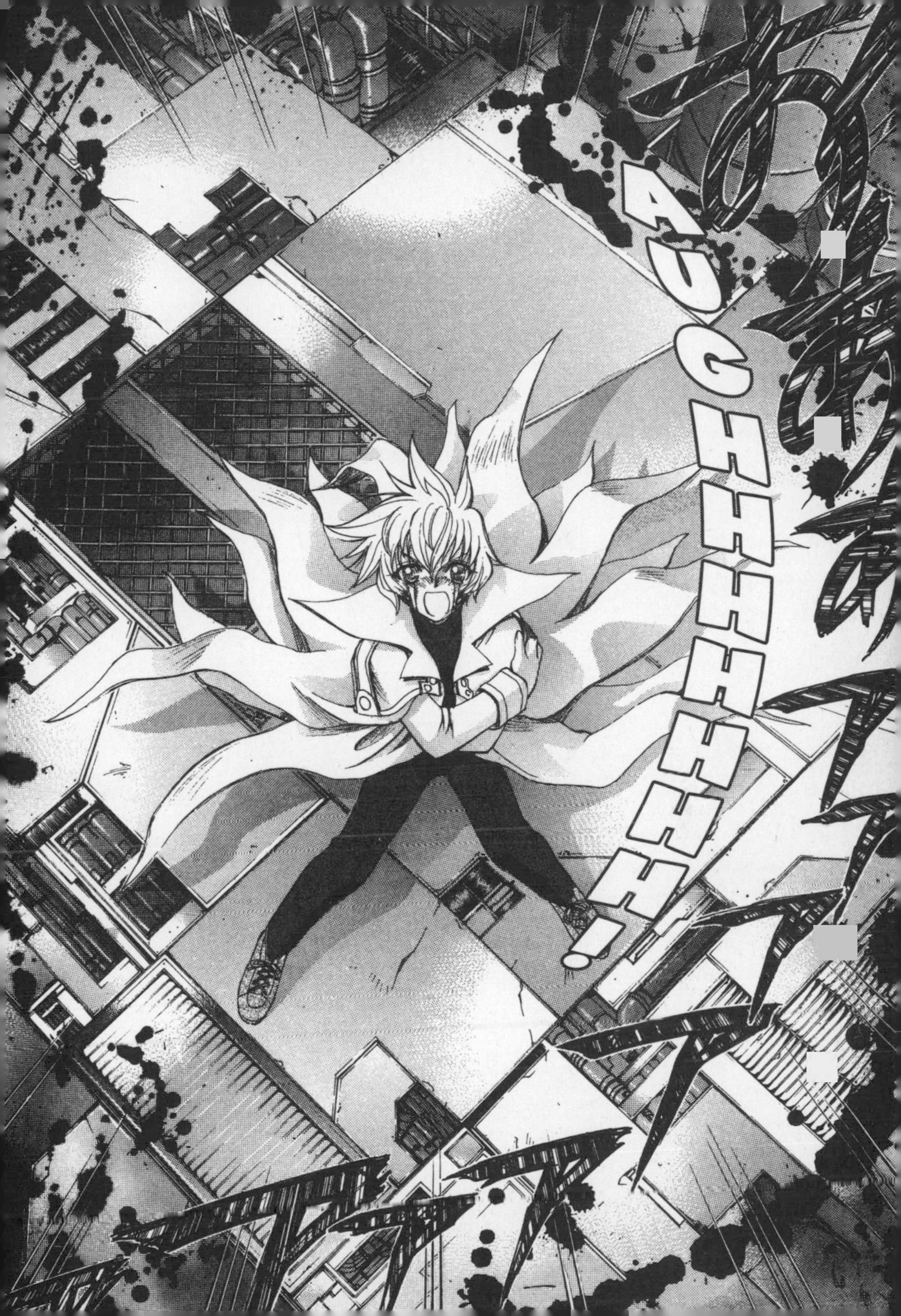
AUGHHHHHHHHH!

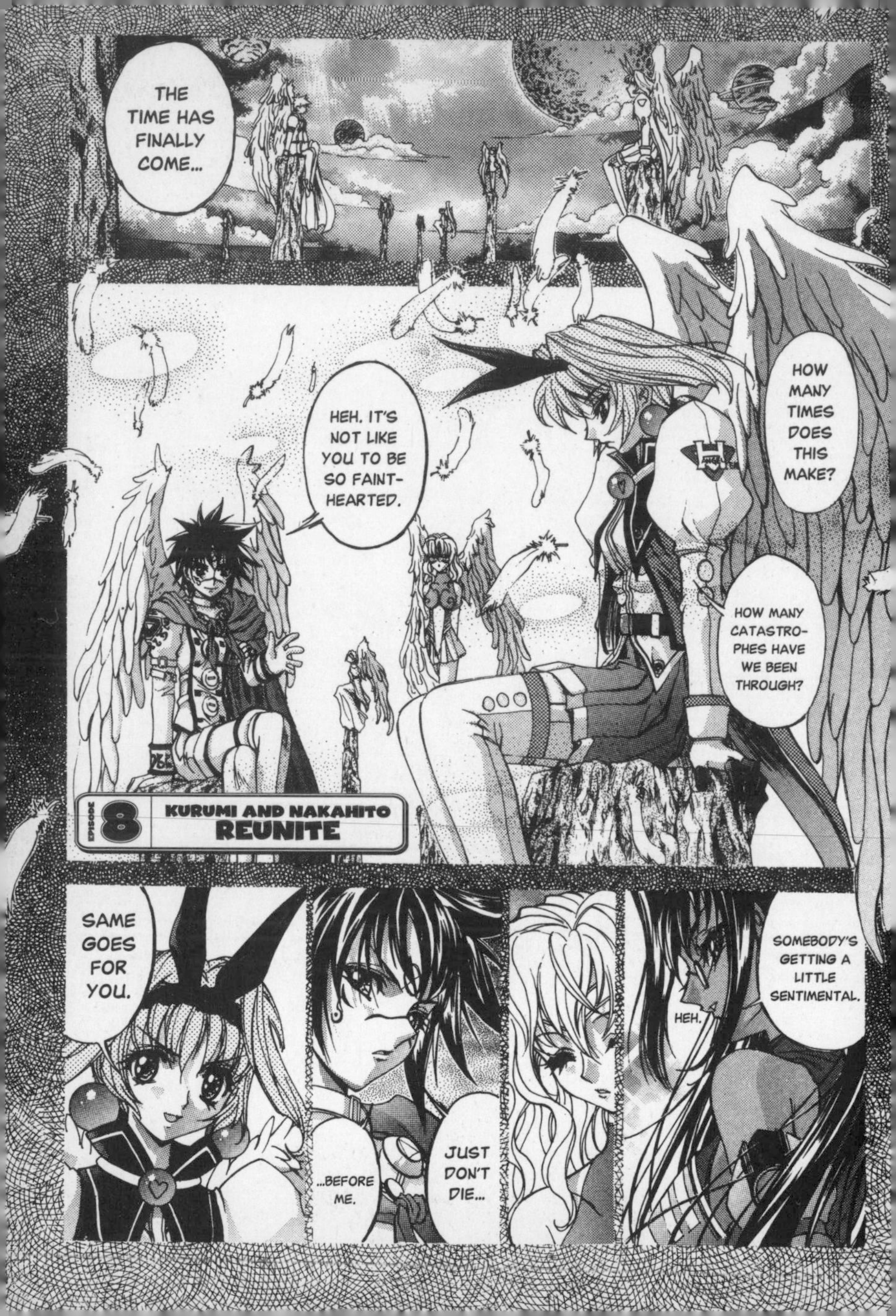
THE TIME HAS FINALLY COME...
HOW MANY TIMES DOES THIS MAKE?
HOW MANY CATASTROPHES HAVE WE BEEN THROUGH?
HEH. IT'S NOT LIKE YOU TO BE SO FAINT-HEARTED.
EPISODE 8
KURUMI AND NAKAHITO REUNITE
SOMEBODY'S GETTING A LITTLE SENTIMENTAL.
HEH.
JUST DON'T DIE...
...BEFORE ME.
SAME GOES FOR YOU.

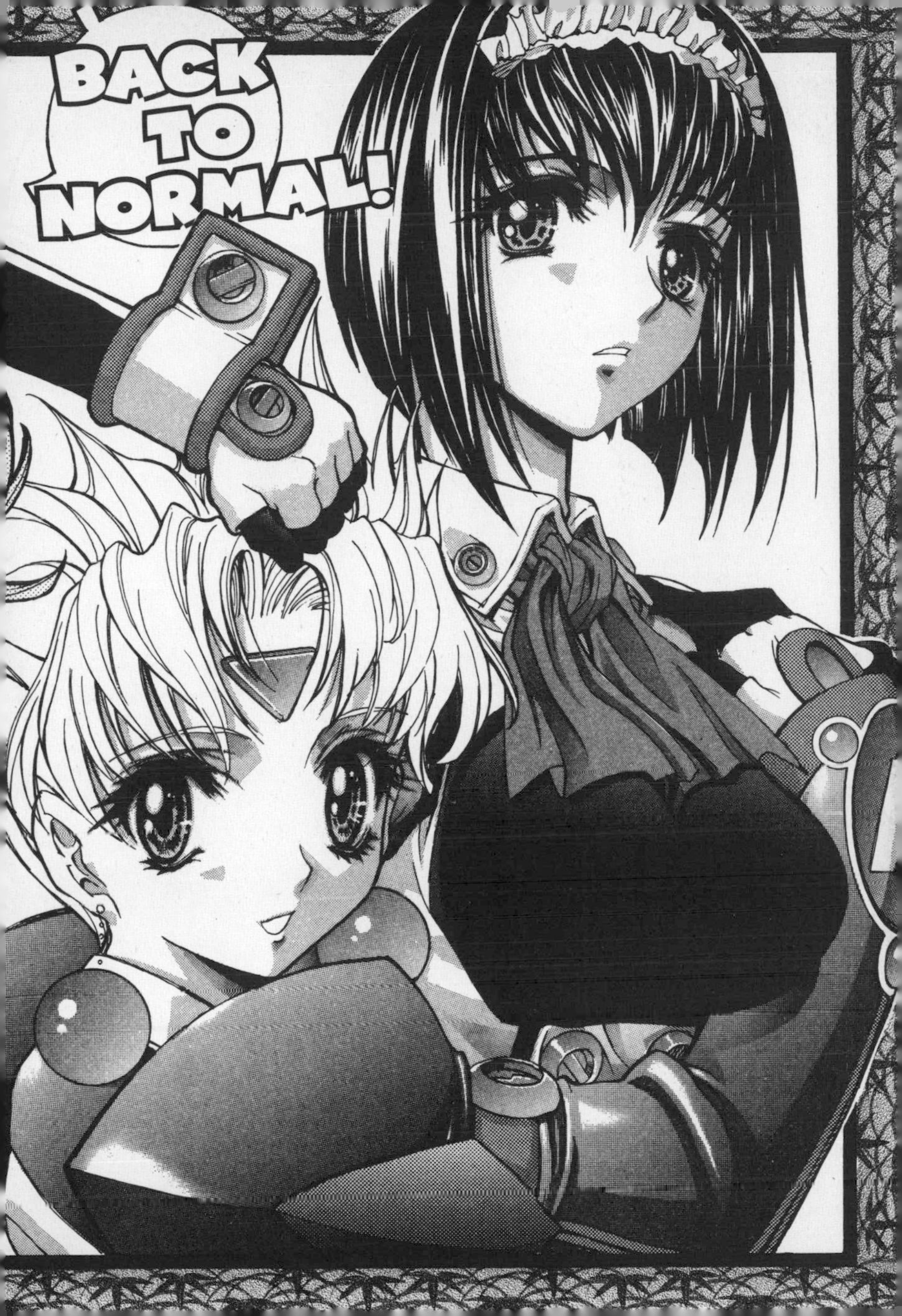
BACK TO NORMAL!

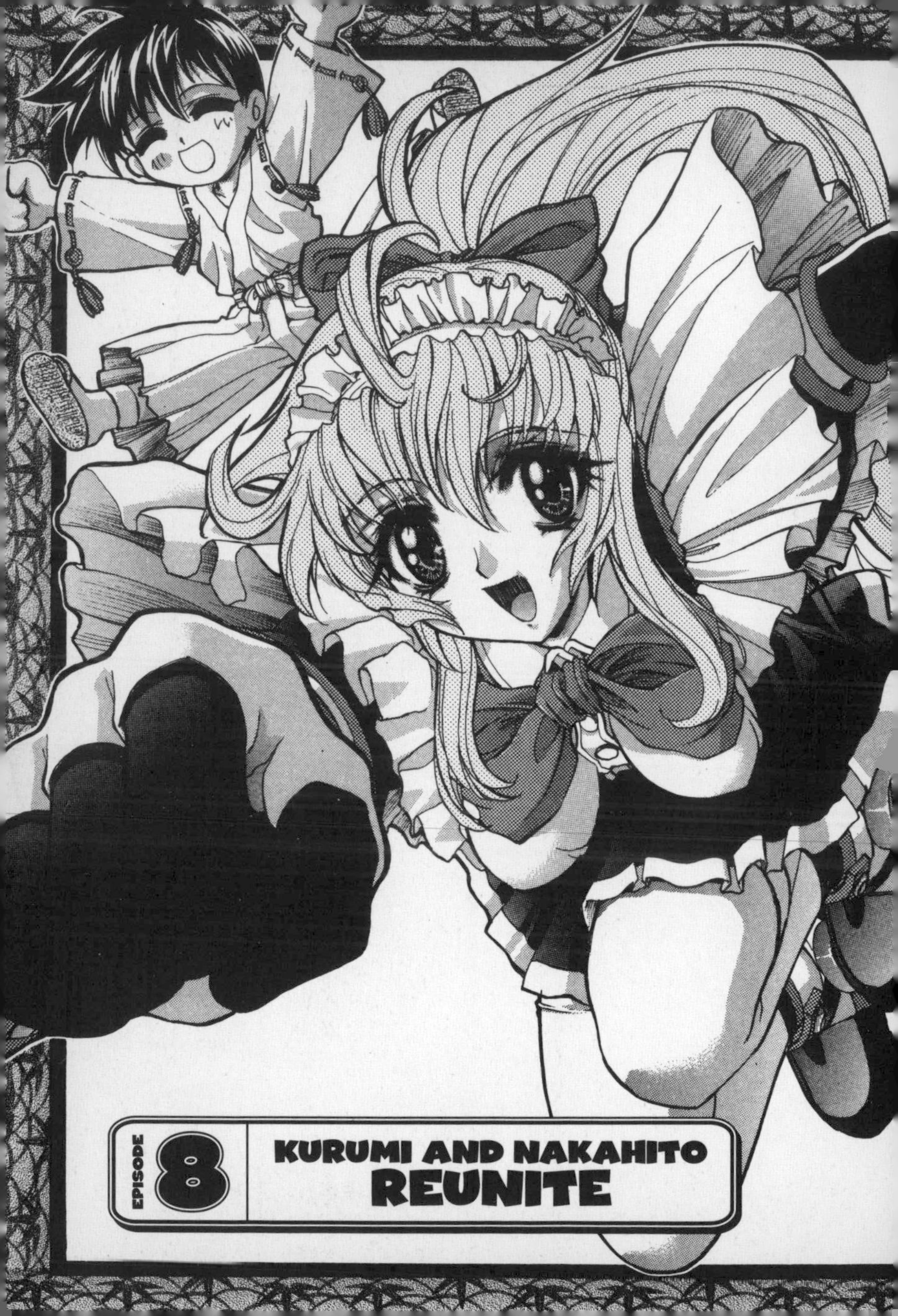
EPISODE 8
KURUMI AND NAKAHITO
REUNITE

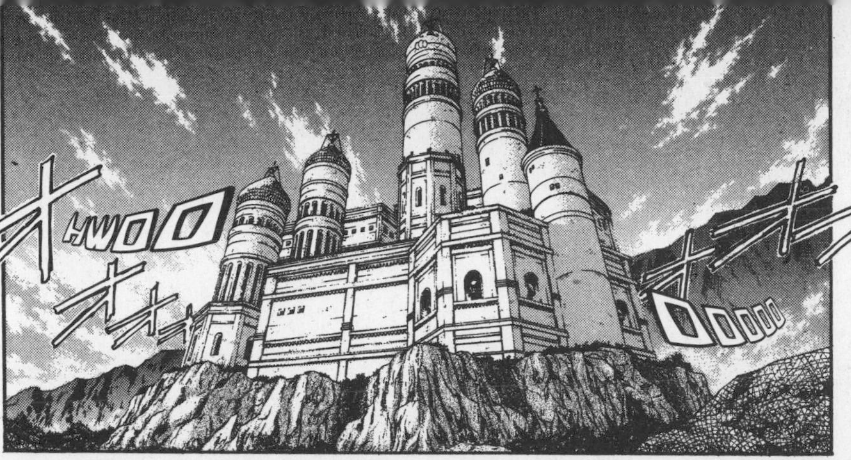
オオオォ…
HWOOO
ォォォ
OOOOO
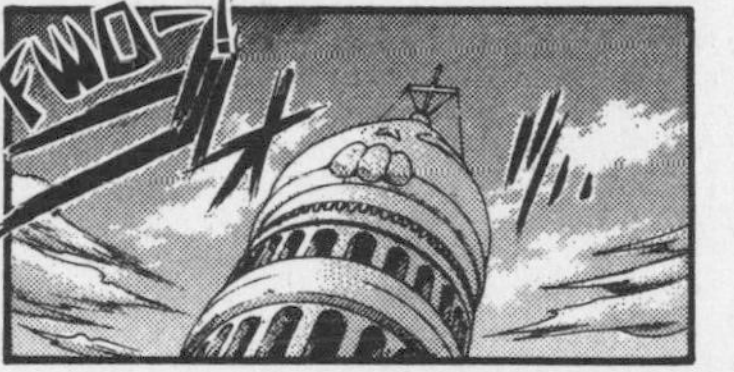
FWOO
フォ！
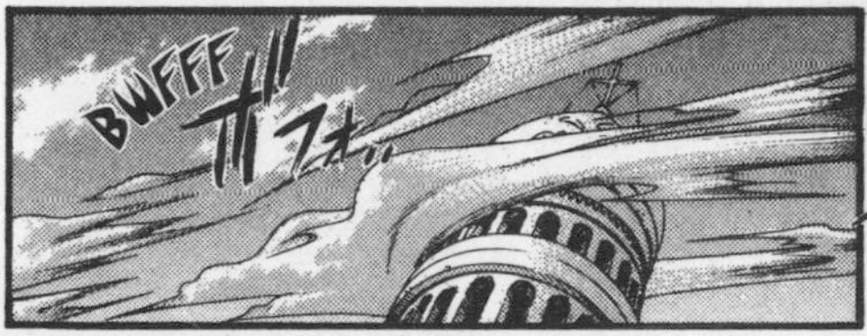
BWFFF
ボフォ…
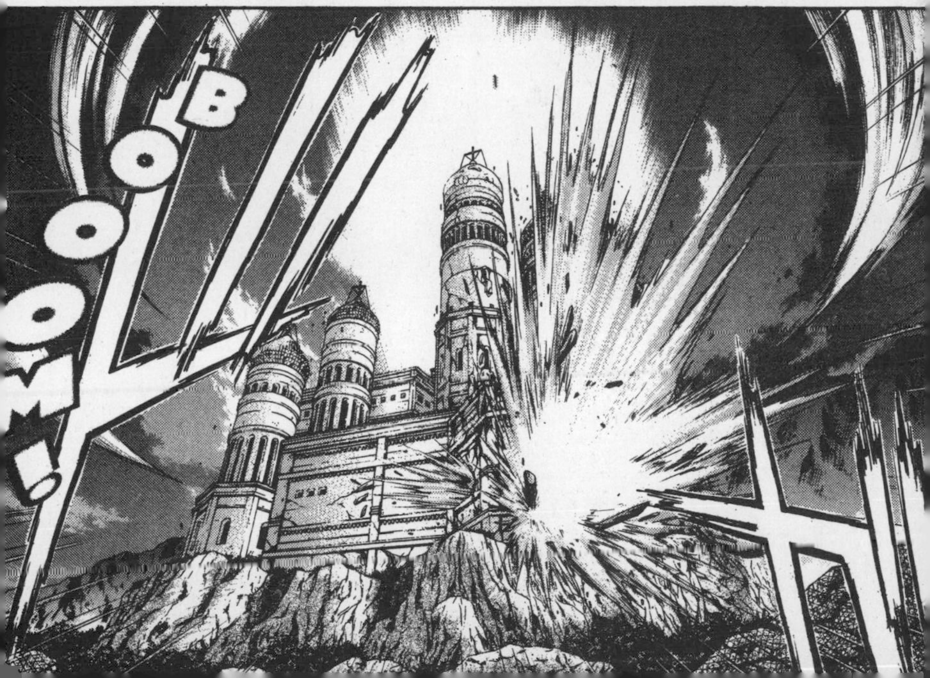
BOOOOM!

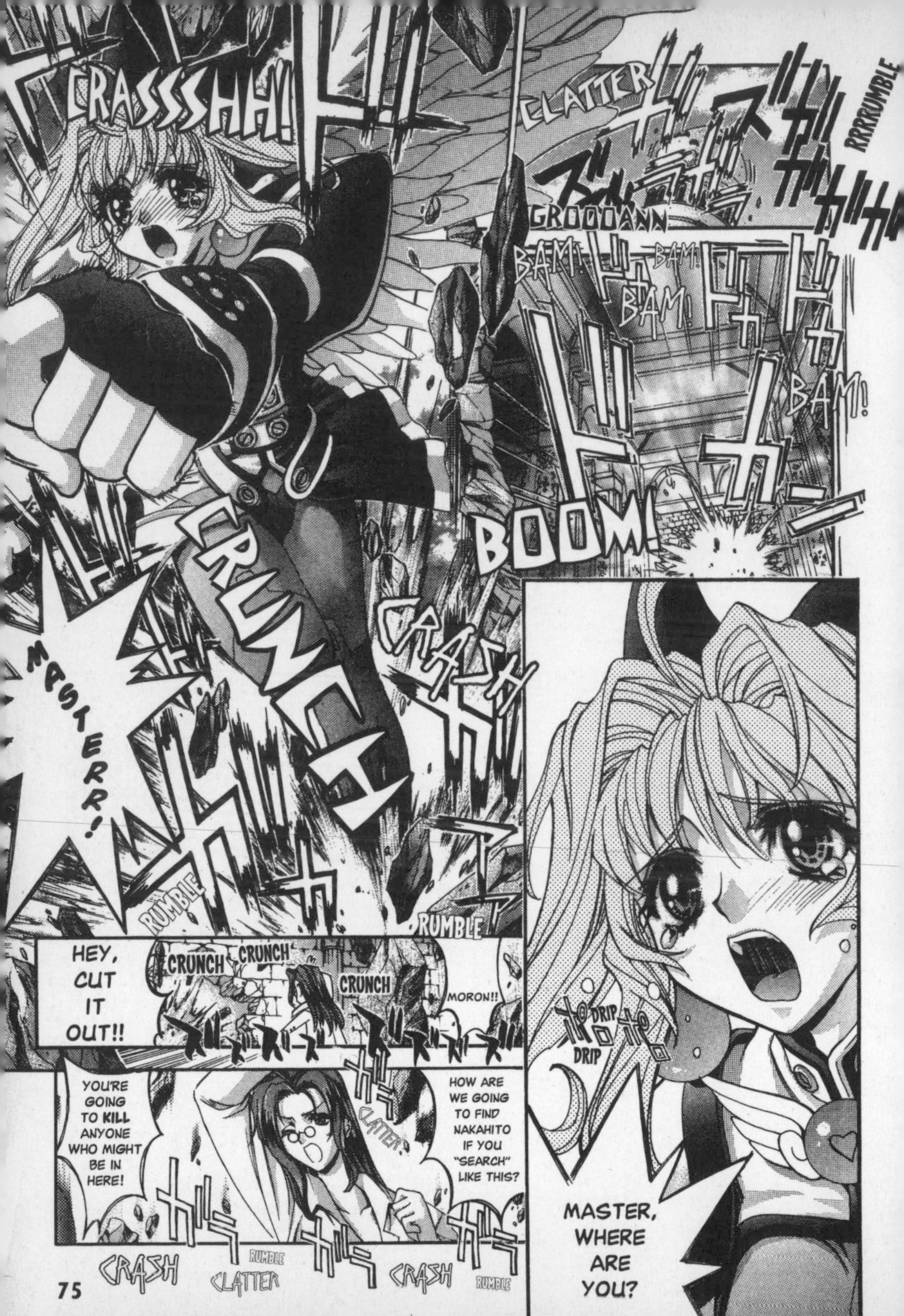
RRRRUMBLE
CLATTER
GROOOANN
BAM!
BAM!
BAM!
BAM!
BOOM!
CRASSSHH!
CRASH
CRUNCH
MASTERR!
RUMBLE
RUMBLE
DRIP
DRIP
MASTER, WHERE ARE YOU?
MORON!!
CRUNCH
CRUNCH
CRUNCH
HEY, CUT IT OUT!!
HOW ARE WE GOING TO FIND NAKAHITO IF YOU "SEARCH" LIKE THIS?
YOU'RE GOING TO **KILL** ANYONE WHO MIGHT BE IN HERE!
CLATTER
RUMBLE
CRASH
CLATTER
RUMBLE
CRASH

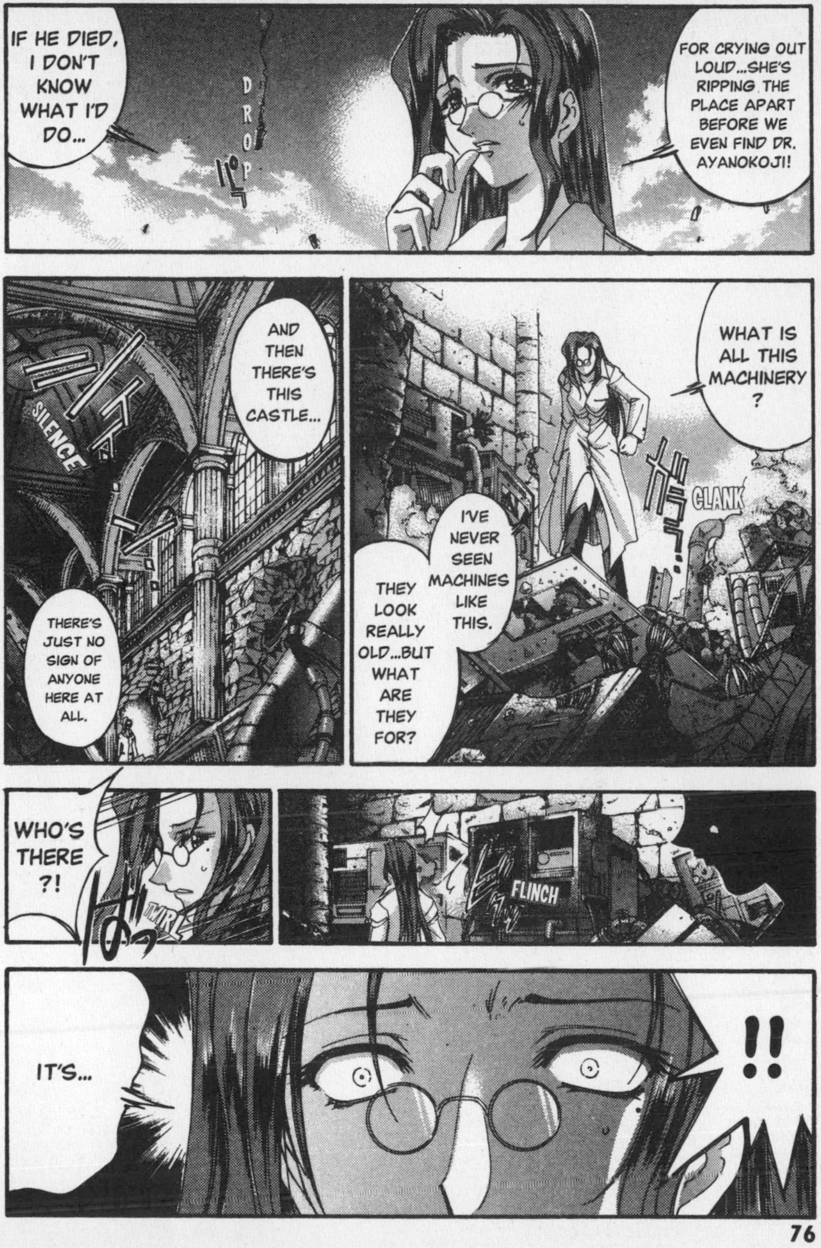
FOR CRYING OUT LOUD...SHE'S RIPPING THE PLACE APART BEFORE WE EVEN FIND DR. AYANOKOJI!
IF HE DIED, I DON'T KNOW WHAT I'D DO...
DROP
WHAT IS ALL THIS MACHINERY?
CLANK
I'VE NEVER SEEN MACHINES LIKE THIS.
THEY LOOK REALLY OLD...BUT WHAT ARE THEY FOR?
AND THEN THERE'S THIS CASTLE...
SILENCE
THERE'S JUST NO SIGN OF ANYONE HERE AT ALL.
FLINCH
WHO'S THERE?!
TWIRL
!!
IT'S...

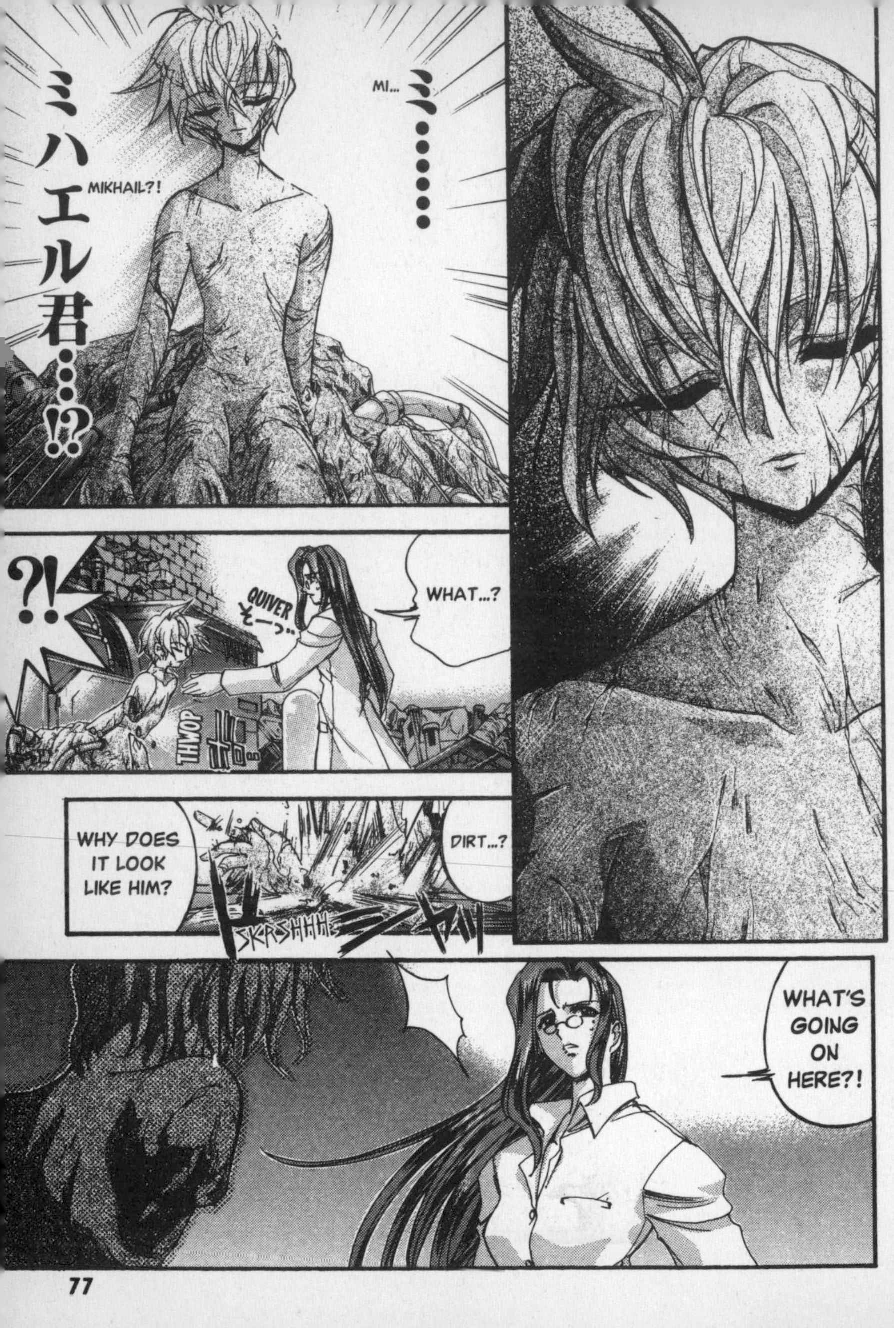
ミ……
MI...
ミハエル君……!?
MIKHAIL?!
WHAT...?
?!
そーっ
QUIVER
ボロ..
THWOP
DIRT...?
WHY DOES IT LOOK LIKE HIM?
SKRSHHH
WHAT'S GOING ON HERE?!

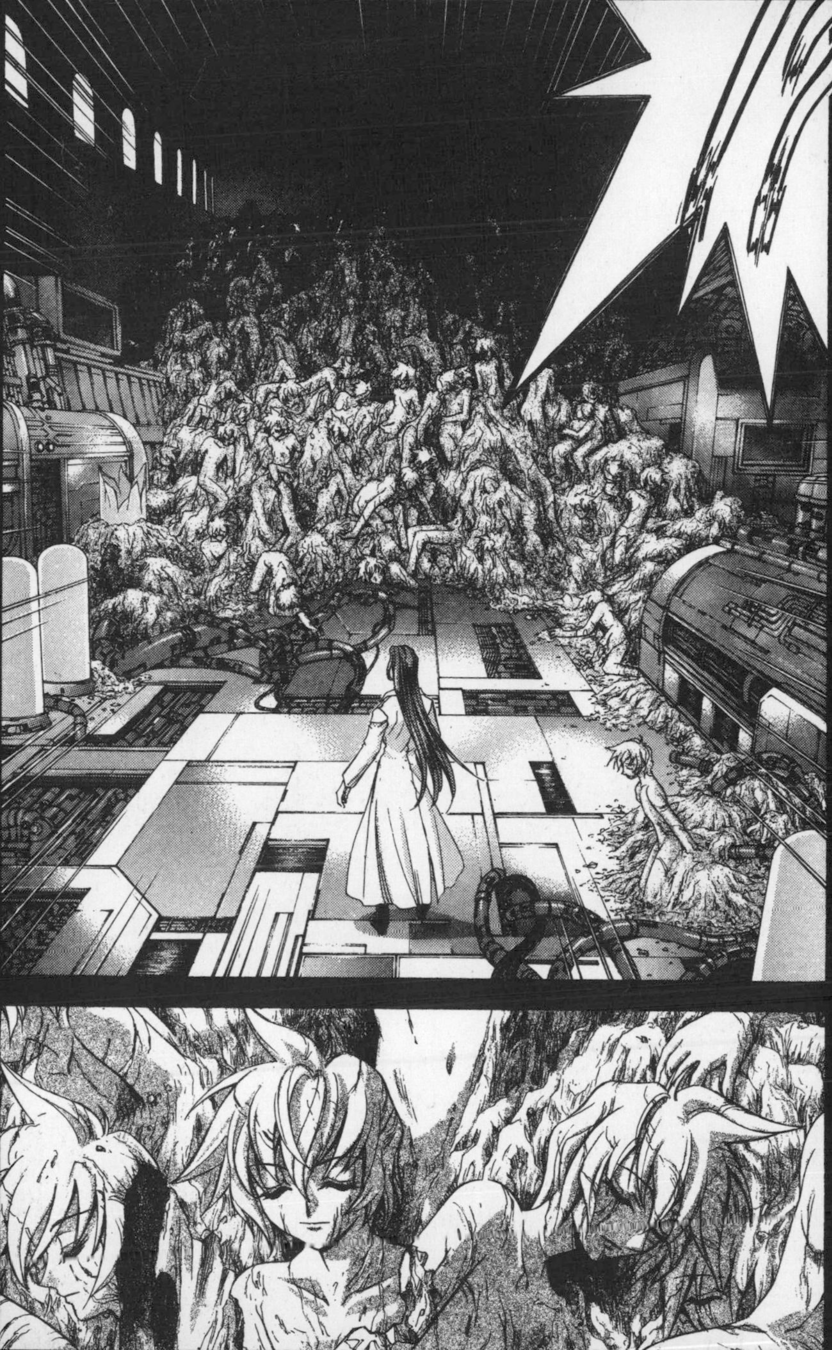

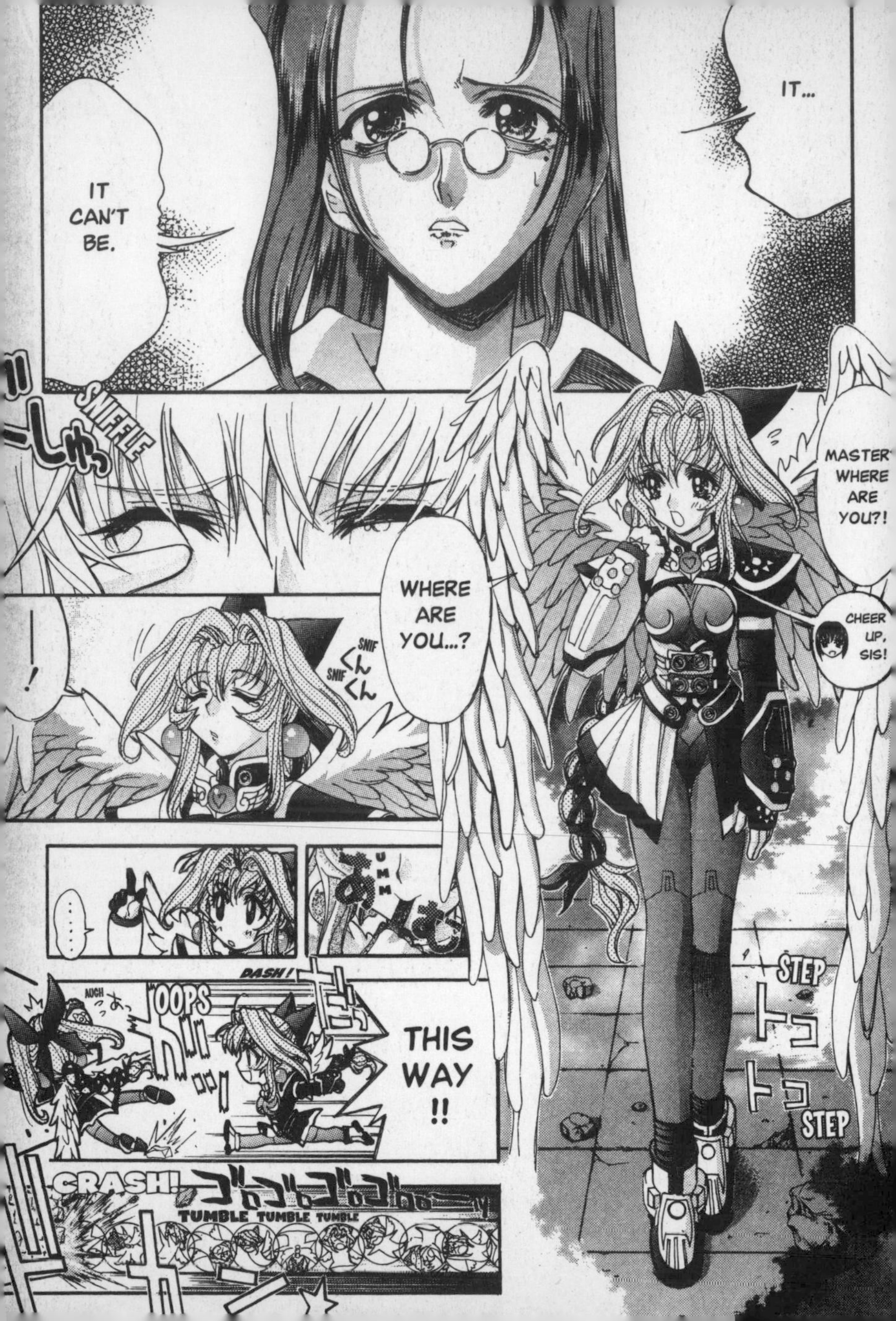
IT...
IT CAN'T BE.
MASTER WHERE ARE YOU?!
CHEER UP, SIS!
STEP
トコ
トコ
STEP
SNIFFLE
WHERE ARE YOU...?
SNIF くん
SNIF くん
!
UMM
......
DASH!
THIS WAY !!
OOPS
AUGH
CRASH!
TUMBLE TUMBLE TUMBLE

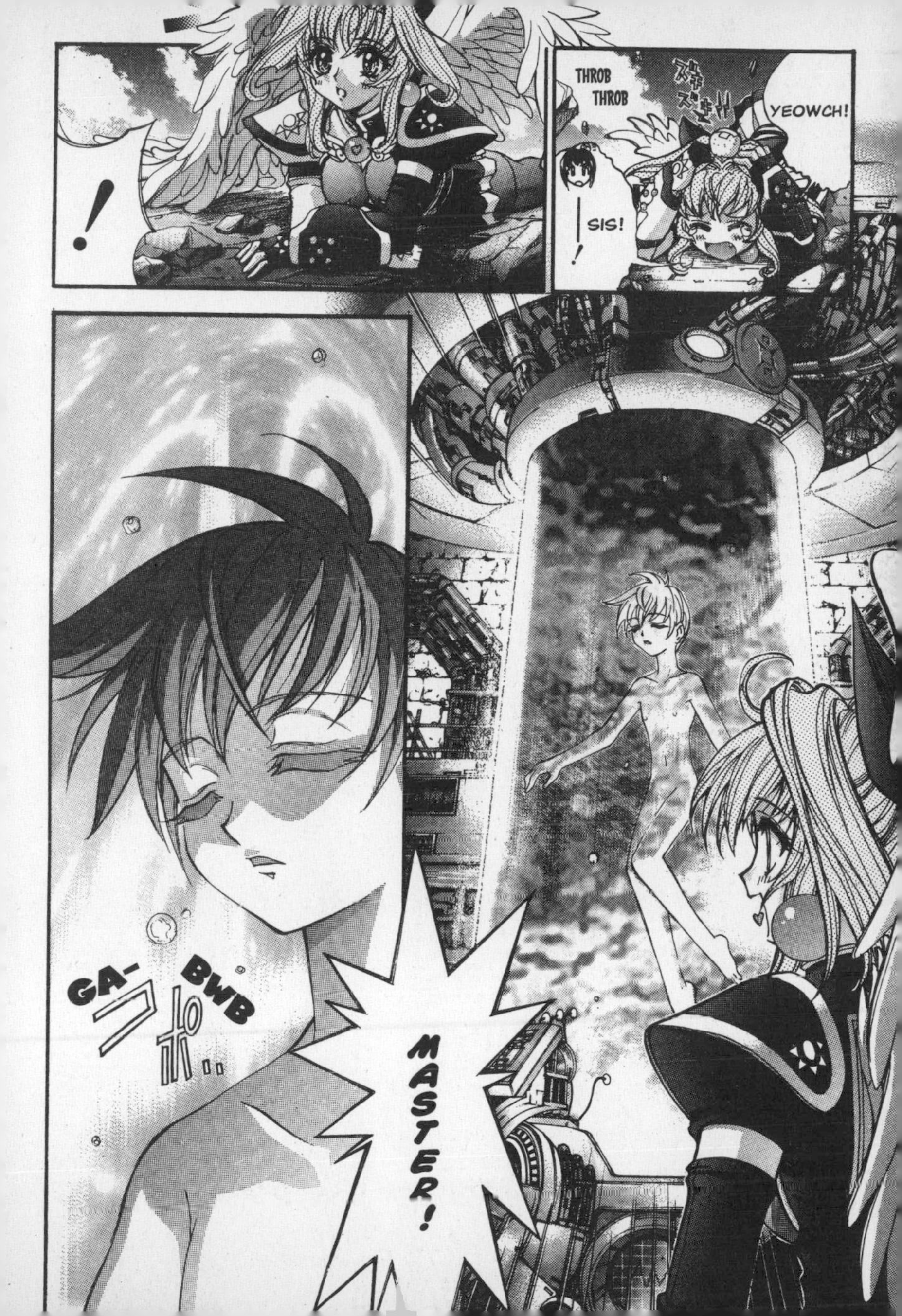
YEOWCH!
THROB THROB
SIS!
!
!
MASTER!
GA-BWB

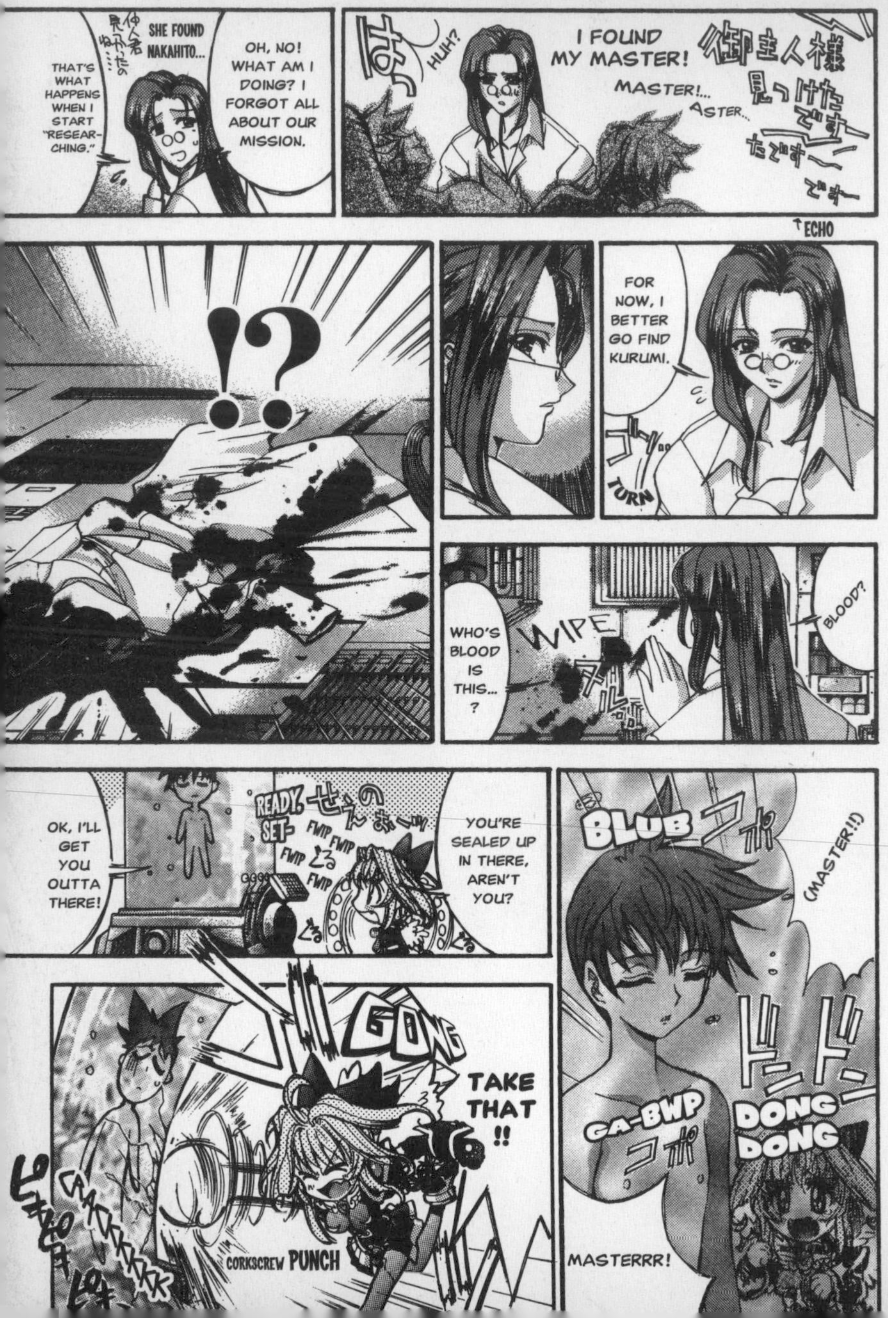

御主人様見っけたです〜
I FOUND MY MASTER!
MASTER!...
ASTER...
たです〜
です〜
↑ECHO
はっ
HUH?
OH, NO! WHAT AM I DOING? I FORGOT ALL ABOUT OUR MISSION.
SHE FOUND NAKAHITO...
仲人君見つけたの
THAT'S WHAT HAPPENS WHEN I START "RESEARCHING."
FOR NOW, I BETTER GO FIND KURUMI.
TURN
BLOOD?
WIPE
WHO'S BLOOD IS THIS... ?
!?
BLUB
(MASTER!!)
ドンドン
DONG DONG
GA-BWP
MASTERRR!
YOU'RE SEALED UP IN THERE, AREN'T YOU?
READY, SET
FWIP FWIP FWIP FWIP
OK, I'LL GET YOU OUTTA THERE!
GONG
TAKE THAT !!
CORKSCREW PUNCH
CRACKCKKKKK

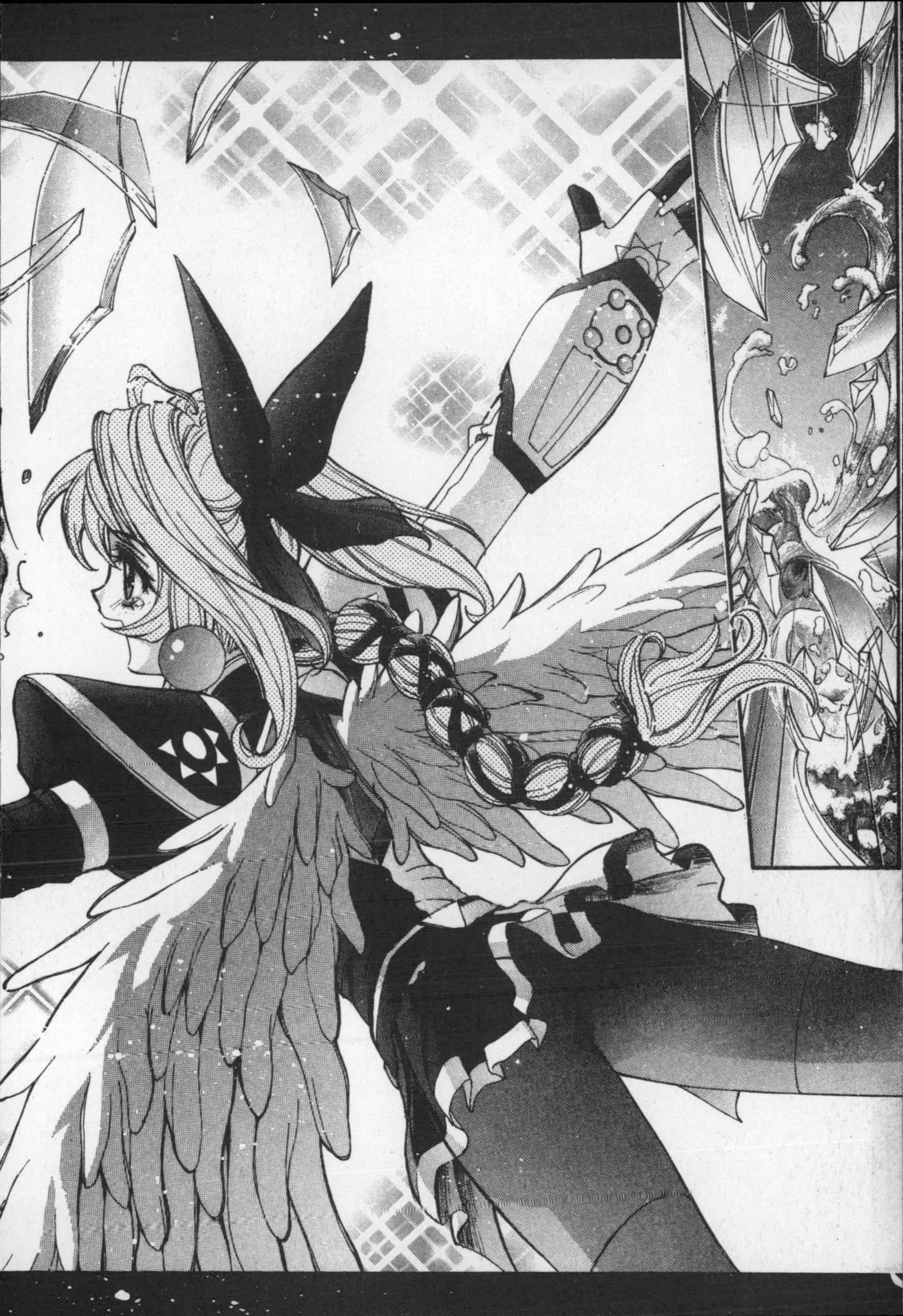

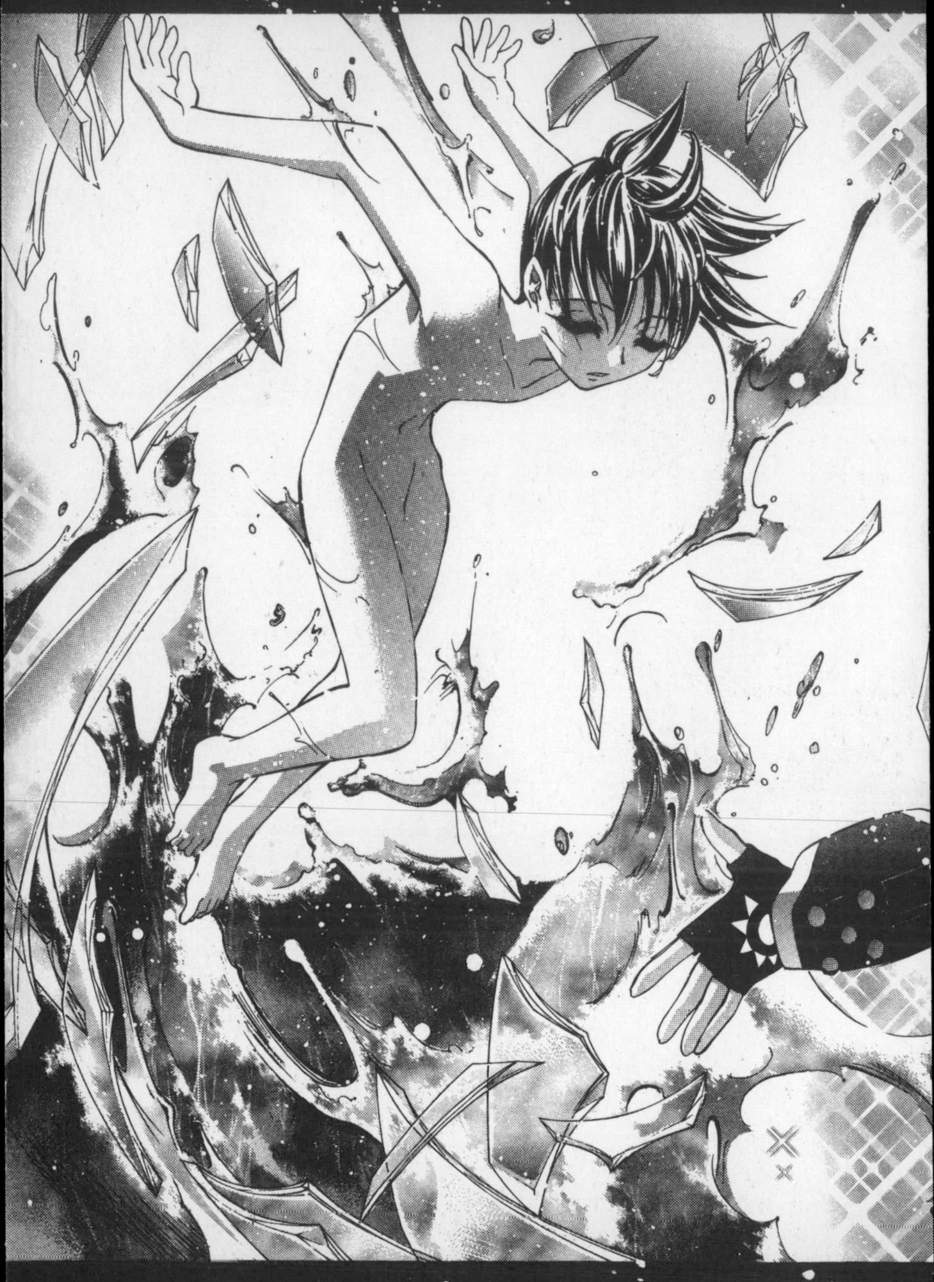

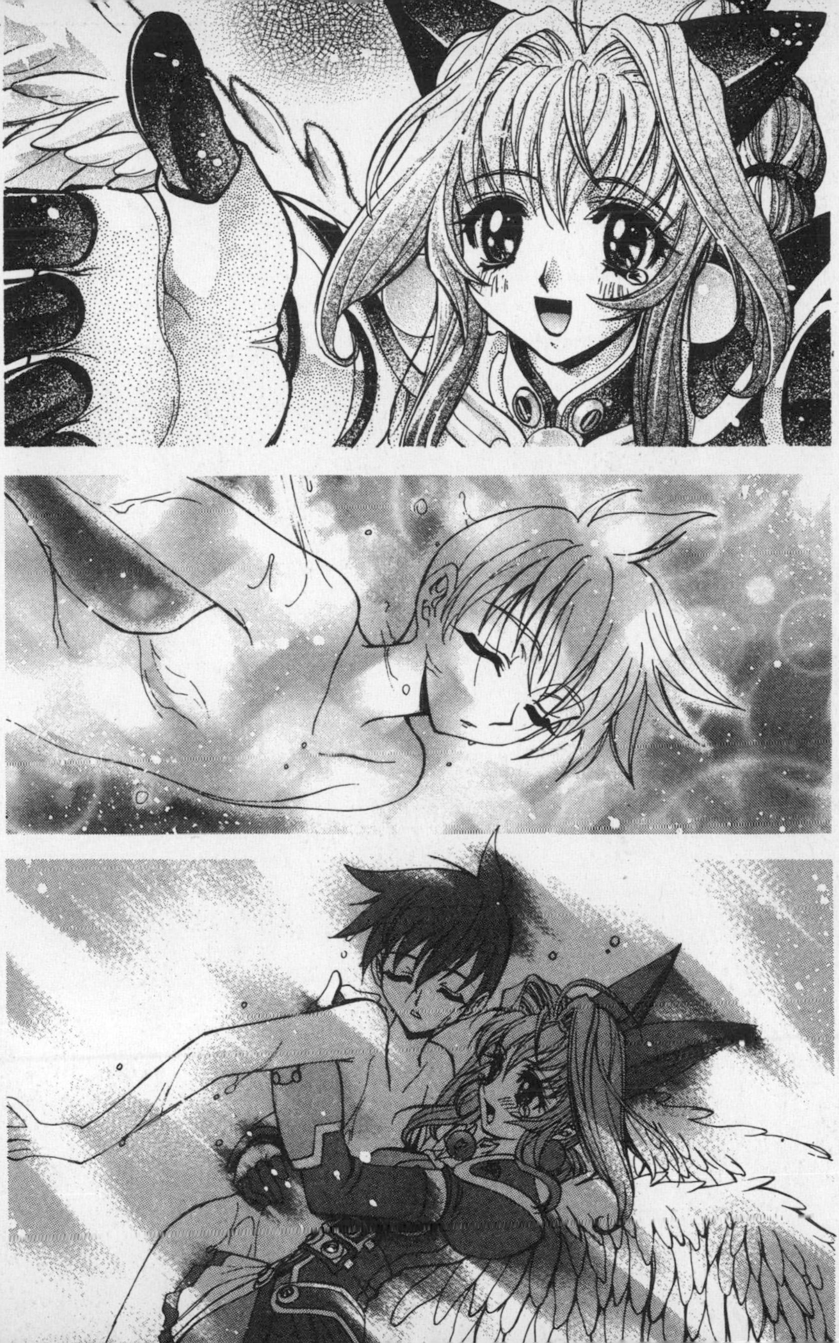

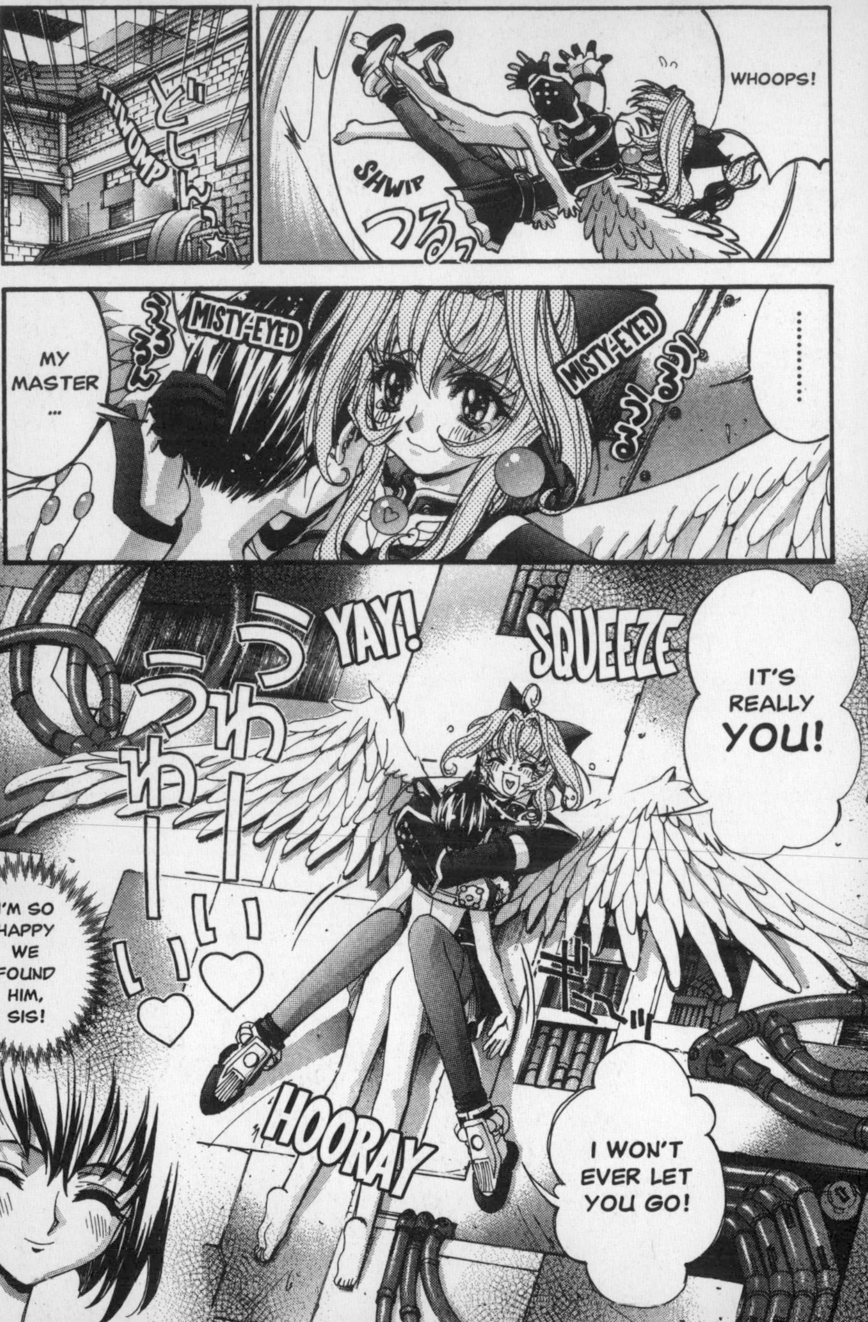
WHOOPS!
SHWIP
つるっ
THWUMP
どしんっ☆
......
MISTY-EYED
MISTY-EYED
MY MASTER ...
IT'S REALLY YOU!
SQUEEZE
YAY!
I WON'T EVER LET YOU GO!
HOORAY
I'M SO HAPPY WE FOUND HIM, SIS!

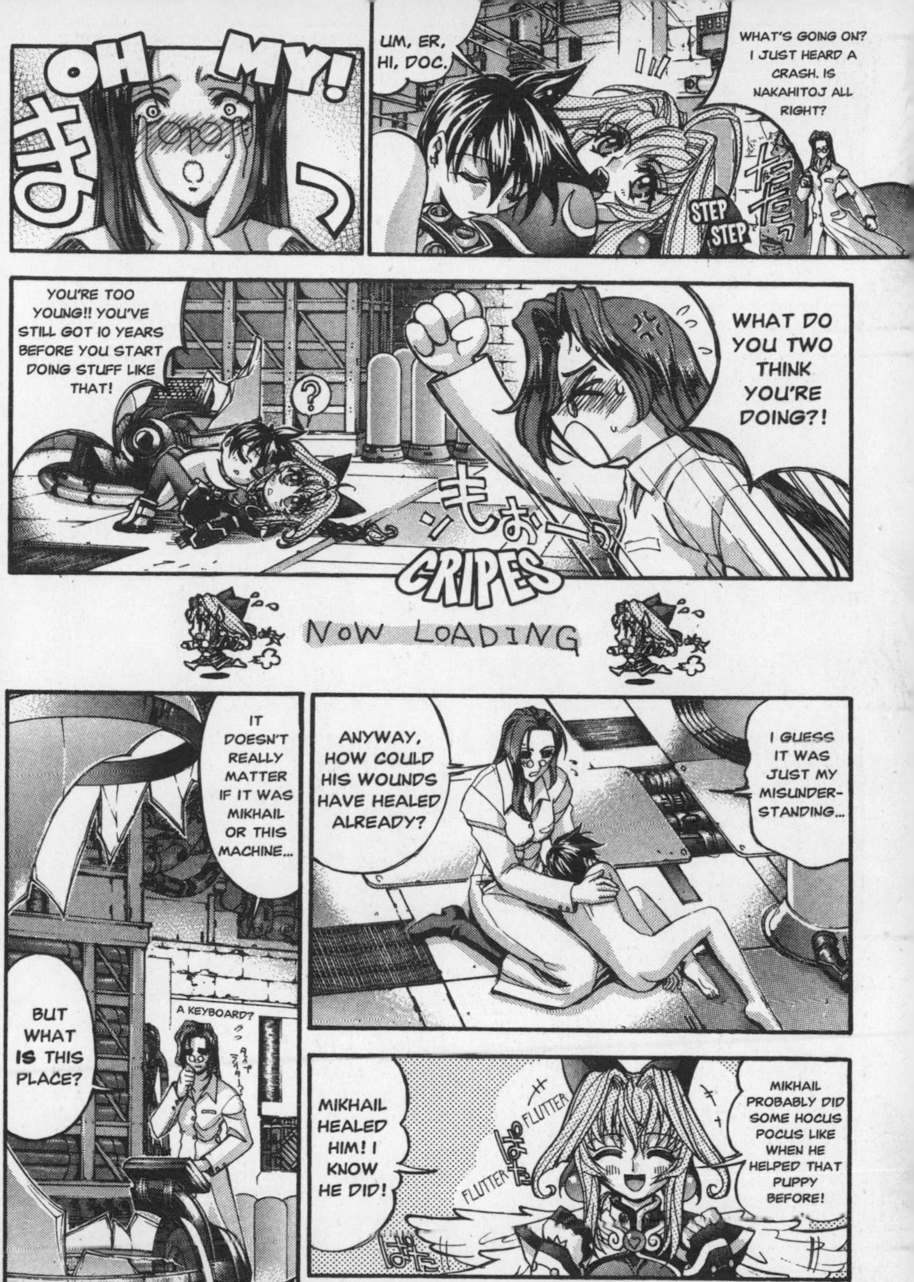
WHAT'S GOING ON? I JUST HEARD A CRASH. IS NAKAHITOJ ALL RIGHT?
UM, ER, HI, DOC.
STEP STEP
OH MY!
まっ
WHAT DO YOU TWO THINK YOU'RE DOING?!
YOU'RE TOO YOUNG!! YOU'VE STILL GOT 10 YEARS BEFORE YOU START DOING STUFF LIKE THAT!
?
CRIPES
NOW LOADING
I GUESS IT WAS JUST MY MISUNDER-STANDING...
ANYWAY, HOW COULD HIS WOUNDS HAVE HEALED ALREADY?
MIKHAIL PROBABLY DID SOME HOCUS POCUS LIKE WHEN HE HELPED THAT PUPPY BEFORE!
MIKHAIL HEALED HIM! I KNOW HE DID!
FLUTTER
FLUTTER
IT DOESN'T REALLY MATTER IF IT WAS MIKHAIL OR THIS MACHINE...
BUT WHAT IS THIS PLACE?
A KEYBOARD?

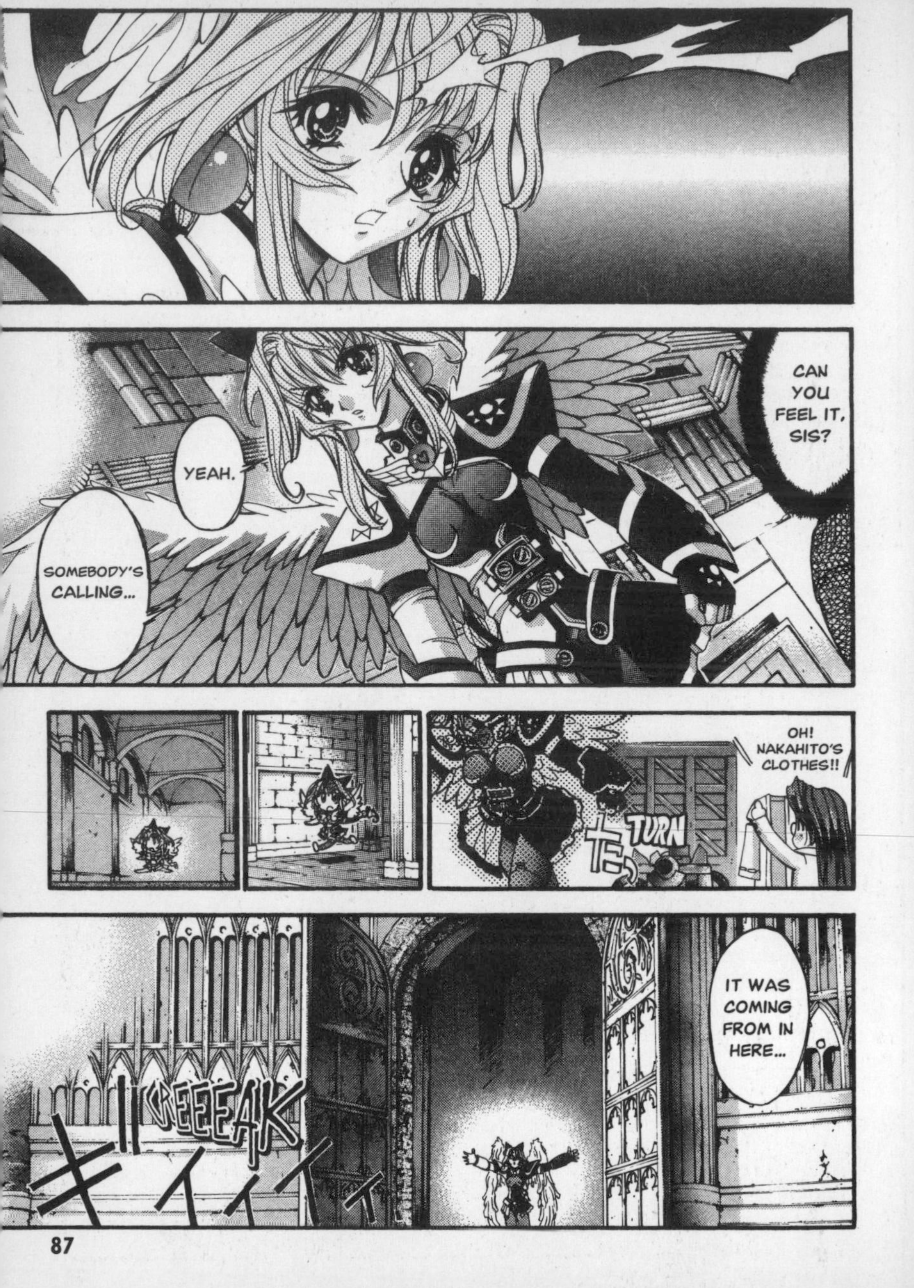
CAN YOU FEEL IT, SIS?
YEAH.
SOMEBODY'S CALLING...
OH! NAKAHITO'S CLOTHES!!
TURN
IT WAS COMING FROM IN HERE...
CREEEAK

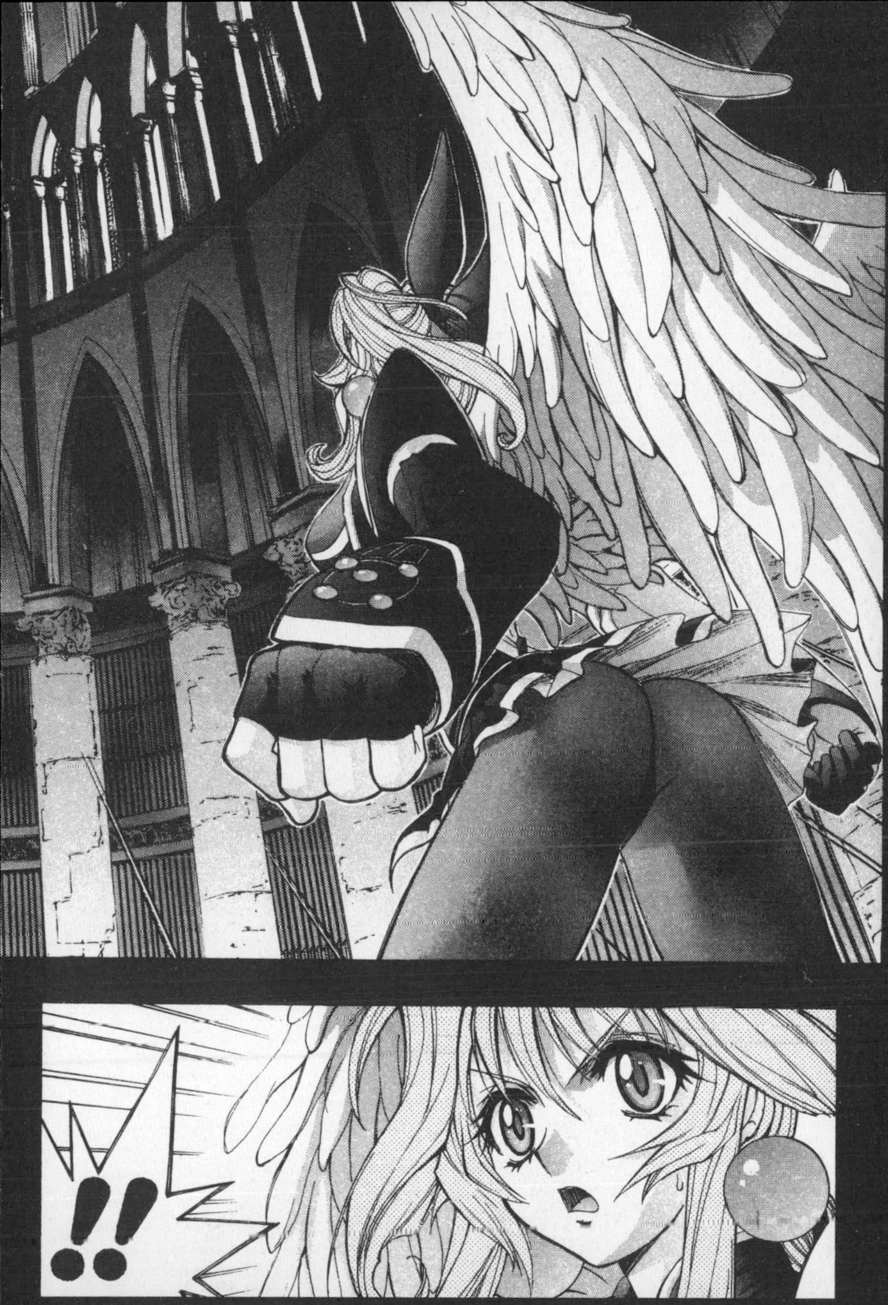
!!

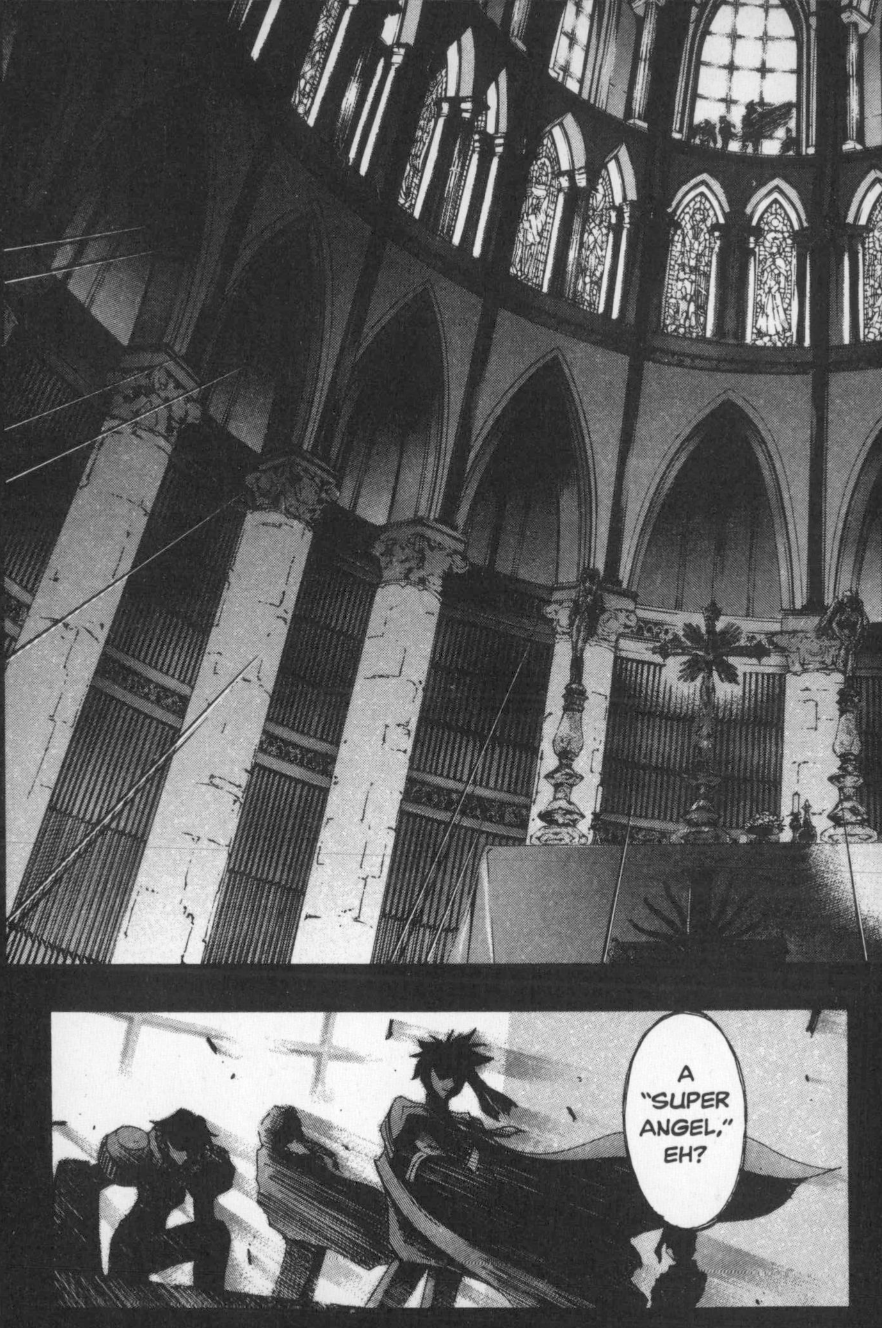
A "SUPER ANGEL," EH?

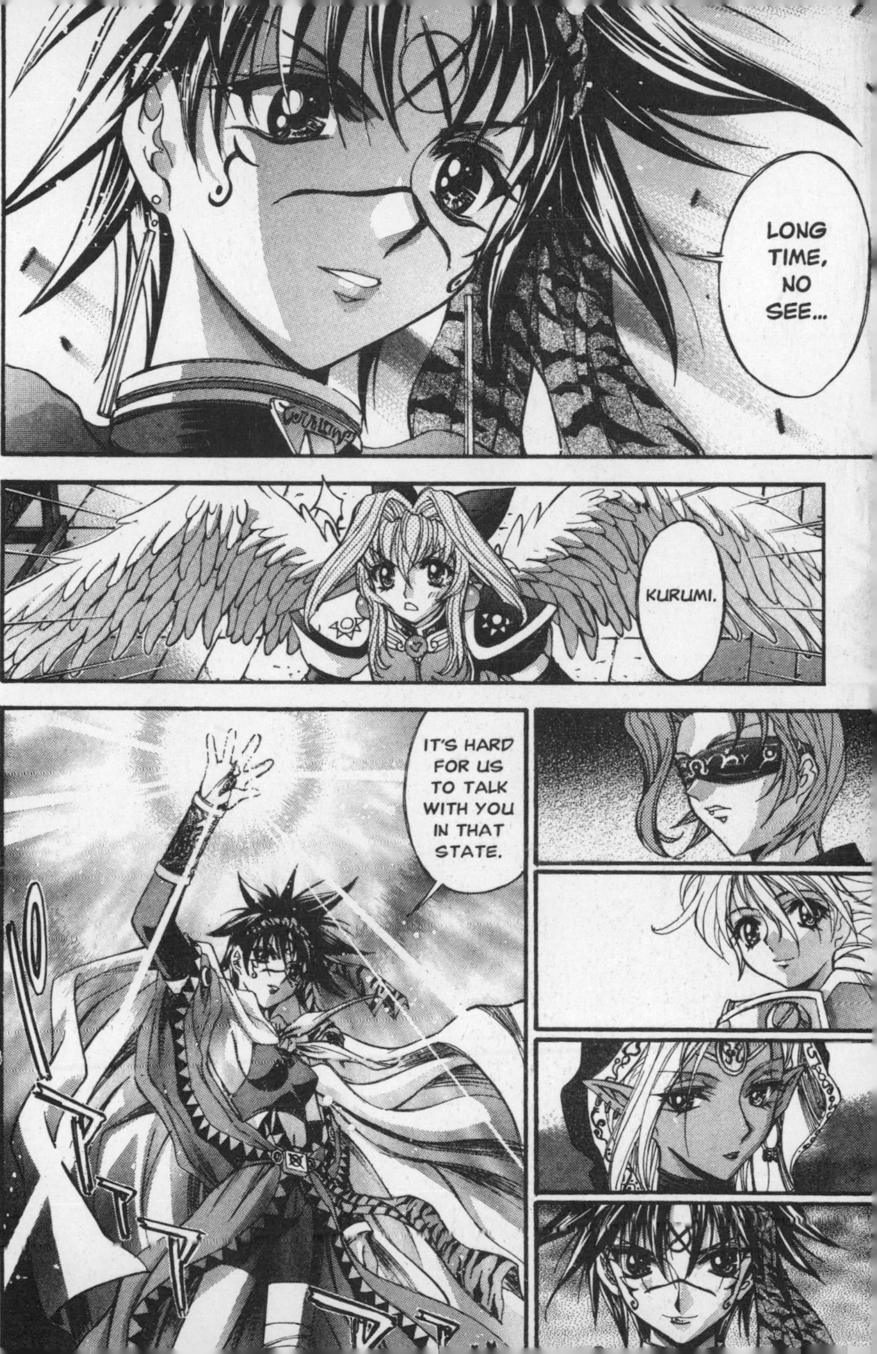
LONG TIME, NO SEE...
KURUMI.
IT'S HARD FOR US TO TALK WITH YOU IN THAT STATE.

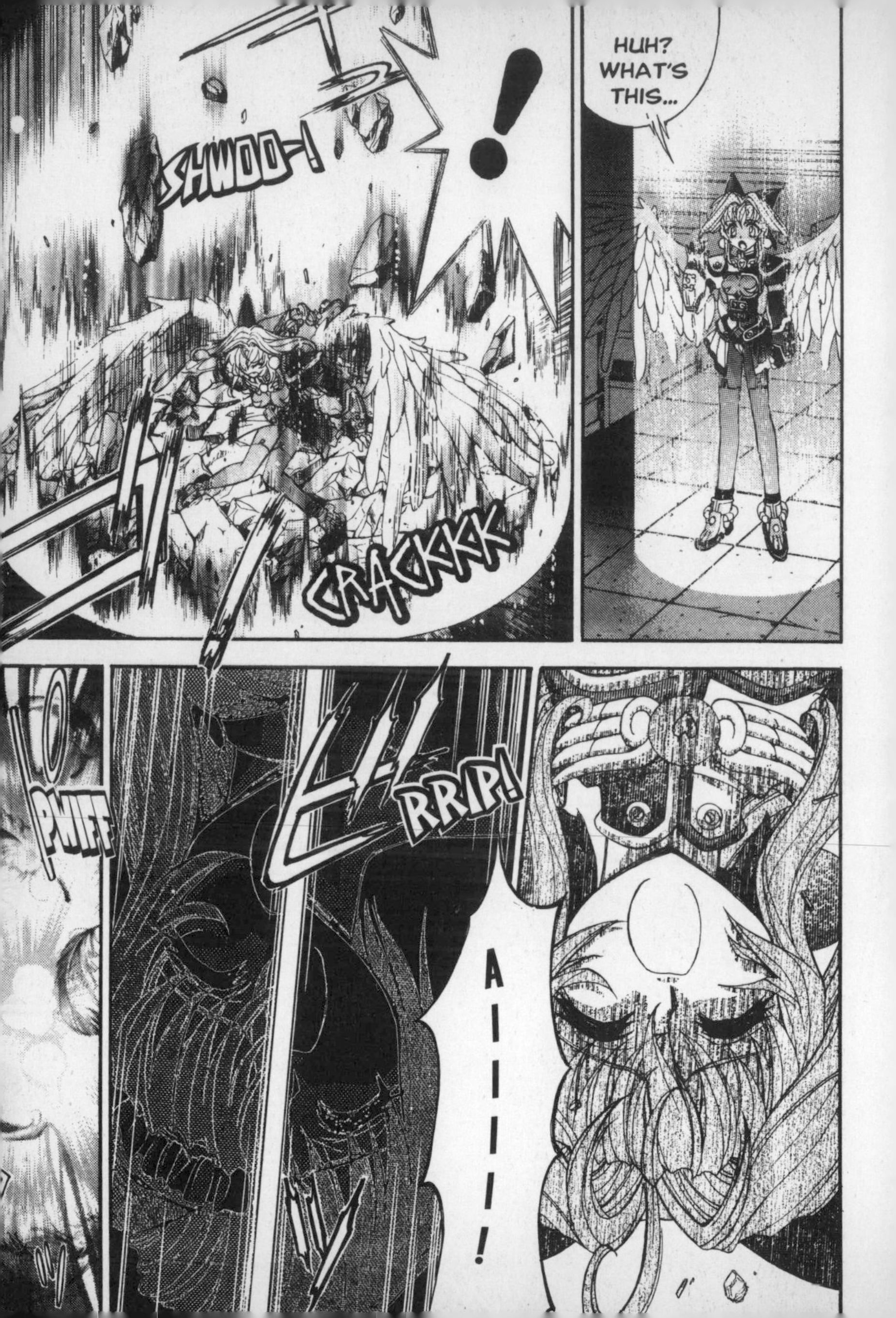
HUH? WHAT'S THIS...
!
SHWOO-!
CRACKKK
A———!
RRIP!
PWIFF

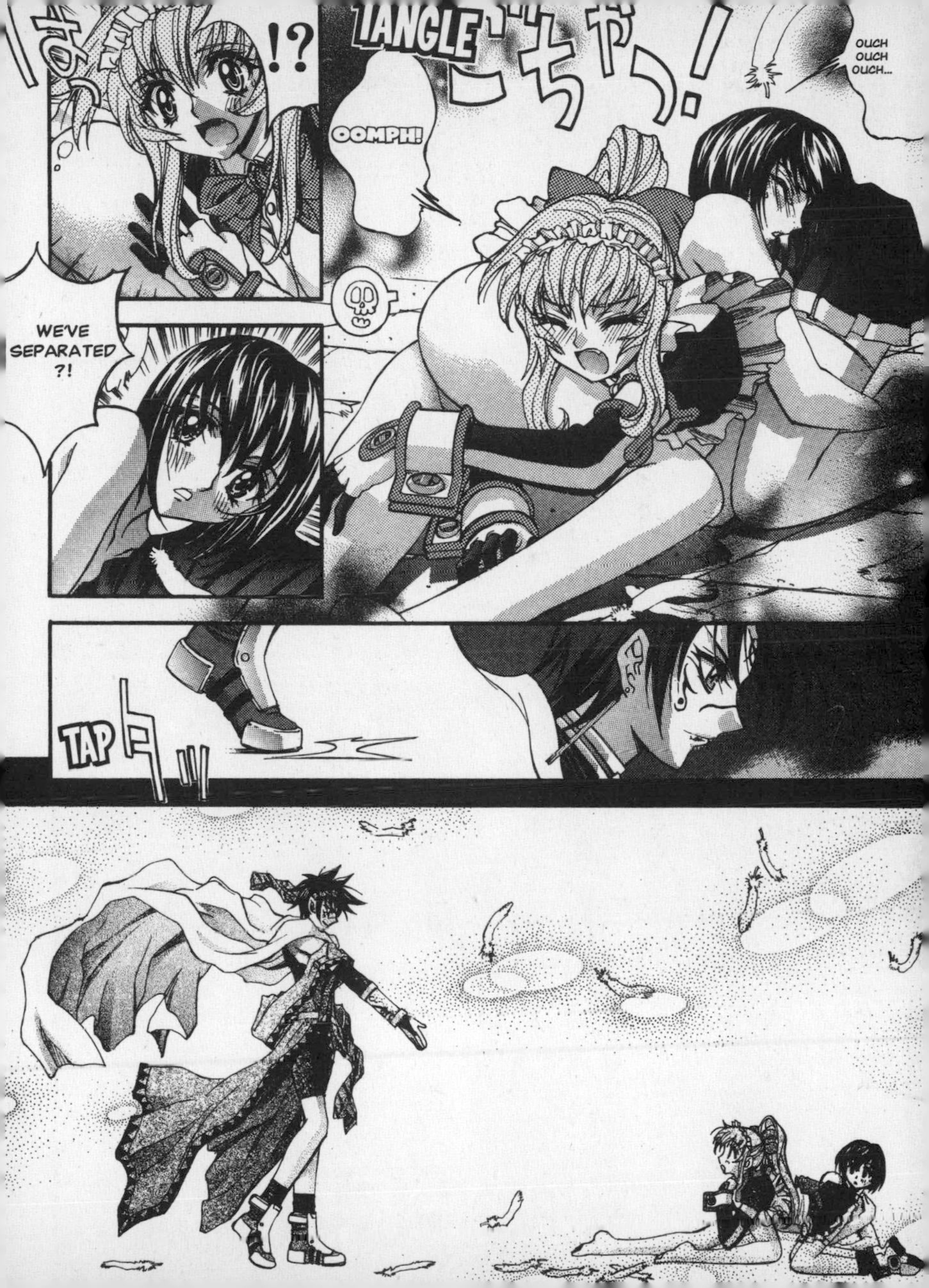
OUCH OUCH OUCH...
TANGLE ごちゃっ!
OOMPH!
はっ!?
WE'VE SEPARATED ?!
TAP トッ

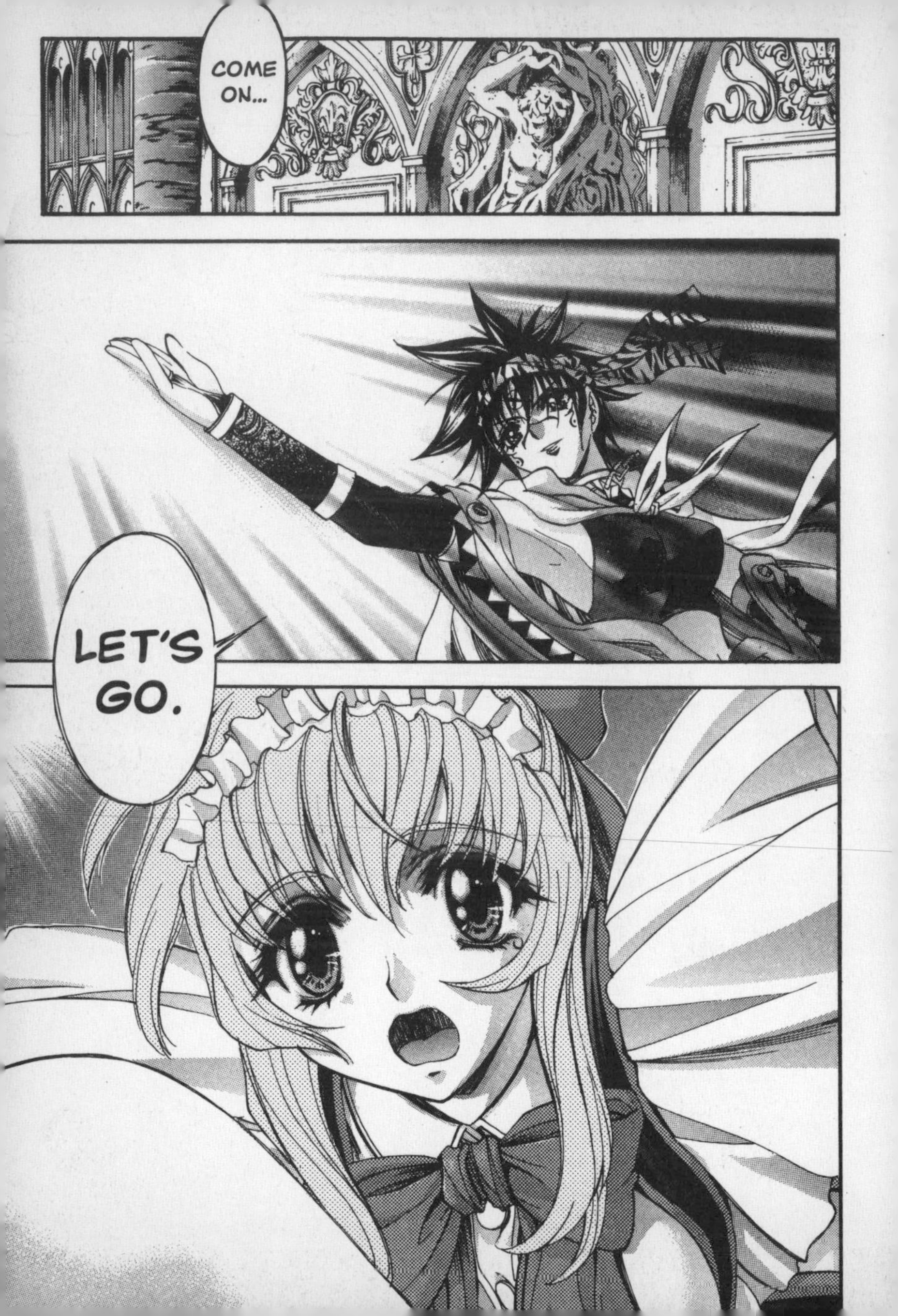

COME ON...
LET'S GO.

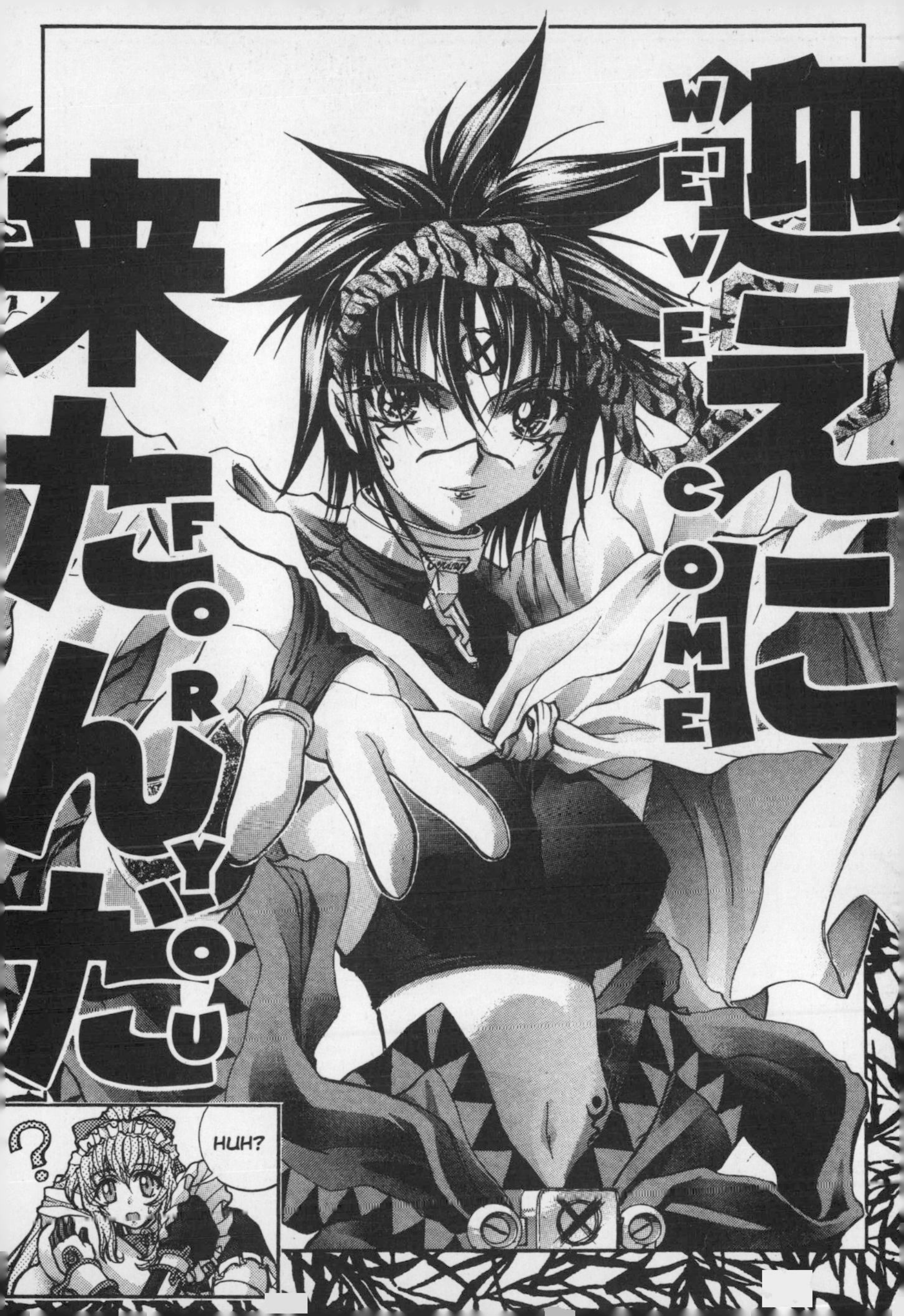
迎えに
WE'VE COME
FOR YOU
来たんだ
HUH?

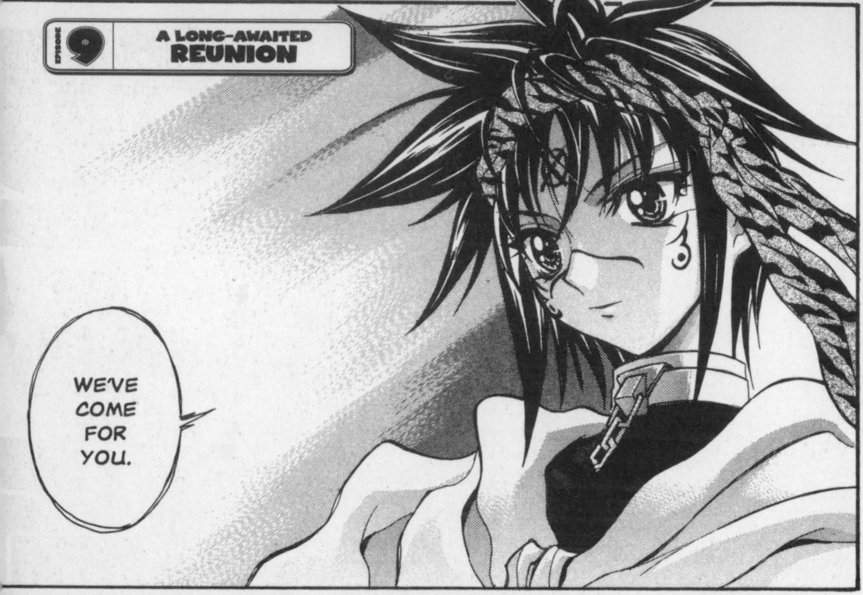
EPISODE 9
A LONG-AWAITED REUNION
WE'VE COME FOR YOU.

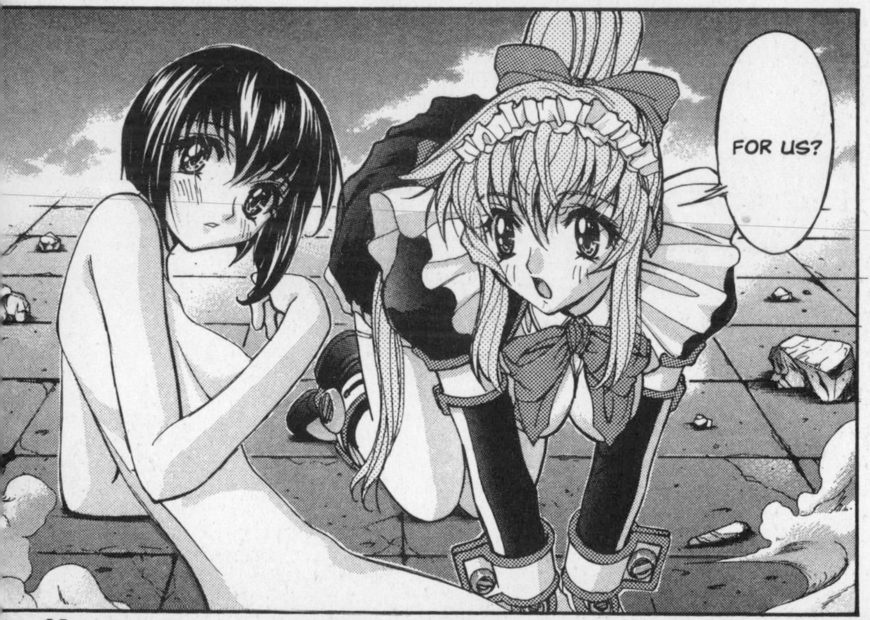
FOR US?

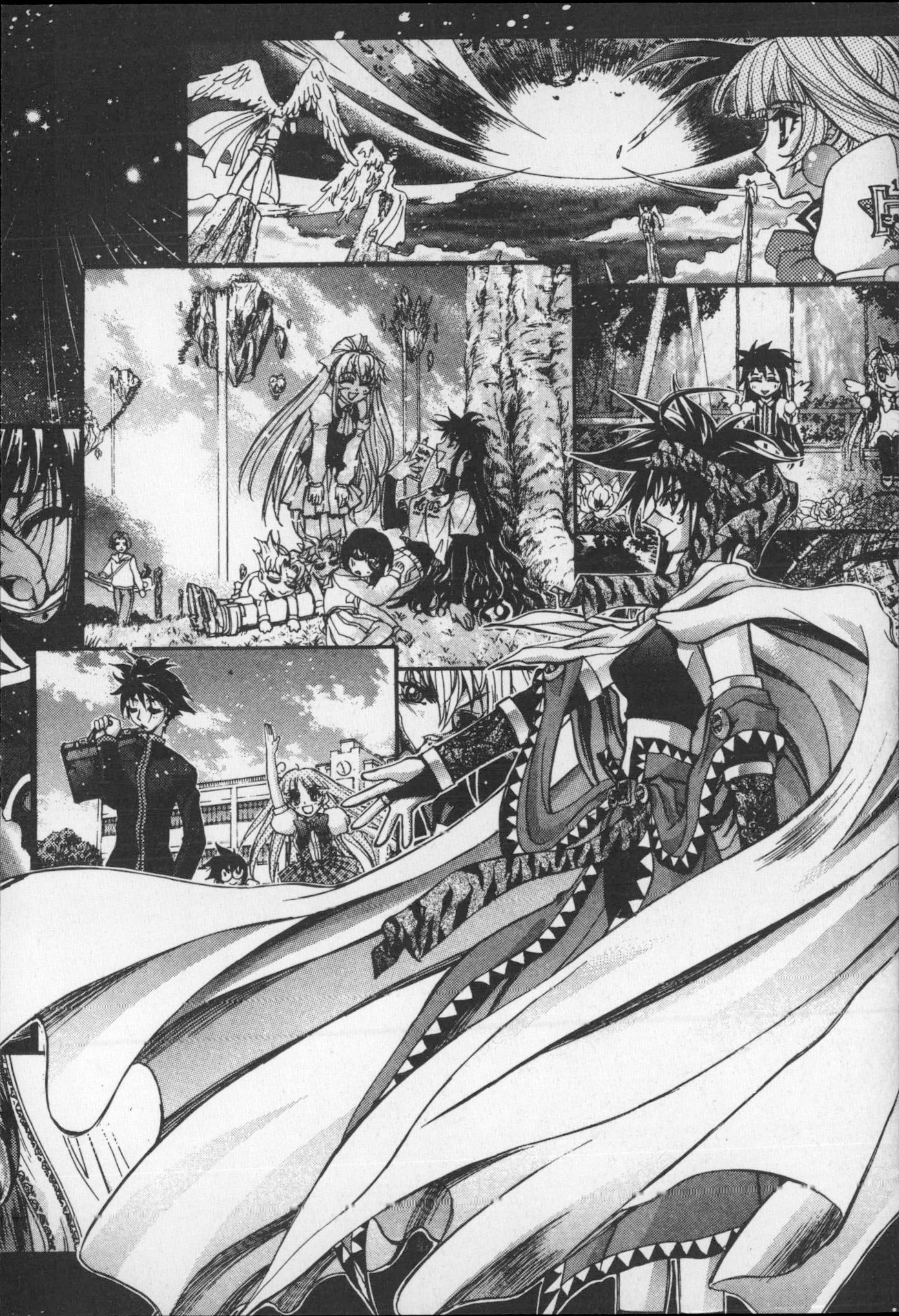

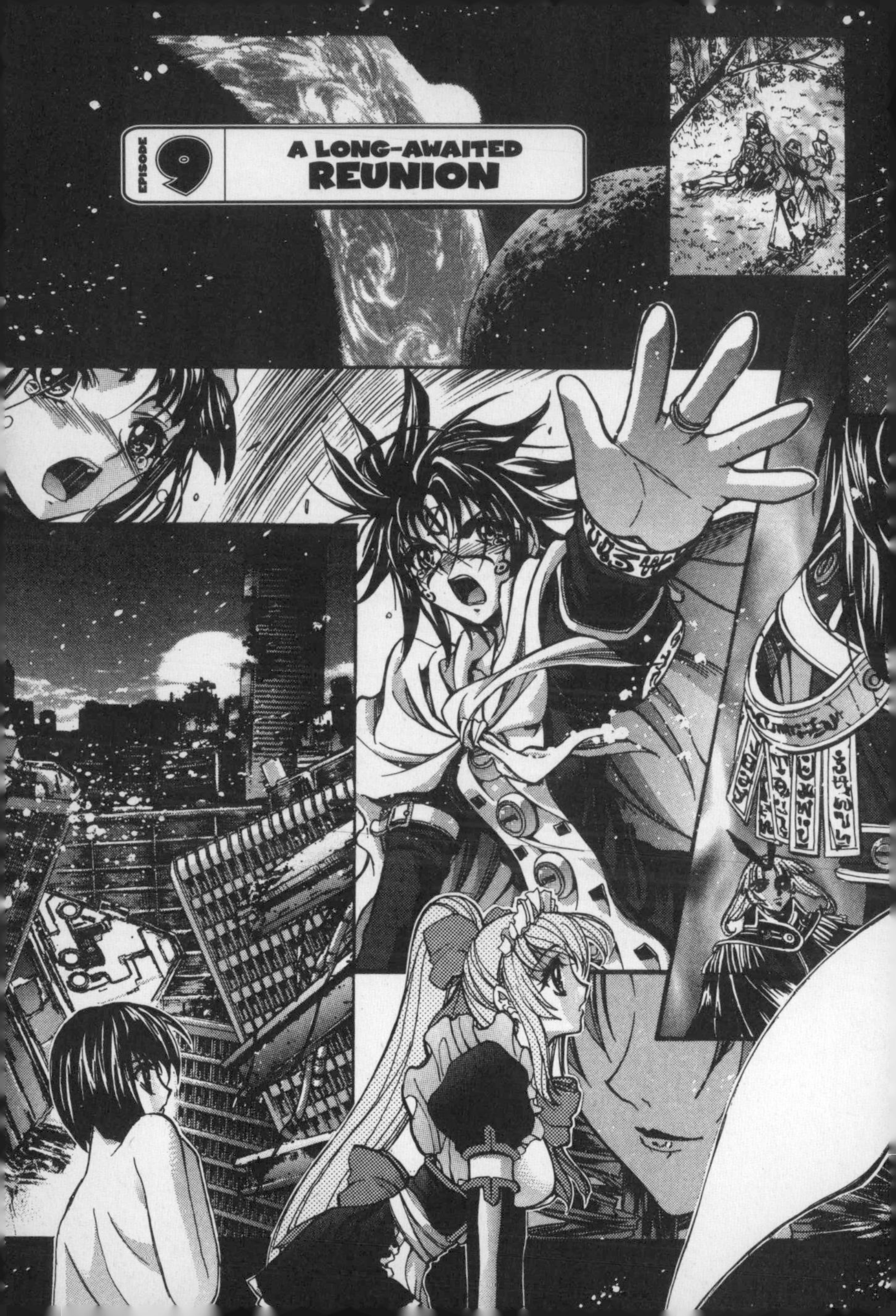
EPISODE 9
A LONG-AWAITED REUNION

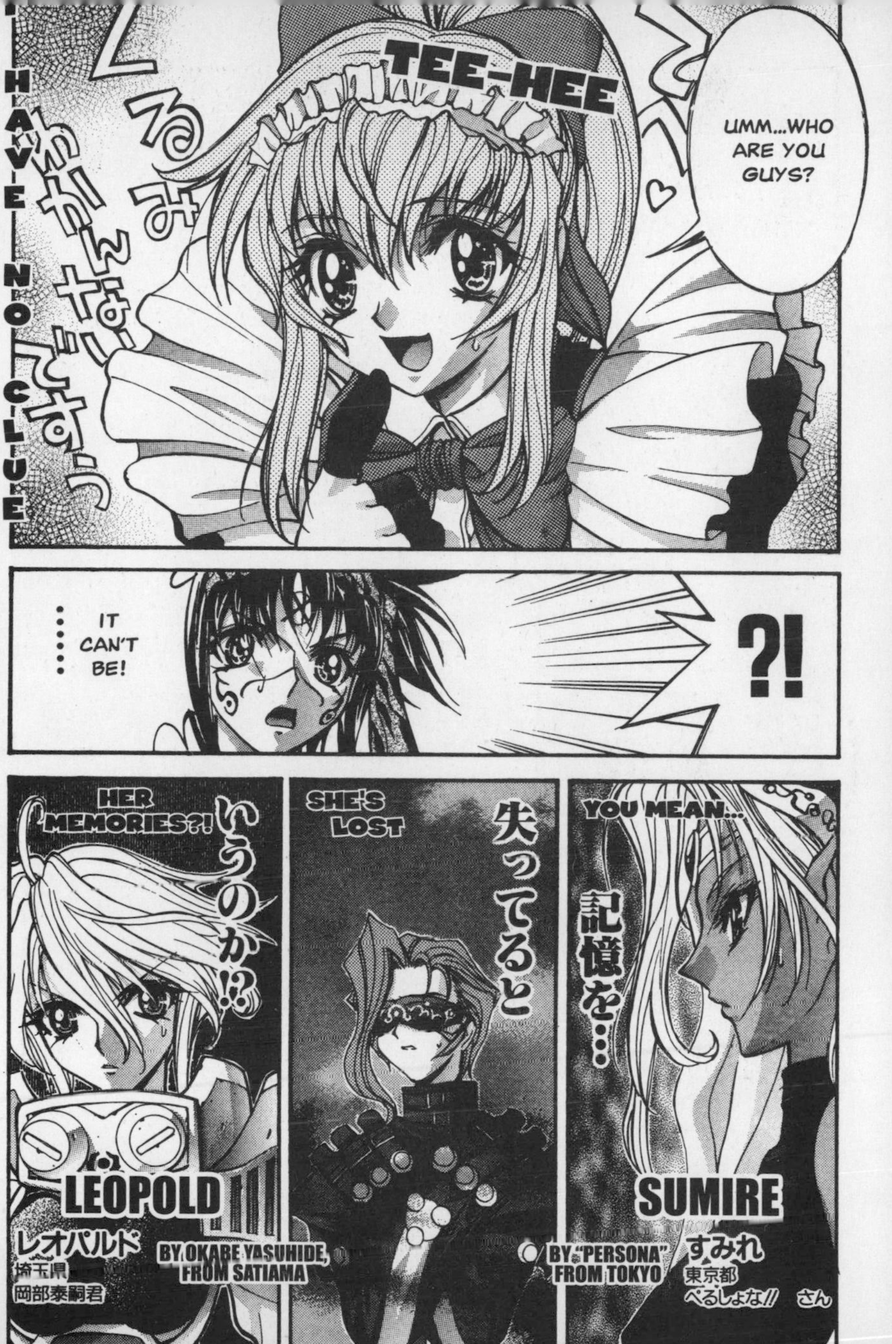
TEE-HEE
UMM...WHO ARE YOU GUYS?
I HAVE NO CLUE
?!
...... IT CAN'T BE!
YOU MEAN...
記憶を…
SHE'S LOST
失ってると
HER MEMORIES?!
いうのか!?
SUMIRE
BY "PERSONA" FROM TOKYO
すみれ
東京都
ぺるしょな!! さん
LEOPOLD
BY OKABE YASUHIDE, FROM SATIAMA
レオパルド
埼玉県
岡部泰嗣君

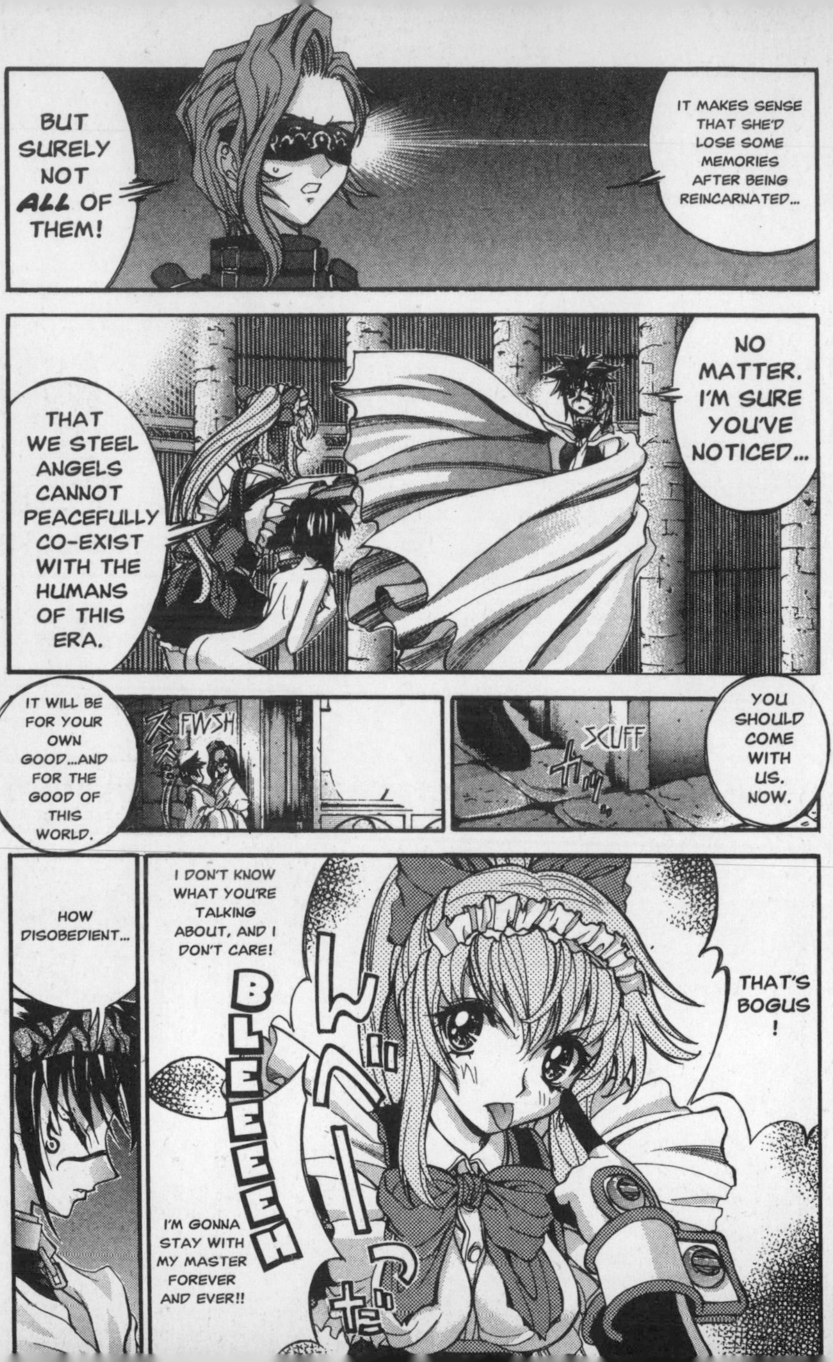
IT MAKES SENSE THAT SHE'D LOSE SOME MEMORIES AFTER BEING REINCARNATED...
BUT SURELY NOT ALL OF THEM!
NO MATTER. I'M SURE YOU'VE NOTICED...
THAT WE STEEL ANGELS CANNOT PEACEFULLY CO-EXIST WITH THE HUMANS OF THIS ERA.
SCUFF
YOU SHOULD COME WITH US. NOW.
FWSH
IT WILL BE FOR YOUR OWN GOOD...AND FOR THE GOOD OF THIS WORLD.
THAT'S BOGUS!
I DON'T KNOW WHAT YOU'RE TALKING ABOUT, AND I DON'T CARE!
BLEEEEEH
I'M GONNA STAY WITH MY MASTER FOREVER AND EVER!!
HOW DISOBEDIENT...

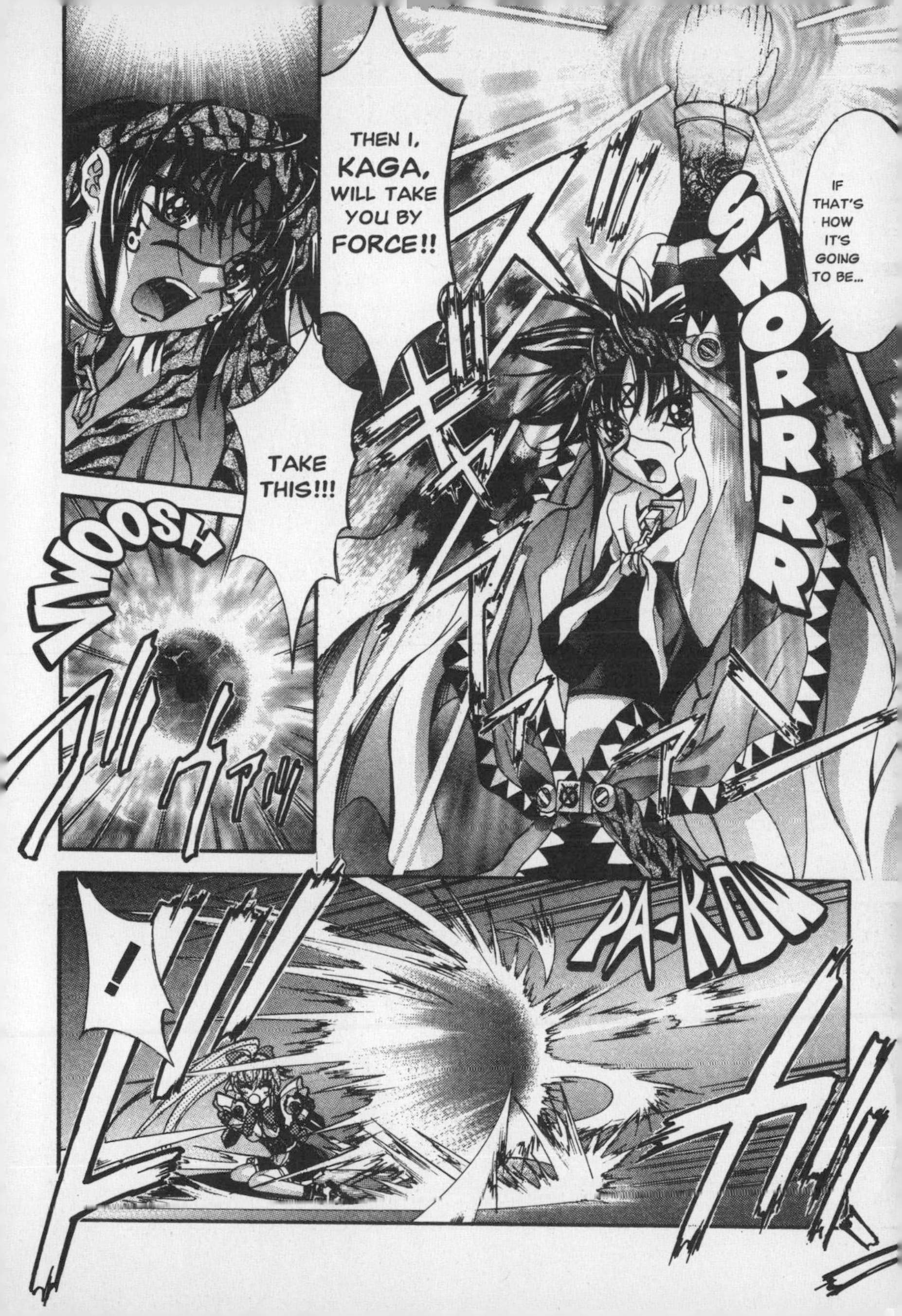
IF THAT'S HOW IT'S GOING TO BE...
SWORRR
THEN I, KAGA, WILL TAKE YOU BY FORCE!!
TAKE THIS!!!
WOOSH
PA-KOW
!

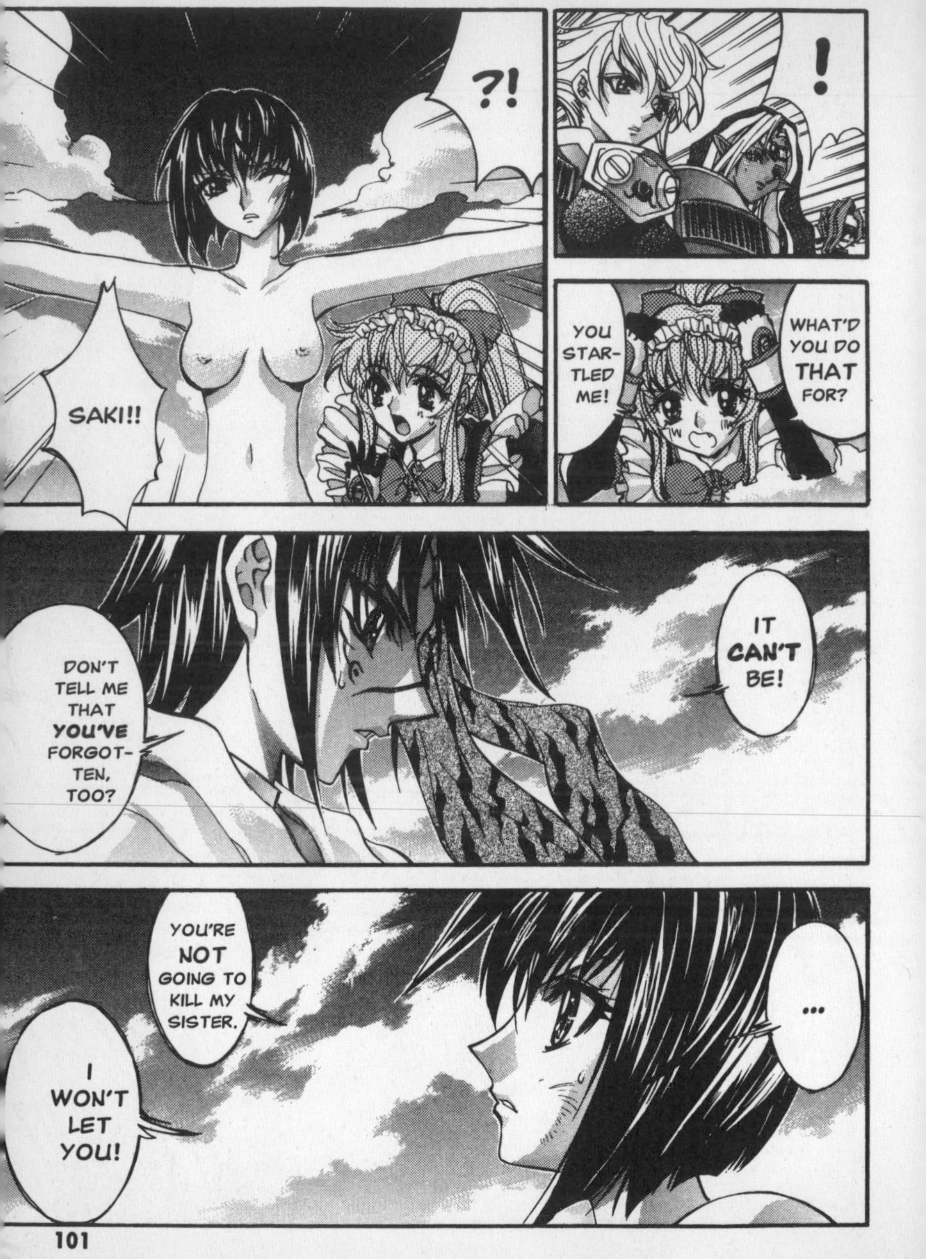
!
WHAT'D YOU DO THAT FOR?
YOU STAR-TLED ME!
?!
SAKI!!
IT CAN'T BE!
DON'T TELL ME THAT YOU'VE FORGOT-TEN, TOO?
...
YOU'RE NOT GOING TO KILL MY SISTER.
I WON'T LET YOU!

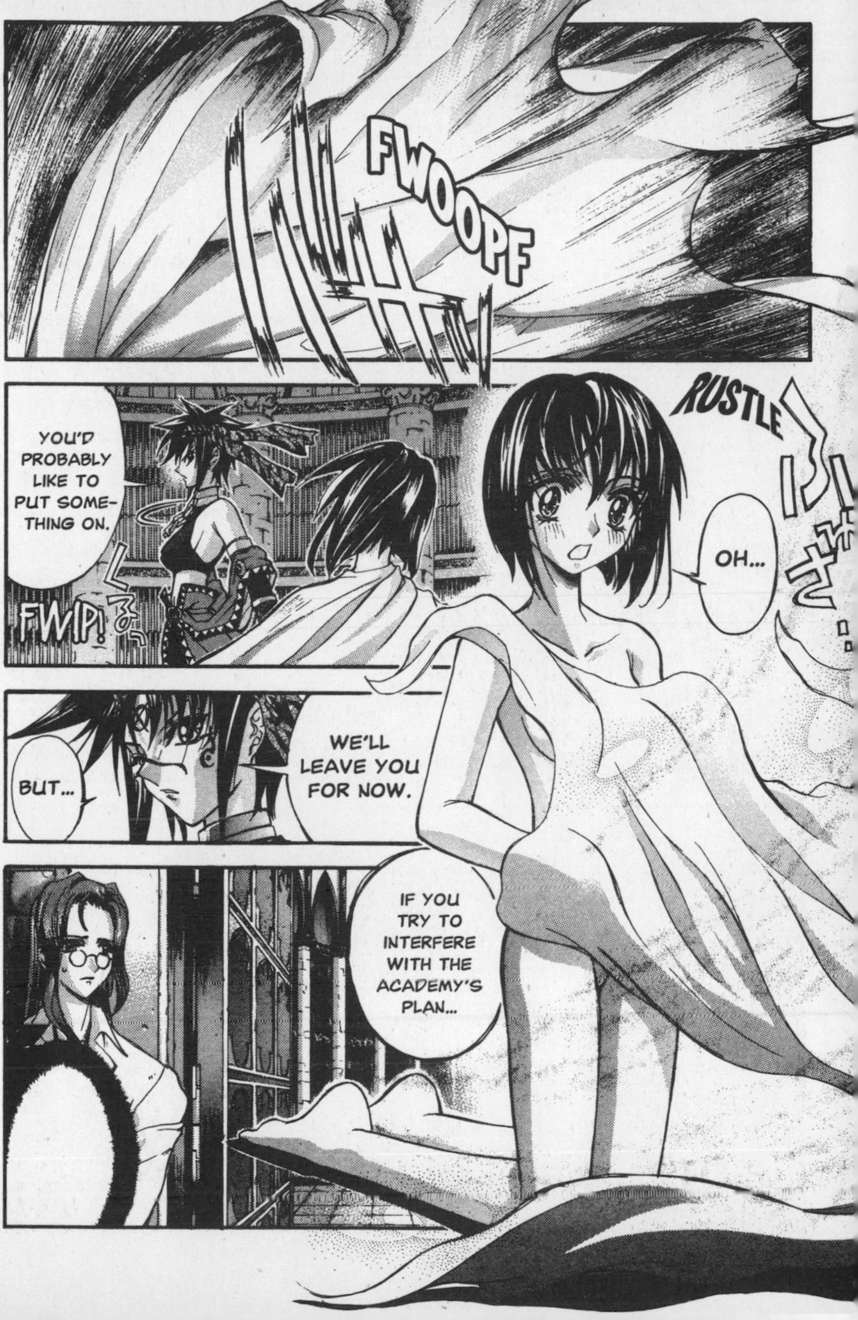
FWOOPF
RUSTLE
OH...
YOU'D PROBABLY LIKE TO PUT SOME-THING ON.
FWIP!
WE'LL LEAVE YOU FOR NOW.
BUT...
IF YOU TRY TO INTERFERE WITH THE ACADEMY'S PLAN...

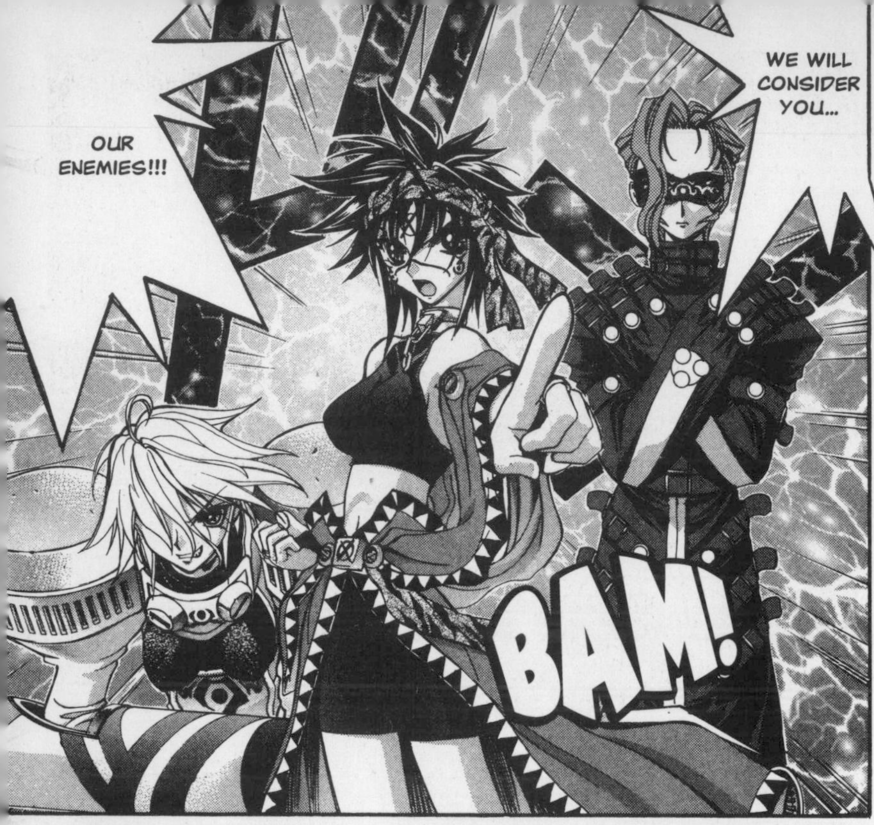
WE WILL CONSIDER YOU...
OUR ENEMIES!!!
BAM!

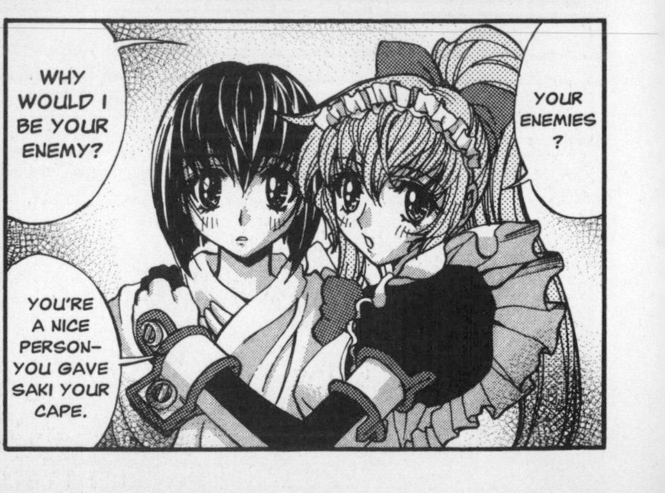
YOUR ENEMIES ?
WHY WOULD I BE YOUR ENEMY?
YOU'RE A NICE PERSON— YOU GAVE SAKI YOUR CAPE.

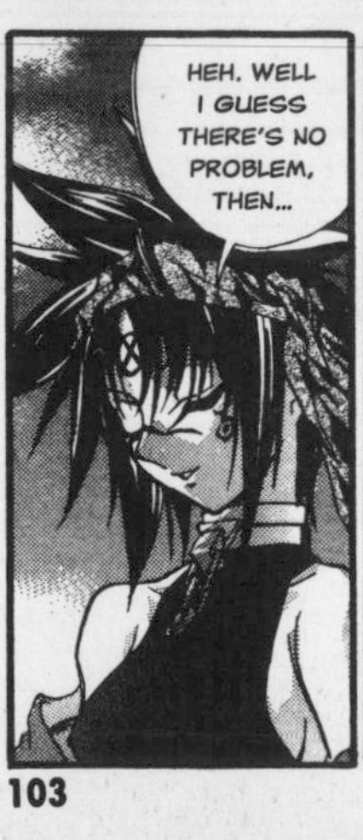
HEH. WELL I GUESS THERE'S NO PROBLEM, THEN...

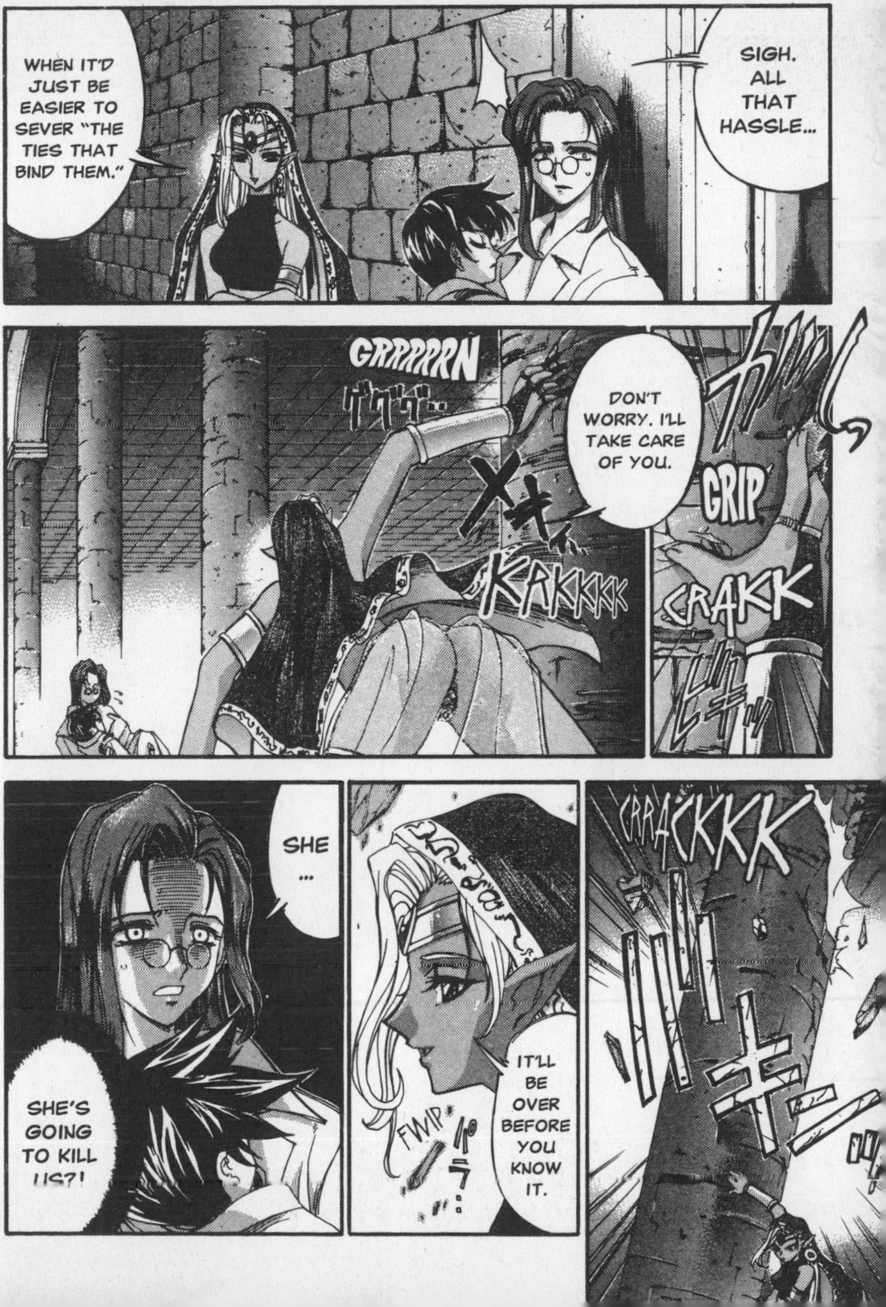
SIGH. ALL THAT HASSLE...
WHEN IT'D JUST BE EASIER TO SEVER "THE TIES THAT BIND THEM."
GRIP
CRAKK
DON'T WORRY. I'LL TAKE CARE OF YOU.
GRRRRRN
KRKKKKK
CRRACKKK
IT'LL BE OVER BEFORE YOU KNOW IT.
FWIP
SHE ...
SHE'S GOING TO KILL US?!

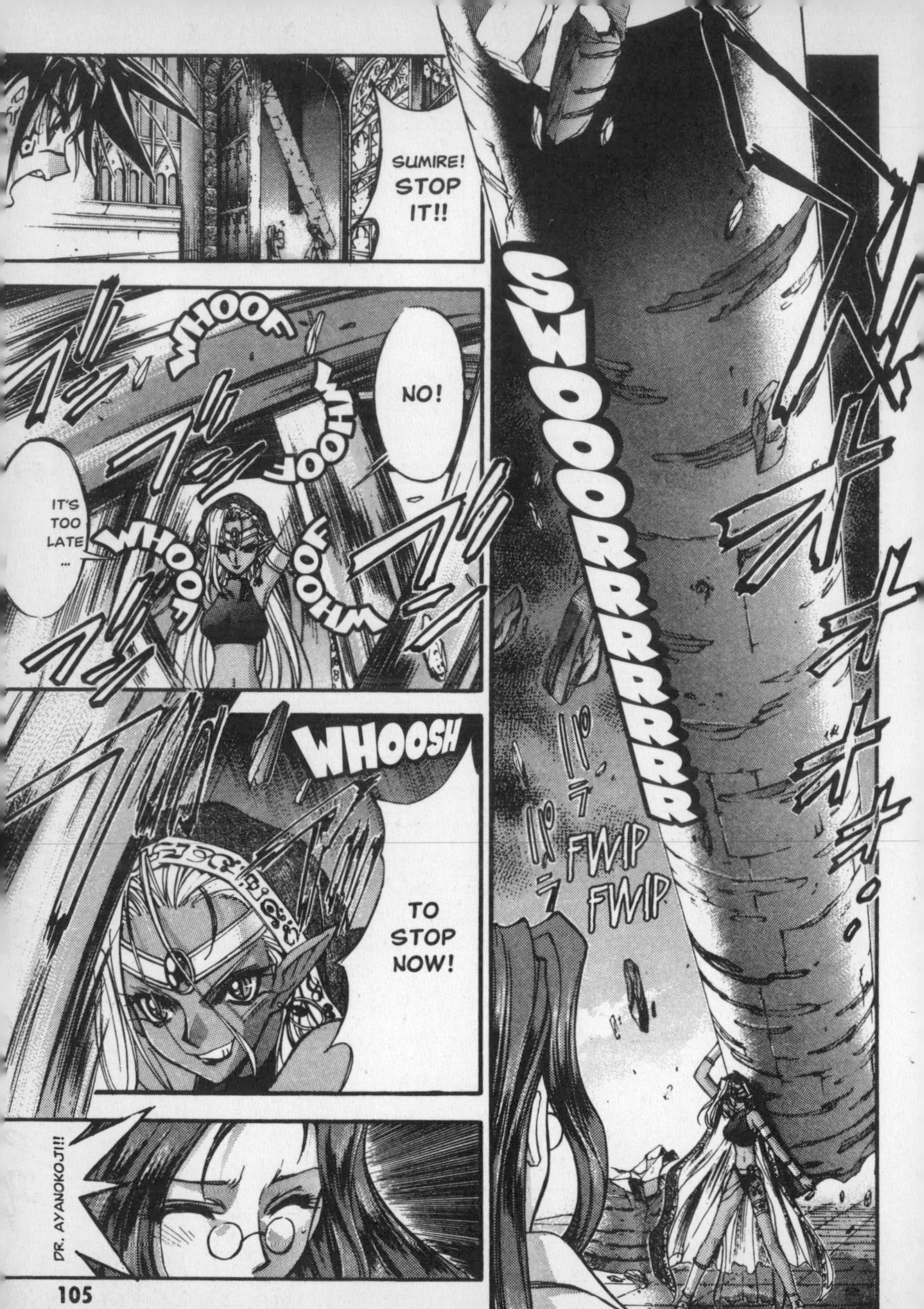
SWOOORRRRRR
FWIP
FWIP
SUMIRE! STOP IT!!
NO!
WHOOF
WHOOF
IT'S TOO LATE...
WHOOF
WHOOF
WHOOSH
TO STOP NOW!
DR. AYANOKOJI!!

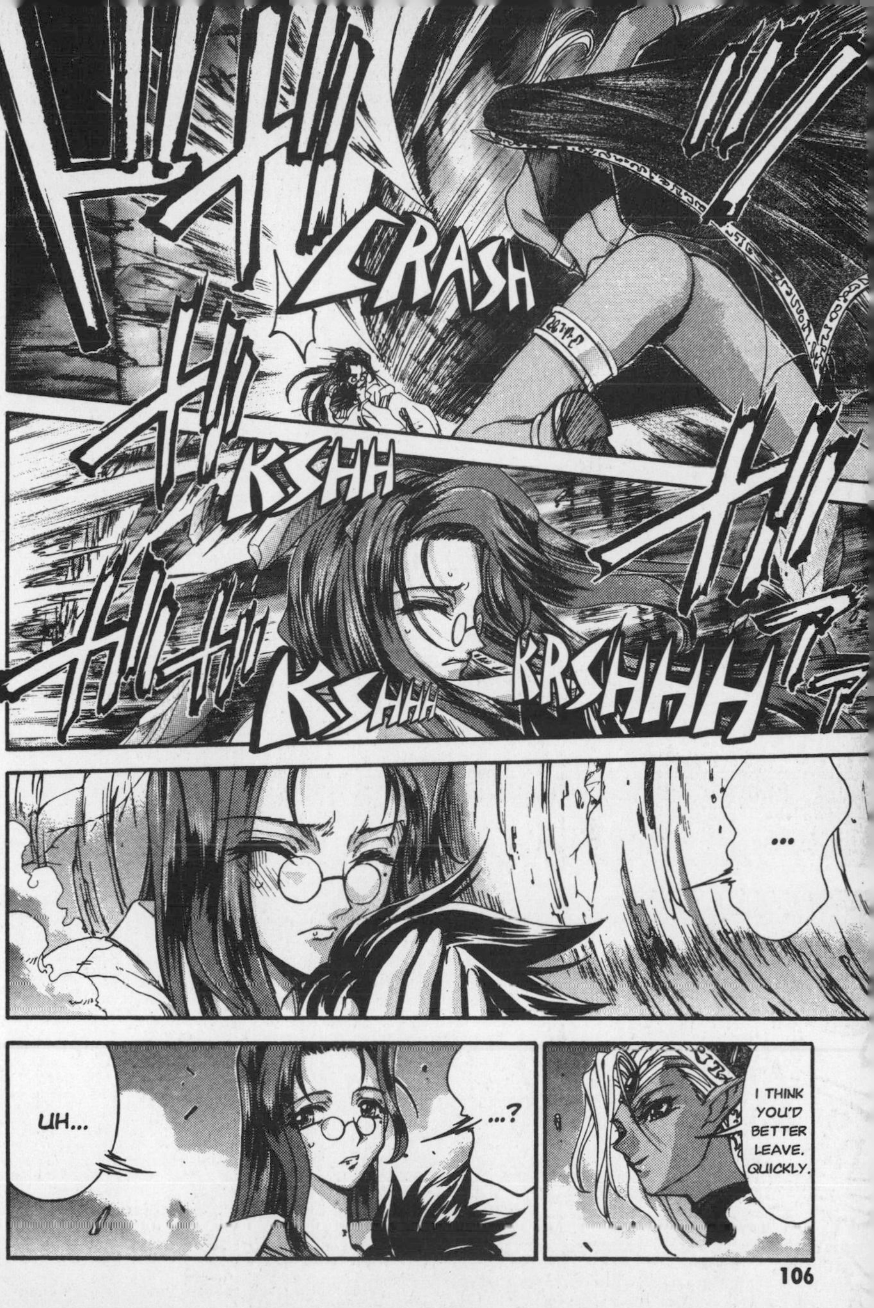
CRASH
KRSHH
KRSHHHH
KSHHH
...
I THINK YOU'D BETTER LEAVE. QUICKLY.
...?
UH...

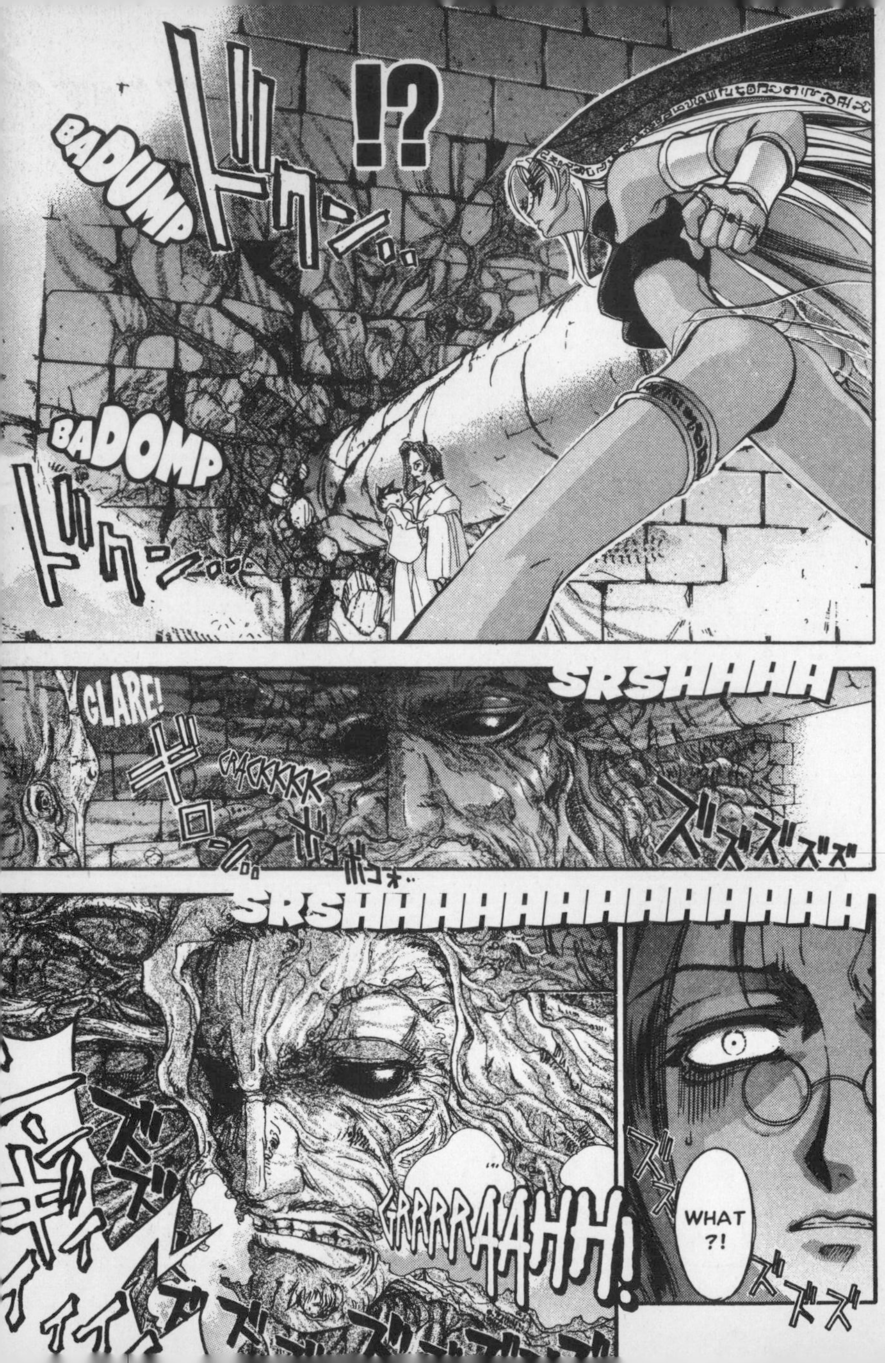
!?
BADUMP
BADOMP
SRSHHHH
GLARE!
CRACKKKKK
SRSHHHHHHHHHHHHHHHH
WHAT ?!
GRRRRAAHH!

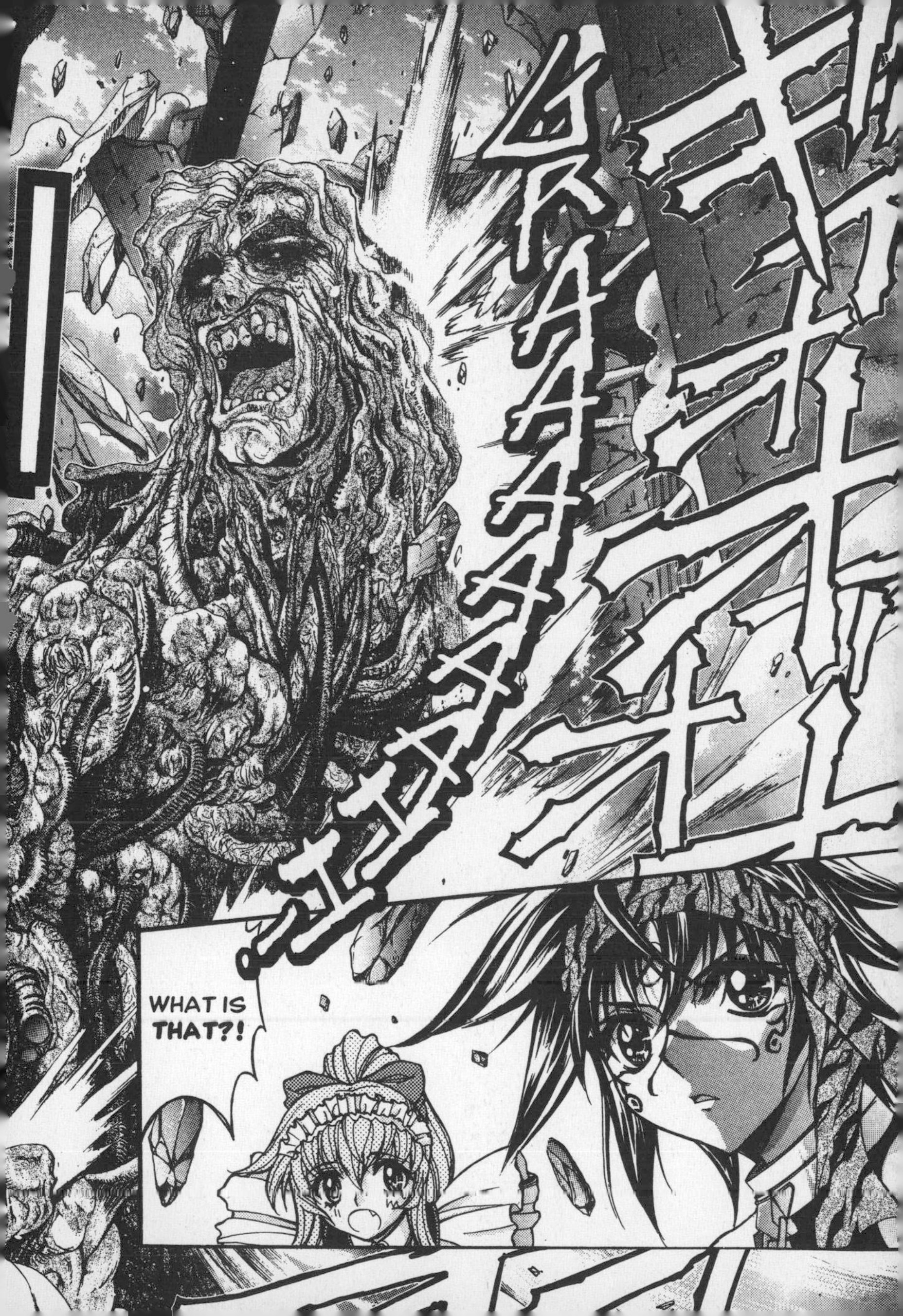
WHAT IS THAT?!

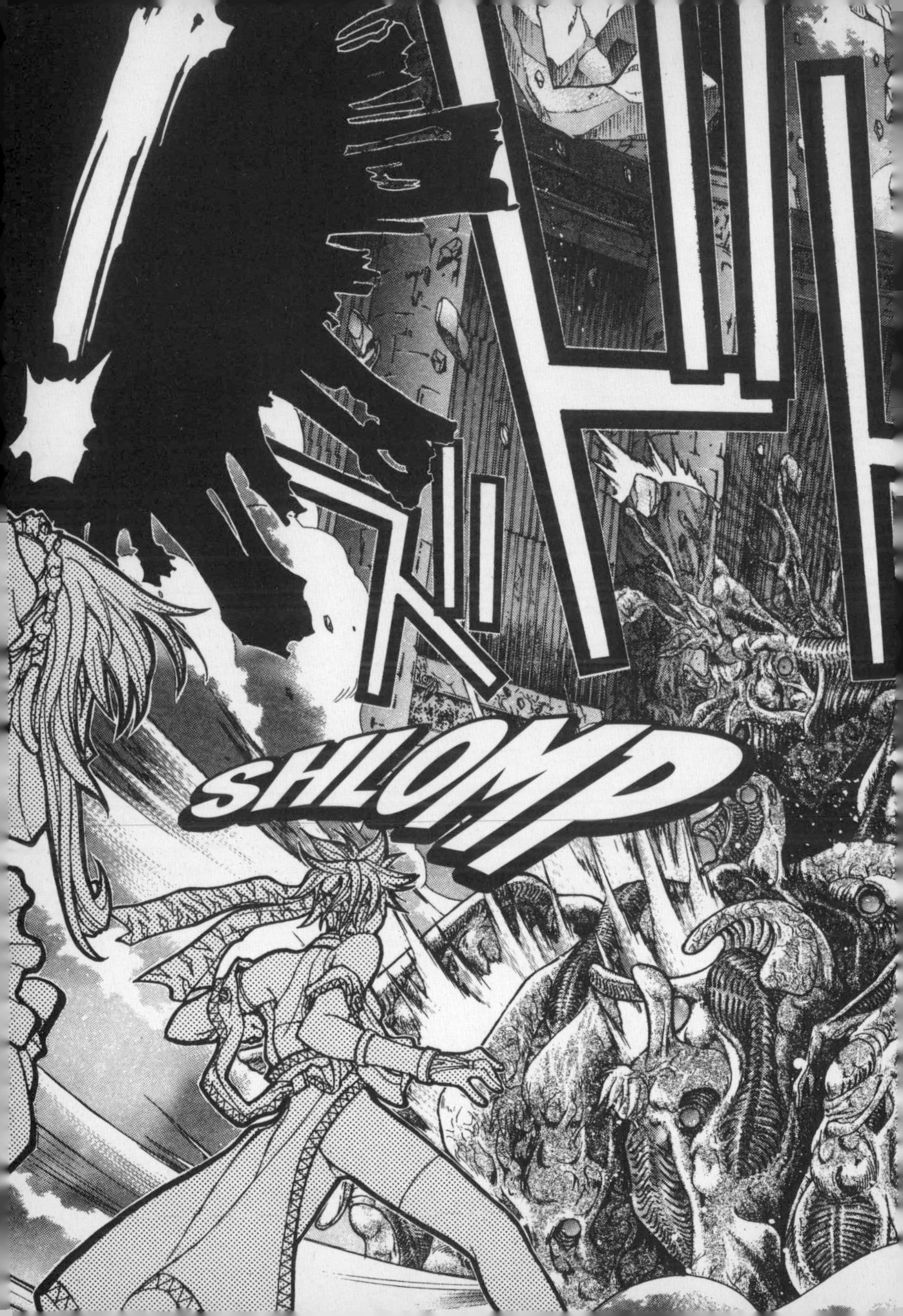
SHLOMP

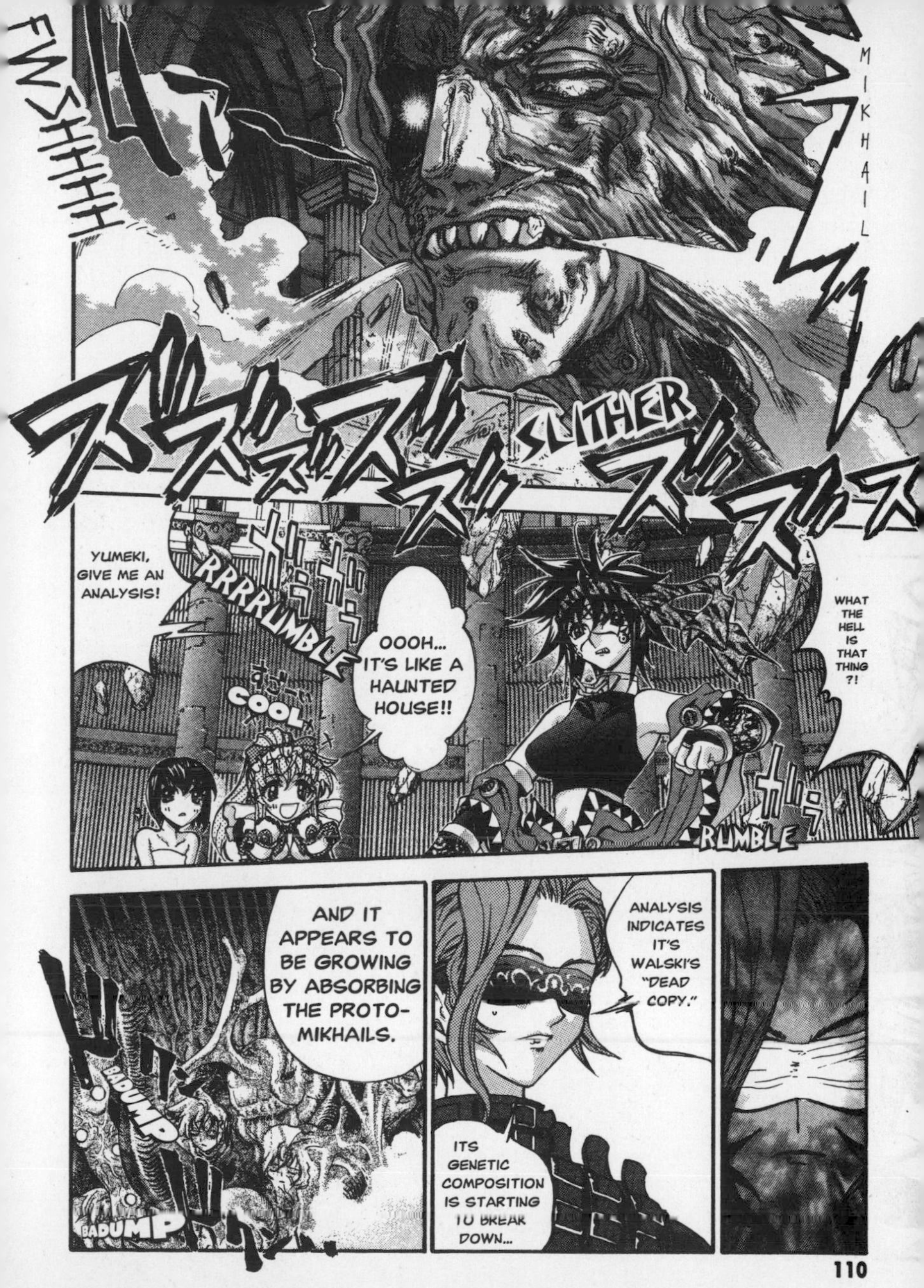
MIKHAIL
FWSHHHH
SLITHER
WHAT THE HELL IS THAT THING?!
RUMBLE
OOOH... IT'S LIKE A HAUNTED HOUSE!!
COOL
RRRRUMBLE
YUMEKI, GIVE ME AN ANALYSIS!
ANALYSIS INDICATES IT'S WALSKI'S "DEAD COPY."
ITS GENETIC COMPOSITION IS STARTING TO BREAK DOWN...
AND IT APPEARS TO BE GROWING BY ABSORBING THE PROTO-MIKHAILS.
BADUMP
BADUMP

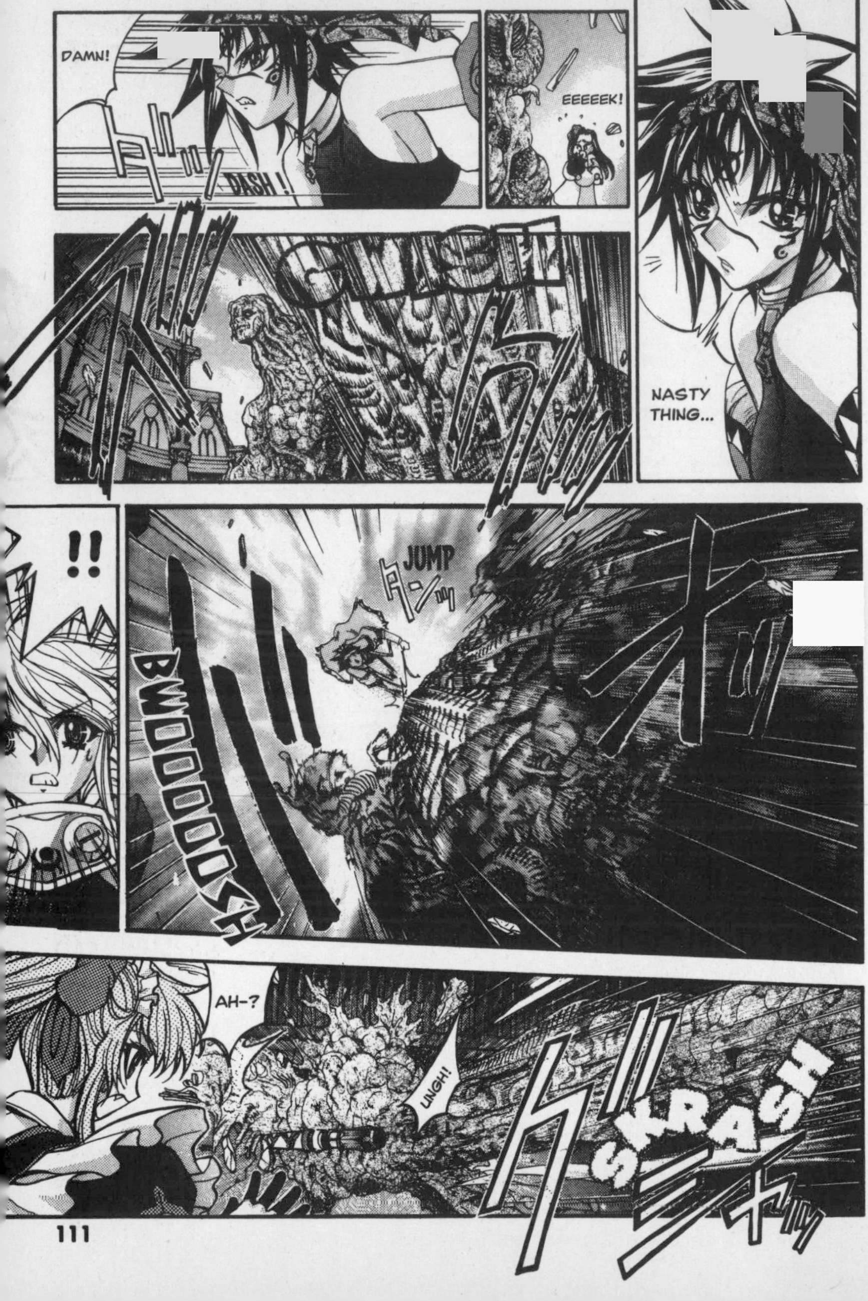
NASTY THING...
EEEEEK!
DAMN!
DASH!
GUSH
JUMP
BWOOOOOSH
!!
SKRASH
UNGH!
AH-?

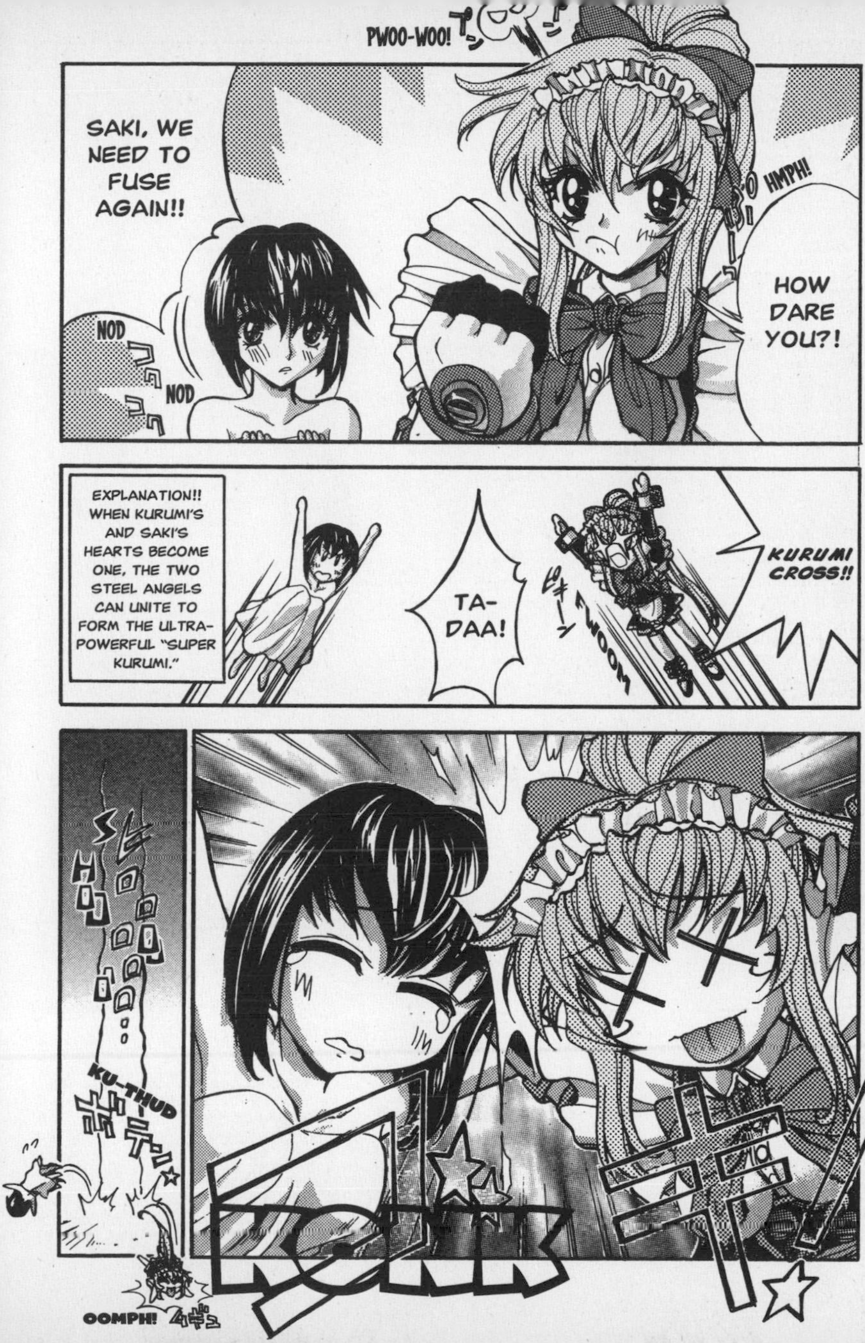
PWOO-WOO!
HMPH!
HOW DARE YOU?!
SAKI, WE NEED TO FUSE AGAIN!!
NOD
NOD
KURUMI CROSS!!
FWOOM
TA-DAA!
EXPLANATION!! WHEN KURUMI'S AND SAKI'S HEARTS BECOME ONE, THE TWO STEEL ANGELS CAN UNITE TO FORM THE ULTRA-POWERFUL "SUPER KURUMI."
KU-THUD
OOMPH!

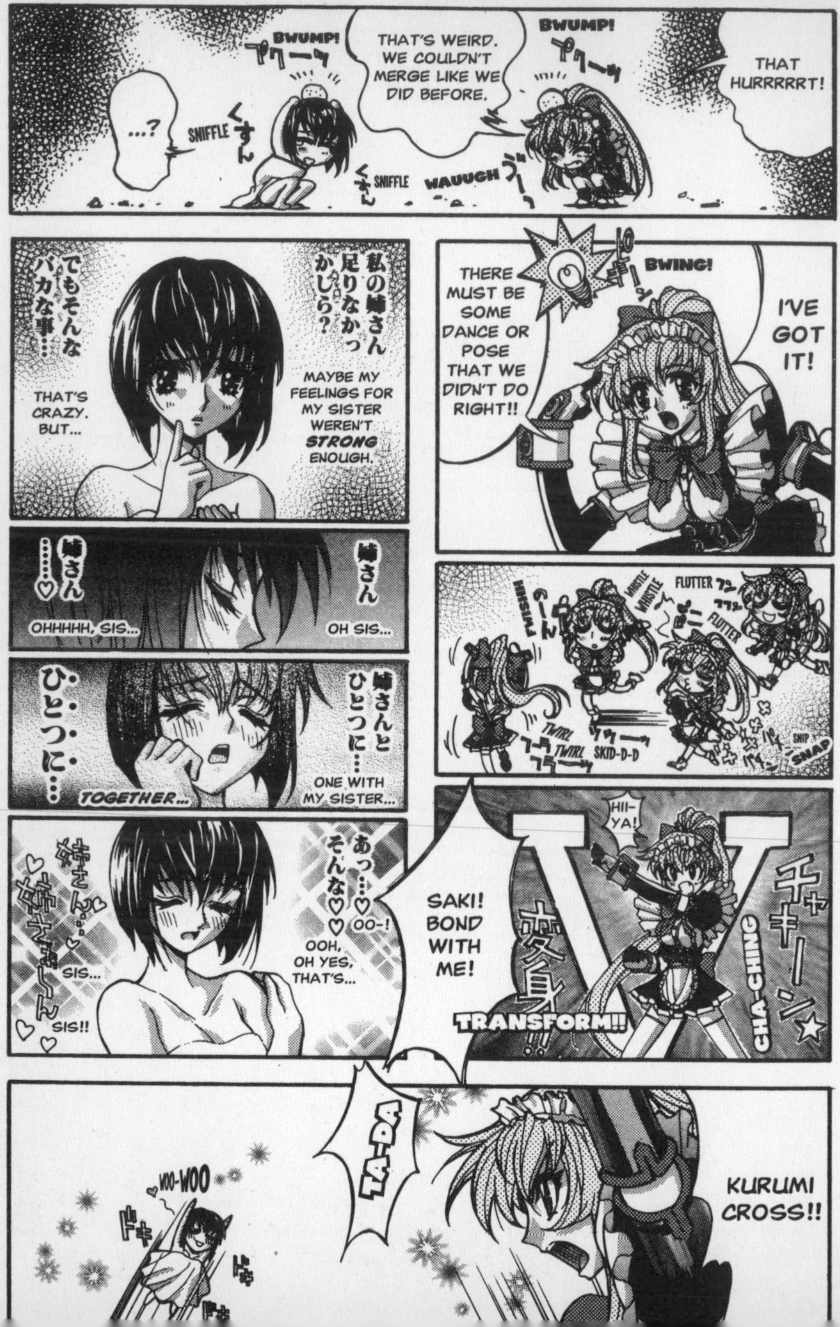
THAT HURRRRRT!
BWUMP! アクーッ
THAT'S WEIRD. WE COULDN'T MERGE LIKE WE DID BEFORE.
WAUUGH うーっ
BWUMP! アクーッ
SNIFFLE くすん
...?
SNIFFLE くすん
I'VE GOT IT!
BWING!
THERE MUST BE SOME DANCE OR POSE THAT WE DIDN'T DO RIGHT!!
私の姉さん足りなかっかしら？
MAYBE MY FEELINGS FOR MY SISTER WEREN'T STRONG ENOUGH.
でもそんなバカな事…
THAT'S CRAZY. BUT...
FLUTTER
WHISTLE
WHISTLE
FLUTTER
FWISHHH
TWIRL
TWIRL
SKID-D-D
SNIP
SNAP
姉さん
OH SIS...
姉さん……♡
OHHHHH, SIS...
姉さんとひとつに…
ONE WITH MY SISTER...
ひとつに…
TOGETHER...
HII-YA!
チャキーン☆
CHA-CHING
変身!!
TRANSFORM!!
SAKI! BOND WITH ME!
あっ…♡そんな♡
OO-!
OOH, OH YES, THAT'S...
SIS...
SIS!!
KURUMI CROSS!!
TA-DA
WOO-WOO
ドキ

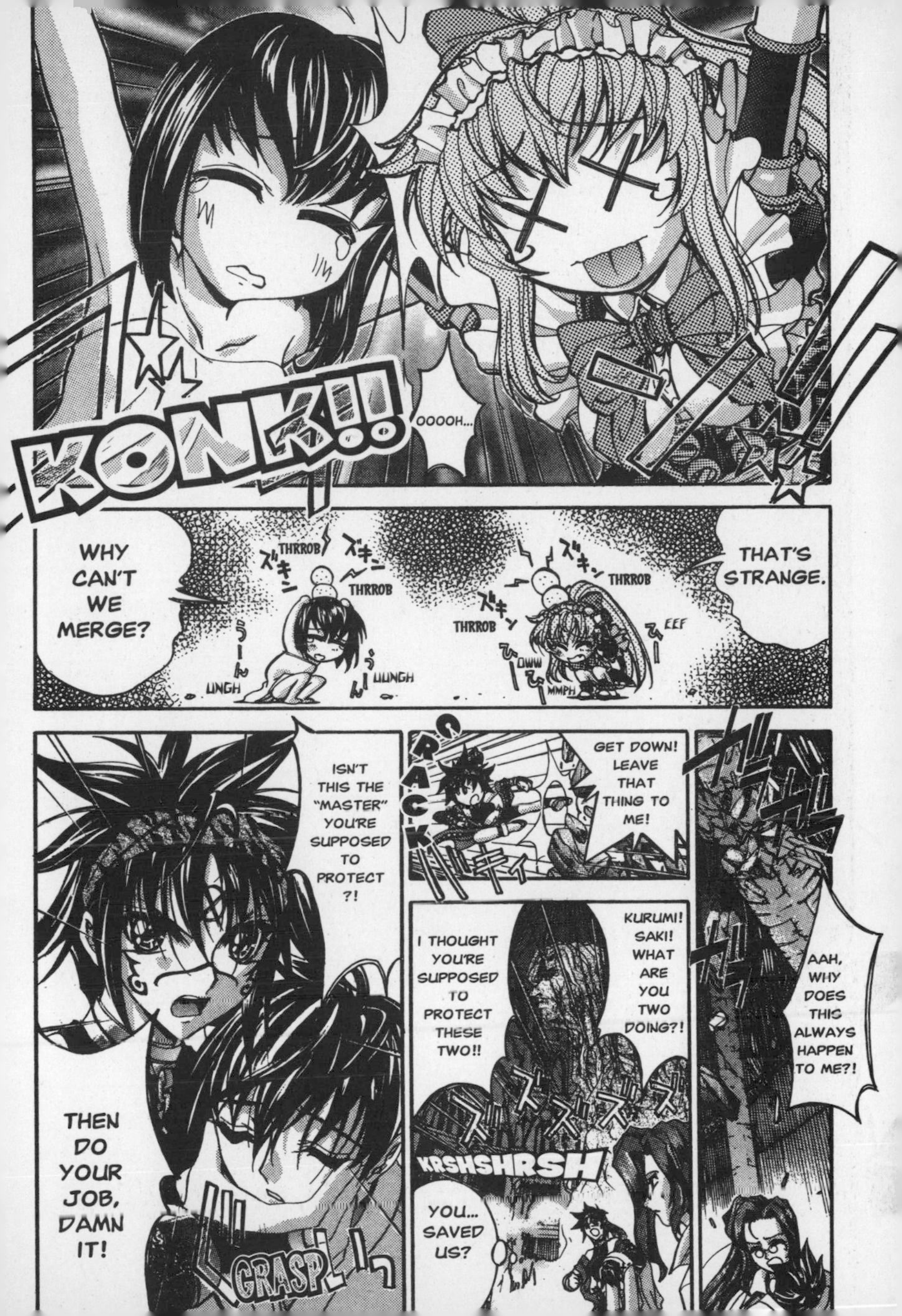
KONK!!
OOOOH...
THAT'S STRANGE.
THRROB
THRROB
EEF
OWW
MMPH
WHY CAN'T WE MERGE?
THRROB
THRROB
UNGH
UUNGH
AAH, WHY DOES THIS ALWAYS HAPPEN TO ME?!
GET DOWN! LEAVE THAT THING TO ME!
CRACK
KURUMI! SAKI! WHAT ARE YOU TWO DOING?!
I THOUGHT YOU'RE SUPPOSED TO PROTECT THESE TWO!!
KRSHSHRSH
YOU... SAVED US?
ISN'T THIS THE "MASTER" YOU'RE SUPPOSED TO PROTECT?!
THEN DO YOUR JOB, DAMN IT!
GRASP

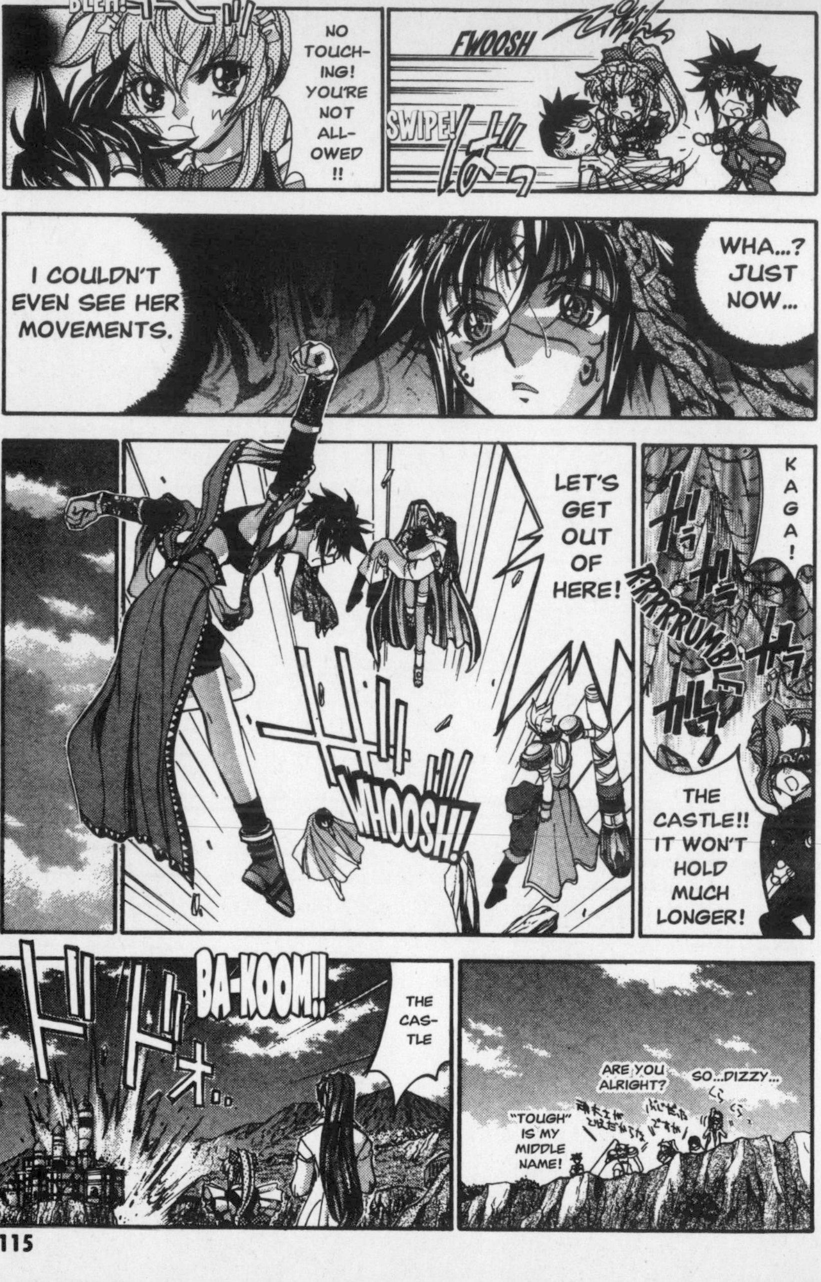
FWOOSH
SWIPE!
BLEH!
NO TOUCHING! YOU'RE NOT ALLOWED !!
WHA...? JUST NOW...
I COULDN'T EVEN SEE HER MOVEMENTS.
KAGA!
RRRRRRUMBLE
THE CASTLE!! IT WON'T HOLD MUCH LONGER!
LET'S GET OUT OF HERE!
WHOOSH!!
SO...DIZZY...
ARE YOU ALRIGHT?
"TOUGH" IS MY MIDDLE NAME!
THE CASTLE
BA-KOOM!!

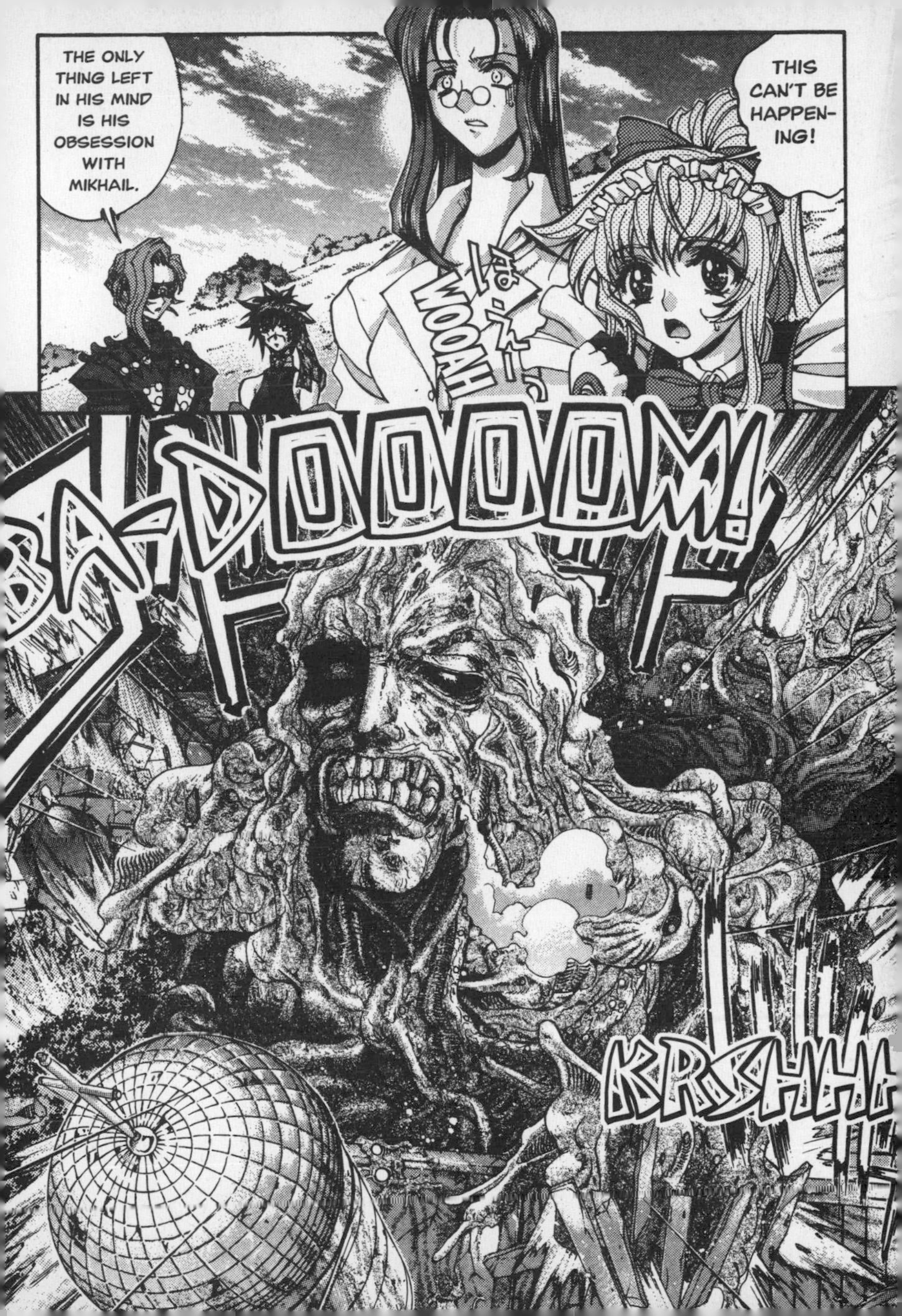
THIS CAN'T BE HAPPEN-ING!
ほえ～っ
WOOAH!
THE ONLY THING LEFT IN HIS MIND IS HIS OBSESSION WITH MIKHAIL.
BA-DOOOOOM!
KRSHHH

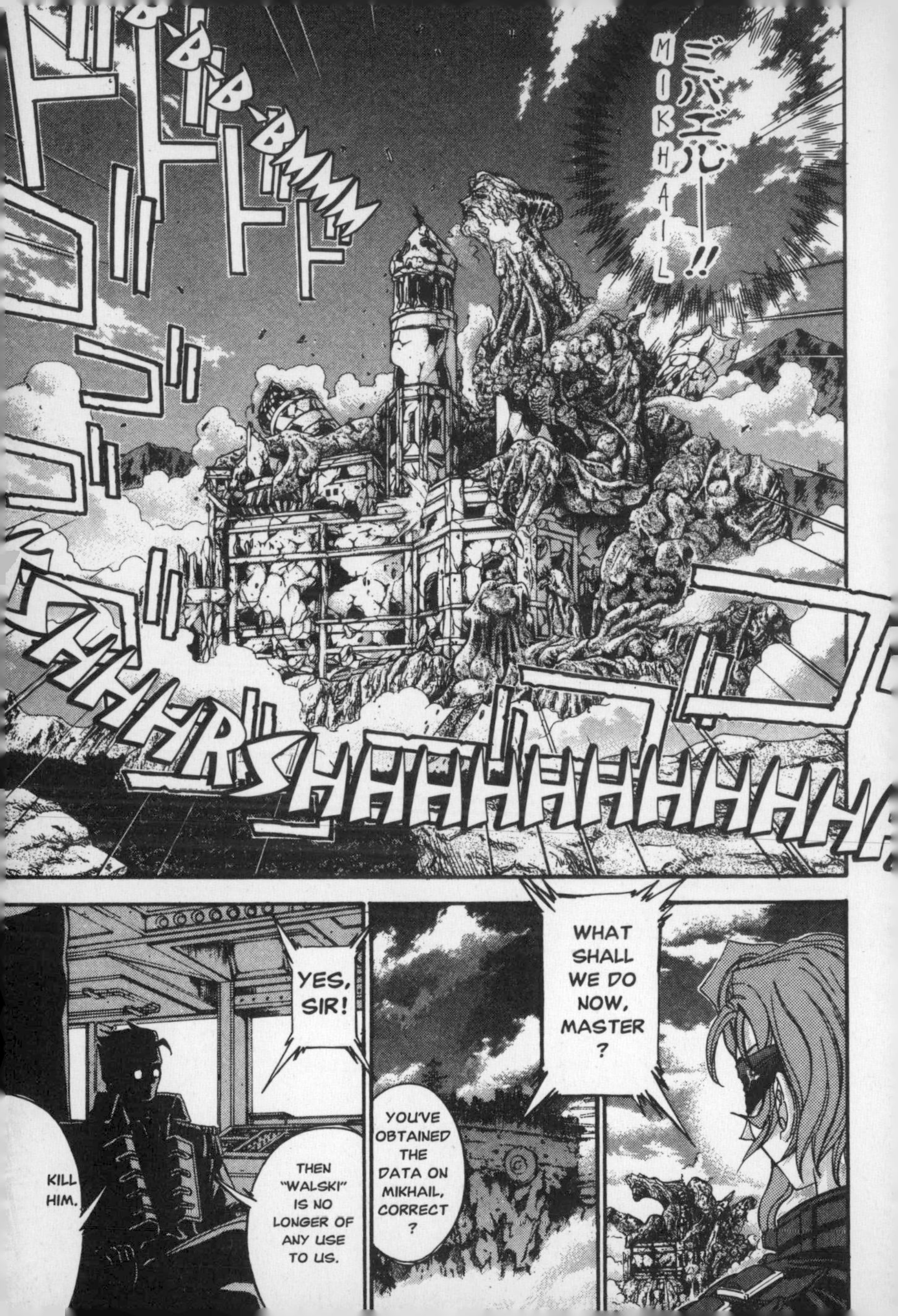
MIKHAIL!!
B-B-B-BMMMMM
SHHHRSHHHHHHHHHHHHH
WHAT SHALL WE DO NOW, MASTER?
YOU'VE OBTAINED THE DATA ON MIKHAIL, CORRECT?
THEN "WALSKI" IS NO LONGER OF ANY USE TO US.
KILL HIM.
YES, SIR!

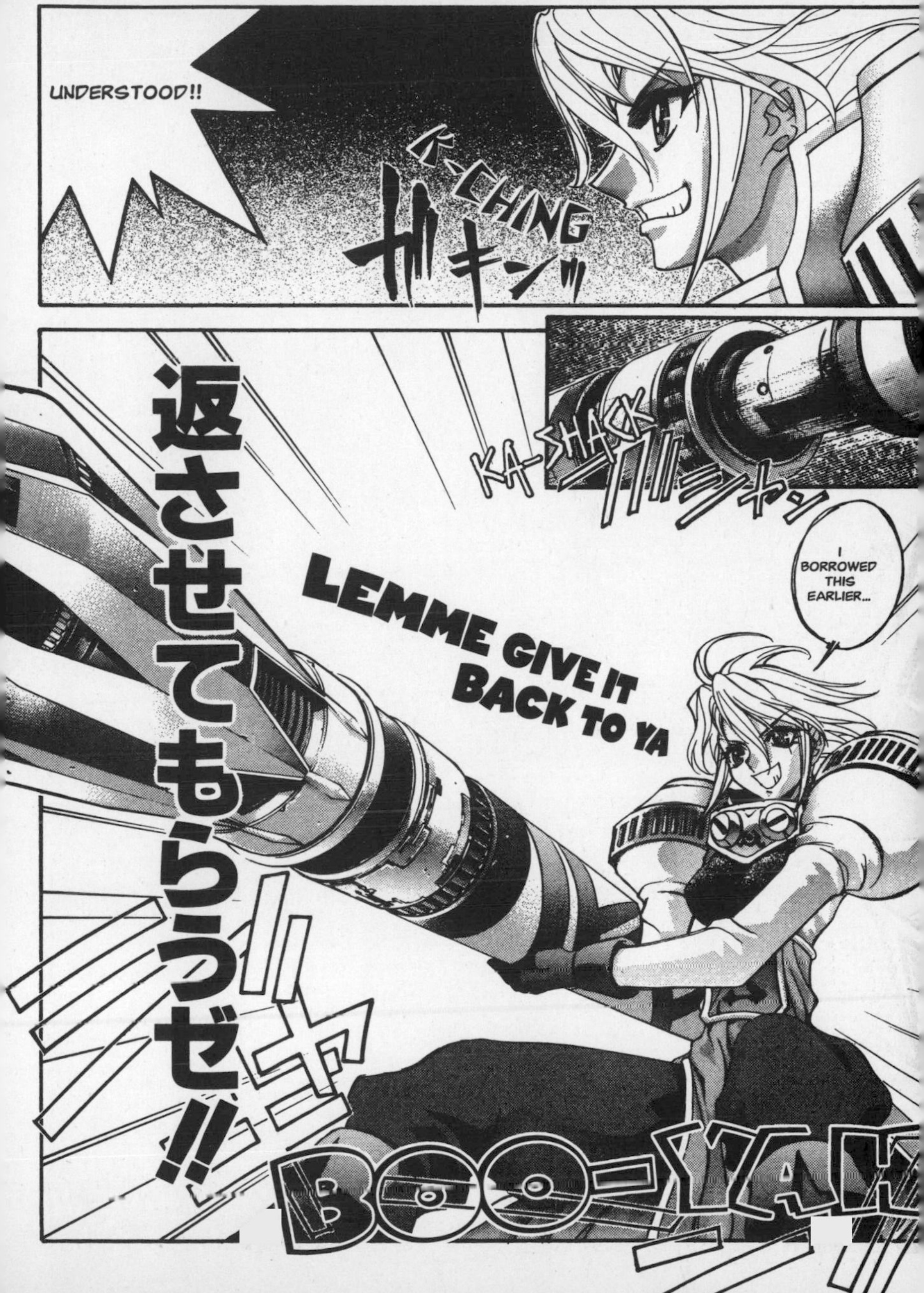
UNDERSTOOD!!
K-CHING
ガキンッ
KA-SHACK
ガシャッ
I BORROWED THIS EARLIER...
LEMME GIVE IT BACK TO YA
返させてもらうぜ!!
BOO-YAH

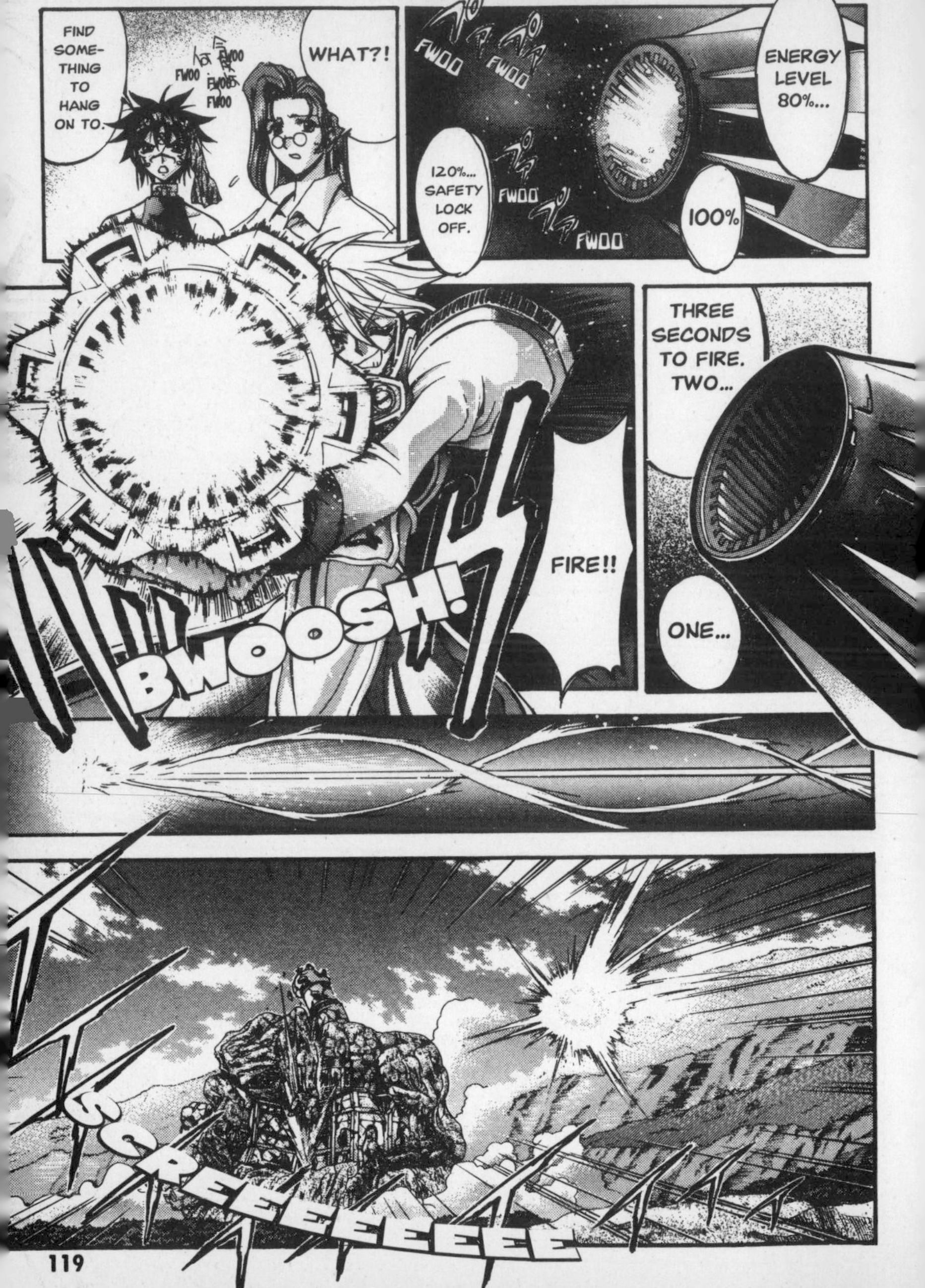
ENERGY LEVEL 80%...
FWOO
FWOO
100%
120%... SAFETY LOCK OFF.
FWOO
FWOO
WHAT?!
FIND SOME-THING TO HANG ON TO.
FWOO
FWOO
THREE SECONDS TO FIRE. TWO...
ONE...
FIRE!!
BWOOSH!
SCREEEEEEEEE

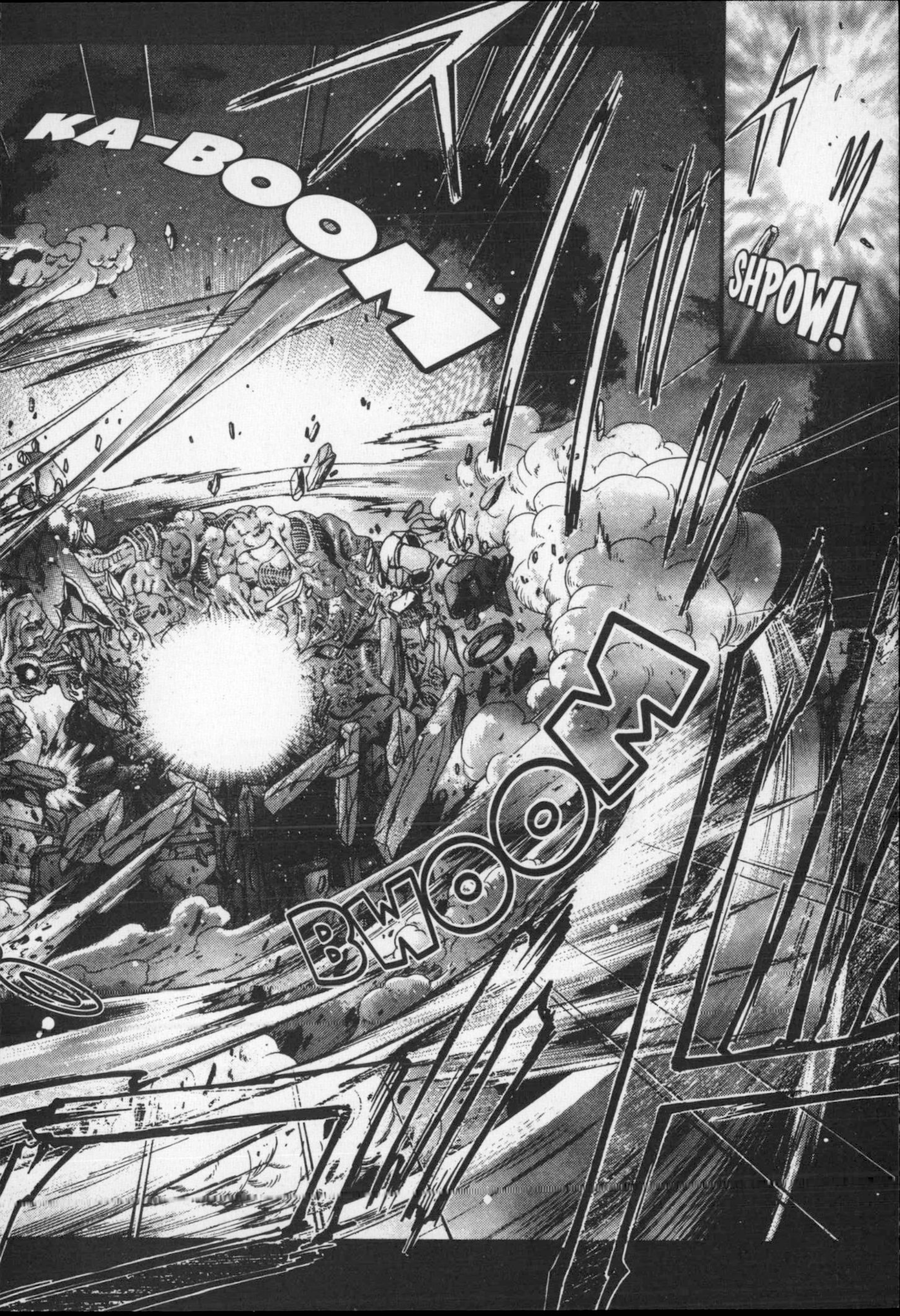
SHPOW!
KA-BOOM
BWOOM

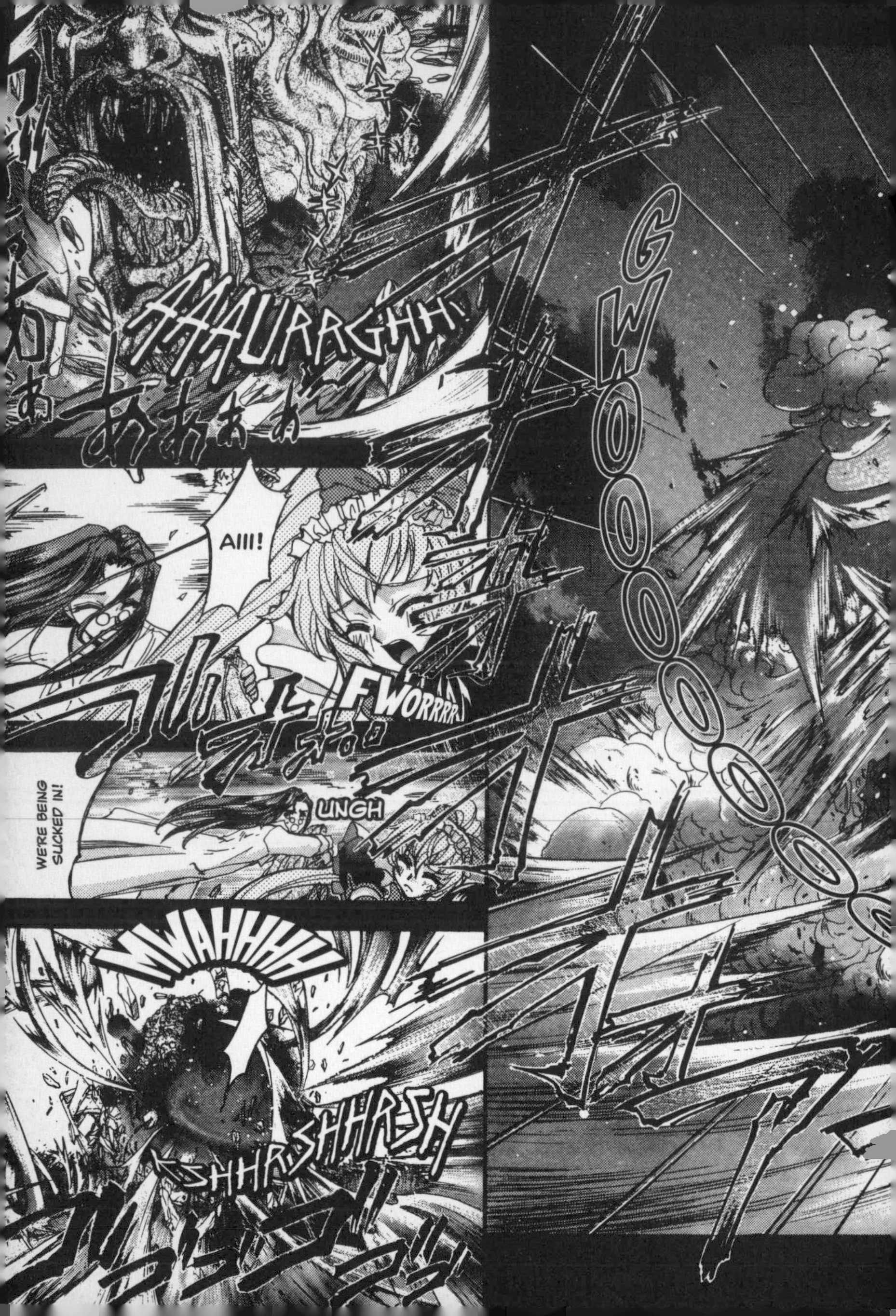
GWOOOOOOOOO
AAAURRGHH!
AIII!
FWORRRR
WE'RE BEING SUCKED IN!
UNGH
MWAHHHH
KSHHRSHHRSH

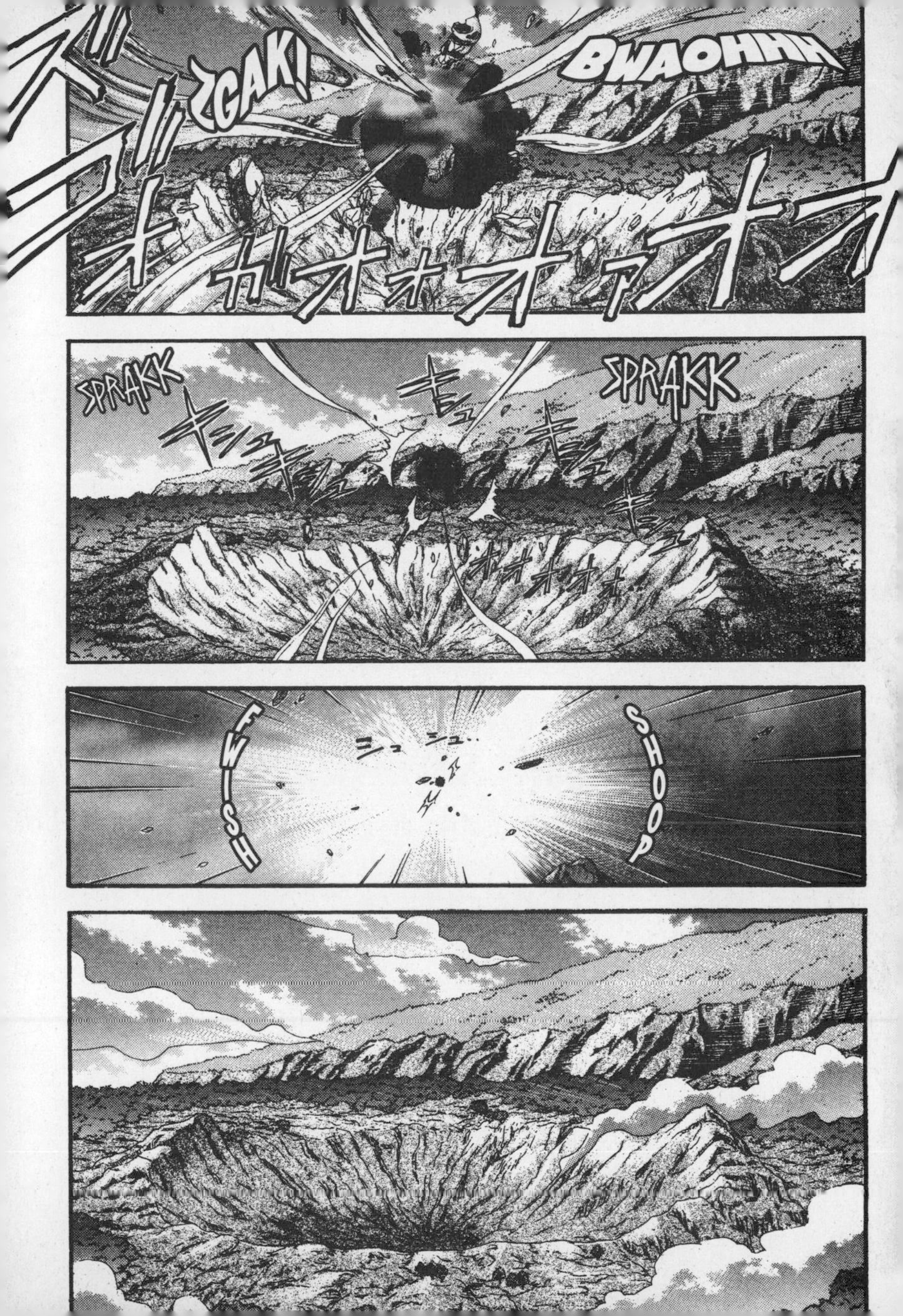
BWAOHHH
ZGAK!
SPRAKK
SPRAKK
SHOOP
シュ シュ‥
FWISH

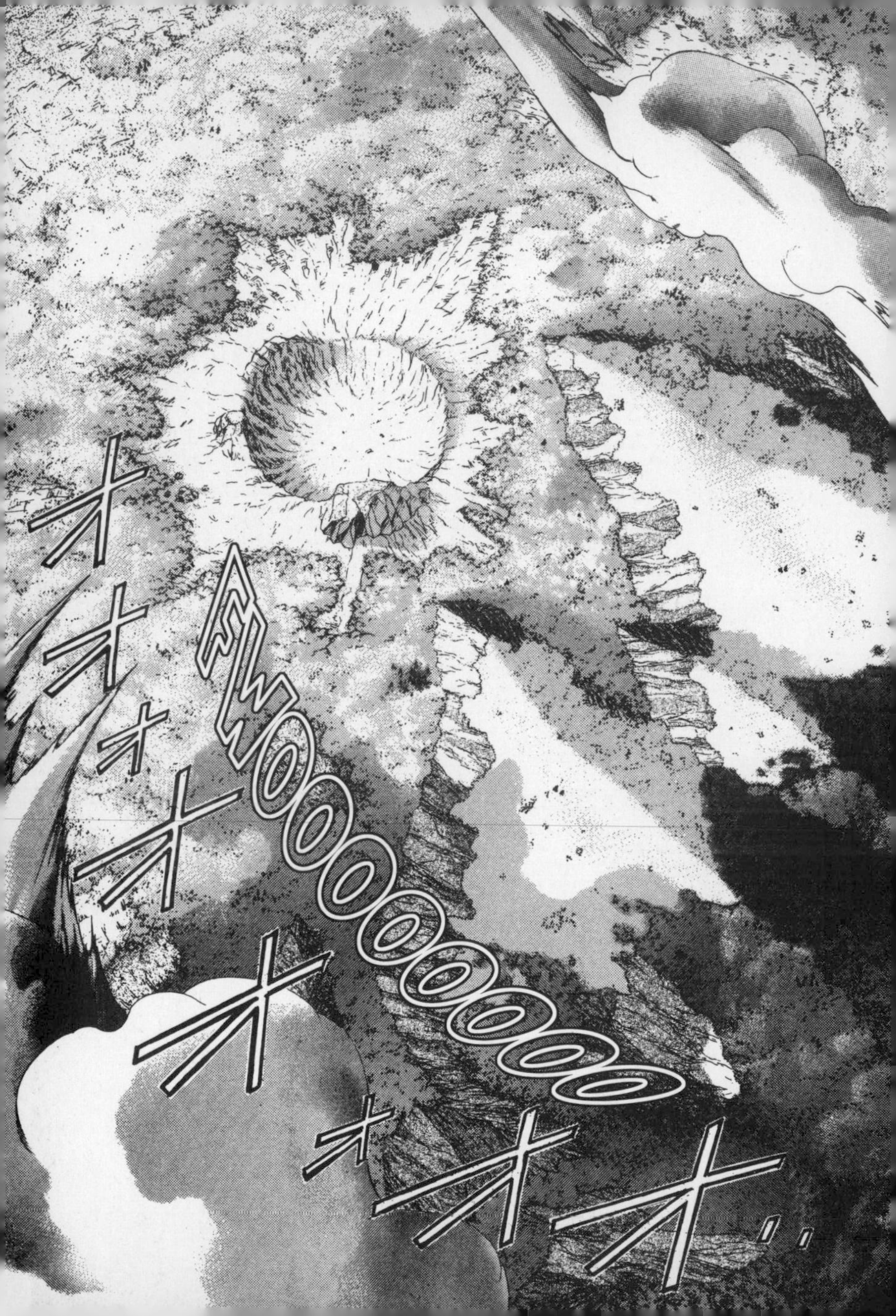
オオォオオォオオ゛
ZWOOOOOOOOO

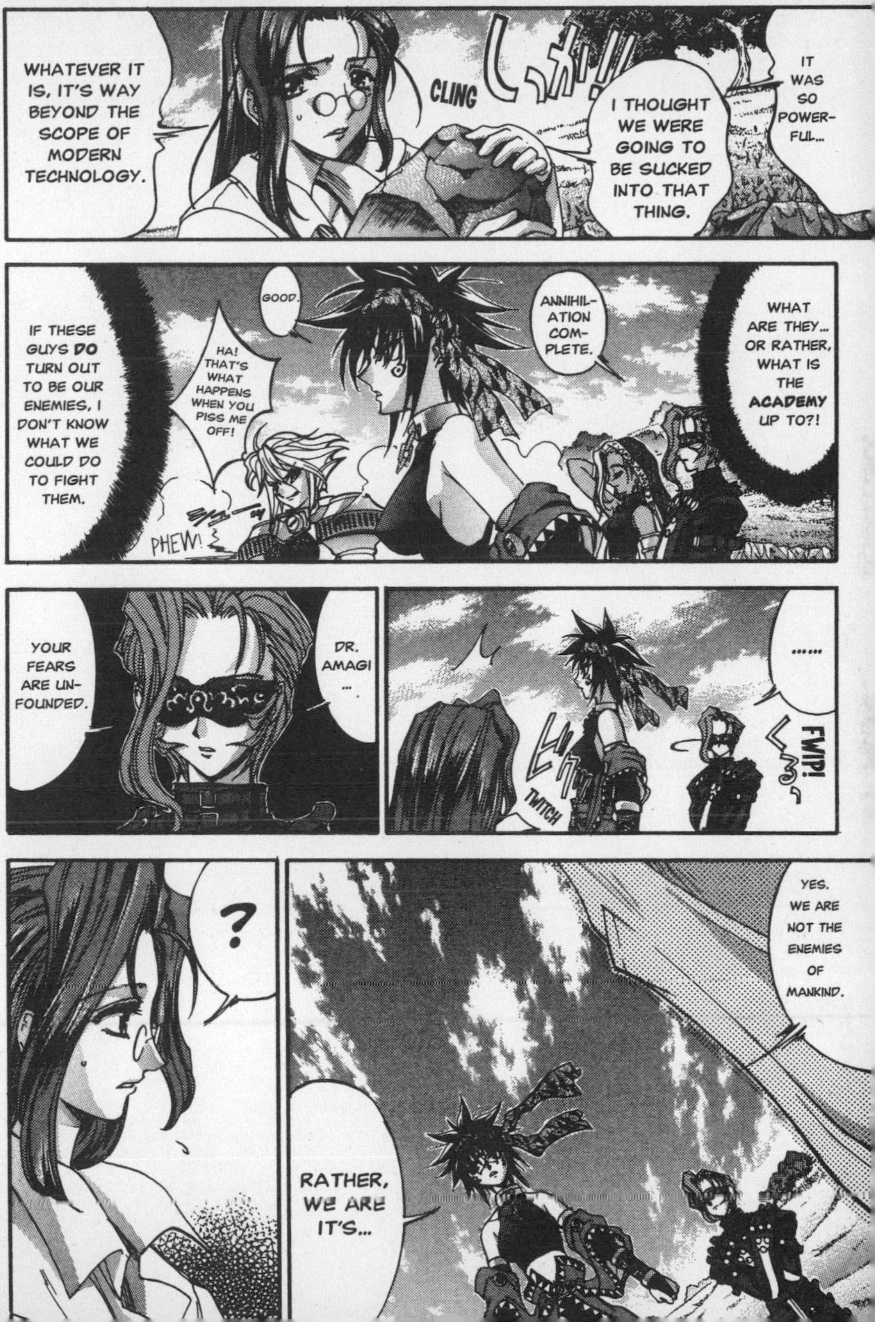
IT WAS SO POWERFUL...
I THOUGHT WE WERE GOING TO BE SUCKED INTO THAT THING.
CLING
WHATEVER IT IS, IT'S WAY BEYOND THE SCOPE OF MODERN TECHNOLOGY.
WHAT ARE THEY... OR RATHER, WHAT IS THE ACADEMY UP TO?!
ANNIHILATION COMPLETE.
GOOD.
HA! THAT'S WHAT HAPPENS WHEN YOU PISS ME OFF!
IF THESE GUYS DO TURN OUT TO BE OUR ENEMIES, I DON'T KNOW WHAT WE COULD DO TO FIGHT THEM.
PHEW!
......
FWIP!
TWITCH
DR. AMAGI ...
YOUR FEARS ARE UNFOUNDED.
YES. WE ARE NOT THE ENEMIES OF MANKIND.
RATHER, WE ARE IT'S...
?

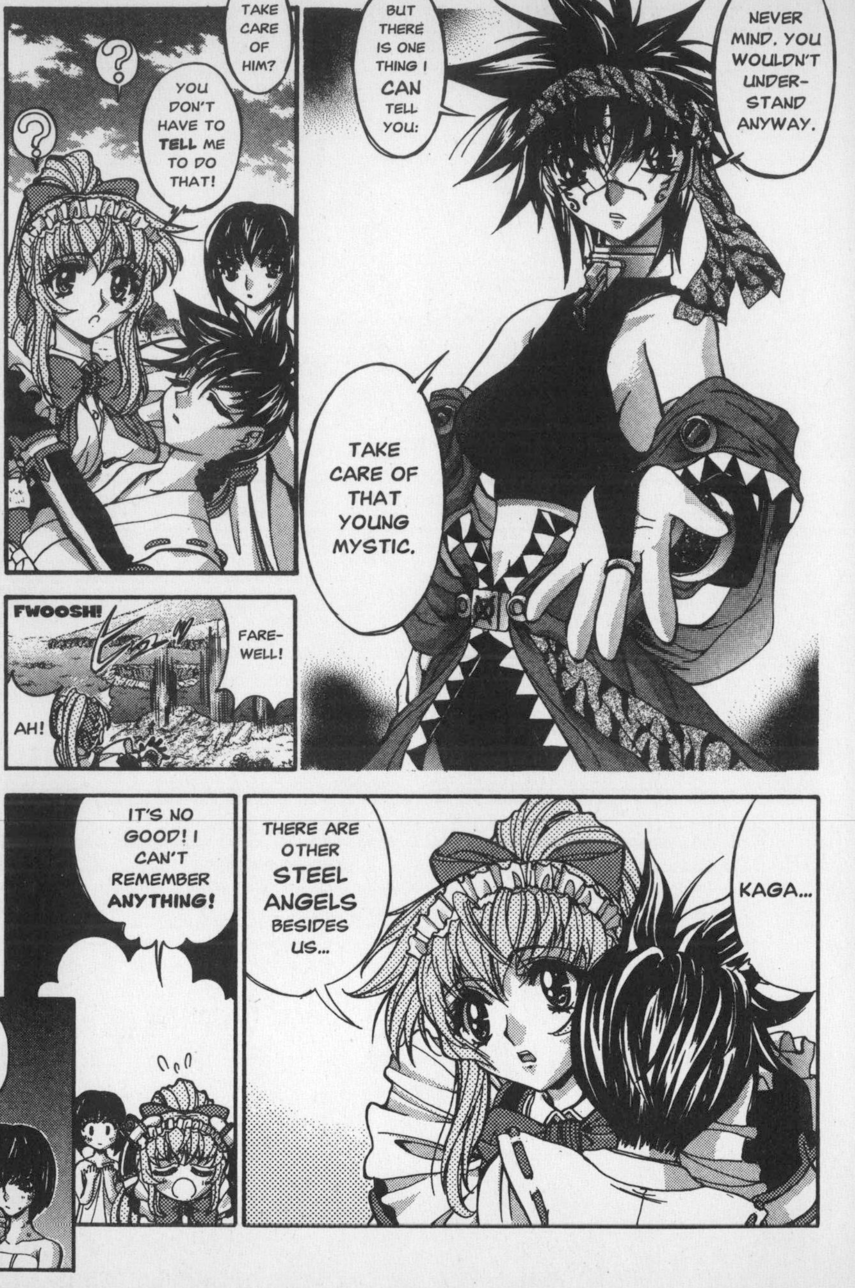
NEVER MIND. YOU WOULDN'T UNDER-STAND ANYWAY.
BUT THERE IS ONE THING I CAN TELL YOU:
TAKE CARE OF THAT YOUNG MYSTIC.
TAKE CARE OF HIM?
YOU DON'T HAVE TO TELL ME TO DO THAT!
FWOOSH!
FARE-WELL!
AH!
KAGA...
THERE ARE OTHER STEEL ANGELS BESIDES US...
IT'S NO GOOD! I CAN'T REMEMBER ANYTHING!
...

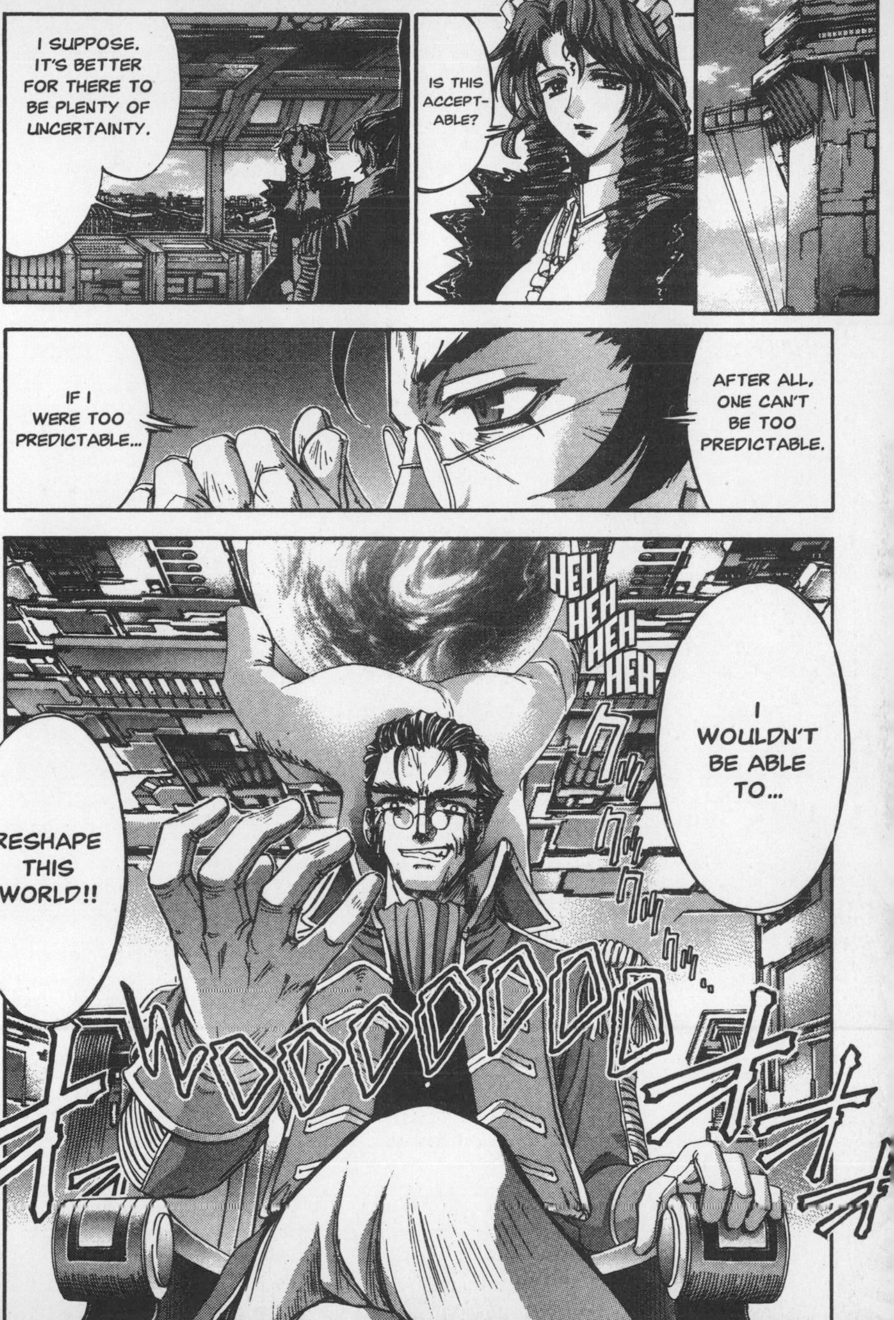
IS THIS ACCEPTABLE?
I SUPPOSE. IT'S BETTER FOR THERE TO BE PLENTY OF UNCERTAINTY.
AFTER ALL, ONE CAN'T BE TOO PREDICTABLE.
IF I WERE TOO PREDICTABLE...
HEH HEH HEH HEH
I WOULDN'T BE ABLE TO...
RESHAPE THIS WORLD!!
WOOOOOOOOOO

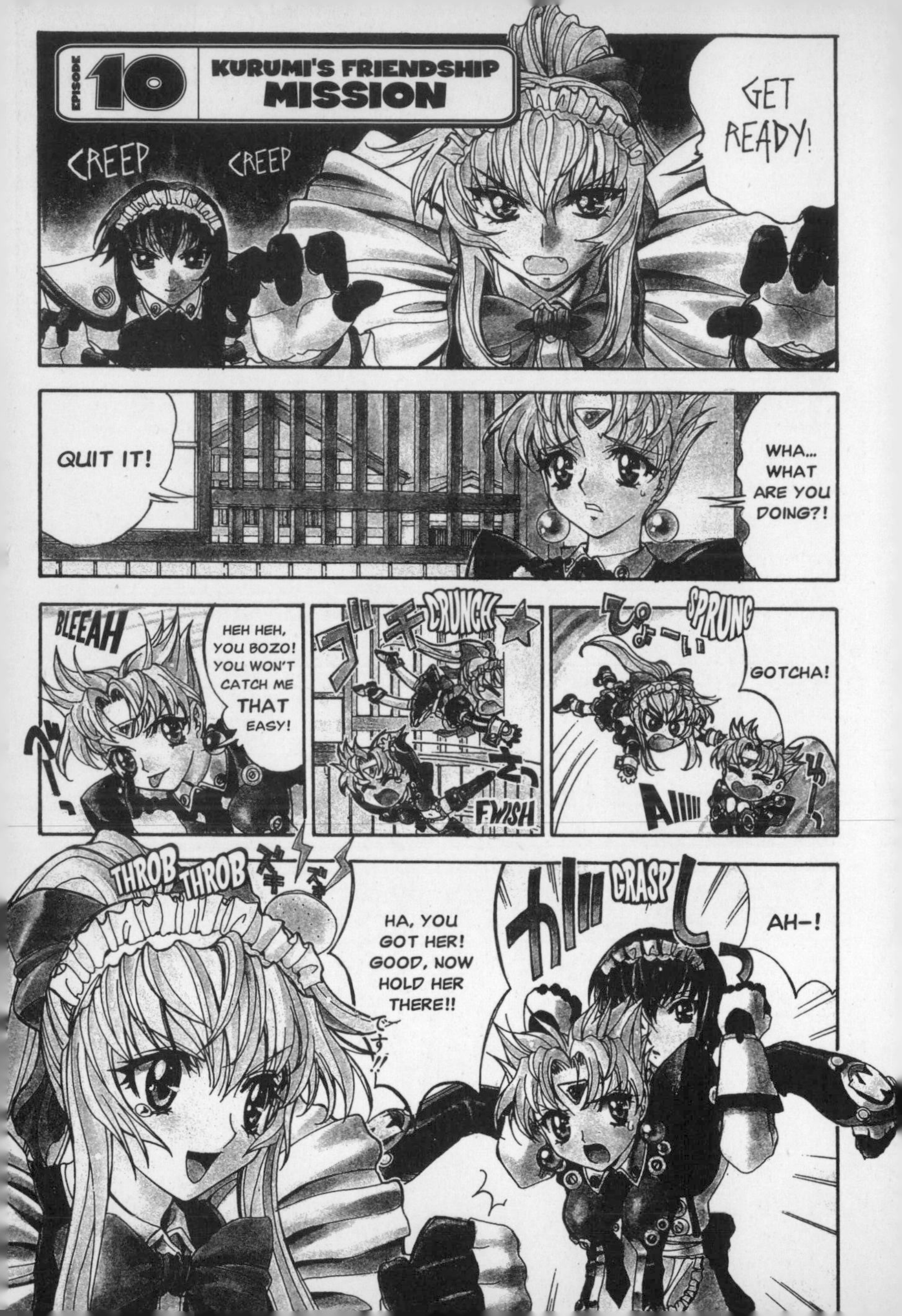
EPISODE 10
KURUMI'S FRIENDSHIP MISSION
GET READY!
CREEP
CREEP
WHA... WHAT ARE YOU DOING?!
QUIT IT!
SPRUNG
GOTCHA!
AIIII
CRUNCH
FWISH
BLEEAH
HEH HEH, YOU BOZO! YOU WON'T CATCH ME THAT EASY!
AH–!
GRASP
HA, YOU GOT HER! GOOD, NOW HOLD HER THERE!!
THROB THROB

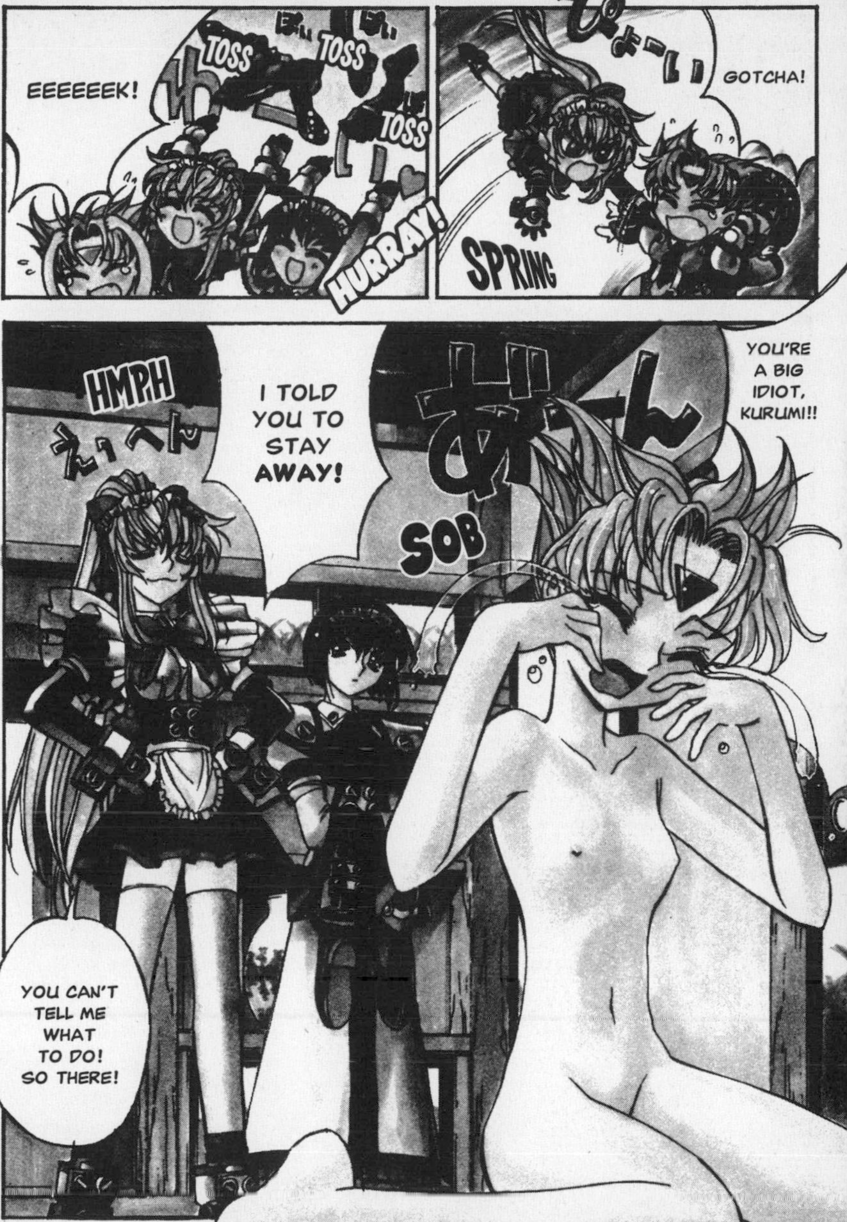
GOTCHA!
SPRING
EEEEEEK!
TOSS TOSS TOSS
わーい
HURRAY!
YOU'RE A BIG IDIOT, KURUMI!!
SOB
I TOLD YOU TO STAY AWAY!
HMPH
えっへん
YOU CAN'T TELL ME WHAT TO DO! SO THERE!

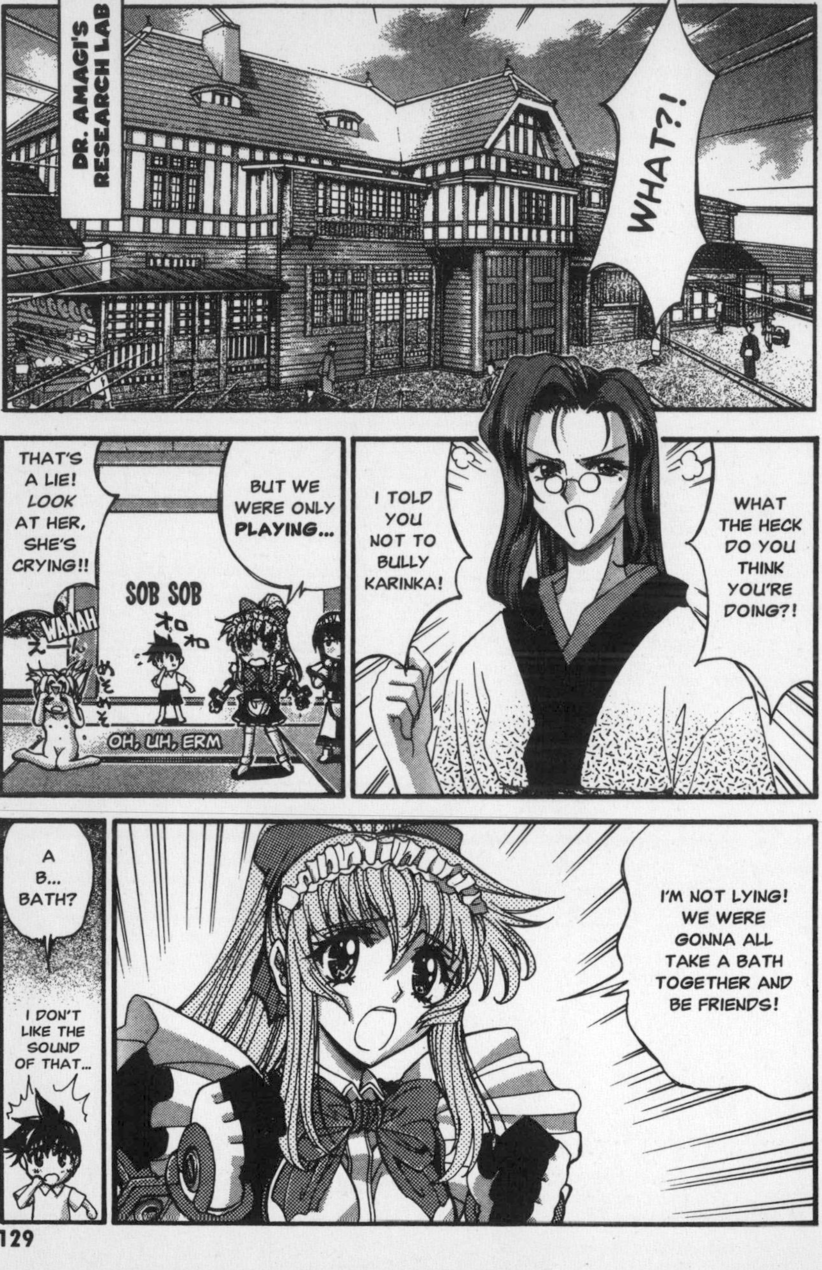
DR. AMAGI'S RESEARCH LAB
WHAT?!
WHAT THE HECK DO YOU THINK YOU'RE DOING?!
I TOLD YOU NOT TO BULLY KARINKA!
BUT WE WERE ONLY PLAYING...
THAT'S A LIE! LOOK AT HER, SHE'S CRYING!!
SOB SOB
WAAAH
えーん
OH, UH, ERM
I'M NOT LYING! WE WERE GONNA ALL TAKE A BATH TOGETHER AND BE FRIENDS!
A B... BATH?
I DON'T LIKE THE SOUND OF THAT...

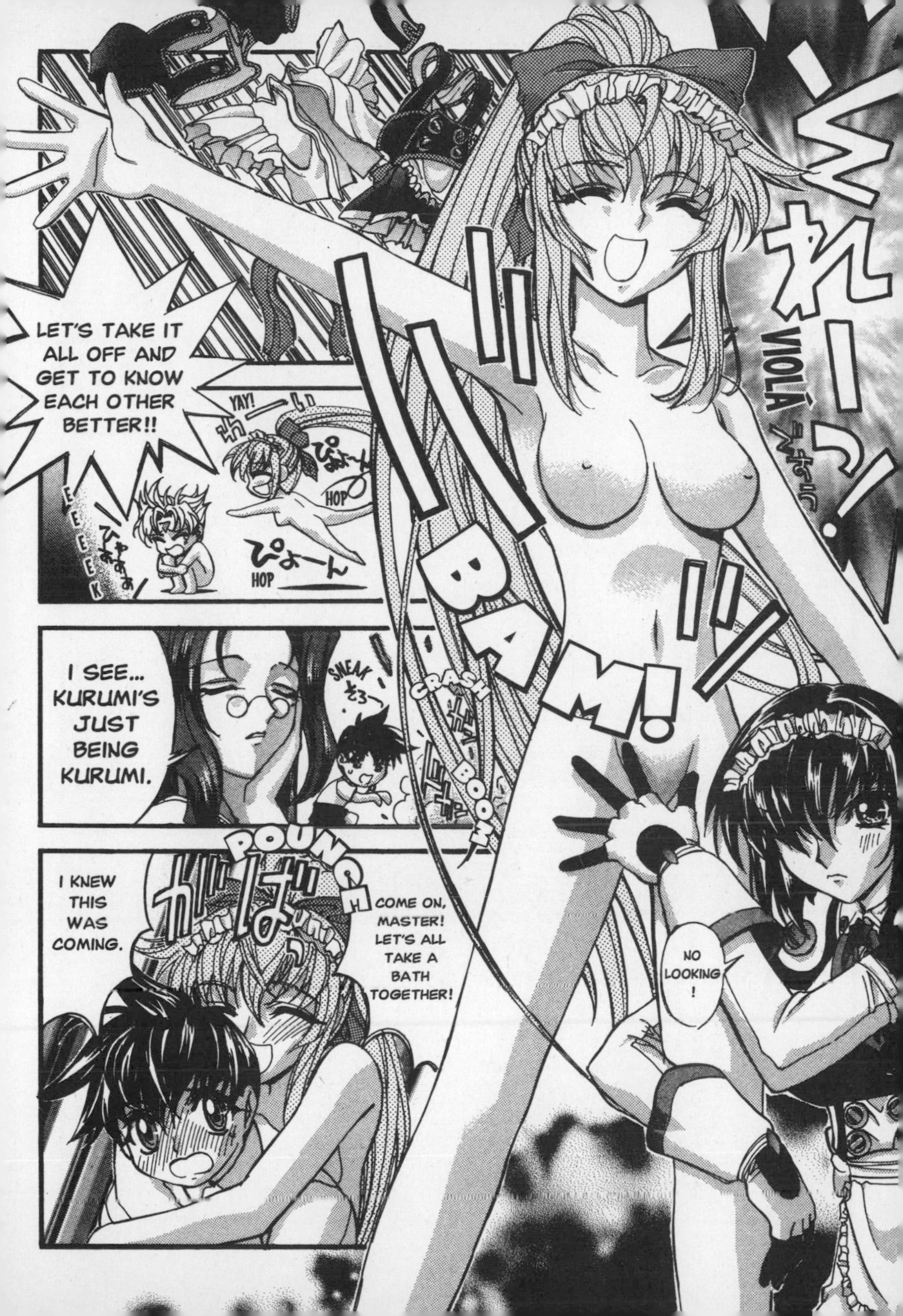

VIOLÀ
BAM!
NO LOOKING!
LET'S TAKE IT ALL OFF AND GET TO KNOW EACH OTHER BETTER!!
YAY!
HOP
ぴょーん
HOP
EEEEEK
I SEE... KURUMI'S JUST BEING KURUMI.
SNEAK
CRASH
BOOM
POUNCE
COME ON, MASTER! LET'S ALL TAKE A BATH TOGETHER!
I KNEW THIS WAS COMING.

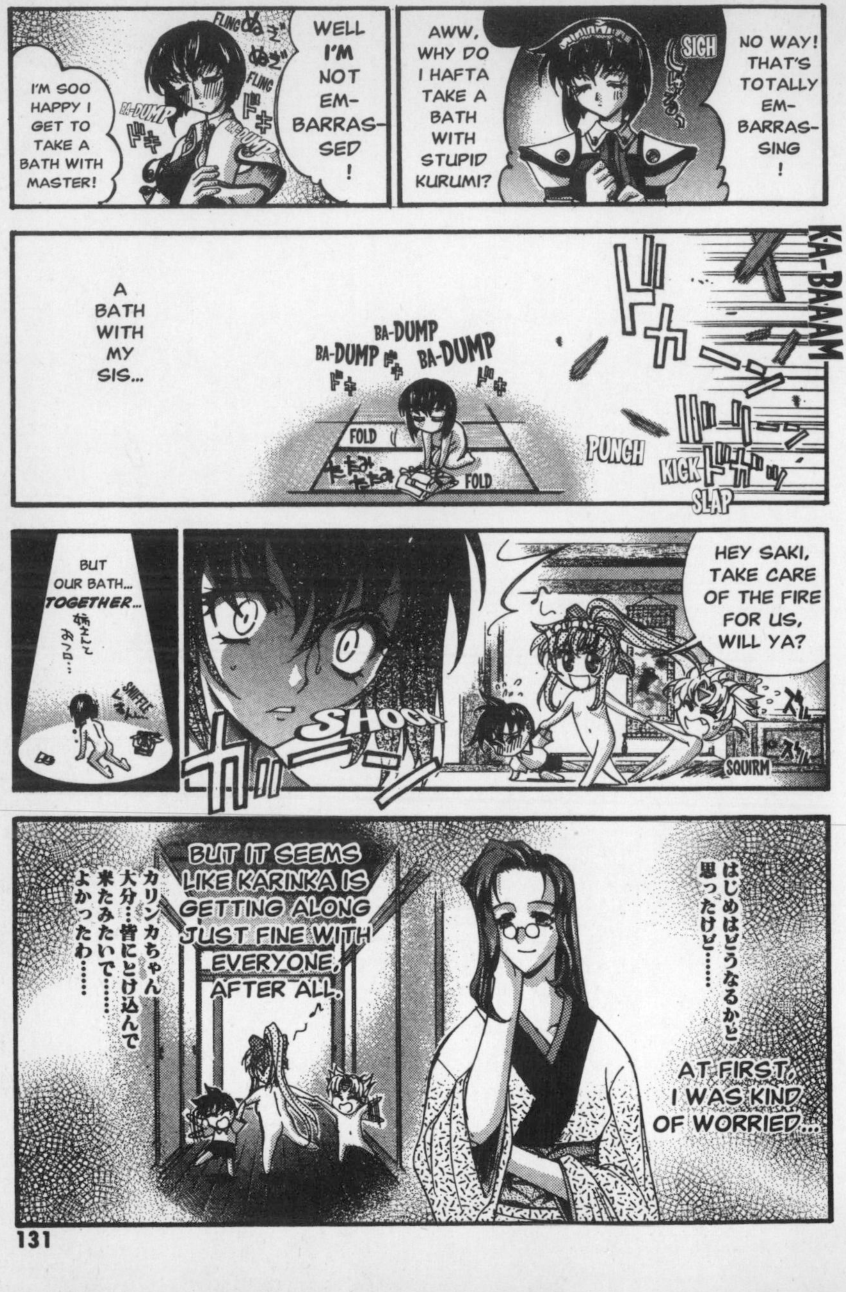
NO WAY! THAT'S TOTALLY EM-BARRAS-SING!
SIGH
AWW, WHY DO I HAFTA TAKE A BATH WITH STUPID KURUMI?
WELL I'M NOT EM-BARRAS-SED!
FLING
FLING
BA-DUMP
BA-DUMP
I'M SOO HAPPY I GET TO TAKE A BATH WITH MASTER!
KA-BAAAM
PUNCH
KICK
SLAP
BA-DUMP
BA-DUMP
BA-DUMP
FOLD
FOLD
A BATH WITH MY SIS...
HEY SAKI, TAKE CARE OF THE FIRE FOR US, WILL YA?
SQUIRM
SHOCK
BUT OUR BATH... TOGETHER...
姉さんとおフロ…
SNIFFLE
AT FIRST, I WAS KIND OF WORRIED...
はじめはどうなるかと思ったけど……
BUT IT SEEMS LIKE KARINKA IS GETTING ALONG JUST FINE WITH EVERYONE, AFTER ALL.
カリンカちゃん大分…皆にとけ込んで来たみたいでよかったわ……

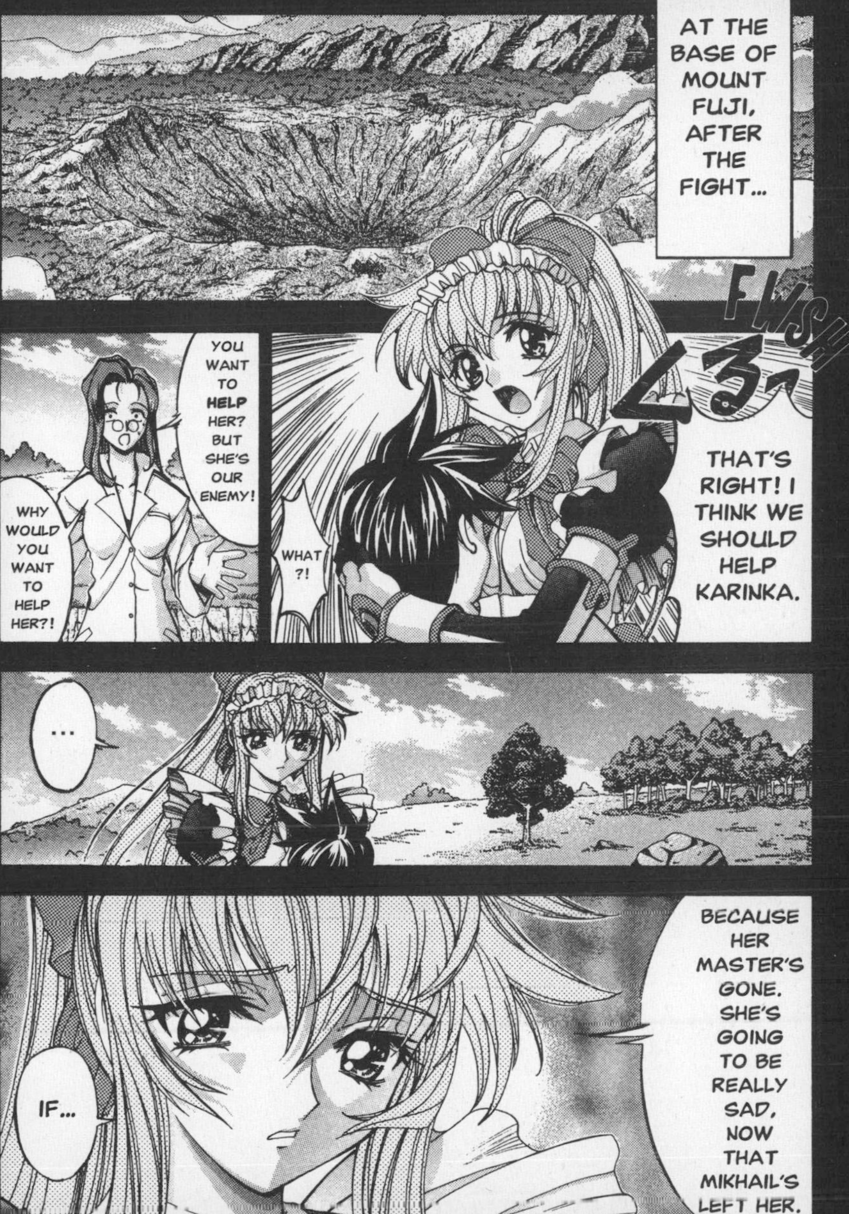

AT THE BASE OF MOUNT FUJI, AFTER THE FIGHT...
FWSH
THAT'S RIGHT! I THINK WE SHOULD HELP KARINKA.
WHAT?!
YOU WANT TO HELP HER? BUT SHE'S OUR ENEMY!
WHY WOULD YOU WANT TO HELP HER?!
...
BECAUSE HER MASTER'S GONE. SHE'S GOING TO BE REALLY SAD, NOW THAT MIKHAIL'S LEFT HER.
IF...

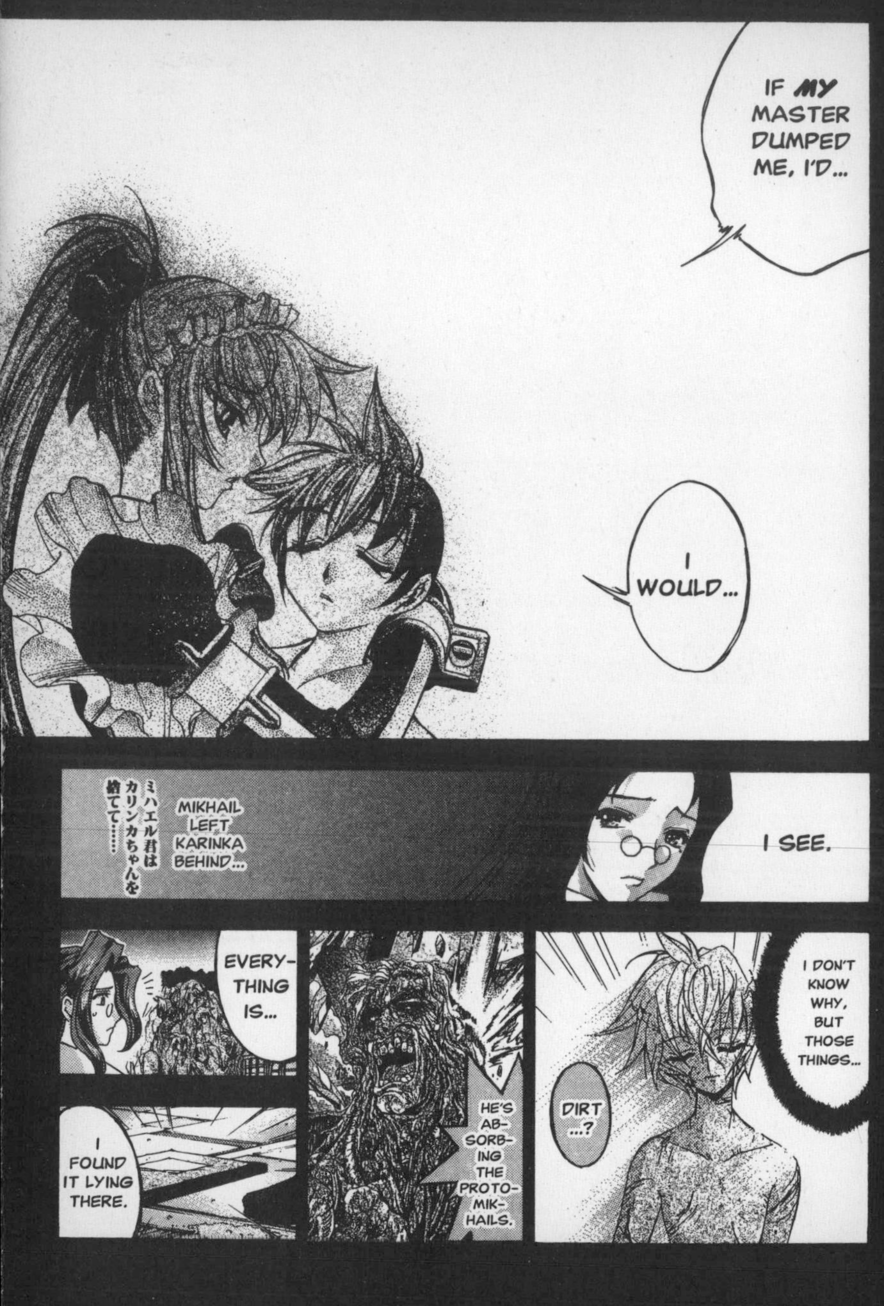
IF MY MASTER DUMPED ME, I'D...
I WOULD...
I SEE.
ミハエル君はカリンカちゃんを捨てて……
MIKHAIL LEFT KARINKA BEHIND...
I DON'T KNOW WHY, BUT THOSE THINGS...
DIRT ...?
HE'S ABSORBING THE PROTO-MIKHAILS.
EVERYTHING IS...
I FOUND IT LYING THERE.

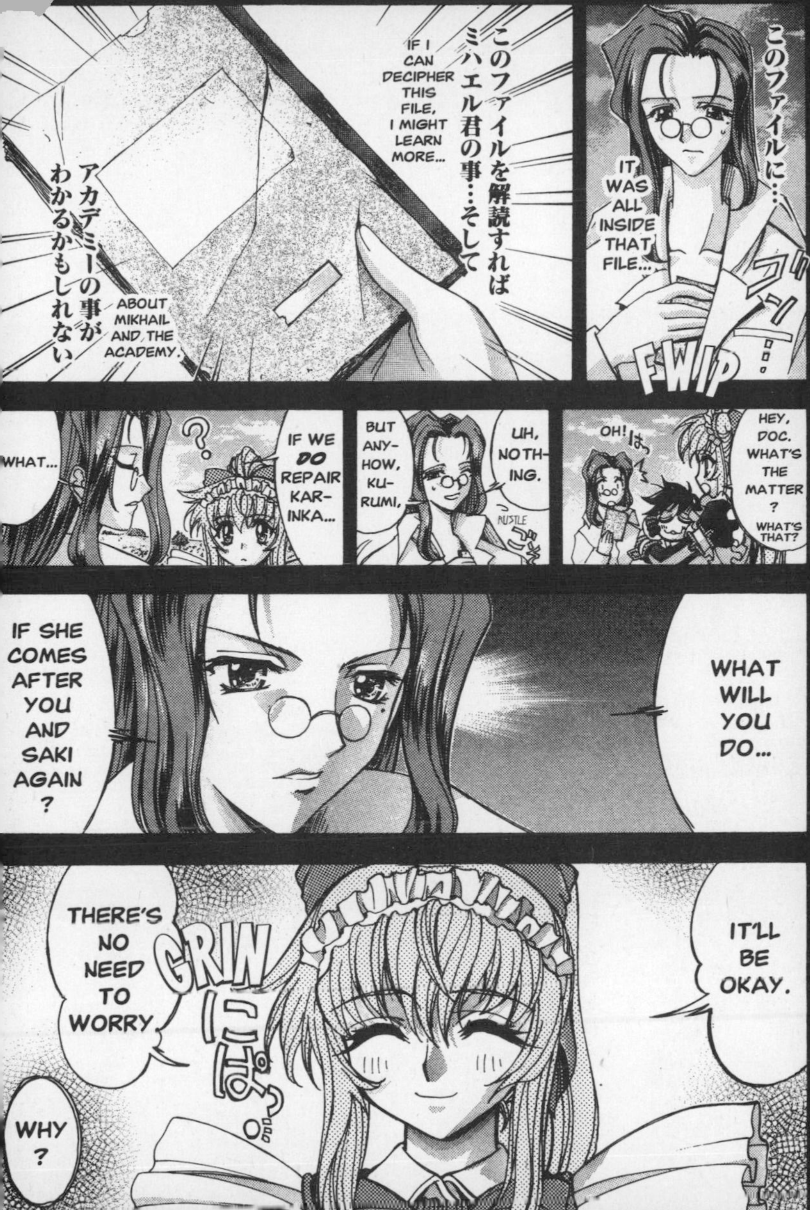
このファイルに…
IT WAS ALL INSIDE THAT FILE...
FWIP
このファイルを解読すればミハエル君の事…そして
IF I CAN DECIPHER THIS FILE, I MIGHT LEARN MORE...
アカデミーの事がわかるかもしれない
ABOUT MIKHAIL AND THE ACADEMY.
HEY, DOC. WHAT'S THE MATTER?
OH! はっ
WHAT'S THAT?
UH, NOTHING.
BUT ANYHOW, KURUMI,
RUSTLE
IF WE DO REPAIR KARINKA...
?
WHAT...
WHAT WILL YOU DO...
IF SHE COMES AFTER YOU AND SAKI AGAIN?
IT'LL BE OKAY.
GRIN
にぱっ
THERE'S NO NEED TO WORRY.
WHY?

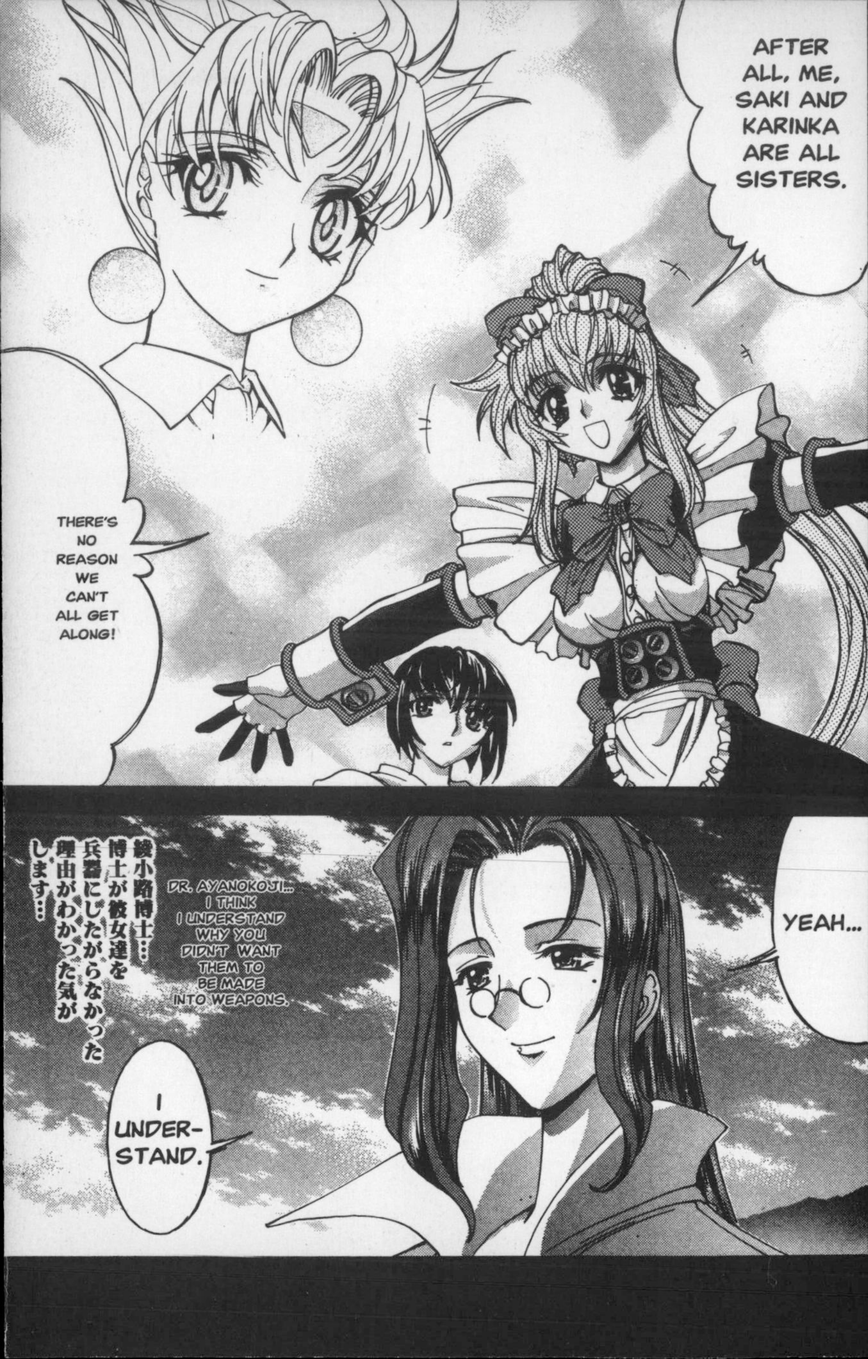
AFTER ALL, ME, SAKI AND KARINKA ARE ALL SISTERS.
THERE'S NO REASON WE CAN'T ALL GET ALONG!
YEAH...
綾小路博士…博士が彼女達を兵器にしたがらなかった理由がわかった気がします…
DR. AYANOKOJI... I THINK I UNDERSTAND WHY YOU DIDN'T WANT THEM TO BE MADE INTO WEAPONS.
I UNDER-STAND.

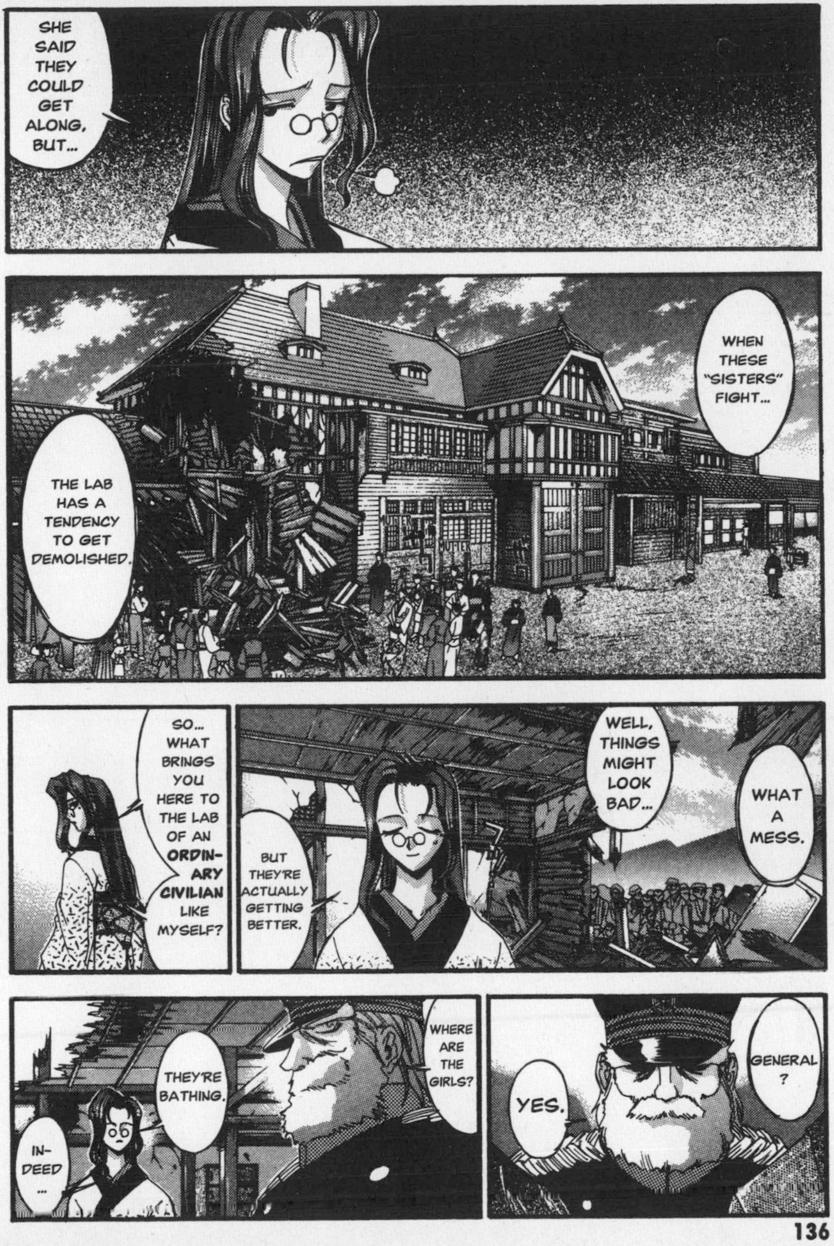
SHE SAID THEY COULD GET ALONG, BUT...
WHEN THESE "SISTERS" FIGHT...
THE LAB HAS A TENDENCY TO GET DEMOLISHED.
WHAT A MESS.
WELL, THINGS MIGHT LOOK BAD...
BUT THEY'RE ACTUALLY GETTING BETTER.
SO... WHAT BRINGS YOU HERE TO THE LAB OF AN **ORDINARY CIVILIAN** LIKE MYSELF?
GENERAL?
YES.
WHERE ARE THE GIRLS?
THEY'RE BATHING.
INDEED...

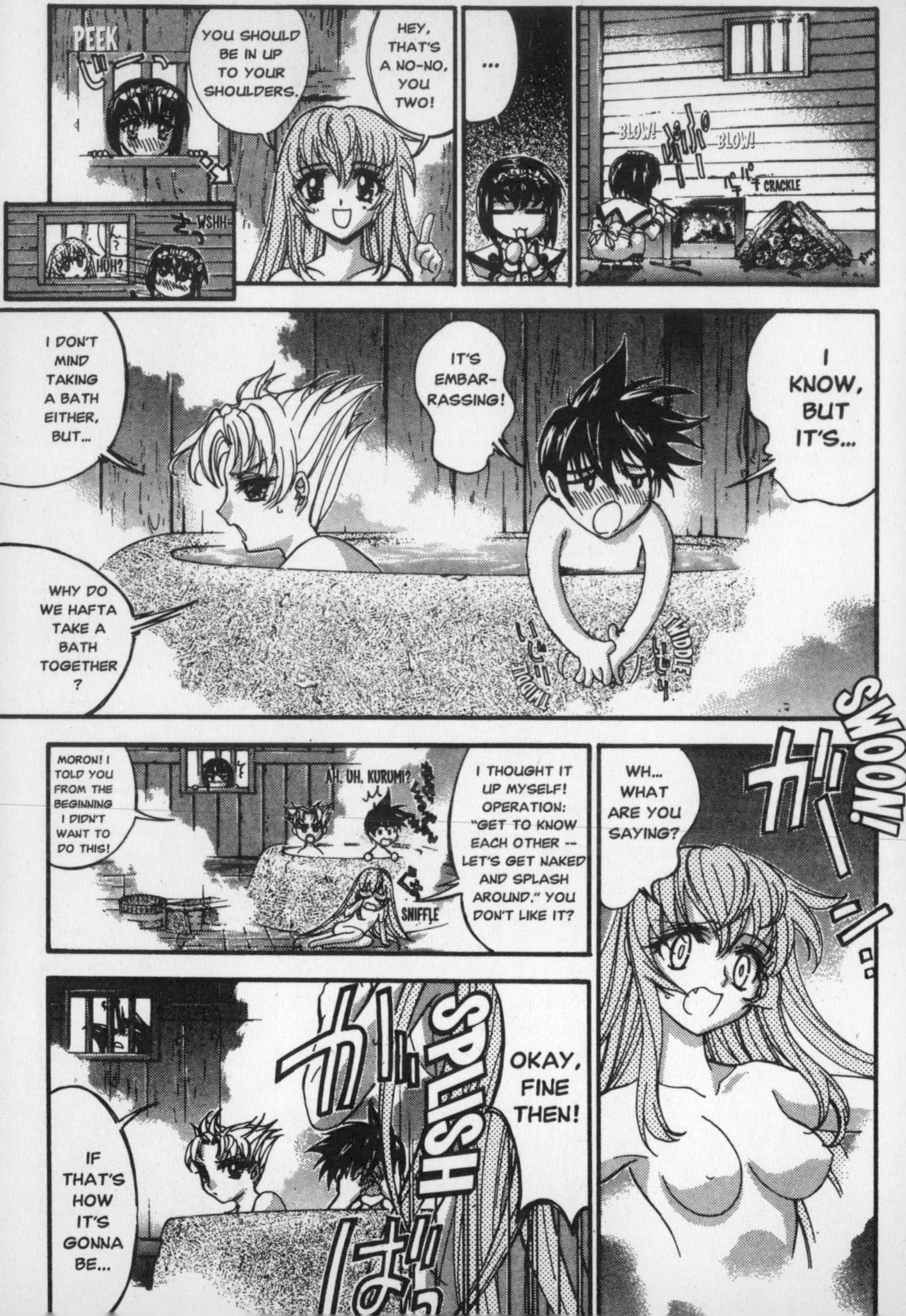
BLOW!
BLOW!
CRACKLE
...
HEY, THAT'S A NO-NO, YOU TWO!
YOU SHOULD BE IN UP TO YOUR SHOULDERS.
PEEK
WSHH
HUH?
I KNOW, BUT IT'S...
IT'S EMBARRASSING!
I DON'T MIND TAKING A BATH EITHER, BUT...
WHY DO WE HAFTA TAKE A BATH TOGETHER?
TWIDDLE
TWIDDLE
SWOON!
WH... WHAT ARE YOU SAYING?
I THOUGHT IT UP MYSELF! OPERATION: "GET TO KNOW EACH OTHER -- LET'S GET NAKED AND SPLASH AROUND." YOU DON'T LIKE IT?
AH, UH, KURUMI?
MORON! I TOLD YOU FROM THE BEGINNING I DIDN'T WANT TO DO THIS!
SNIFFLE
SPLASH
OKAY, FINE THEN!
IF THAT'S HOW IT'S GONNA BE...

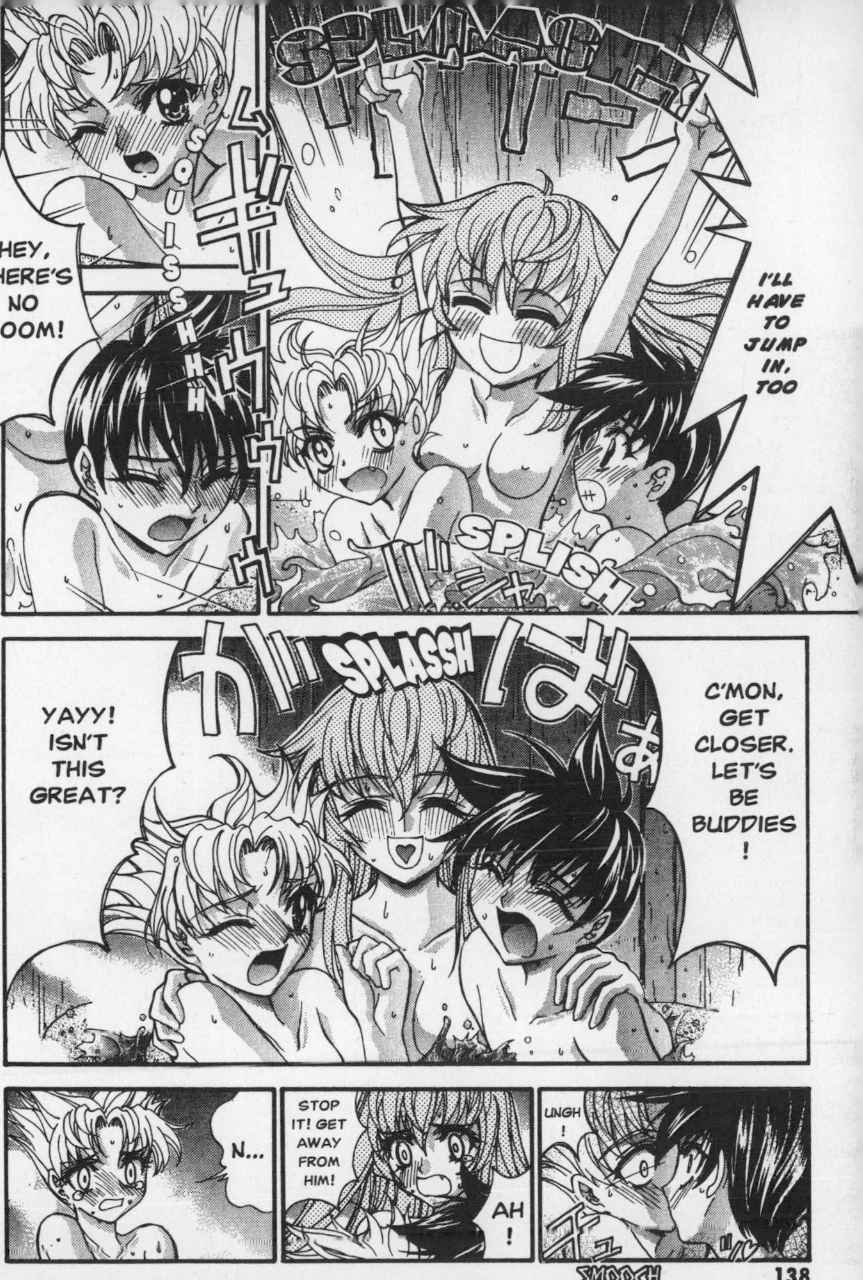
SPLUMMASH
I'LL HAVE TO JUMP IN, TOO
SPLISH
HEY, THERE'S NO ROOM!
SQUISSHHH
C'MON, GET CLOSER. LET'S BE BUDDIES!
SPLASSH
YAYY! ISN'T THIS GREAT?
UNGH!
SMOOCH
STOP IT! GET AWAY FROM HIM!
AH!
N...

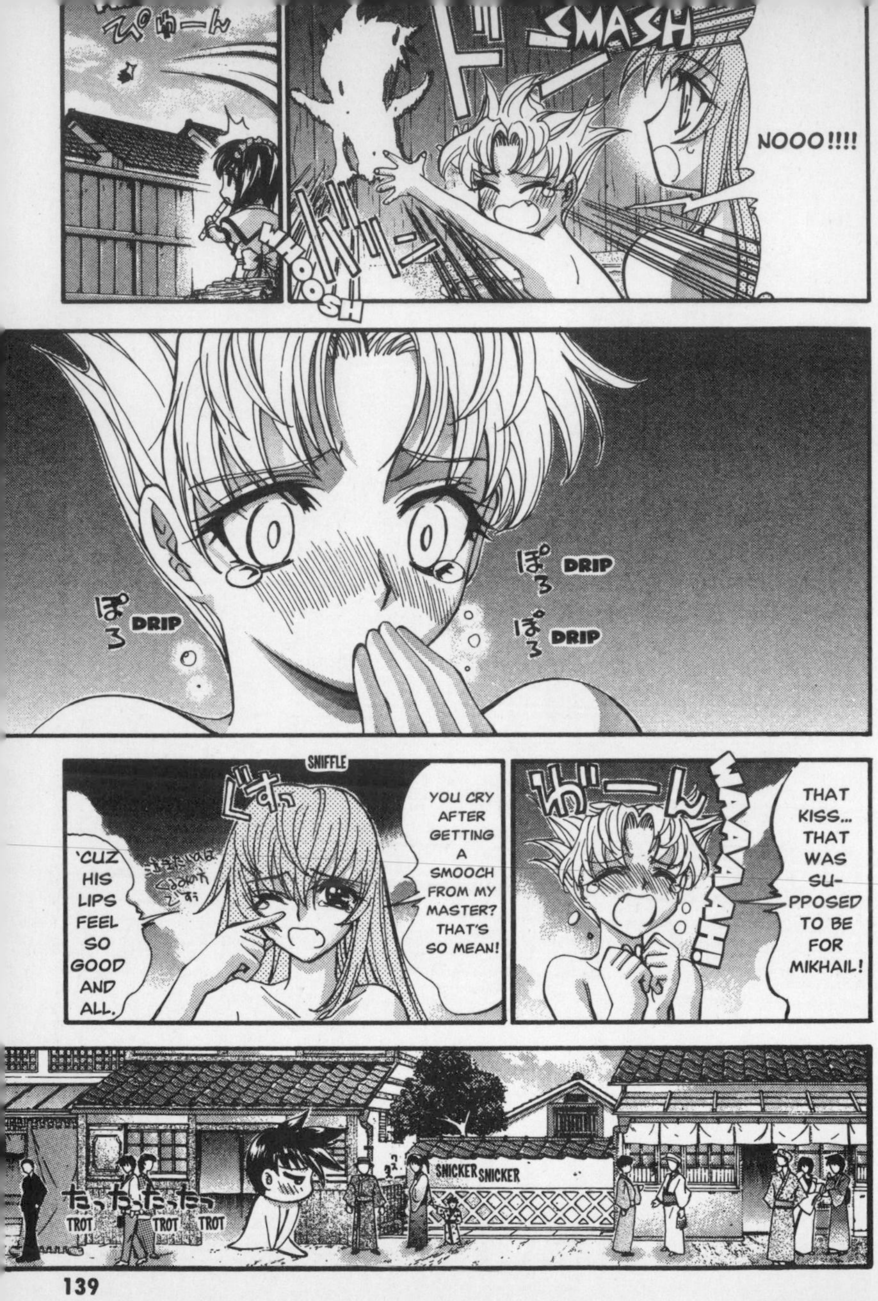
SMASH
NOOO!!!!
WHOOSH
ぴゅーん
ぽろ DRIP
ぽろ ぽろ DRIP
ぽろ DRIP
ぐすっ
WAAAAAH!
THAT KISS... THAT WAS SU-PPOSED TO BE FOR MIKHAIL!
SNIFFLE
YOU CRY AFTER GETTING A SMOOCH FROM MY MASTER? THAT'S SO MEAN!
'CUZ HIS LIPS FEEL SO GOOD AND ALL.
たったったったっ
TROT TROT TROT
SNICKER SNICKER

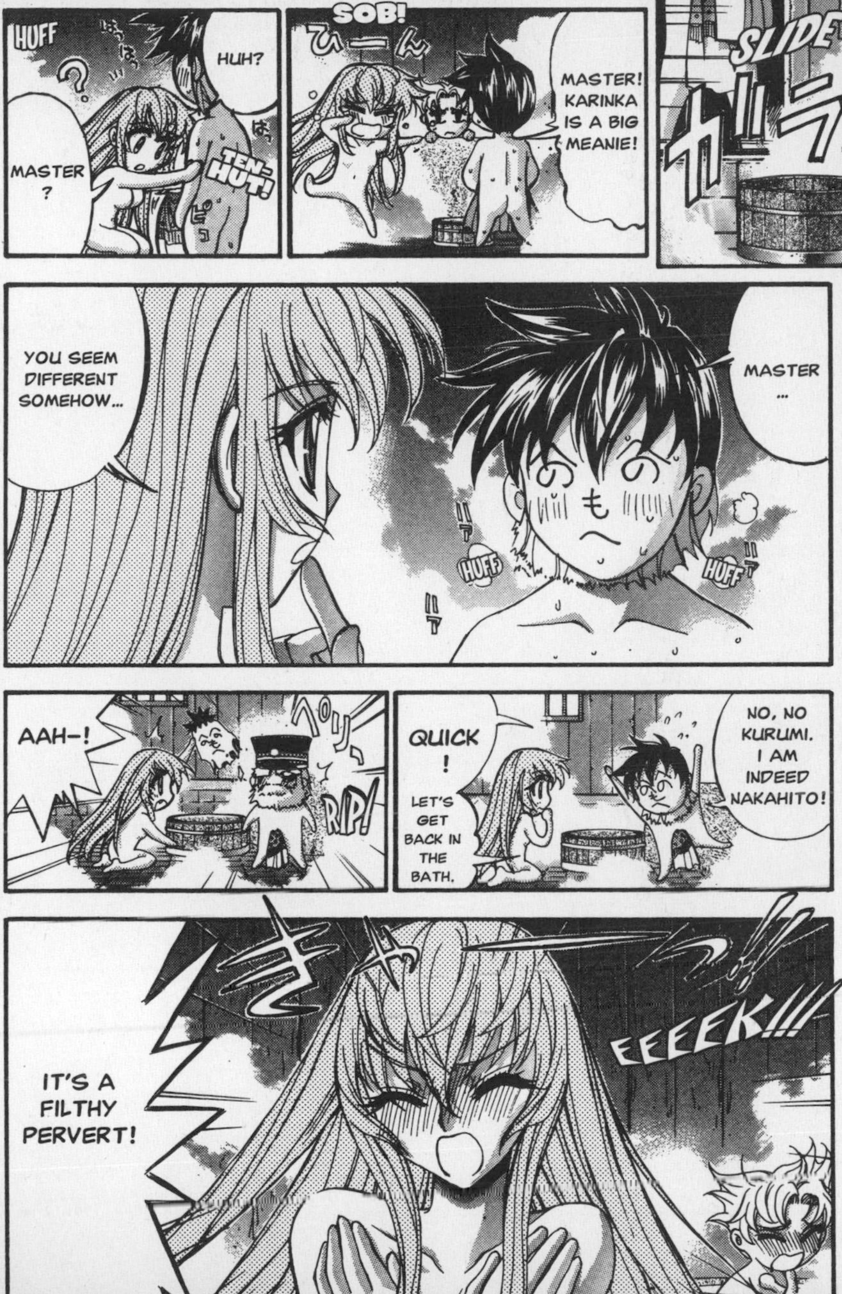
SLIDE
SOB!
ひーん
MASTER! KARINKA IS A BIG MEANIE!
HUH?
HUFF
MASTER ?
TEN-HUT!
MASTER ...
YOU SEEM DIFFERENT SOMEHOW...
HUFF
HUFF
NO, NO KURUMI. I AM INDEED NAKAHITO!
QUICK!
LET'S GET BACK IN THE BATH.
AAH-!
RIP!
EEEEK!!!
IT'S A FILTHY PERVERT!

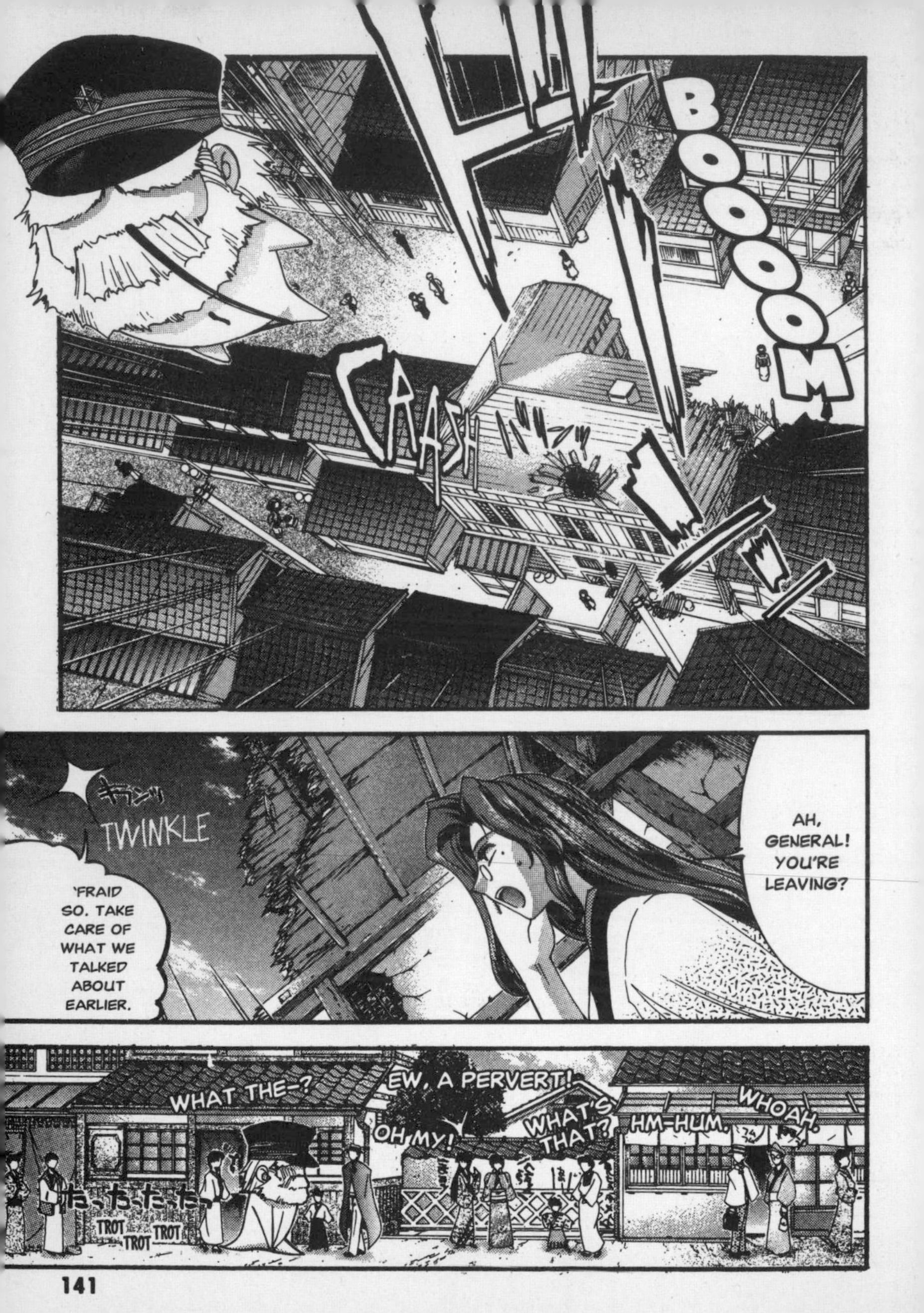
BOOOOOM
CRASH
AH, GENERAL! YOU'RE LEAVING?
TWINKLE
'FRAID SO. TAKE CARE OF WHAT WE TALKED ABOUT EARLIER.
WHOAH.
HM-HUM.
WHAT'S THAT?
OH MY!
EW, A PERVERT!
WHAT THE–?
TROT TROT TROT

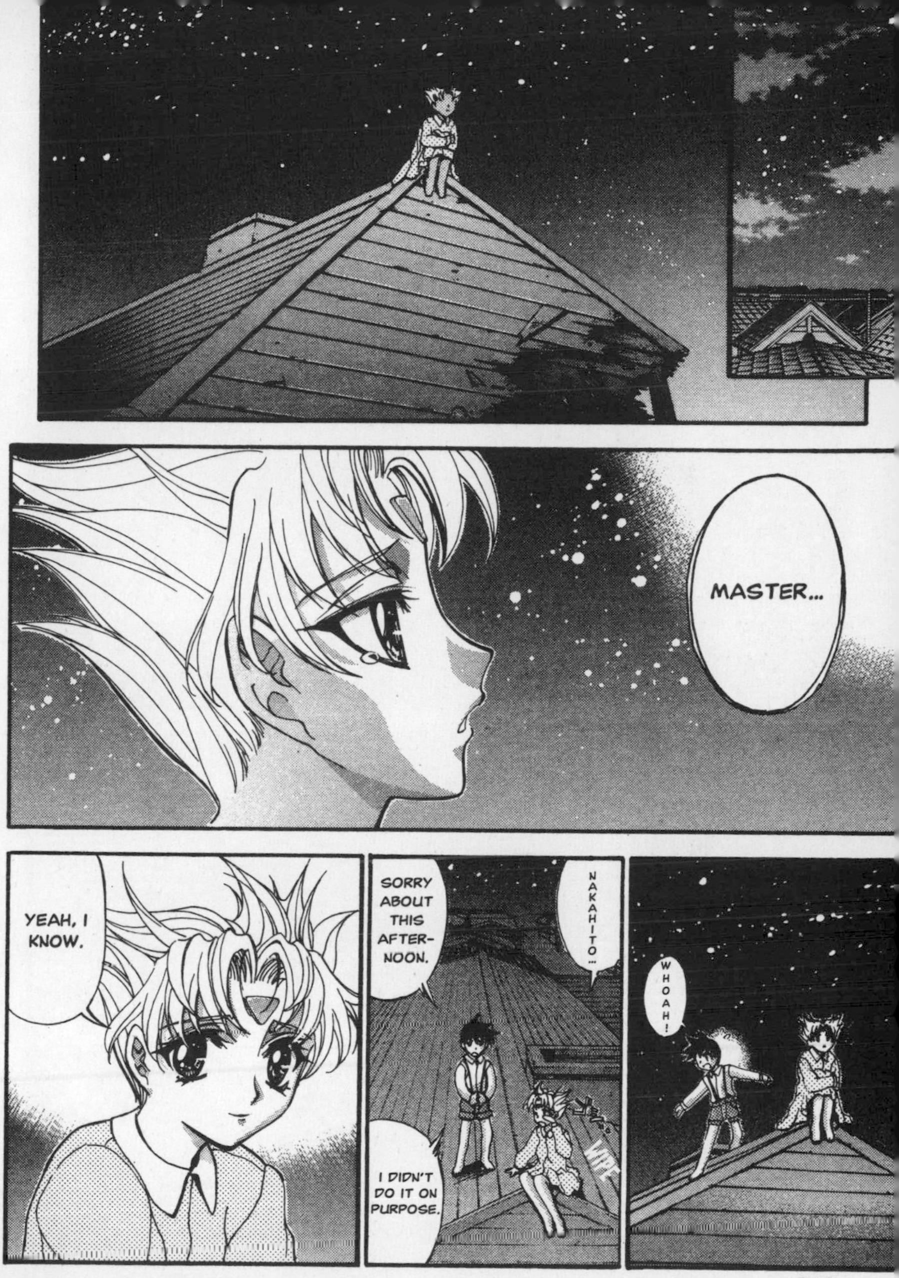
MASTER...
WHOAH!
NAKAHITO...
SORRY ABOUT THIS AFTERNOON.
WIPE
I DIDN'T DO IT ON PURPOSE.
YEAH, I KNOW.

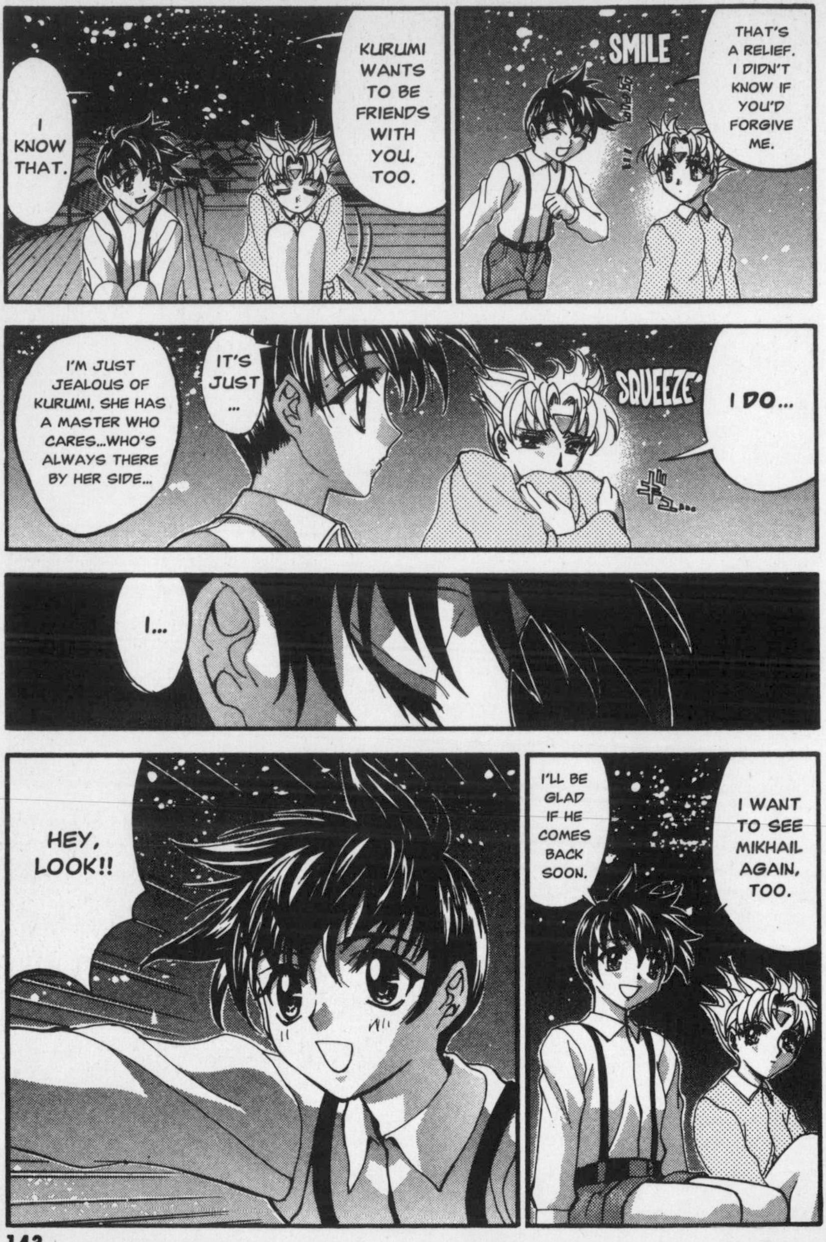
THAT'S A RELIEF. I DIDN'T KNOW IF YOU'D FORGIVE ME.
SMILE
KURUMI WANTS TO BE FRIENDS WITH YOU, TOO.
I KNOW THAT.
I DO...
SQUEEZE
IT'S JUST ...
I'M JUST JEALOUS OF KURUMI. SHE HAS A MASTER WHO CARES...WHO'S ALWAYS THERE BY HER SIDE...
I...
I WANT TO SEE MIKHAIL AGAIN, TOO.
I'LL BE GLAD IF HE COMES BACK SOON.
HEY, LOOK!!

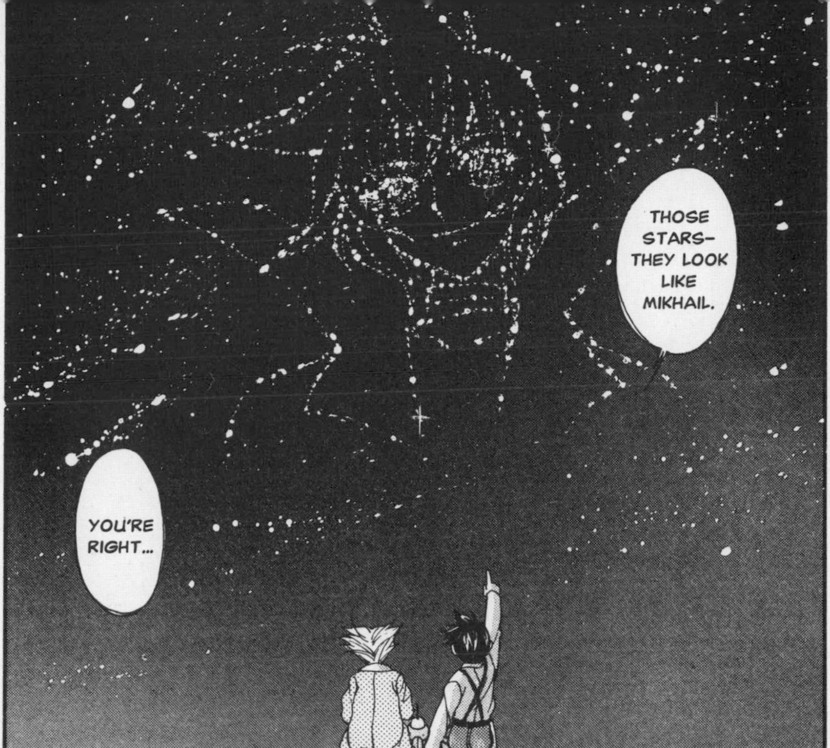
THOSE STARS– THEY LOOK LIKE MIKHAIL.
YOU'RE RIGHT...

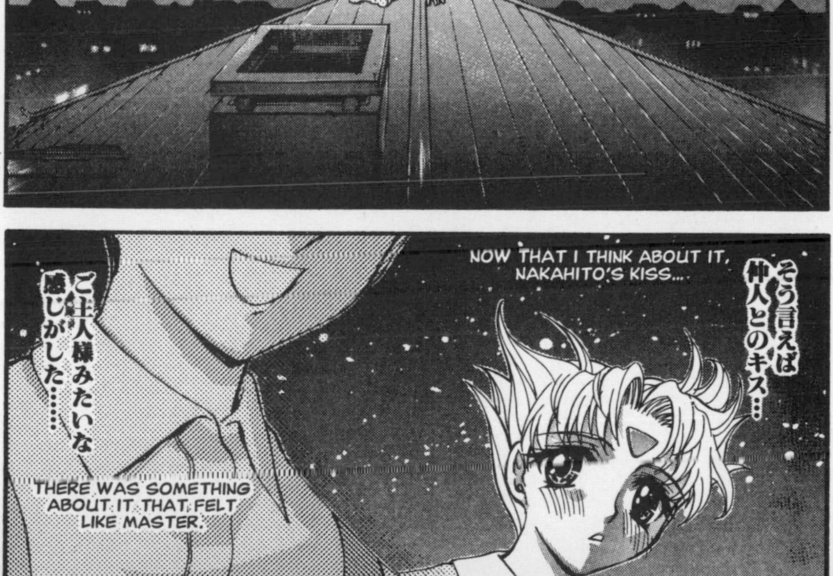
NOW THAT I THINK ABOUT IT, NAKAHITO'S KISS...
そう言えば仲人とのキス…
ご主人様みたいな感じがした……
THERE WAS SOMETHING ABOUT IT THAT FELT LIKE MASTER.

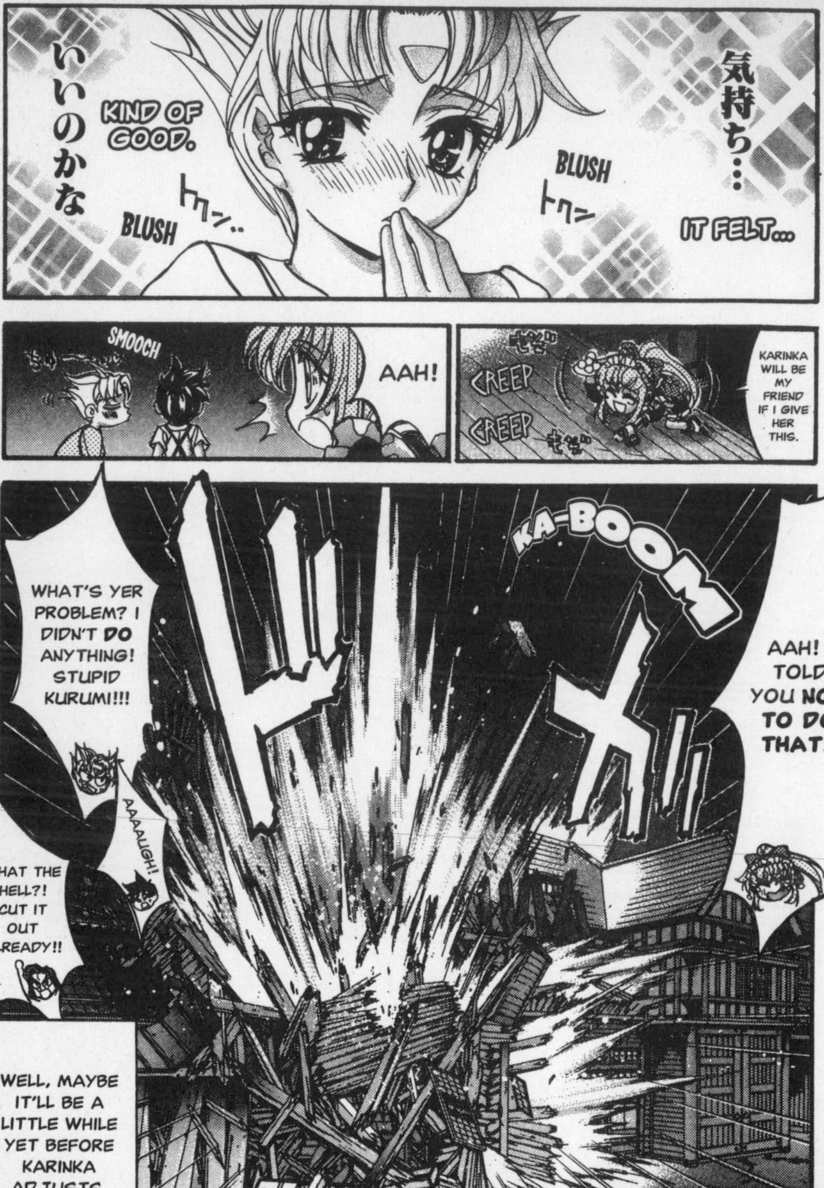
気持ち…
IT FELT...
BLUSH
トクン
いいのかな
KIND OF GOOD.
トクン..
BLUSH
KARINKA WILL BE MY FRIEND IF I GIVE HER THIS.
CREEP
CREEP
AAH!
SMOOCH
KA-BOOM
AAH! I TOLD YOU NOT TO DO THAT!!
WHAT'S YER PROBLEM? I DIDN'T DO ANYTHING! STUPID KURUMI!!!
AAAALIGH!
WHAT THE HELL?! CUT IT OUT ALREADY!!
WELL, MAYBE IT'LL BE A LITTLE WHILE YET BEFORE KARINKA ADJUSTS.

EPISODE 11 KURUMI'S SPY MISSION

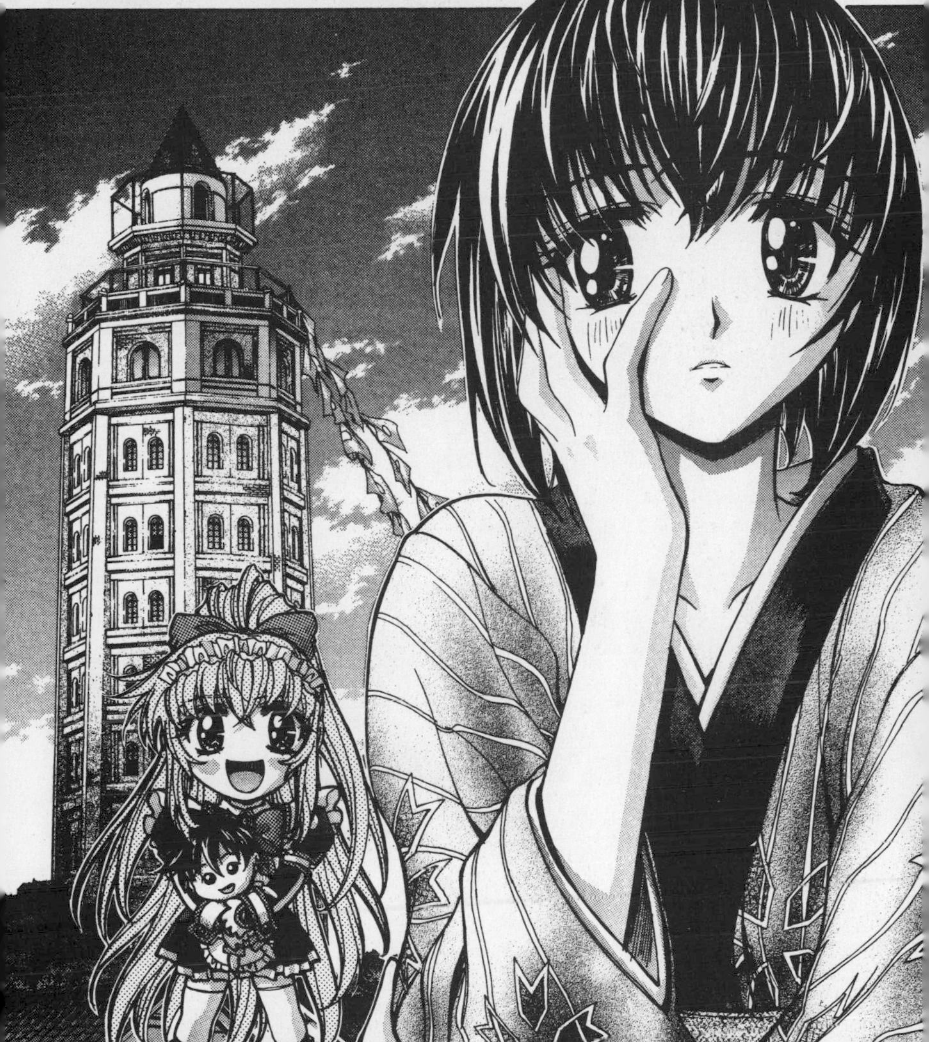

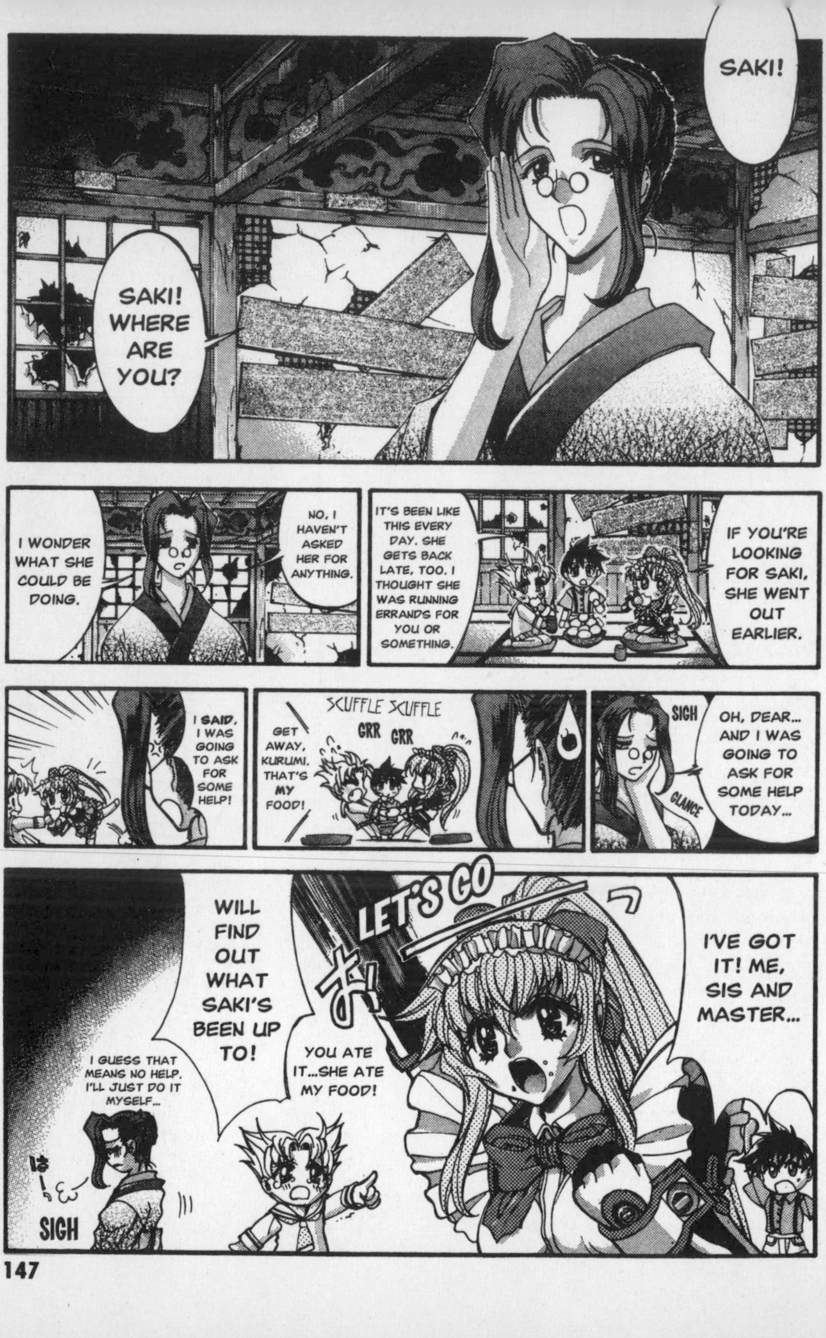
SAKI!
SAKI! WHERE ARE YOU?
IF YOU'RE LOOKING FOR SAKI, SHE WENT OUT EARLIER.
IT'S BEEN LIKE THIS EVERY DAY. SHE GETS BACK LATE, TOO. I THOUGHT SHE WAS RUNNING ERRANDS FOR YOU OR SOMETHING.
NO, I HAVEN'T ASKED HER FOR ANYTHING.
I WONDER WHAT SHE COULD BE DOING.
SIGH
OH, DEAR... AND I WAS GOING TO ASK FOR SOME HELP TODAY...
GLANCE
SCUFFLE SCUFFLE
GRR GRR
GET AWAY, KURUMI. THAT'S MY FOOD!
I SAID, I WAS GOING TO ASK FOR SOME HELP!
I'VE GOT IT! ME, SIS AND MASTER...
LET'S GO
お!
WILL FIND OUT WHAT SAKI'S BEEN UP TO!
YOU ATE IT...SHE ATE MY FOOD!
I GUESS THAT MEANS NO HELP. I'LL JUST DO IT MYSELF...
SIGH

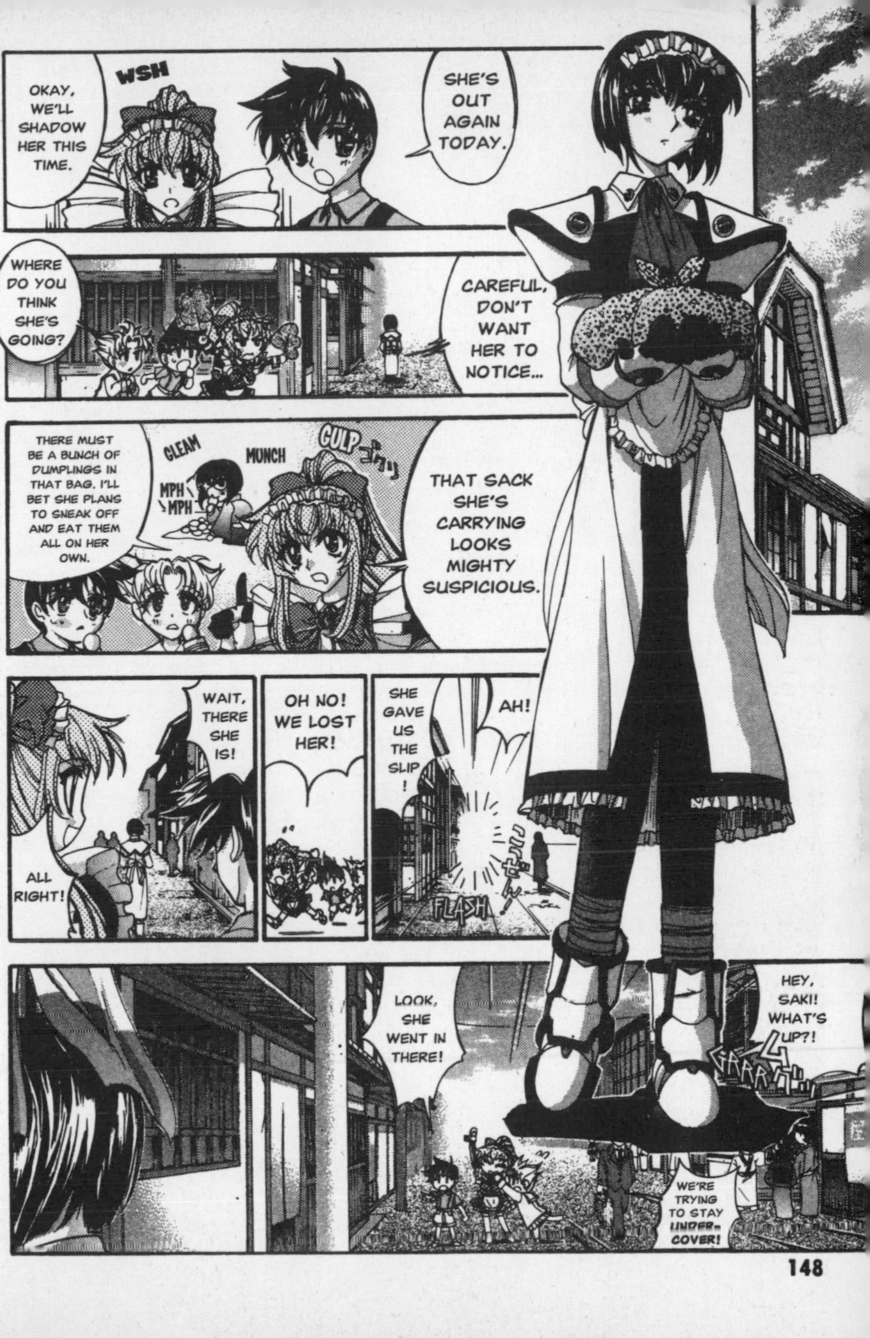
SHE'S OUT AGAIN TODAY.
WSH
OKAY, WE'LL SHADOW HER THIS TIME.
CAREFUL, DON'T WANT HER TO NOTICE...
WHERE DO YOU THINK SHE'S GOING?
THAT SACK SHE'S CARRYING LOOKS MIGHTY SUSPICIOUS.
GULP
MUNCH
GLEAM
MPH MPH
THERE MUST BE A BUNCH OF DUMPLINGS IN THAT BAG. I'LL BET SHE PLANS TO SNEAK OFF AND EAT THEM ALL ON HER OWN.
AH!
SHE GAVE US THE SLIP!
FLASH
OH NO! WE LOST HER!
WAIT, THERE SHE IS!
ALL RIGHT!
HEY, SAKI! WHAT'S UP?!
WE'RE TRYING TO STAY UNDER-COVER!
LOOK, SHE WENT IN THERE!

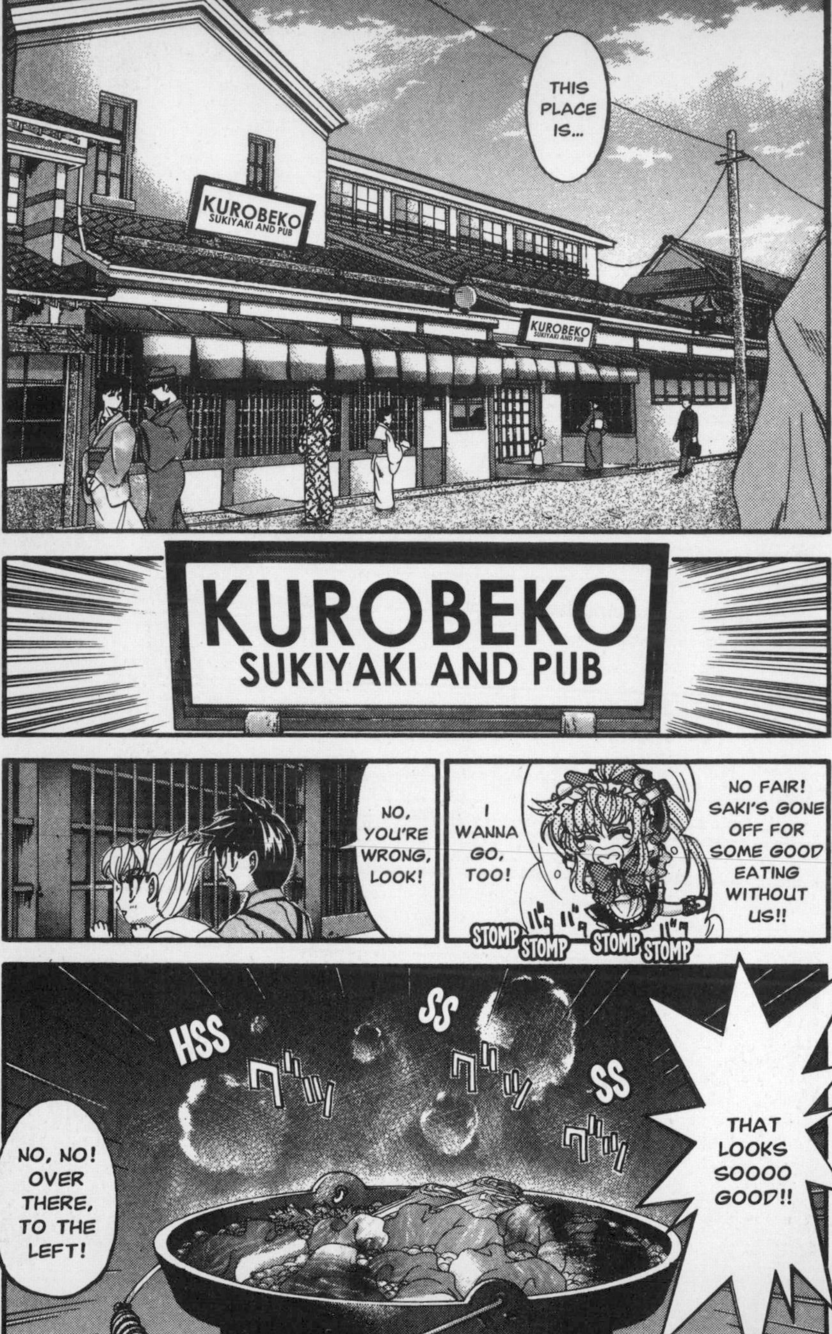
KUROBEKO
SUKIYAKI AND PUB
KUROBEKO
SUKIYAKI AND PUB
THIS PLACE IS...
KUROBEKO
SUKIYAKI AND PUB
NO FAIR! SAKI'S GONE OFF FOR SOME GOOD EATING WITHOUT US!!
I WANNA GO, TOO!
STOMP STOMP STOMP STOMP
NO, YOU'RE WRONG, LOOK!
THAT LOOKS SOOOO GOOD!!
SS
SS
HSS
NO, NO! OVER THERE, TO THE LEFT!

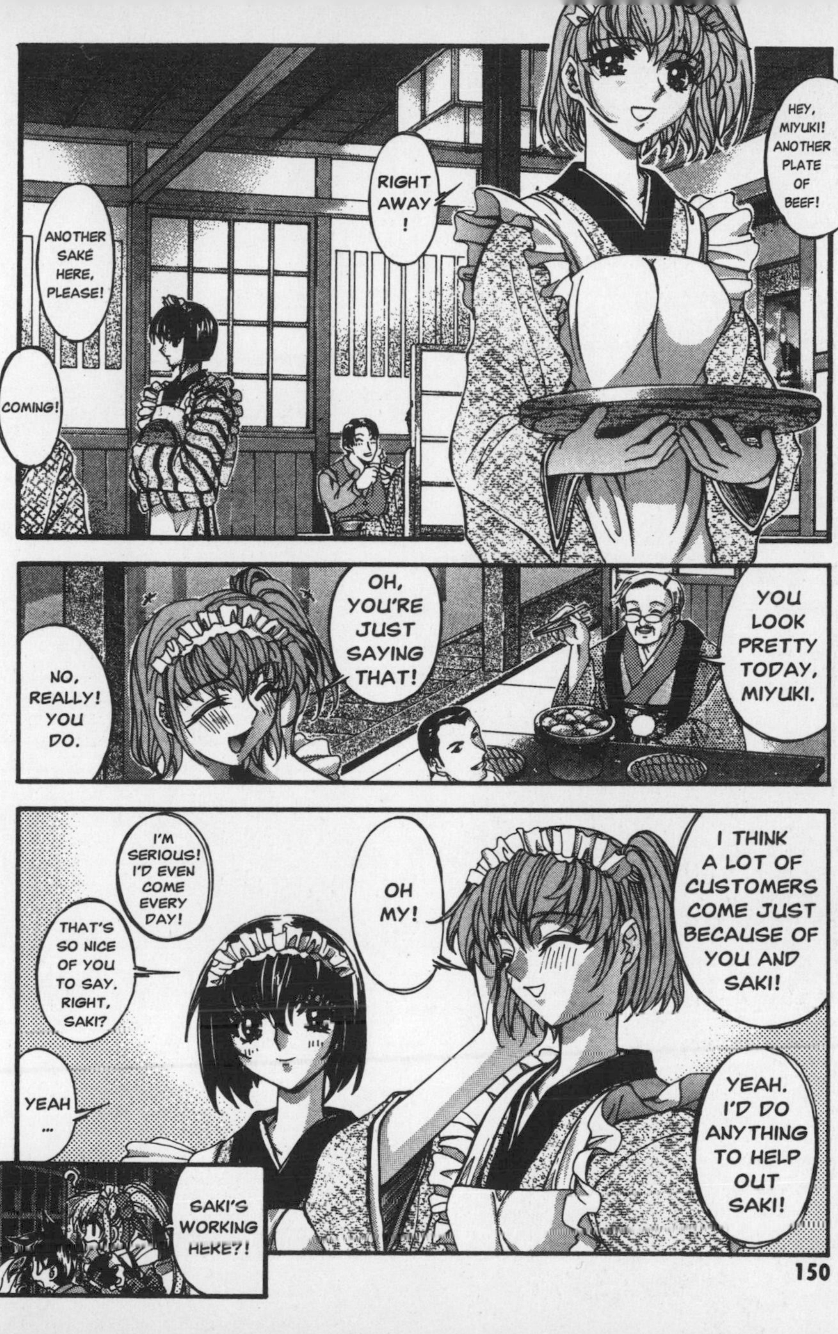
HEY, MIYUKI! ANOTHER PLATE OF BEEF!
RIGHT AWAY!
ANOTHER SAKÉ HERE, PLEASE!
COMING!
YOU LOOK PRETTY TODAY, MIYUKI.
OH, YOU'RE JUST SAYING THAT!
NO, REALLY! YOU DO.
I THINK A LOT OF CUSTOMERS COME JUST BECAUSE OF YOU AND SAKI!
OH MY!
I'M SERIOUS! I'D EVEN COME EVERY DAY!
THAT'S SO NICE OF YOU TO SAY. RIGHT, SAKI?
YEAH. I'D DO ANYTHING TO HELP OUT SAKI!
YEAH ...
SAKI'S WORKING HERE?!

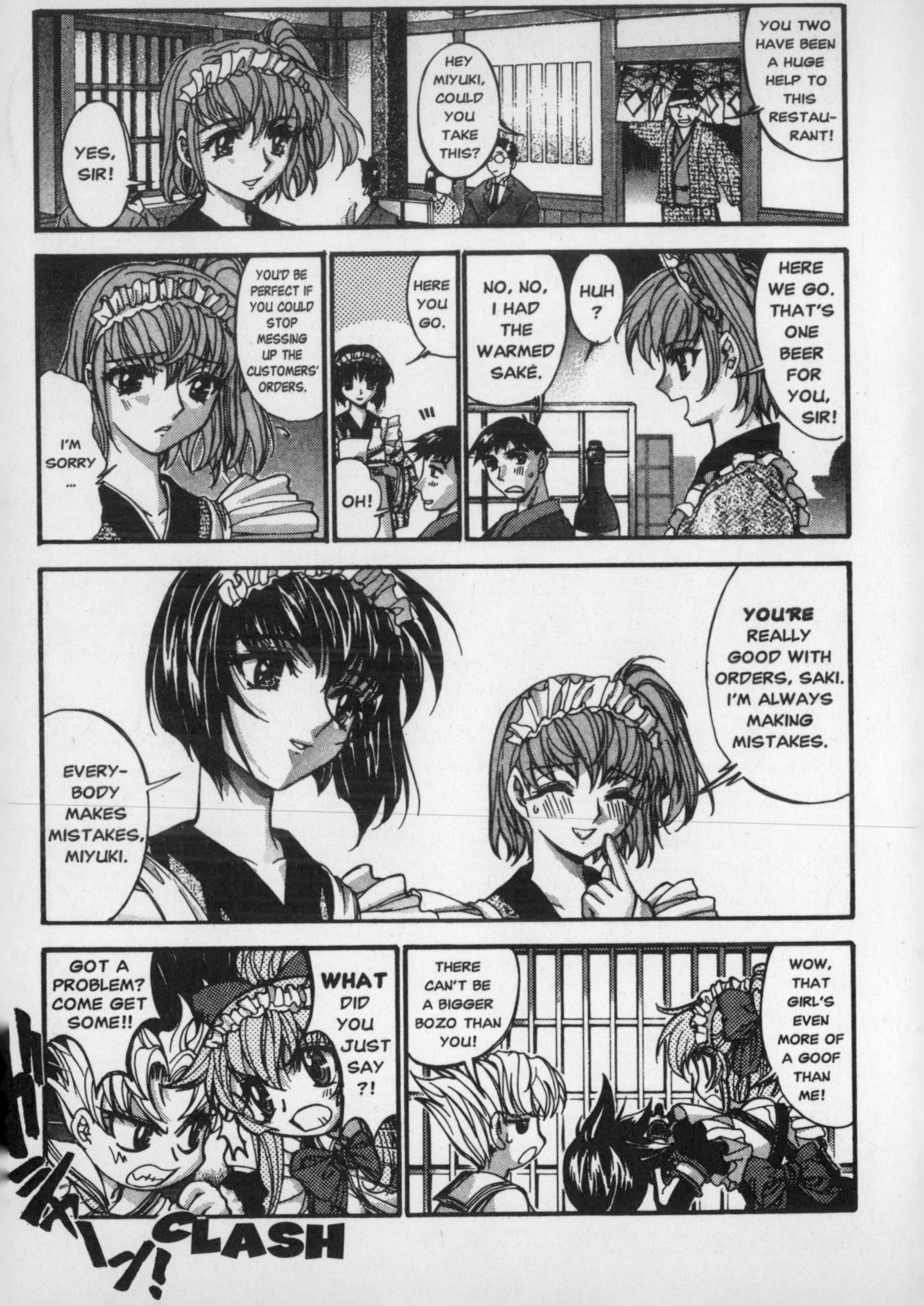
YOU TWO HAVE BEEN A HUGE HELP TO THIS RESTAU-RANT!
HEY MIYUKI, COULD YOU TAKE THIS?
YES, SIR!
HERE WE GO. THAT'S ONE BEER FOR YOU, SIR!
HUH ?
NO, NO, I HAD THE WARMED SAKÉ.
HERE YOU GO.
OH!
YOU'D BE PERFECT IF YOU COULD STOP MESSING UP THE CUSTOMERS' ORDERS.
I'M SORRY ...
YOU'RE REALLY GOOD WITH ORDERS, SAKI. I'M ALWAYS MAKING MISTAKES.
EVERY-BODY MAKES MISTAKES, MIYUKI.
WOW, THAT GIRL'S EVEN MORE OF A GOOF THAN ME!
THERE CAN'T BE A BIGGER BOZO THAN YOU!
WHAT DID YOU JUST SAY ?!
GOT A PROBLEM? COME GET SOME!!
CLASH

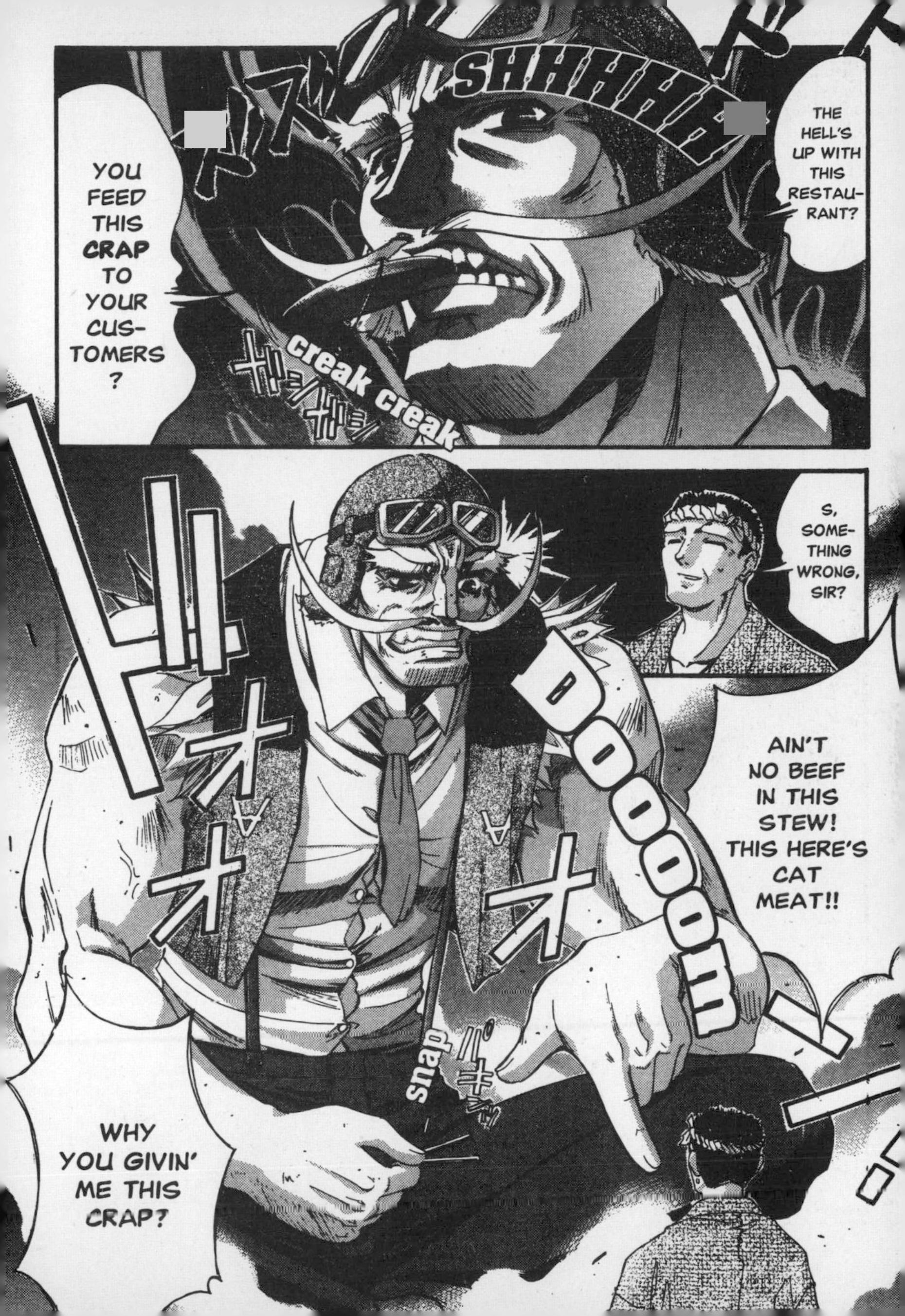
SHHHHH
THE HELL'S UP WITH THIS RESTAURANT?
YOU FEED THIS CRAP TO YOUR CUSTOMERS?
creak creak
S, SOMETHING WRONG, SIR?
Doooom
AIN'T NO BEEF IN THIS STEW! THIS HERE'S CAT MEAT!!
snap
WHY YOU GIVIN' ME THIS CRAP?

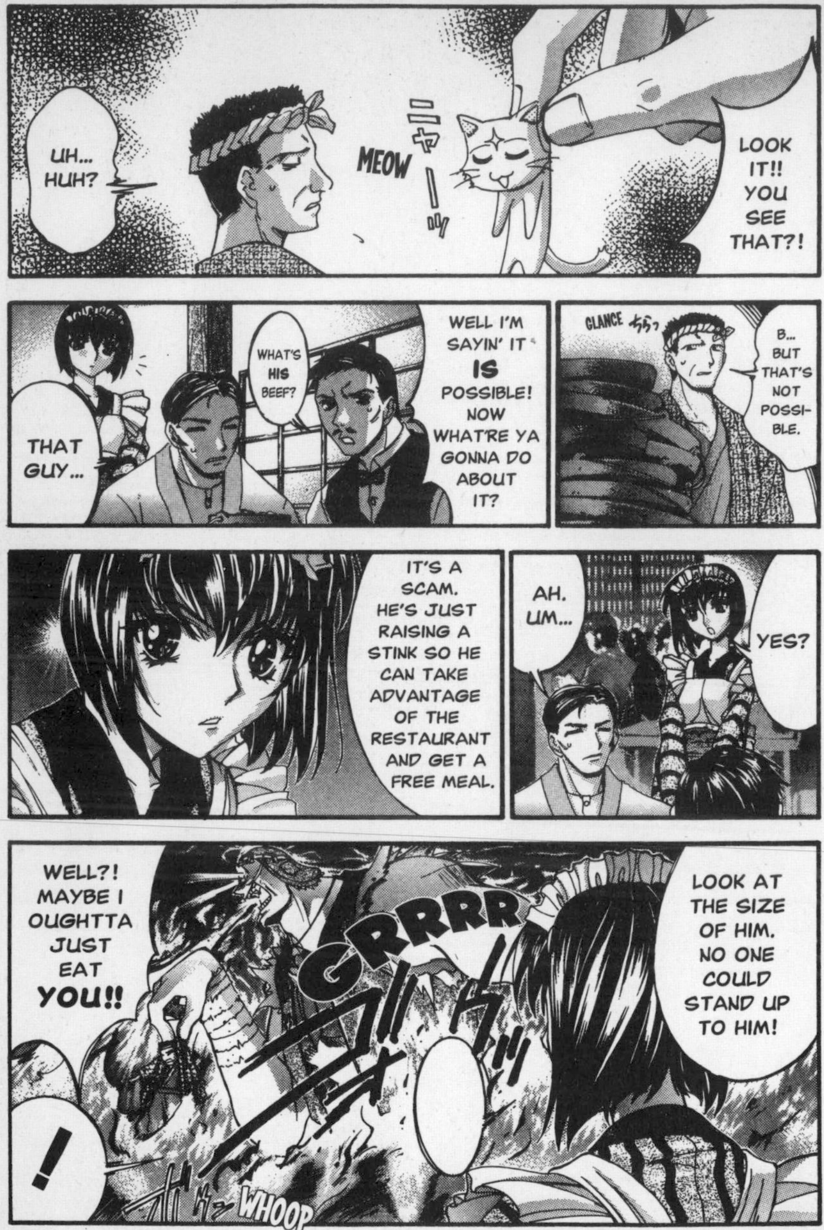
LOOK IT!! YOU SEE THAT?!
MEOW
ニャーッ
UH... HUH?
GLANCE ちらっ
B... BUT THAT'S NOT POSSIBLE.
WELL I'M SAYIN' IT **IS** POSSIBLE! NOW WHAT'RE YA GONNA DO ABOUT IT?
WHAT'S **HIS** BEEF?
THAT GUY...
YES?
AH. UM...
IT'S A SCAM. HE'S JUST RAISING A STINK SO HE CAN TAKE ADVANTAGE OF THE RESTAURANT AND GET A FREE MEAL.
LOOK AT THE SIZE OF HIM. NO ONE COULD STAND UP TO HIM!
GRRRR
WELL?! MAYBE I OUGHTTA JUST EAT **YOU!!**
!
WHOOP

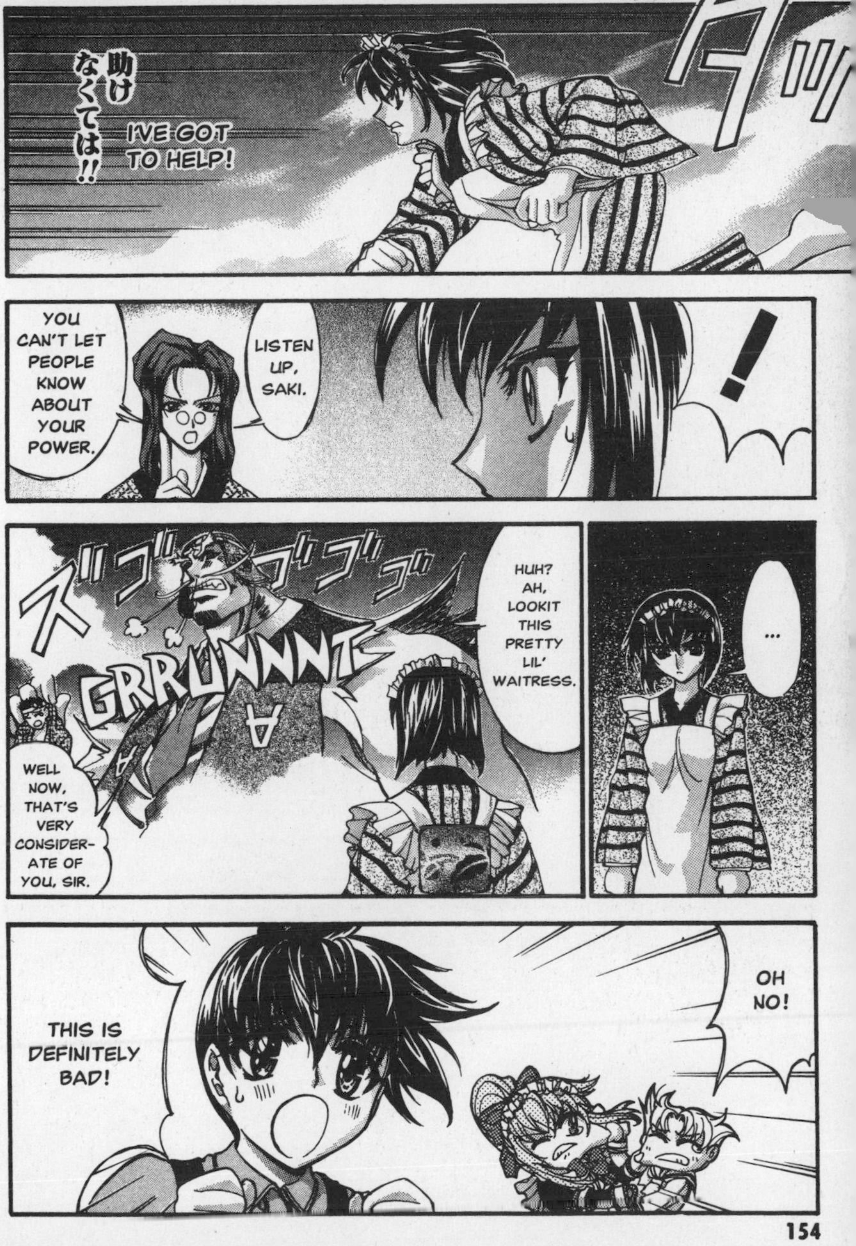
DASH!
タッ
助けなくては!!
I'VE GOT TO HELP!
!
LISTEN UP, SAKI.
YOU CAN'T LET PEOPLE KNOW ABOUT YOUR POWER.
...
HUH? AH, LOOKIT THIS PRETTY LIL' WAITRESS.
ズゴゴゴゴ
GRRUNNNT
WELL NOW, THAT'S VERY CONSIDER-ATE OF YOU, SIR.
OH NO!
THIS IS DEFINITELY BAD!

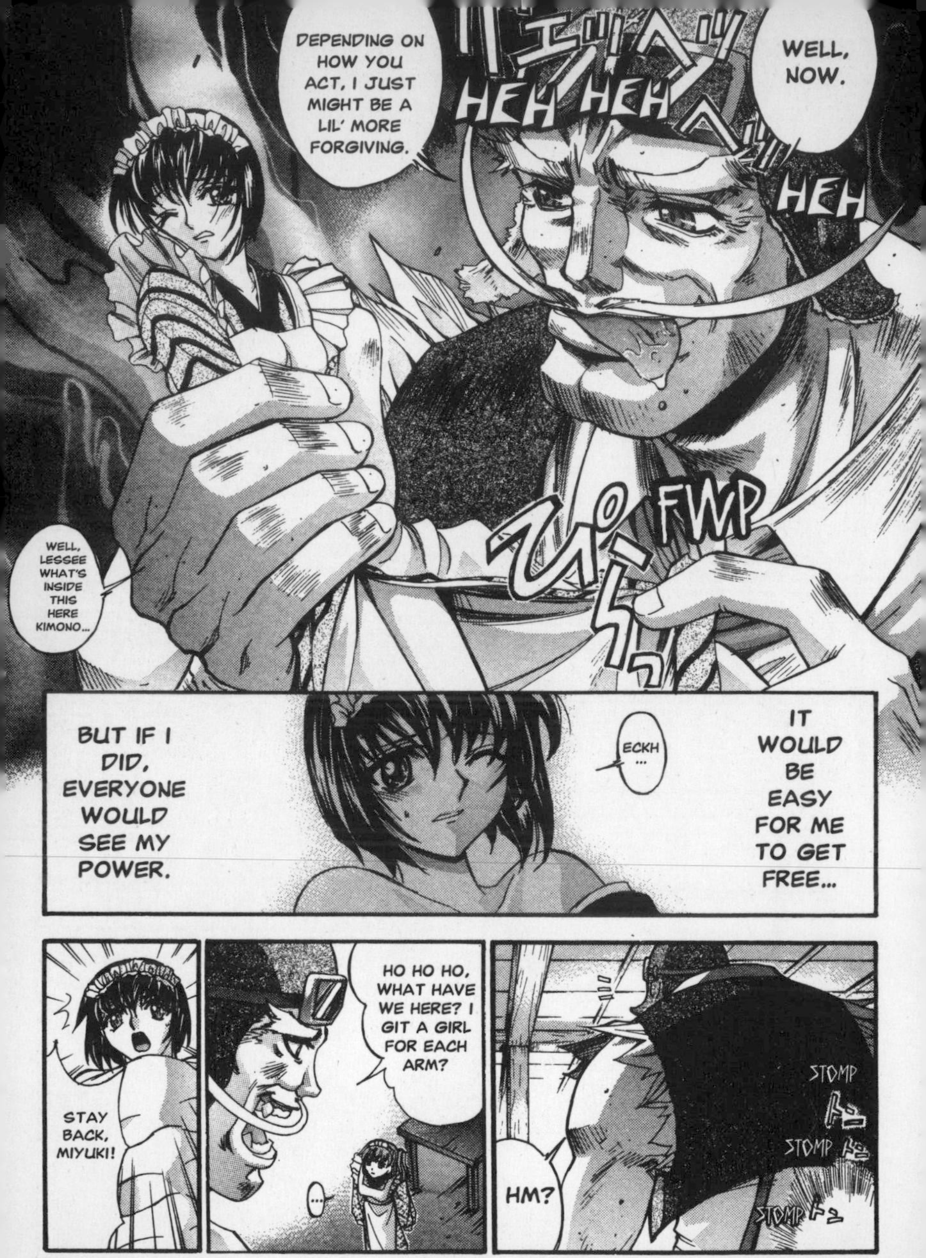
WELL, NOW.
HEH HEH HEH
DEPENDING ON HOW YOU ACT, I JUST MIGHT BE A LIL' MORE FORGIVING.
FWP
WELL, LESSEE WHAT'S INSIDE THIS HERE KIMONO...
IT WOULD BE EASY FOR ME TO GET FREE...
ECKH...
BUT IF I DID, EVERYONE WOULD SEE MY POWER.
STOMP
STOMP
STOMP
HM?
HO HO HO, WHAT HAVE WE HERE? I GIT A GIRL FOR EACH ARM?
...
STAY BACK, MIYUKI!

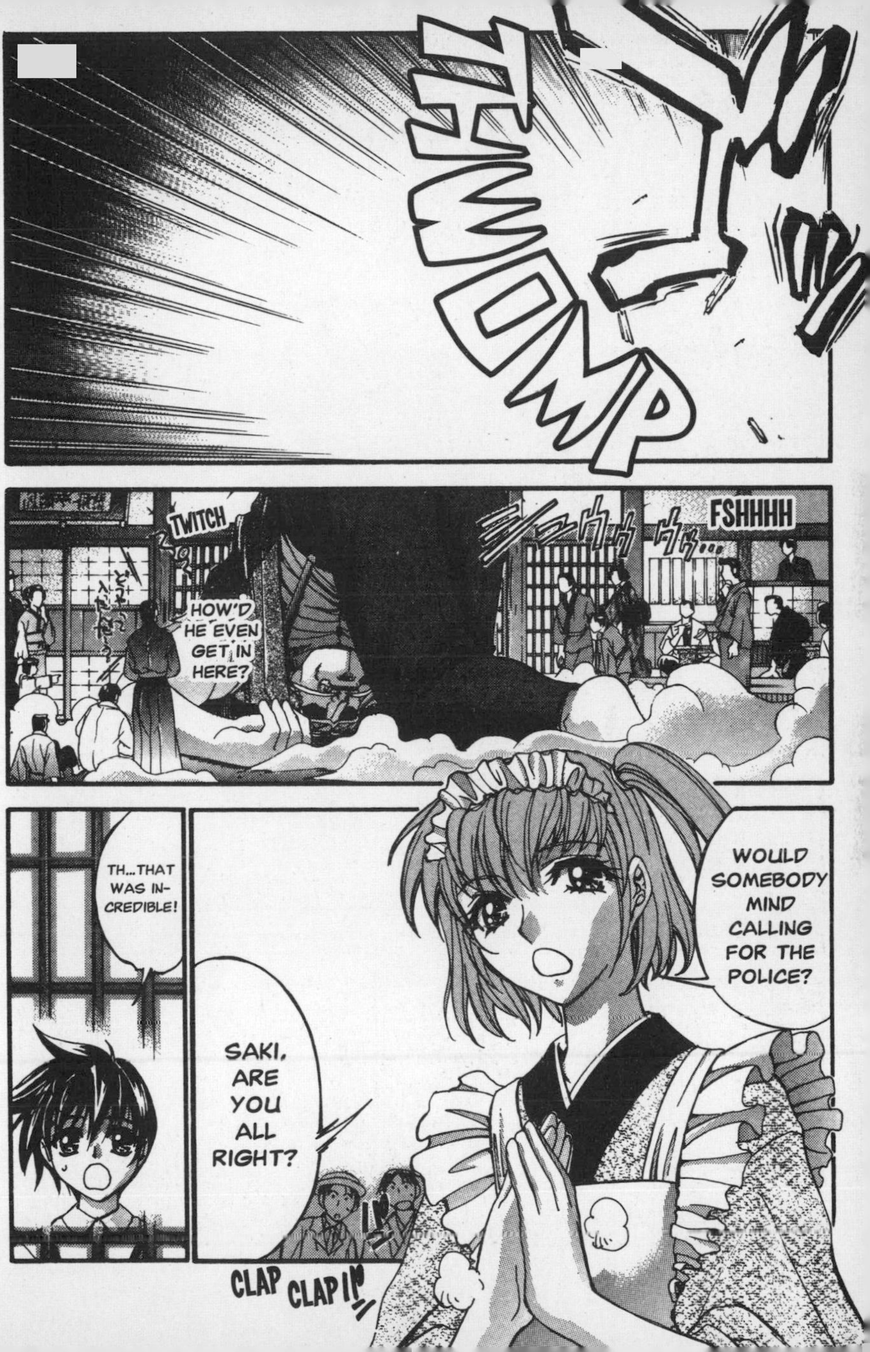
THWOMP
FSHHHH
TWITCH
HOW'D HE EVEN GET IN HERE?
WOULD SOMEBODY MIND CALLING FOR THE POLICE?
SAKI, ARE YOU ALL RIGHT?
CLAP CLAP!!
TH...THAT WAS IN-CREDIBLE!

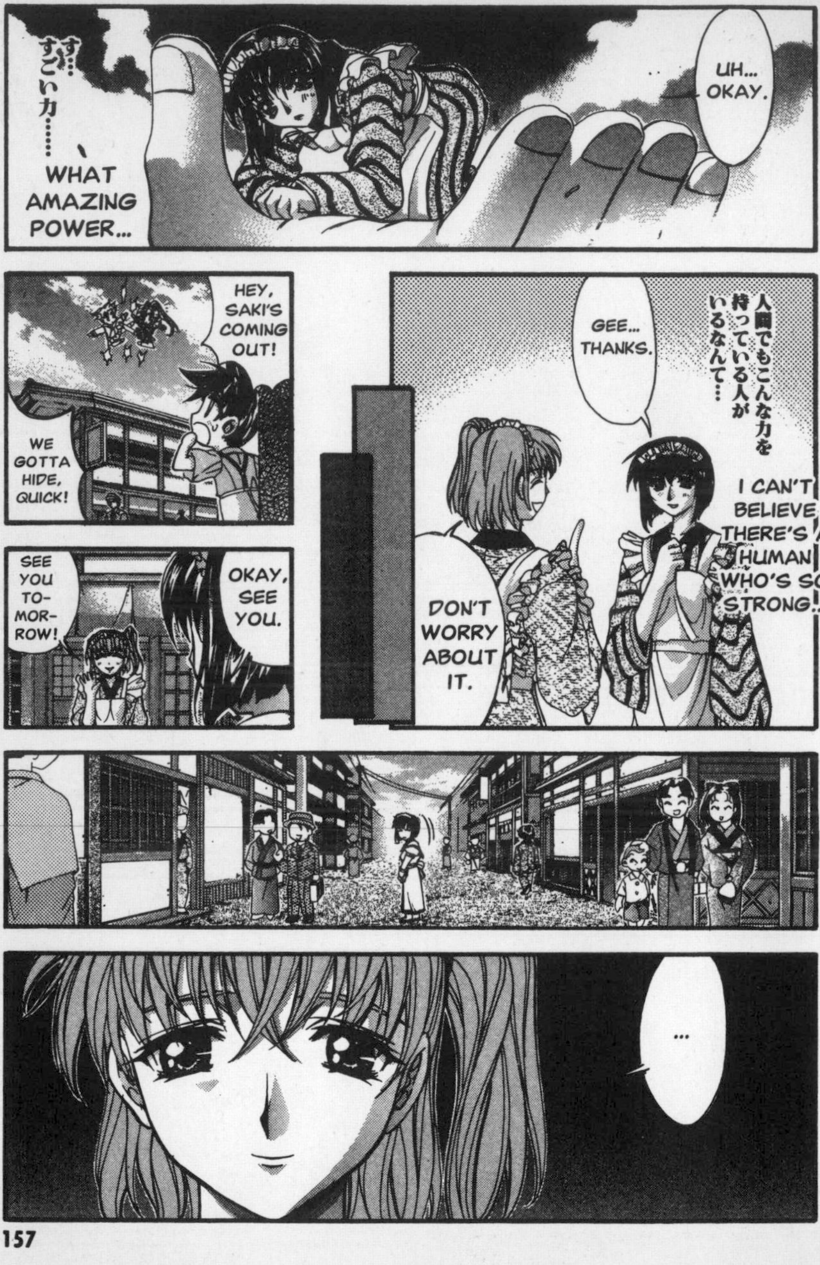
UH... OKAY.
す…すごい力……、
WHAT AMAZING POWER...
人間でもこんな力を持っている人がいるなんて…
GEE... THANKS.
I CAN'T BELIEVE THERE'S A HUMAN WHO'S SO STRONG...
DON'T WORRY ABOUT IT.
HEY, SAKI'S COMING OUT!
WE GOTTA HIDE, QUICK!
OKAY, SEE YOU.
SEE YOU TO-MOR-ROW!
...

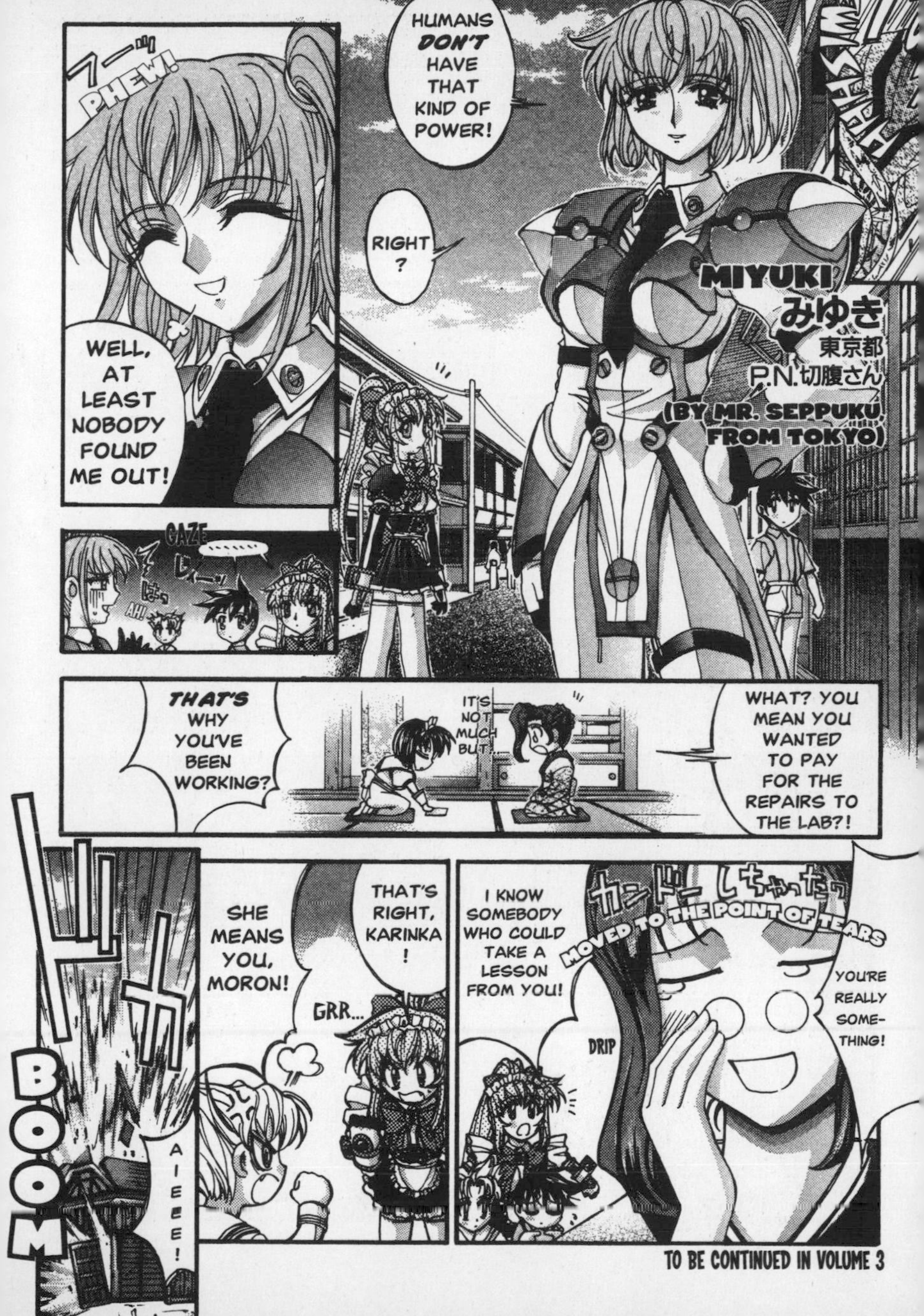
WHASH
MIYUKI
みゆき
東京都
P.N.切腹さん
(BY MR. SEPPUKU FROM TOKYO)
HUMANS *DON'T* HAVE THAT KIND OF POWER!
RIGHT?
PHEW!
WELL, AT LEAST NOBODY FOUND ME OUT!
GAZE
AH!
WHAT? YOU MEAN YOU WANTED TO PAY FOR THE REPAIRS TO THE LAB?!
IT'S NOT MUCH BUT...
THAT'S WHY YOU'VE BEEN WORKING?
MOVED TO THE POINT OF TEARS
I KNOW SOMEBODY WHO COULD TAKE A LESSON FROM YOU!
YOU'RE REALLY SOME-THING!
DRIP
THAT'S RIGHT, KARINKA!
SHE MEANS YOU, MORON!
GRR...
BOOM
AIEEE!

TO BE CONTINUED IN VOLUME 3

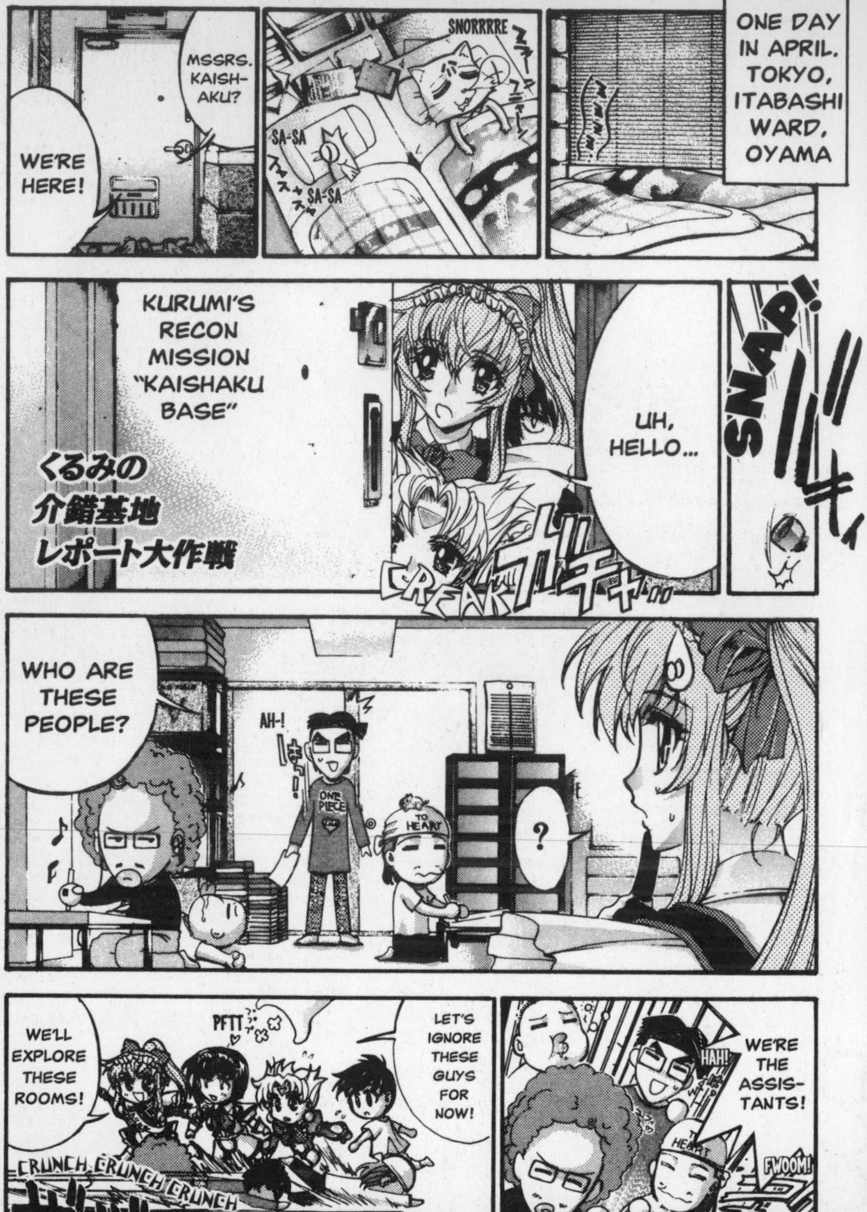
ONE DAY IN APRIL. TOKYO, ITABASHI WARD, OYAMA
SNORRRRE
SA-SA
SA-SA
MSSRS. KAISHAKU?
WE'RE HERE!
SNAP!
UH, HELLO...
CREAK
KURUMI'S RECON MISSION "KAISHAKU BASE"
くるみの
介錯基地
レポート大作戦
?
AH-!
WHO ARE THESE PEOPLE?
HAH!
WE'RE THE ASSISTANTS!
FWOOM!
LET'S IGNORE THESE GUYS FOR NOW!
PFTT
WE'LL EXPLORE THESE ROOMS!
CRUNCH CRUNCH CRUNCH CRUNCH

A FIRST IN JAPAN -IT'S KAISHAKU BASE 99!

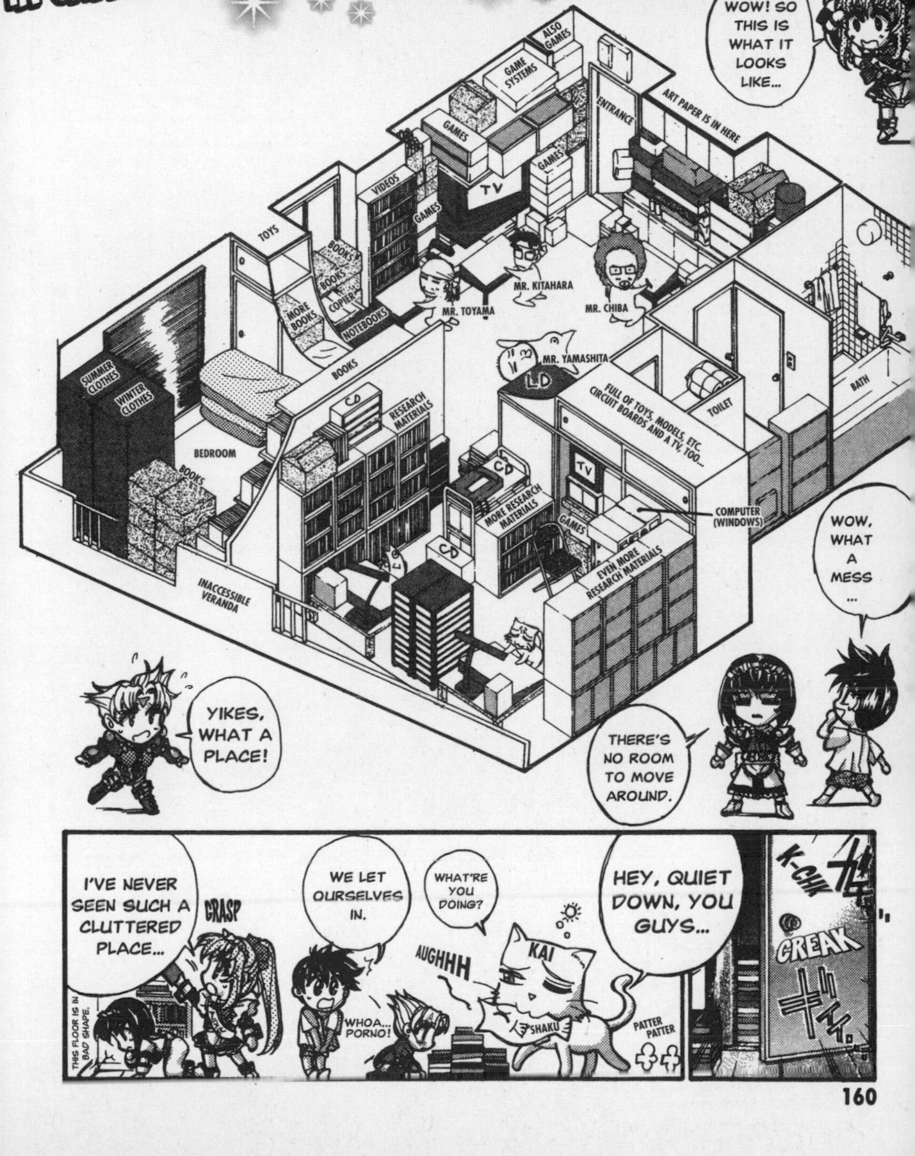
WOW! SO THIS IS WHAT IT LOOKS LIKE...
ALSO GAMES
GAME SYSTEMS
ENTRANCE
ART PAPER IS IN HERE
GAMES
GAMES
TV
GAMES
VIDEOS
TOYS
BOOKS
BOOKS
COPIER
MORE BOOKS
NOTEBOOKS
MR. KITAHARA
MR. TOYAMA
MR. CHIBA
MR. YAMASHITA
LD
BATH
TOILET
FULL OF TOYS, MODELS, ETC. CIRCUIT BOARDS AND A TV, TOO...
TV
BOOKS
CD
RESEARCH MATERIALS
SUMMER CLOTHES
WINTER CLOTHES
BEDROOM
BOOKS
CD
MORE RESEARCH MATERIALS
GAMES
COMPUTER (WINDOWS)
CD
EVEN MORE RESEARCH MATERIALS
INACCESSIBLE VERANDA
WOW, WHAT A MESS...
THERE'S NO ROOM TO MOVE AROUND.
YIKES, WHAT A PLACE!
K-CHIK
CREAK
HEY, QUIET DOWN, YOU GUYS...
PATTER PATTER
KAI
SHAKU
AUGHHH
WHAT'RE YOU DOING?
WE LET OURSELVES IN.
WHOA... PORNO!
CRASP
I'VE NEVER SEEN SUCH A CLUTTERED PLACE...
THIS FLOOR IS IN BAD SHAPE.

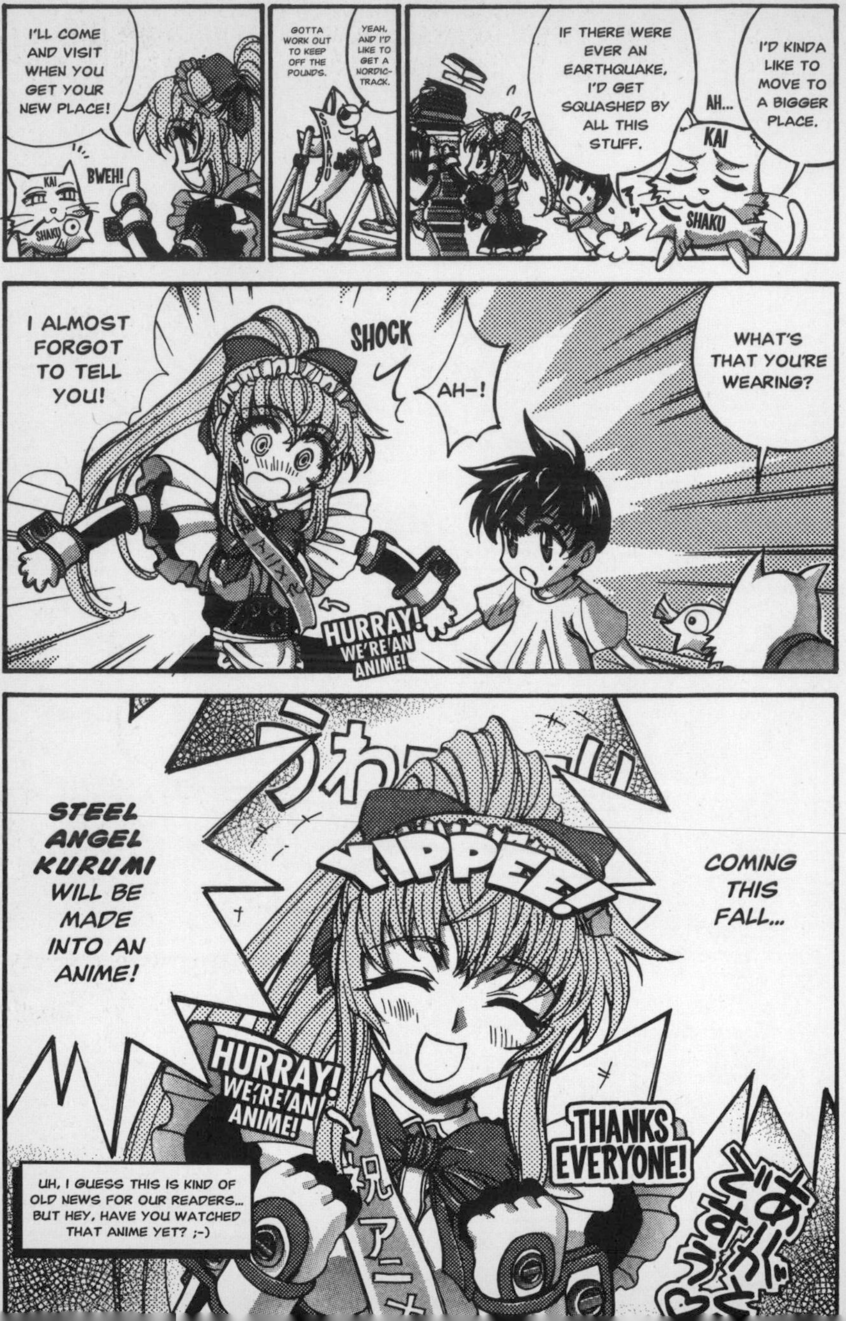
I'D KINDA LIKE TO MOVE TO A BIGGER PLACE.
AH...
KAI
SHAKU
IF THERE WERE EVER AN EARTHQUAKE, I'D GET SQUASHED BY ALL THIS STUFF.
YEAH, AND I'D LIKE TO GET A NORDIC-TRACK.
GOTTA WORK OUT TO KEEP OFF THE POUNDS.
SHAKU
I'LL COME AND VISIT WHEN YOU GET YOUR NEW PLACE!
BWEH!
KAI
SHAKU
WHAT'S THAT YOU'RE WEARING?
AH-!
SHOCK
I ALMOST FORGOT TO TELL YOU!
HURRAY! WE'RE AN ANIME!
COMING THIS FALL...
YIPPEE!
STEEL ANGEL KURUMI WILL BE MADE INTO AN ANIME!
THANKS EVERYONE!
HURRAY! WE'RE AN ANIME!
UH, I GUESS THIS IS KIND OF OLD NEWS FOR OUR READERS... BUT HEY, HAVE YOU WATCHED THAT ANIME YET? ;-)

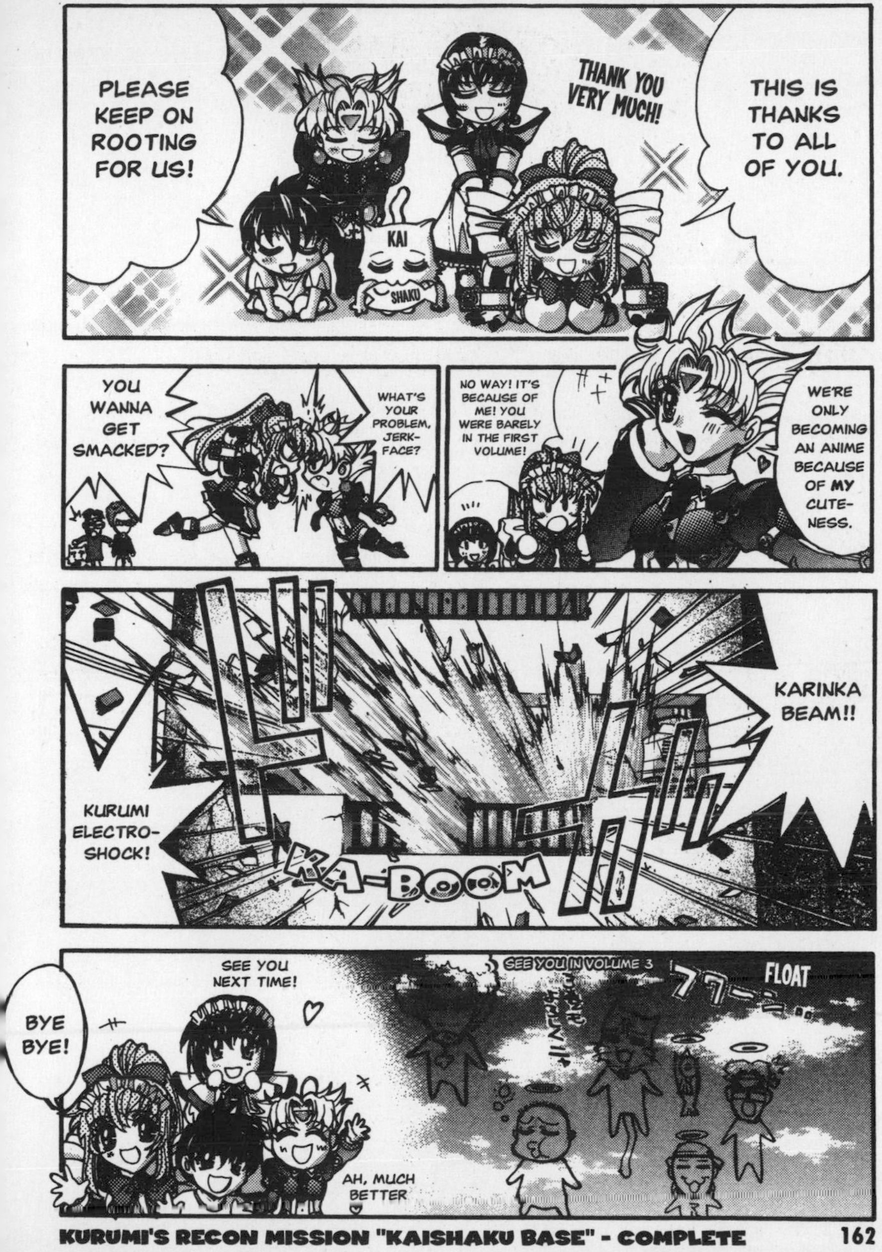
THIS IS THANKS TO ALL OF YOU.
THANK YOU VERY MUCH!
PLEASE KEEP ON ROOTING FOR US!
KAI
SHAKU
WE'RE ONLY BECOMING AN ANIME BECAUSE OF MY CUTENESS.
NO WAY! IT'S BECAUSE OF ME! YOU WERE BARELY IN THE FIRST VOLUME!
WHAT'S YOUR PROBLEM, JERK-FACE?
YOU WANNA GET SMACKED?
KARINKA BEAM!!
KURUMI ELECTRO-SHOCK!
KA-BOOM
SEE YOU IN VOLUME 3
FLOAT
SEE YOU NEXT TIME!
BYE BYE!
AH, MUCH BETTER

KURUMI'S RECON MISSION "KAISHAKU BASE" - COMPLETE

TRANSLATOR'S NOTES

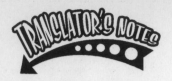

Steel Angel Kurumi Vol 02

PG. 12 All three of these are take-offs of Japanese dramas that aired sometime in the 80s. Each show featured high school dropouts and outlaw female high school students.

PG. 31 The kanji on the back of Nakahito's hand has two meanings—not only is it the symbol for "god/spiritualism" (which is significant as Nakahito belongs to a family of divine sorcerers), it is the first symbol in his family name of "Kagura."

PG. 34 "Nine Cuts Mudra." Mudra is a Sanskrit word meaning "sign" or "seal." It is often used to refer to gestures, esp. those that have meaning or are for the channeling of power. The mudra that Nakahito performs is called *kuji-kiri* (Japanese, lit. "nine cuts"), and is accompanied by a chant that calls forth a sacred, spiritual energy meant to banish evil.

PG. 47 Series vs. Parallel circuits: Series circuits are more powerful, but do not last as long. Parallel circuits are less powerful but last longer. The difference is in their design. If the symbol "||" represents a power source (like a battery) and a line represents a wire, this is what the circuits would look like:

(Series)

(Parallel)

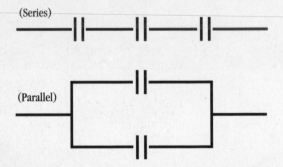

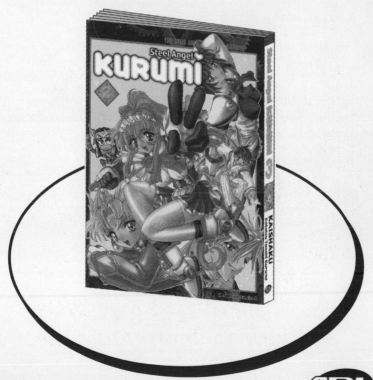

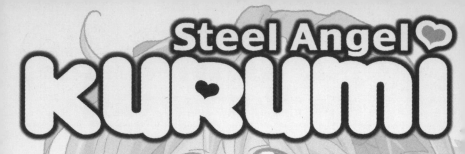

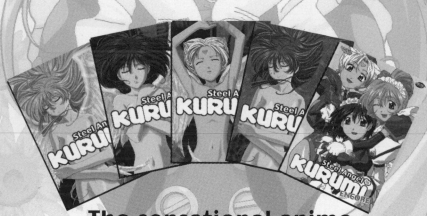

The sensational anime is available on five DVDs, exclusively from ADV Films!

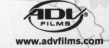

AFTER YOU'VE READ THE MANGA, DON'T FORGET TO WATCH THE ANIME!

Coming in March 2004 exclusively from ADV Films!

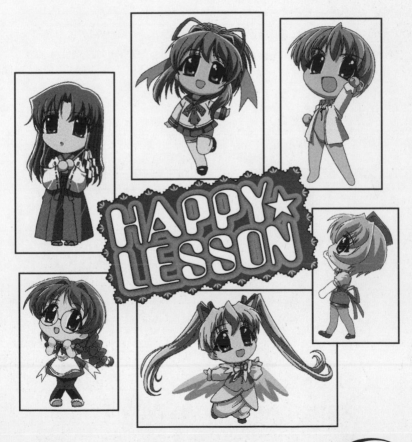

TOO MUCH ATTENTION
can be HAZARDOUS to a man's health!!

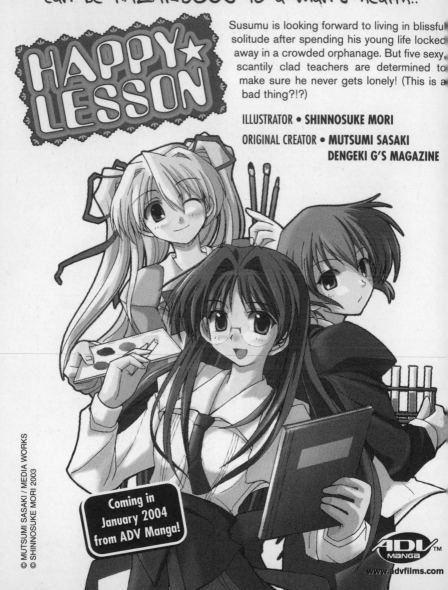

HAPPY☆LESSON

Susumu is looking forward to living in blissful solitude after spending his young life locked away in a crowded orphanage. But five sexy, scantily clad teachers are determined to make sure he never gets lonely! (This is a bad thing?!?)

ILLUSTRATOR • **SHINNOSUKE MORI**

ORIGINAL CREATOR • **MUTSUMI SASAKI**
DENGEKI G'S MAGAZINE

**Coming in
January 2004
from ADV Manga!**

ADV MANGA™

www.advfilms.com

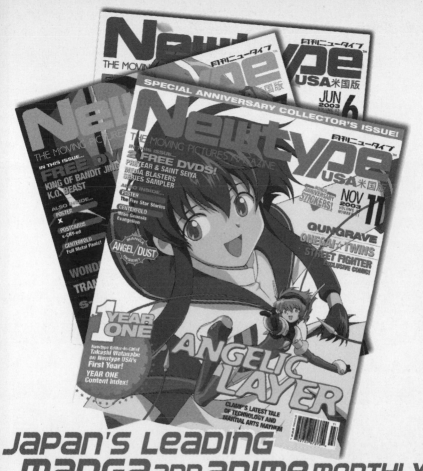
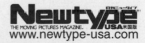

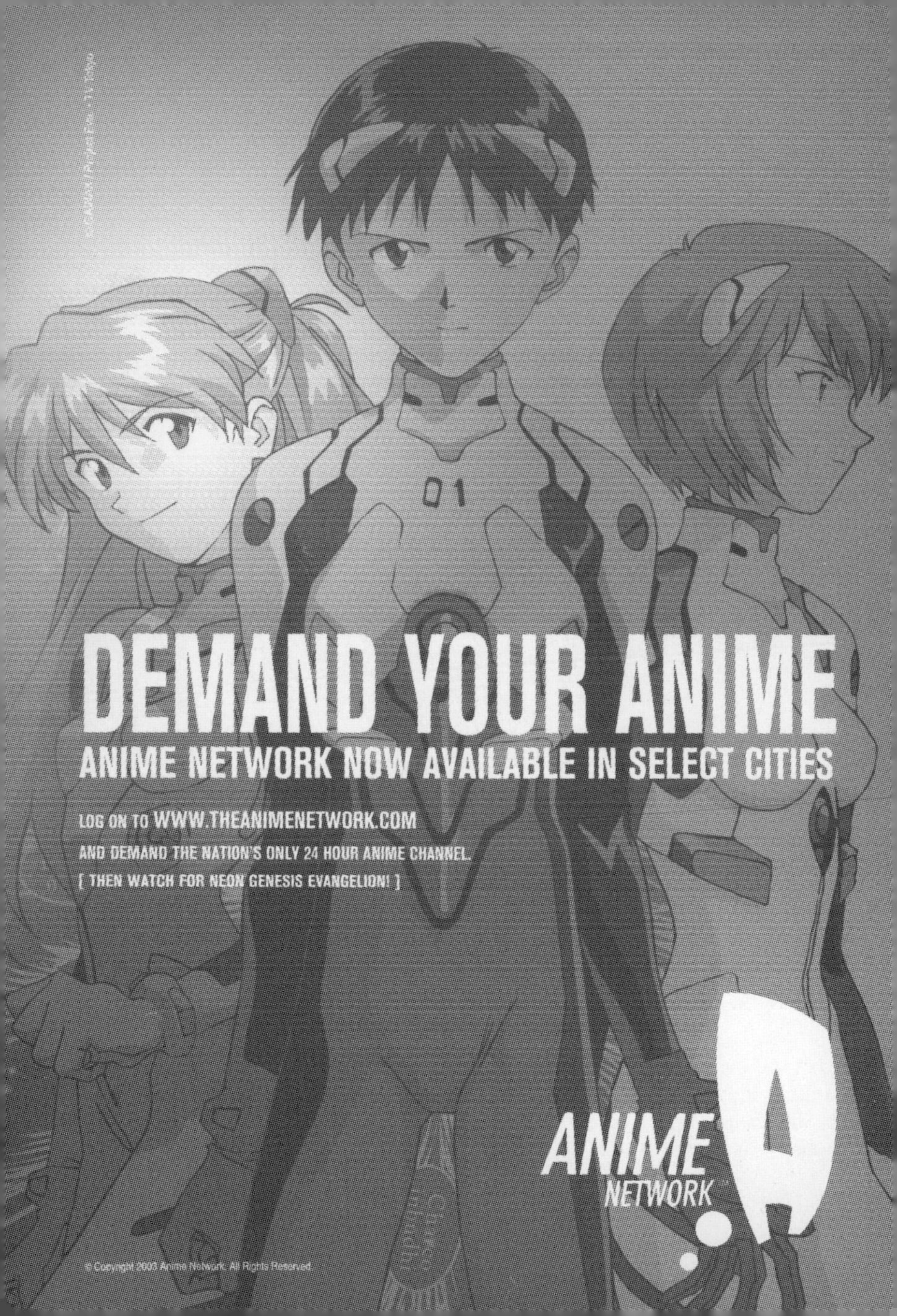

DEMAND YOUR ANIME
ANIME NETWORK NOW AVAILABLE IN SELECT CITIES
LOG ON TO WWW.THEANIMENETWORK.COM
AND DEMAND THE NATION'S ONLY 24 HOUR ANIME CHANNEL.
[THEN WATCH FOR NEON GENESIS EVANGELION!]
ANIME NETWORK
© Copyright 2003 Anime Network. All Rights Reserved.

Steel Angel KURUMI
Volume Two
Creator KAISHAKU

© KAISHAKU 1999

Originally published in Japan in 1999 by
KADOKAWA SHOTEN PUBLISHING CO., LTD., Tokyo.
English translation rights arranged with
KADOKAWA SHOTEN PUBLISHING CO., LTD., Tokyo.

Translator **KAY BERTRAND**
ADV Manga Translation Staff **JAVIER LOPEZ,
AMY FORSYTH, BRENDAN FRAYNE, EIKO McGREGOR**
Print Production/Art Studio Manager **LISA PUCKETT**
Graphic Designer **JORGE ALVARADO**
Graphic Artists **WINDI MARTIN, RYAN MASON, KRISTINA MILESKI,
SHANNON RASBERRY, GEORGE REYNOLDS, LANCE SWARTOUT**
Research/ Traffic Coordinator **MARSHA ARNOLD**

International Coordinators **TORU IWAKAMI, ATSUSHI KANBAYASHI**

Publishing Editor **SUSAN ITIN**
Assistant Editor **MARGARET SCHAROLD**
Editorial Assistant **VARSHA BHUCHAR**
Proofreader **SHERIDAN JACOBS**

President, C.E.O & Publisher **JOHN LEDFORD**

Email: editor@adv-manga.com
www.adv-manga.com
www.advfilms.com

For sales and distribution inquiries please call 1.800.282.7202

ADV MANGA is a division of A.D. Vision, Inc.
10114 W. Sam Houston Parkway, Suite 200, Houston, Texas 77099

ISBN: 1-4139-0012-7
First printing, January 2004
10 9 8 7 5 4 3 2 1
Printed in Canada

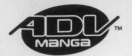

ANIME SURVEY

PLEASE MAIL THE COMPLETED FORM TO: EDITOR – ADV MANGA
℅ A.D. Vision, Inc. 10114 W. Sam Houston Pkwy., Suite 200 Houston, TX 77099

Name: ____________________
Address: ____________________
City: State: Zip: ____________________

E-Mail: ____________________
Male ☐ Female ☐ Age: ____________________
Cable Provider: ____________________

☐ ***CHECK HERE IF YOU WOULD LIKE TO RECEIVE OTHER INFORMATION OR FUTURE OFFERS FROM ADV.***

1. Annual Household Income (*Check only one*)

- ☐ Under $25,000
- ☐ $25,000 to $50,000
- ☐ $50,000 to $75,000
- ☐ Over $75,000

2. How do you hear about new Anime releases? (*Check all that apply*)

- ☐ Browsing in Store
- ☐ Internet Reviews
- ☐ Anime News Websites
- ☐ Direct Email Campaigns
- ☐ Online forums (message boards and chat rooms)
- ☐ Carrier pigeon
- ☐ Other: __________
- ☐ Magazine Ad
- ☐ Online Advertising
- ☐ Conventions
- ☐ TV Advertising

3. Which magazines do you read? (*Check all that apply*)

- ☐ Wizard
- ☐ SPIN
- ☐ Animerica
- ☐ Rolling Stone
- ☐ Maxim
- ☐ DC Comics
- ☐ URB
- ☐ Polygon
- ☐ Original Play Station Magazine
- ☐ Entertainment Weekly
- ☐ YRB
- ☐ EGM
- ☐ Newtype USA
- ☐ SciFi
- ☐ Starlog
- ☐ Wired
- ☐ Vice
- ☐ BPM
- ☐ I hate reading
- ☐ Other:

4. Would you subscribe to digital cable if you could get a 24 hour/7 day a week anime channel (like the Anime Network)?

☐ Yes
☐ No

5. Would you like to see the Anim

☐ Yes
☐ No

6. Would you pay $6.99/month for the Anime Network?

☐ Yes
☐ No

7. What genre of manga and anime would you like to see from ADV? (*Check all that apply*)

☐ adventure
☐ romance
☐ detective
☐ fighting
☐ horror
☐ sci-fi/fantasy
☐ sports

8. How many manga titles have you purchased in the last year?

☐ none
☐ 1-4
☐ 5-10
☐ 11+

9. Where do you make your manga purchases? (*Check all that apply*)

☐ comic store
☐ bookstore
☐ newsstand
☐ online
☐ other: ____________________
☐ department store
☐ grocery store
☐ video store
☐ video game store

10. What's your favorite anime-related website?

☐ advfilms.com
☐ anipike.com
☐ rightstuf.com
☐ animenewsservice.com
☐ animenewsnetwork.com
☐ animeondvd.com
☐ animenation.com
☐ animeonline.net
☐ planetanime.com
☐ other: ________________

All information provided will be used for internal purposes only. We promise not to sell or otherwise divulge your information.